EDITING TECHNIQUES WITH FINAL CUT PRO

2ND EDITION

MICHAEL WOHL

PEACHPIT PRESS
BERKELEY, CALIFORNIA

EDITING TECHNIQUES WITH FINAL CUT PRO, 2ND EDITION
Michael Wohl

Peachpit Press
1249 Eighth Street
Berkeley, CA 94710
510/524-2178
510/524-2221 (fax)

Find us on the World Wide Web at: www.peachpit.com
To report errors, please send a note to errata@peachpit.com

Peachpit Press is a division of Pearson Education

Editor: Douglas Cruickshank
Production Editor: Lisa Brazieal
Technical Editor: Alexis Van Hurkman
Compositor: Owen Wolfson
Indexer: Ron Strauss
Cover Designers: Mimi Heft, Lupe Edgar
Interior Designer: Mimi Heft
Storyboard Artist: Joel Cardinal
Illustrations: Peter Hoey
Sample Frames: courtesy of Bare Witness Productions, Brett Shapiro (images from *The Chocolate Curse*), Slant Rhyme Productions, and Grottofilms (images from David Munro's *Compulsory Breathing*).

Notice of Rights

Notice of Liability

Trademarks

ISBN 0-321-16887-9

9 8 7 6 5 4 3 2 1

Printed and bound in the United States of America

DEDICATION

To all of the dreamers who cherish the independent spirit. Follow your dreams!

ACKNOWLEDGEMENTS:

I would like to thank:

My editor, Douglas Cruickshank, tech editor Alexis Van Hurkman, our production editor Lisa Brazieal, and the whole staff at Peachpit—especially executive editor Marjorie Baer, whose enthusiasm and patience contributed immeasurably to this book.

All of the film editors who agreed to be interviewed. I only wish I could include everyone's ideas—I learned so much from all of you.

Mark at A.C.E., the countless agents and agents' assistants who helped to set up the interviews, and Dawn Walters who transcribed them.

The cast and crew of *Want*, the entire Bare Witness Productions crew, Eric Peltier, Xandra, and David at Grotto films, and, of course, Daniel Gamburg who has always been willing to do whatever I ask, no matter how strange or difficult (even if I'm taking pictures).

Brian, Randy, Will, and the rest of the Yak Herders, past and present. We done changed the world. Please keep on making it better.

Lisa Brenneis for giving me the crazy idea to take this thing on in the first place and for supporting me throughout, even if it was just to see someone share her pain.

My loving family, PSW, KAW, AJW, HDR, and KFM.

And most of all, I would like to thank Divi Crockett for so very much help, support, trust, dedication, inspiration, and love.

—Michael Wohl

CONTENTS

CHAPTER TWO: FILM LANGUAGE   31

CHAPTER THREE: EDITING PATTERNS   93

CHAPTER FOUR: PREPARING TO EDIT 149

CHAPTER SIX: ADVANCED EDITING 279

CHAPTER EIGHT: SPECIAL EFFECTS 411

The Invisible Art

Unless you're a film professional or a serious fan, you may have never heard names like Walter Murch or Thelma Schoonmaker—even though they are editing geniuses without whose work films like *The English Patient* and *Raging Bull* would never have been possible. In the filmmaking industry, they are more than merely famous; they are superstars.

So why don't you know their names?

Because at its best film editing is an invisible art. While the cinematographer shoots pretty pictures that catch your eye and movie stars' faces grab your attention (they'd better, considering how much they cost), the editor's job is to make her work completely invisible. Although some filmmakers, such as Oliver Stone and Jean-Luc Godard, have chosen a cinematic style that draws attention to the filmmaking process, if you work professionally as a film editor (or aspire to), you're usually trying as hard as you can to keep anyone from noticing your editing work. In fact, the better the editing, the harder it is to observe and explain.

It's All Film

I use the terms "film," "video," "program," "show," and "movie" more or less interchangeably. Even though most of the content you'll be working with probably originates on video and may end up being distributed on video, "film" is still widely accepted as the best way to refer to the media that combine moving images with sound. Thus, in this book, the term "filmmaking" refers to the art of creating projects in all those different media.

Thousands of film and video editors are at work every day, cutting TV programs, news reports, video games, corporate training videos, movies, commercials, and countless other projects. And whether you know it or not, in many cases when you say to yourself, "Wow, that film was great!" it's the work of the editor that you're applauding.

THE MAN BEHIND THE EDITING MACHINE

When I first became interested in filmmaking, I went to my local theater and watched Francis Ford Coppola's *Apocalypse Now* more than 20 times in a row. I went back every day, until the ticket taker started letting me in for free. I'm not sure if it was out of admiration or pity.

The reason I kept going back was that I was trying to deconstruct the film and figure out why it was so powerful—a difficult process, since films are designed precisely to defeat that kind of analysis. Every day I would sit there watching the screen, trying to catalogue the visual, aural, and story elements. And every day I got caught up in the film's seductive dramatic content and technique, and I would lose track of my analysis. Still, each day I got a little further into the film before I lost focus, until finally I could describe how the film was constructed, shot by shot.

Most people don't want to know how film works; they don't want anything to spoil the magic. Because deep down film *is* magic—which is part of what attracts some of us to learning how it works. Personally, I've always been drawn to things that seem impossible: I seek to understand the things that baffle me. So ever since my experience with *Apocalypse Now,* whenever a particular film really appeals to me, I go to see it again and again, until I can deconstruct it.

Becoming a Filmmaker

It wasn't long before I decided to try my hand at making movies, so in 1988 I enrolled in San Francisco State University. SFSU boasts a small, intensive film-production program that's highly respected in the filmmaking community. The focus is on film as a medium for artistic expression, rather than as a tool for entertainment or, God forbid, commerce.

Of course, if you're looking for a career in the real world of filmmaking, it's useful to know a particular skill set and excel at it. So I supplemented my artistic education at SFSU with an internship at a corporate video production house, where I honed my editing skills. I had also been writing screenplays for many years, and as I became more interested in directing, I looked for opportunities to work with actors.

Shortly after I graduated from film school, I produced, directed, and edited my first fiction film, *Theatereality,* but I kept working at the production house as an editor, assistant director, and video technician. Because I had taught myself basic computer skills, I also became the company's computer expert.

Building Final Cut Pro

One thing led to another, and one day I woke up to find myself working at Adobe Systems, testing an early version of Adobe Premiere—one of the first digital desktop editing systems. Almost no one on the design team had any experience actually editing video; that was where I came in. Working closely with Randy Ubillos, the architect and lead engineer of Premiere, I reported bugs and helped design features for the forthcoming release.

When Randy resigned from Adobe to create a new division at Macromedia—one that would be responsible for building the ultimate next-generation tool for desktop video production—he invited me to join the team designing what would eventually become Final Cut Pro. Part of my job was heading a mini production studio within Macromedia where we could test the software on real-world projects.

The development of Final Cut Pro took nearly four years—far longer than had been expected—and in the meantime, Macromedia decided that a professional video editing tool no longer fit the company's product strategy. In the summer of 1998, Apple took over the project and guided our focus squarely towards DV. Nine months later, Final Cut Pro version 1.0 was born.

During its entire development, I was using the software at whatever prototype stage it was at to cut my shows. This allowed me to make recommendations about improving the workflow and how the features would hold up in the real world. The engineers could look over my shoulder and observe how the program worked on an actual project. Everyone agreed that this process was one reason Final Cut Pro became such a useful—and successful—application. Indeed, many other software projects of all types (including Adobe Premiere) have adopted this technique as part of their development cycle. Perhaps it's this, more than the specific features of Final Cut Pro, which constitutes my real legacy to the world of software development.

Once Final Cut Pro was out in the world, my job was to teach people how to use it. In addition to building the tutorial that shipped with the software, and constructing the demos Apple used at trade shows and sales meetings, I taught Final Cut Pro to Apple sales teams, product reps, and demo artists.

Back to the World of Filmmaking

All this was fun, but it was taking me farther and farther away from filmmaking. Finally, in September 1999, I left Apple to get back to *using* the tools rather than building them. I didn't totally give up on teaching, though. In the last few years I've led classes on Final Cut Pro, digital video production, cinema as an online medium, and related topics for places like the American Film Institute, DV Creators, and San Francisco State University.

These days, I'm able to devote more time and energy to creating digital video projects of my own. Before leaving Apple, I co-founded a theater company called Bare Witness Productions that produces short films using improvisational techniques both in front of and behind the camera. We would go to real locations and use wireless mics and tiny DV cameras to perform and record improvised dramatic scenes. Then we edited the pieces and posted the results on a Web site. Several of these shorts played in film festivals and some have won awards.

Following that success, I wrote, produced, directed, and edited *Want,* a feature film about dot com mania and sex addiction. *Want* was shot in the winter of 2001 and edited over the course of the next year. It was complete by the fall of 2002 and our premiere was held in Victoria, British Columbia in February 2003. Since then it has been screened at numerous film festivals and we are in negotiations for broader distribution.

I will be using examples and anecdotes from my recent real life projects throughout this book to illustrate and elaborate on various editing techniques and concepts. I hope this real world anchor will give these lessons an element of truth that will help turn dry concepts into practices and techniques that are alive and easy to remember.

FINAL CUT AND THE DIGITAL REVOLUTION

The last few years have seen nothing less than a bona fide revolution in the world of filmmaking. This is due in large part to new technologies, particularly DV; digital editing systems like the Final Cut family; *FireWire;* the Internet; and computers powerful enough to process huge data files without taking all day to do it.

What makes these technologies revolutionary is not so much their capability as their affordable price. Less than ten years ago, it would have cost at least $250,000 to set up a modest digital film production facility. Today, you can buy equipment and software that let you achieve the same professional production level for $25,000 or less.

All this is having a profound impact on our society—and it's far broader than simply making it possible to produce professional video on the cheap. Revolutionary technology is opening up the powerful medium of film to millions of people who had no previous access. This means we'll be hearing more voices—and that means new ways of shooting, editing, and thinking that will inevitably transform film in ways that are unimaginable today.

But the technology just gets you started. To become a successful film editor, you need to learn how to see the invisible art, how to understand and speak the secret visual language that editors use to build effective film sequences.

LANGUAGE CLASS, LESSON ONE

Whether you call it film or video, the moving image is a universal language, one that the whole world understands but only a limited few have taken the time to learn to speak.

As an editor, the biggest part of your job is to learn to deconstruct and understand the components of film language. You need to be able to do it in your sleep. I must warn you here and now that this may have a significant and detrimental impact on your ability to actually enjoy popular culture. Rather than relaxing and letting the filmmakers take you for a pleasant ride, you'll find yourself obsessively analyzing the media you see. This can have a dire effect on your personal relationships as well. Nothing spoils a first date like a detailed dissertation on the continuity errors in the romantic comedy you're watching.

Learning the Language

You'll also need to understand the common terms and specialized vocabulary used in the world of film and video production, as well as some terms that are specific to computer use and software operation. As we go along, I'll italicize terms that are potentially confusing or obscure. You'll find the definitions in a glossary in the back of the book.

Turn Off the Sound

Want to see how it works? Turn off the sound.

Get a copy of your favorite movie or television show, and watch it *with the sound turned off.* Without the distraction of dialogue, sound effects, or musical score, it's easier to pay close attention to the visual elements that make up a sequence. For instance, duration: How long are the *shots?* Are they consistent or inconsistent in length (long and short shots intermixed)?

Are the shots connected by *cuts? Dissolves? Wipes?* Other special visual effects?

Watch the sequence again without sound. This time pay attention to the *edit points* in each shot—the precise moment when one shot ends and the following shot begins. What's happening before and after each edit point? How are the pictures on either side of the edit point connected? Is the connection visual? Spatial? Emotional?

Now go back and watch the show a third time—this time with the sound on. What are the elements that make up the soundtrack? Music? On-camera dialogue? Off-camera speech? Sound effects? Background noise or *room tone?*

Listen to how the sound interacts with the visual elements, how it bridges transitions and complements or contrasts with the visual content. Pay attention to the edit points for the sound: Where does each sound element start and end? Compare the audio edit points to the visual edit points. Notice how much, or how little, the sound affects the visual content.

The more you learn how to deconstruct the media you watch, the better you'll get at creating media of your own. After trying this exercise a few times, you'll start to do this sort of deconstruction automatically as you watch, without having to roll the show back. And you'll discover that your visual vocabulary is growing fast, making you a more effective editor and filmmaker.

THE GAME PLAN

Even if you don't plan to become a full-time editor, or if producing video content is only a hobby or a small part of your current job, knowing the tools of this trade will benefit you in ways you may not realize. Consider that 15 years ago basic computer skills were widely seen as geeky esoterica; today they are a prerequisite for nearly any job. In just the same way, as technology continues to advance, video will become more and more commonplace in all types of communication. This book will teach you the fundamental editing concepts you'll need to prepare for that day.

We'll start by going over the basic elements of what film editing is all about. Then I'll move on to show you how to use Final Cut like a pro. You'll learn to edit with skill and finesse and make the most of the software. Some of the techniques we'll explore are basic, and some are quite advanced.

Final Cut Pro Not Required

Final Cut Pro is a powerful, versatile tool for sound editing, video editing, performing some kinds of special effects, and managing the *post-production* of film and video projects. And because it is my tool of choice, I will generally refer to it when I describe how to perform various editing operations.

However, this book is aimed at teaching you how to become a competent, professional editor, not just a technician who knows the ins and outs of one particular software program. The editing strategies I'll describe don't depend on using Final Cut Pro or Final Cut Express. They should be equally useful no matter what editing system you're using, whether it's an Avid, an old-fashioned splicing block, or some hot new software neither you nor I have heard of yet. Sometimes, finding the best solution to a particular problem may require a tool other than Final Cut Pro. In such cases I'll show you how to integrate that tool with the rest of your workspace.

Pro vs. Express

Final Cut Pro and Final Cut Express share the vast majority of their functionality. Because all of the basic editing functions are identical across the two programs, this book is applicable to users of either software. There are only a handful of specific features in Final Cut Pro that are not in Final Cut Express and vice versa. When I am describing such a feature, you will see an identifying icon in the left margin and a dotted vertical line that runs parallel to the relevant text. Unless a section is marked in this manner, it applies equally to both programs.

The main areas of functionality exclusive to Final Cut Pro 4 include Customizability; Logging (both covered in Chapter 4); Keyframing of Effects; Time Remapping (both covered in Chapter 8); and the Audio Mixer (covered in Chapter 7). In addition, several features were redesigned in Final Cut Pro 4, such as track targeting (covered in Chapter 5). In this case, the functionality described for Final Cut Express also applies to earlier versions of Final Cut Pro.

What This Book Isn't

Now that you have some idea what this book is, let me tell you what it is *not:*

This book is not a comprehensive manual. Final Cut Pro 4 comes with a 1,400-page tome (spread across three volumes) detailing every option of every feature. Final Cut Express also comes with a robust User Guide. Lisa Brenneis's *Final Cut Pro 4 for Macintosh: Visual QuickPro Guide,* and *Final Cut Express: Visual Quickstart Guide,* both published by Peachpit Press, are also great resources to help you learn how each tool and feature works.

Nor is this book intended for absolute beginners at digital video. I won't tell you how to install your software, or what hardware you should buy, or how to hook it up. You'll need a basic familiarity with Macintosh operating procedures, and it will be extremely helpful if you have access to a Final Cut workstation (Pro or Express) in order to try out the techniques described herein.

MORE THAN MAKING MARKS ON PAPER

We are all media consumers. Virtually anyone living in today's technological culture sees thousands of hours of professionally produced video and film every year. Images are used to communicate information, entertain, educate, and persuade—sometimes all at the same time. But even with the latest technology at your fingertips, filmmaking is not a simple medium to master. Sure, the tools are getting cheaper and simpler to use, but it is still easy to tell the work of a professional from that of an amateur.

Merely having paper and pencil does not make someone a writer. Writing is more than making marks on paper. It's a craft that requires a deep understanding of language, principles, and techniques—all of which will vary widely depending on the intended result. Film editing is just the same. Sure, anyone with a couple of thousand dollars can buy a computer and a video-editing application like Final Cut—but that doesn't mean he knows how to edit.

By the time you complete this book, you will have learned to recognize a wide variety of editing situations and know exactly how the pros handle them. (You don't have to follow the "rules," of course, but at least you'll know which ones you're breaking.) And no matter what type of shows you'll be editing, the quality of your work will improve.

Not only will this book change the way you use your editing software, it will change the way you think about film.

Keystroke Names

Whenever I specify a single-letter keystroke (as in, "To access the razor blade tool, press ⓑ") that letter will be printed in uppercase for readability. However, that doesn't mean you should type it in uppercase. In fact, I want you to hit that key without pressing [Shift]. On the rare occasions that I'll ask you to type something in uppercase, I'll include [Shift] followed by a hyphen, as in, "Press [Shift]-ⓑ." (The hyphen means press both keys simultaneously.) Bottom line: Unless you see a [Shift], all letter keys should be typed lowercase.

CHAPTER ONE

The Editor's Job

A movie is shaped three times. It is written; then it is produced; and finally, it is edited.

It all begins when a screenwriter lays out a vision for the film. He conceives characters and their dialogue or narration. He structures the dramatic events that constitute the plot, and interweaves the themes that ultimately give meaning to the work.

Next, a producer acquires the rights to the script, and assembles a cast and crew to transform the written words into moving images and sounds that will be recorded on film or tape.

The most important person the producer will hire is the director, who instills the script with her own interpretation, emphasizing certain elements and downplaying others, adding tiny touches and deeper insights. Together, these collaborators revise the script to work within the financial restrictions and limitations of production logistics. Then they pick locations, hire actors, specify shots and *camera angles,* and start filming the scenes. With every individual decision they make, they shape the raw material of the film in their own unique way.

WHERE THE EDITOR FITS IN

Once a film is shot, the raw footage is handed over to a team of editors—a principal editor (usually called simply "the editor") and various assistant editors—who continue to revise and adapt the material, shaping it into its final form. The editor will make her own changes to the now collective vision—sometimes out of necessity (for instance, to compensate for missing shots or ones that are technically flawed), sometimes as an expression of her artistic judgment. Although final authority for such choices usually rests with the director, the editor exercises a great deal of control over the way the story is told. She may change the order of scenes, or shots within a scene, to prolong a sense of mystery or suspense. She might decide to omit a shot that tells the audience what to think, or she might add one that foreshadows a dramatic event.

Sometimes a story is actually rewritten in the editing room—which can mean revamping everything from its basic structure to the emotional tone, the underlying theme, and the way the audience feels about the characters. Often decisions made in the editing room reveal elements previously undiscovered in the original story or shooting script. There may be ideas present in the material but latent in the script, or concealed in the director's unconscious choices that are invisible to either writer or director. A great editor can perceive these hidden themes and through editing technique, bring them to light.

For instance, several years ago I cut a show called *Ron's World* about a developmentally disabled man who was trying to find love. The director had an annoying habit of composing his shots with some foreground object obscuring part of the frame. When I asked him why, he said he liked the way it looked. But as I assembled the scenes, I began to see how the images reflected Ron's difficulty seeing the world clearly and his inability to interact with those around him. I was able to put that realization to good use.

Although the obscured shots cropped up throughout the film, I decided to use them most often in the early scenes. Then, after the climax, when Ron makes a real emotional connection with the woman he loves, I stopped using them entirely. The result was a subtle but effective way to help the audience understand the character's unique view of the world.

The writer creates a story, and the director gives it vision—but it's the editor who tells it.

THE EDITING PROCESS

Editing involves a lot more than simply choosing and arranging shots. An experienced editor knows how to work in creative collaboration with the director, the producer, and even the writer. And he understands that most editing decisions are based on the special nature and design of every film or video project. Part of the craft of editing is treating each project uniquely, shaping it to find how the material can best be communicated.

What Kind of Film Are You Making?

Often it's the big questions that never get asked, and the biggest question of all is: What the heck are you trying to do, anyway? People make films for all sorts of reasons, but for the most part they can be sorted into four main categories: films that inform, films that educate, films that persuade, and films that entertain. Once you know which category (or categories) your film falls into, you'll be able to determine the answers to the many smaller questions that will occur during the editing process.

These four goals will lead you in four different editing directions. Confusing them, or trying to follow too many of them at once, may destroy the integrity of the project and undermine its potential. If you're making an instructional video about building materials, don't get caught up trying to entertain when your goal is to educate. Likewise, if you're creating an ad to sell designer perfume, don't try to teach the viewer how to make her own.

Of course, there's always overlap. Some projects may inform at one point, educate at another, and entertain at a third. And some films fall outside of this simplified structure altogether. Still, knowing where you stand in terms of your intent will help you make a better show.

Films That Inform

By "inform" I mean providing facts about a given subject. For instance, an informative film about eggs would not attempt to convince the audience that eggs are good or bad for people's health, but might show, among other things, how they are brought to market in rural China. Two categories of film that might be classified as informative are documentary and corporate communications. If your goal is to inform, some editing strategies might be:

- Clearly identify the content as factual information, as opposed to opinion or interpretation, and make it easy for your audience to comprehend each point you want to make. For example, you might use a map showing egg production centers or an animated line following the egg's path through the factory. Or you might implement subtler editing techniques, such as manipulating the pacing. For example, you might choose to tell your story in chronological order, stopping at important points to discuss their significance.

- Summarize important content. At the end of each section, or at the end of the film, reiterate the essential information that you want the audience to take home with them. You can do this with a graphic chart or a list, or sometimes by replaying selected scenes with a narrator reminding the viewer what their significance is.

Films That Educate

While "informing" and "educating" do overlap a bit, the goal of an educational film is generally not just to supply viewers with information but to show them how to use that information. For instance, if the egg documentary were re-edited to be educational or instructional, it might explain how to select eggs at a market; how to identify their origin, age, and cholesterol content; and how to ensure you don't take home a carton with a cracked egg in it. If your goal is to educate, some editing strategies might be:

- Break down the subject or task into small, clearly identifiable parts. For example, tell your viewers that when choosing eggs they should note their expiration date, check the level of refrigeration they're stored at, inspect each egg for cracks, and check the carton for signs of contamination. You would probably use specific shots or sequences to illustrate each of these steps.

- Provide assignments or tasks to help the viewer apply and reinforce what she's learned. For example, send the viewer out to buy some eggs, and include a sequence where she can compare the eggs she's bought to a sample package you show on screen.

- Repeat important steps. Learning is based on repetition. The more you repeat critical information, the more likely the viewer is to retain it.

Films That Persuade

Persuading is a cross between informing and entertaining. A good persuasive film convinces the viewer without ever feeling preachy or didactic. At their best, such films are entertainment that leaves you with a particular message: For instance, if you want to persuade your audience that eggs are the best food for breakfast, lunch, and dinner, you might base your show around a happy family that eats lots of eggs. If your goal is to persuade, some editing strategies might be:

- Show both sides of an issue. Neglecting to acknowledge the opposing view leaves an audience suspicious. For instance, you could acknowledge that because eggs don't have much fiber, the happy family might want to eat some salad on the side now and then with their omelets.

- Focus on the micro view first, and then extrapolate to the macro. For example, start by telling the story of one family and its egg consumption habits, and then expand to show how the whole community benefits.

- Pay extra attention to your soundtrack. Music will affect the emotions of your viewers far more powerfully than purely visual information (see the "Designing Sound" section in Chapter 7).

Films That Entertain

Entertainment refers to shows whose primary purpose is to amuse or divert the audience. They may be humorous, dramatic, suspenseful, or provide some other form of emotional release, such as empathy. An entertaining egg movie might tell the story of a chicken desperate to keep her eggs from being eaten. She follows a customer home and devises elaborate obstacles to prevent his family from cooking her eggs. If your goal is to entertain your audience, some editing strategies might be:

- Hide the evidence of filmmaking artifice. You want to disguise the fact that a crew of 52 people worked for three days in order to make a scene that runs for only ten minutes onscreen. A great deal of editing technique is about concealing this artifice.

- Use editing techniques that emphasize suspense, humor, and action (see Chapter 3, "Editing Patterns").

- Create an emotionally engaging story through the basic dramatic structures such as cause and effect, building tension, and conventional pacing (also covered in Chapter 3, "Editing Patterns").

Getting to Know Your Tools

Whether you're editing with Final Cut Pro, Avid, or on a Steenbeck flatbed, the better you know your production tools, the better work you'll do. Of course, just knowing which toolbar holds which features and controls won't tell you when to use them. But familiarizing yourself with time-saving shortcuts and compound features available in your editing suite will free up more of your brain power for making those creative decisions.

It's equally important to know what your tool *can't* do. Sure, you can drive nails with a screwdriver, it sort of works. But wouldn't you be happier using a hammer? For example, Final Cut has some robust *compositing* and audio capabilities (see Chapter 8, "Special Effects," and Chapter 7, "Cutting the Track"), but other tools, like Discreet Combustion or Avid ProTools, are better suited for accomplishing complex tasks in those areas. Likewise, you could probably edit a feature film in Adobe After Effects, but since it's geared toward creating special effects, why would you want to?

Most professional editors have a big "box" of tools, each one suited for a different job. Knowing which tool is right for which job is one of the things that differentiates a pro from a novice—but this kind of knowledge comes only from experience. If you're still learning, be patient: Read books like this, and exchange ideas with more seasoned editors via user groups, online forums, and so on. You'll learn a lot.

Most important, *practice*. Edit everything you can get your hands on. Nothing can teach you better than actually doing the job. The beauty of the new technology is that it's easier (and cheaper) than ever to gain experience by actually producing video projects. If you've got some downtime between paying gigs, go ahead and put together a project to keep you busy. Try doing a public service announcement for a nonprofit you admire, or a music video for a friend's band. Every hour you spend editing will make you a better editor. You will hone your craft, develop a personal style, and of course, add clips to your résumé and reel.

The Importance of Knowing Your Audience

You can't edit well if you don't know your audience. Editing a film aimed at teenage girls will be very different than editing one targeted at middle-aged businessmen. A good editor never forgets who will be watching the film, and she bases every edit decision on that knowledge. Hopefully, the writer, director, and production crew all kept the audience in mind, too, as they carried out their roles. But as editor, you are the final gatekeeper, the ultimate arbiter of how best to communicate the film's message.

All the same, never presume that you can guess what your audience wants. Nothing turns off an audience quicker than a film that feels patronizing or "targeted." To learn what viewers want, find some and ask them. For instance, imagine you're making a film meant for single working mothers. Find someone in that demographic and quiz her about what television shows she watches and what kinds of movies she tends to see. You'll probably be surprised at what you find. Are you making a show that's supposed to be exciting for kids? Great! Go out and find some kids, ask these same questions. If possible, ask them to be your sample viewers, show them a *rough cut* of your film, and invite specific feedback. And whoever your informants are—single working mothers, ten year-olds, whoever—listen to their answers and implement them in your next cut.

The Value of Getting Involved Early

It's your job to cut the movie and make it look as good as you can, but this can be tough if you have no control over what got shot in the first place. Is this an unfair predicament? Of course, but try telling that to your producer after the film bombs.

Smart editors get involved in the production as early as possible so they can ensure that adequate *coverage* (a variety of angles) is shot. Sometimes coverage is so bad that you simply can't cut the scene without changing its structure. On smaller productions, the producer and director may not have the foresight or budget to bring in an editor before finalizing their *shot lists,* but it's very much in your interest—and theirs—for you to look over those shot lists and (if necessary) talk with the producer and director before production begins.

What should you look for? Every scene should be covered from multiple angles: long shots, close-ups, reverse angles (see Chapter 2, "Film Language"). Action sequences require even more coverage than static scenes. Objects that play an important role in the scene should be captured in *inserts,* and emotional content should be emphasized with close-ups of the actors' faces. Always insist on *cutaways* for every scene. And remind the audio recordist to record *room ton*e for every location and mic position.

Another thing to watch out for is scene transitions. What's the editing plan to get out of one scene and into the next? If this is overlooked during production, the editor will have to scrounge up something for a suitable bridge.

Also, the earlier you get involved, the more opportunity you'll have to become familiar with the story and the details of the footage.

If you can swing it, it's great to be physically present on set during filming. Here's why:

- You may get ideas for cutaways or additional coverage once you see the actual location.

- If time is running short on set, shots are often dropped or combined. Sometimes that's OK, but it will end up being your problem if the crew fails to get adequate coverage or if the *D.P.* hurriedly places a shot on the wrong side of the *axis*.

Sometimes it's nice for an editor to come onto a job completely "clean"—without any knowledge of, or attachment to, what occurred during production. For instance, someone who suffered through an 18-hour day when the rave scene was shot may have a harder time trimming it. A totally mercenary editor can cut more ruthlessly and may make a better final program. But usually, even just 30 seconds on set can save you many hours of post-production agony.

Meeting Your Team

If at all possible, take time to discuss the film with the writer and director before you start editing. You want to fully understand where the story originated and how it's been interpreted before you got involved. You will need to work closely with the director to find out if he wants to highlight or downplay certain script elements. This will provide valuable clues about how to approach the editing process.

For instance, in *Want* I intended it to seem as though the moon was watching over the main character, so throughout the film the cinematographer frequently chose high-angle shots to simulate the moon's point of view. Regardless of what was photographed, the choice and placement of these shots was an editorial decision. Another example would be the director asking the editor to use a certain sound effect every time a particular character or location is seen.

The relationship between the editor and the director is one of the most crucial associations in the production. Some directors spend many hours in the editing room, looking over the editor's shoulder and taking an active role in the editing process. Others assume that the editor has done her homework and leave it to her to get the job done. In either case, good communication with your director will result in a clear editorial vision that illuminates the project in its best light. A bad relationship may lead to a situation where the directorial vision and the editing style are so incompatible that they compete, confusing or distracting the audience and diluting the impact of the film.

Working With the Director

The director is responsible for the overall look and feel of the program. As editor, your job is to implement that look and feel, while stepping around the land mines inherent in the footage. For the decisions made during production and those made in post-production to match stylistically, the editor must understand and share the director's vision.

The best directors are fluent in the language and grammar of film, and many of them have a background in editing, which can make your collaboration with them easier. Unfortunately, many directors don't know anything about editing. If you're working with one of them, the first thing you should do is buy him a copy of this book—OK, you can lend him yours, but make sure he reads it. A director needn't be able to use an editing tool like Final Cut, but the more familiar he is with the details of the editor's job, the more effective your communication will be.

Protocol in the Editing Room

Different people work differently. You need to figure out what your own preferences are so you can do your best work—and then make sure everyone understands how you want your editing room to run. Sometimes a director will look over your shoulder throughout the editing process. Other times she will leave you alone as long as you turn in a daily or weekly report. Which model makes you most comfortable? Do you enjoy the collaborative nature of having the director in the room, or does that destroy your concentration?

Make sure you find out how often you are supposed to turn in work to the director and producer. Different plans may be appropriate depending on the length of the program.

Creating a Realistic Schedule

One of the biggest mistakes an editor can make is underestimating how long a project will take—and underbidding the price. The fact is, it can be very difficult to guess how long a film will take to edit, especially since so many factors that affect the schedule are beyond your control. Still, unless you help your producer and director set realistic expectations, you may be in for an unpleasant experience.

This may seem like an intrusion of business advice into the middle of what's supposed to be a creative guide, but in the film industry, creativity and business are inextricably connected. Depending on various factors, it can take anywhere from one day to one week to complete editing one minute of film. Coming up with an accurate overall estimate will mean the difference between a good edit and a sloppy rush job.

Also keep the 80/20 rule in mind: The last 20 percent of the process invariably takes 80 percent of the time. You may complete a rough cut quickly, but that doesn't necessarily mean the fine cut will be equally fast.

Here are some of the factors that will have an impact on your editing schedule.

The Footage   Before you come up with an estimate for editing time, take a look at the footage. Ideally, you should screen some of that footage before taking the job in the first place. What you mostly need to find out is how much coverage was shot. A show with very little coverage means fewer choices for you when it's time to build a sequence. Also, you want to check whether the camera angles match and the quality of the production sound is usable.

The Budget   Is there enough money for reshoots? Pickups? ADR and proper sound design? How about color correction? How flexible is the budget for post? All of this will have an impact on your schedule and the ultimate quality of the show.

The Vision   How clear is the director's vision? Does the footage serve that vision? How well do you understand it? If the director's vision isn't clear at the start, you may need to re-edit a show multiple times while you and he try to figure out what it is. This will affect how long the project takes and your satisfaction in editing it.

The Schedule   Of course, someone on the producer's staff has already decided how long the project will take to edit, and she will expect you to work within her schedule. While it is not impossible for someone to estimate correctly, in my experience most estimates fall somewhere between overly optimistic and wildly unrealistic. Shows that are budgeted for three weeks editing time often take four weeks, and sometimes as many as six.

It's important to be clear on exactly what you are expected to deliver in the allotted time. An assembly? A rough cut? A fine cut? Sound mix? Sometimes dates are flexible; sometimes the schedule is locked down because of a commitment made by the producers. You need to know which is the case before you start, because as soon as you sign on this will be your problem.

How Much Should You Charge?   Sometimes you will sign on for an hourly rate; other times you'll be asked to bid for the job on the basis of a one-time project fee. In most cases, you should try to bill hourly. Otherwise you're going to wind up working a few 20-hour days at your own expense as the schedule draws to a close.

Reading the Script

The most important thing an editor can do to prepare for a job is to become intimately familiar with the processes and creative decisions that preceded her work—starting with the script. The better you know your script, the easier it will be to create an editing style that's consistent with the larger vision of the production.

A good editor should know the script as thoroughly as the writer does—not just the structure of the story and the sequence of events but themes, tone, and style. Is the story about human relationships, or does it explore an inner psychological state? Is it comic? Contemplative? Suspenseful? Understanding the big picture will help you to resolve smaller editing problems as they arise.

Viewing the Footage

You also need to become deeply familiar with all the *footage* available to you. Every shot, every *take*. The better you know the footage, the better you'll be able to edit it. Perhaps there's a two-second shot from scene 31 you can steal to complete an editing sequence in scene 18. Or perhaps there's a moment after the director called "Cut," but before the camera operator stopped shooting, when the actor let her guard down and gave a genuine expression that's exactly what will sell scene 91.

I'll repeat this, because it's supremely important: *You need to review every take of every shot.* It's tempting to simply scan through the takes that the director circled on the shot list or camera log—meaning he thought they were "good"—but again and again I've found that there may be a magical moment, say, at the beginning of an aborted take, that might make all the difference when you construct the final sequence.

Final Cut has very powerful tools for marking and cataloging your media (see Chapter 4, "Preparing to Edit"). Use them! Watch the footage again and again. All of it. Catalogue it, make comments about the shots, and note the things that stand out. If you follow this advice you will find that you have the entire body of footage in your head and at your fingertips when you are editing. And that's exactly what you need.

Budgeting Time for Sound Design

Remember that audio creates more than half the impact of your program. Three kinds of sound are combined to create the final audio track: dialogue, sound effects, and music. Often these will take up dozens of discrete tracks. Thankfully, Final Cut has unlimited audio tracks available to you (see Chapter 7, "Cutting the Track").

The process of assembling and editing audio can become very complex, and large productions typically hire two or three specialized sound editors to help out. One sound editor will cut dialogue while another edits the sound effects tracks.

The music supervisor will secure rights to copyright-protected materials and hire a composer to write an original score. A third editor, the music editor, may be responsible for editing the music and incorporating it into the final sound mix.

On smaller productions, many of these jobs are handled by fewer people, but ultimately you, as editor, will be responsible for bringing together dialogue, sound effects, and music for the final sound mix. For any film that will be dubbed, or distributed in foreign languages, you will be required to provide a separate version of the final mix with everything except the dialogue.

Coordinating Special Effects Production

Similarly, in most big-budget productions, special visual effects will be created and edited by a separate team. The visual effects supervisor will oversee the production of the shots, working with a crew that can range from a team of artists designing models at digital workstations to an entire production crew responsible for shooting plates, making mattes, building models, filming motion control sequences, and so on.

It's critical for the visual effects team to operate in very close coordination with editorial, since the results of each team's work will affect the other's. The editor needs to know the precise length and placement of the special effects shots, and the effects team needs to return *comps* as quickly as possible, so the editor can see how they integrate into her scenes. This process often takes several rounds of back and forth to complete successfully.

Practicing the Art of the Possible

It's essential to understand the realities of your production. Learn to factor budgetary constraints, time constraints, length of the show, and client control into your editing decisions. For instance, sure, the show might be better if you ran the whole thing through the *Cinelook* filter and remixed the sound at a Dolby Surround mixing stage—but before you start making editing decisions based on those expectations, be sure you have the time to do it and the money to pay for it.

A mediocre show that's finished is infinitely better than a brilliant one that never gets completed. Thousands of projects are abandoned every year.

Finally, it's important to know where your responsibilities begin and end. If your director or client has final say over your creative decisions, you need to understand that fact before you pull your hair out over creative differences. She has her reasons, and if you don't like 'em…go out and make your own film!

CHOOSING THE SHOT

One of the most important parts of the editor's job is to discard unusable footage. A typical production shoots between 20 and 100 times more footage than the editor will use in the final program. (This is what filmmakers mean when they refer to a 20:1 or 100:1 *shooting ratio.*) That means the editor must eliminate (in the former case) 19 minutes of footage for every minute she uses. How do you decide what to toss?

Usually you'll have *heads and tails* (extra footage at the beginning and end of each shot) that inflate the shooting ratio a little. Depending on the nature of the production, you may have lots of different shots of each scene (coverage), you may have lots of takes of each shot, or you may have both.

How do you tell a good shot from a bad one? Here are some criteria professional editors use to make the cut.

Composition

An editor has to be able to recognize the elements of good composition. Composition refers to the arrangement of objects within the frame, and the elements therein include both positive and negative space (**Figure 1.1**).

To some extent defining "good" composition and "bad" composition is an aesthetic exercise involving subjective elements like personal taste—and a good editor should be able to recognize not just her own taste but the varied tastes of her varied audiences. Nonetheless, you can use several quantifiable technical criteria to help eliminate badly composed shots.

Figure 1.1 "Positive space" refers to the areas in the image containing subject matter, and "negative space" refers to the areas without it. Positive and negative space can also be thought of as areas of light and darkness. Good composition requires an appropriate balance between positive and negative space. This image contains a large amount of negative space at one side, which contributes to the dramatic impact of the shot.

Headroom

Good composition requires adequate negative space framing a subject's head. Look for shots with a small but comfortable buffer between the subject's head and the edge of the frame. If the buffer space is too small, the subject will appear cramped or contained. If the buffer space is too large, the subject will appear to be floating loosely in his environment. Both errors make the viewer feel uncomfortable.

There are only two exceptions to this rule:

- Extreme close-ups where it's OK to cut off the top of the head in order to see the jaw move.

- Wide shots where showing the subject in the context of the environment requires placing him far from the edges of the frame (**Figure 1.2**).

Figure 1.2 The images above show proper headroom: The subjects are clearly visible without any wasted space.

The pictures above show incorrect headroom. The image on the left has too much empty space above the subject, and the image on the right cuts off the face of one of the two subjects.

The images above illustrate exceptions to the headroom rule. On the left, this wide shot captures the subject as a silhouette against the surf. The "excessive" space above the subject's head is desirable because it helps to show the environment and the subject's place in it. Tight close-ups typically cut off the top of the subject's head in order to reveal jaw movement, as illustrated on the right.

Noseroom (aka Facespace)

Look for shots with adequate room between the subject and the edge of the frame *in the direction she's facing.* If the subject is too close to the edge of the frame, the audience can't see what she's looking at. This is unsettling and distracts viewers from the subject herself, focusing their attention on the space just offscreen where the subject is looking. This effect becomes amplified when you take into account the various rules and guidelines regarding screen direction, and whether a subject should be looking screen-right or screen-left (**Figure 1.3**). (See the section on screen direction in Chapter 2.)

Figure 1.3 The image on the left shows good noseroom: Since the subject is on the right side of the frame, looking left, the composition provides a comfortable amount of space between her and the edge of frame. The image on the right shows poor noseroom: The subject is on the right side of frame, looking directly into the right frame edge. This unsettles the audience because they can't see what she's looking at.

Also, pay attention to how the character is centered in the frame—which may be significant both in terms of the shot's emotional impact and in identifying the correct reverse shot when dealing with point of view (see the sections on reverse and point-of-view shots in Chapter 2). This will be even more pronounced when working in a wide-screen format like 16:9 or 1:1.85.

The Point of Focus

One of the editor's key tasks is to guide the audience's attention, not just in terms of how the main story is told from the beginning to the end of the film, but in each shot along the way. You need to choose shots with a clear point of focus. That could be a character, an object, a conflict, or an action.

For instance, a *two-shot* (that's any shot with two people in it; see the section on two-shots in Chapter 2) where both subjects' head- or noseroom is compromised in order to see both of them is very distracting. The viewer doesn't know where the point of focus is and loses interest in the narrative (**Figure 1.4**).

Figure 1.4 This shot is badly composed because it doesn't provide a clear point of focus for the viewer. Both characters are partially cut off. This could have been corrected by moving farther away from the subjects or panning to one or the other.

Distracting Background Elements

Shots in which an object appears to be sticking out of the back of someone's head (**Figure 1.5**), or in which a highly legible sign or brightly colored object is creating a distraction in the background, are poorly composed. The objects tend to draw attention away from the subject. Sometimes the distracting element might be a light stand, a *grip,* a mic boom, the boom operator, or maybe just his shadow. Pay special attention to reflections and shadows. Nothing spoils a shot like the camera operator's shadow falling on the subject.

Figure 1.5 While in some cases you can overlook distracting background elements, at other times they are just too glaring. This framing gives the actor an impressive hairstyle that I suspect neither she nor the set stylist intended.

It's general practice in dramatic films to hide the tools of film creation as much as possible. Audiences for some genres, such as documentary or reality-based programs, will tolerate revealing these elements.

Lighting Problems

Badly lit shots can diffuse the viewer's point of focus or destroy it altogether. At worst, they can be so distracting they are unusable.

But perfect lighting is not crucial—although it helps to be able to see the subject. The most important consideration is how well the lighting in a given shot matches the shots around it. If, in a single scene, you cut from a brightly lit shot to a dimly lit one, you pull the viewer's attention away from the subject and toward the construction of the film itself. Scenes that are under- or overexposed can play convincingly as long as all the shots in the sequence are consistent. Pickups can be problematic in this regard, because they are often shot at a different time from the sequence into which they'll be cut and may display different lighting characteristics. In some cases, production lighting errors can be corrected by using color correction filters (see "Correcting Errors," Chapter 8).

In general, look out for *lens flares,* backlit subjects, and shots with conflicting *key lights.* If the key light is coming from the left in the master shot and the right in the single, it won't match (see the sections on master and single shots in Chapter 2).

Audio Problems

Audio that sounds inconsistent across different shots in the same scene is even worse than inconsistent lighting. Visuals convey information, so as long you can see what's going on, the picture will be understood. Audio tends to convey emotional tone, so we're much more sensitive to subtle inconsistencies in the audio. Fortunately, many audio problems can be repaired in post, but this is often expensive and sometimes quite difficult.

Checking It Out on the Big Screen

Never make a final editing decision about anything until you view the sequence in the same format the audience will see. Problems that seem insignificant (or even invisible) on your 13-inch editing monitor can explode into disaster when projected 20 feet tall.

For instance, timing and performances work very differently at different scales, so you should hold off locking down a sequence until you've seen it at full scale. You'll want to pace your scene a little more slowly if the film is going to be projected in a theater and a little more quickly for shows intended for videotape release.

Paper Dolls

One trick you can employ in the editing room is to cut out a paper silhouette of a row of theatergoers and tape it to the bottom of your monitor (**Figure 1.6**).

Figure 1.6 The poor man's screening room.

This may seem silly, but it is remarkable how well it works. Seeing the video playback behind the tiny heads allows you to get a sense of the scale it will have in the theater.

If your final presentation mode will be VHS videotape, don't put the finishing touches on your show until you see what happens to contrast and detail when your high-resolution masters are dubbed down to VHS. Perhaps that shot with borderline exposure problems will become unacceptably murky after it goes through the transfer process. Better to find out before 10,000 tapes have been duplicated.

PERFORMANCE: CHOOSING THE TAKE

The editor is responsible for choosing the performances that best communicate the purpose of the scene—and of the whole piece. Often the director will be involved in these decisions, but if you're lucky, he won't be there all the time.

In most cases someone on set will have kept a *camera log*. Sometimes the best takes will be circled, or flagged with Good, Better, Best indicators. Having this information is invaluable, especially when the director has already provided her recommendations. But don't rely on the log alone; the editor's eye may discern problems that everyone else has missed.

What Constitutes a Good Take?

Occasionally, a flaw that seemed fatal on the set proves to be subtle, unnoticeable, or easily fixable in the editing room. Unfortunately, most of the time the reverse is true—and what was chosen as the "best take" on the set has a lens flare or some audio problem that went unnoticed at the time. Sometimes, the "best take" may not match *continuity* with the "best take" of another shot. In that case the editor must make a trade-off between maintaining continuity and choosing the best performance.

In fact, often the best take is really a combination of several takes. Since you're likely to be cutting back and forth between shots, you can use the beginning of one take, the middle of another, and the end of a third. A shot described on the camera log as aborted or unacceptable may actually have been perfectly successful—until the moment when the light fell over. There's no reason not to use the beginning of that take.

Ultimately, it is up to you to make the best film you can with the footage available to you. The better you know every foot of that footage, the more likely you are to make the wisest choices. You should see every frame of film or tape, and you should see it more than once.

What constitutes a good take? Usually it's a combination of what happens in front of the camera and what happens behind it. Sometimes a mediocre performance can be transformed into a great take by a stellar camera movement. Sometimes the camera operator may reframe subtly at just the wrong time, accidentally anticipating the actor's movement within the frame and ruining the shot. Each take is different and offers different opportunities to a good editor.

STYLE AND HOW TO GET IT

Style is a pretty abstract thing. I use the word to describe a filmmaker's aesthetic approach to the material. Style explains why one editor might choose to edit rhythmically while another prefers a more syncopated pace, and a third uses a technique like jumpcutting (see the section on jumpcutting in Chapter 2). Style is why one director might select wide-angle lenses for a scene or shoot from a crane. Stylistic issues apply equally to audio, lighting, casting, and the script. Although style may seem subtle and of less concern than the content of your program, it can make the difference between a pretty good program and a great one.

Ask Orson Welles, Federico Fellini, or George Lucas. Style is everything.

Where Does Style Come From?

Style starts with the script. Good writing always has style, and good script writing is no exception. At the simplest level you can look at what genre a script is: Comedy? Thriller? Western? Genres like these come with their own traditional styles, elements that an audience will expect. For instance, a thriller drops clues early on that will lure the audience into trying to solve the mystery.

To get an idea of how this works, look at some of your favorite genre films and try to figure out what types of scenes carry the weight of the film. Are the themes conveyed through dialogue or through actions? What are the rhythms of the script, the pacing of the cutting?

At every stage of a film production, as creative film workers do their jobs, they are implementing visual and dramatic style. For instance, the art department sets production style through set design and dressing, costuming and makeup. Although this is most obvious in period dramas, where these elements are more pronounced, you'll see this process at work even in modern comedies.

The D.P. creates visual style by selecting camera position, movement, angle, and lighting design. For instance, Jim Jarmusch's *Stranger Than Paradise* used a unique photographic and editorial style by filming every scene in a static long shot and editing as sparsely as possible. Even the location manager has a big impact when she chooses a particular house or outdoor setting to film a scene.

On set with the actors, a good director will shape performances to serve the overall style of the piece. For instance, in the film *Raising Arizona* the Coen brothers chose an acting style that was broad and exaggerated. For *The Remains of the Day*, James Ivory elected one that was understated and subtle.

During post-production, a talented editor will make countless choices about key elements like pacing and storytelling structure that will impact the final style of the film. Also, sound design is created almost entirely during post, including choices about music, special effects cues, even the equalization characteristics of the primary audio track. These days you may be responsible for color correction and visual effects as well. All of these elements will influence the show's style. Pay attention to the stylistic choices made earlier in the process, and make an effort to understand and complement them.

The key to good style is twofold: First, consistency. Second, appropriateness.

Consistency

In some ways, stylistic consistency is far more important than specific decisions about whether to cut fast or slow, hand-hold the camera, or play a whole scene in a low-angle wide shot. Consistent style may not necessarily be "good," but inconsistent style is always bad. Not only is inconsistency aesthetically unappealing, it interferes with communicating your program's message.

Select an approach and stick with it. Simply being aware of having consciously *selected* a style will often be enough to remind you to make editing decisions consistent with that style.

Appropriateness

Next comes appropriateness. Editing style must complement the content of the film in a way that creates something greater than the sum of its parts.

For example, in *Want* I needed to show how the main character lives in two different worlds: the glamorous public world where he works, shops, eats, and drives; and the darker, personal world where he carries out private activities and makes emotional contacts. The D.P. and I called the two worlds Glamland and Underworld, and we set up a list of stylistic elements for each one: Glamland shots were made from a crane or a tripod, Underworld shots were hand-held or shot from a monopod; Glamland scenes were lit warmly and evenly, Underworld shots were lit with shadowed areas and a cooler look; Glamland used bright colors, while Underworld was muted and monochromatic.

We went through the entire script and identified where each scene fit along the continuum between Glamland and Underworld. This way, during production all we had to do was glance at our chart once per scene to know exactly what the intended style was to be.

In the end, our stylistic vision informed everything about the film, from the costume designs to camera placement and dramatic direction for the scenes. The end result was, I like to think, a film that has a clear and poignant style.

> ### *Breaking the Rules*
>
> *Genre guidelines and traditional styles are rules that can be most striking when they're broken. At one point in the film, Trey (our main character) is starting to slip out of normal life into his inner psychological obsessions. To illustrate this, we shot one scene twice: first in the Glamland style, and then the Underworld style. I wanted to maximize the impact of the different styles, so I cut the whole sequence using Glamland takes—except for one shot, where I cut to a close-up of Trey from the Underworld footage. The effect of breaking my own stylistic guidelines was to emphasize the rules themselves, which accentuated the emotional content of the scene. The visual style reverberated with the content, engaging the audience in a more significant way than either element could have managed alone.*

Developing a Personal Style

Everyone likes to think they have style, and the truth is, they do. Every filmmaker has a unique signature, whether she likes it or not. The question is: Is it aesthetically appealing or provocative, or is it just hard to watch? The more easily you can identify and understand other filmmakers' styles, the more clearly you will be able to identify and understand your own—and make the best of it.

A good craftsperson can mimic others' styles and still have a clear sense of his own. But it takes practice to achieve this kind of mastery. When painters train, they paint copies of masterpieces to understand how they were created. When musicians learn their instruments, they begin by reproducing music composed and recorded by others. Even craftspeople like woodworkers start by reproducing existing designs. It's strange to me that many beginning filmmakers jump right into their own film projects without ever taking this step.

In fact, one of the best ways to understand the aesthetic elements that make up cinematic style is to attempt to copy that style from an existing piece of work. Pick a scene from your favorite movie, TV commercial, or music video. Of course, since film is such a complex medium with so many elements, it may not be possible for you to faithfully reproduce your favorite TV show. But you can make a start.

Pay close attention to the elements that contribute to the finished film: What is the nature of the script or concept? What are the key elements of the art direction (color schemes, arrangement of props and sets, costumes), lighting design, and so on?

Notice the camera choices: Does the camera move a lot? If so, is the movement smooth or jerky? Are the camera angles extremely high or low? Is the camera generally close to the subject or far away? What medium was the project shot on?

Innumerable factors go into style, but since this is a book about editing and post-production, let's focus on editing: How long does each shot last? Does the editor generally use shots that are uniform in length, or is the editing arrhythmic with long and short shots intermixed? Are the edit points marked by cuts or dissolves? How often does the editor repeat shots? Does the film use traditional cutting patterns, or are the basic editing rules bent or broken? Does the editor favor jump cuts, or does he preserve continuity? Are camera angles consistent, or do they change from shot to shot? What can you say about the sound design? Most feature films use 48 to 128 discrete tracks throughout the film. How many different tracks can you identify (dialogue, sound effects, ambiances, music, and so on)?

Once you've identified all the elements that contribute to cinematic style in the show you've chosen, go out and try to reproduce them. See how closely you can replicate the style. Try this a couple of times. What better way to master the tools of your trade? These days the tools of production are cheap enough that you have no excuse *not* to practice your craft—before you put your heart and your pocketbook (or your client's heart and pocketbook) into a real project.

INTERVIEW

Brian Berdan began his career with an apprenticeship on David Lynch's *Blue Velvet.* Since then he's worked with a variety of directors, including Oliver Stone and Peter Bogdanovich, and edited films with a wide diversity of styles. His credits include *Grosse Pointe Blank, Natural Born Killers,* and *Smoke Signals.* When we spoke, he was working on Mark Pellington's *The Mothman Prophecies.* Since then, he has completed *The Big Bounce* for Warner Bros.

MICHAEL WOHL: WHAT'S YOUR FAVORITE PART OF YOUR JOB?

Brian Berdan: I get to dabble in all the different aspects of the creative process. I get a little bit of the music, I get a little bit of the visual effects, I get a little of the sound design and a little of the writing. I've got my fingers in everything. It's one of the most creative jobs next to being the director. During the sound mix is one of my most favorite times. It's when it all comes together and you're seeing the finished product on the screen.

DESCRIBE YOUR PROCESS. HOW DO YOU BEGIN A PROJECT?

It's all based on the script and the story. Once I find a script I like, I'll meet with the director. If we hit it off, off we go. If we have similar ideas about how the story's going to go, we might have an hour long conversation two months before shooting. I try to be involved in the rewriting process, if I can, in any small way. There are usually two or three big problems in the script and I say, "This is not going to work. You've written three scenes in a row in the same location. We've got to do something a little different here."

HOW IMPORTANT IS IT FOR YOU TO WATCH THE DAILIES?

Lately directors haven't been very regimented about watching dailies every night. Part of it's because we have videotapes, and they say, "I'll see it back at the hotel." I like looking at dailies totally raw, never having seen the set. I hate going to the set because that ruins things for me. I see how a room is laid out, and I might assume things while I'm cutting based on that knowledge. But, if I'm just seeing it from the dailies then I have to make the logic work by myself. I'm the first audience member to see something. I make little notes, and then I go back through the footage again and make selects. Just anything that's interesting: A flash frame, a smile. Then I build this huge "selects reel," and from there I'll start refining.

HOW MUCH OF THE SHOW IS CUT BEFORE THE SHOOTING'S FINISHED?

Hopefully, the whole thing is cut three days after shooting's over. I try to keep up to camera. The most important reason you're doing that is so that the production knows that they have all the shots they need. For example, I'll be cutting a scene and realize, "You didn't cover this side of the scene, and you haven't torn the set down yet, so go back and get this shot, please." We're missing one little link and quickly you grab a close-up of somebody.

HOW MANY OF THE SCENE LINKS ARE PLANNED IN THE SCRIPT AND HOW MANY ARE DEVISED IN THE EDITING PROCESS?

It depends on how visual the director is. On *Mothman* we're coming up with all kinds of cool transitions after the fact. A lot of times, you're moving scenes around. We had a scene where we had a great transition, but the order of the scenes didn't work so we had to give up that beautiful transition to make the story work. In fact, rarely have I been on a show where they had meticulously planned out cut points. The only one that actually was kind of cool was *Smoke Signals*. Chris Eyre had worked out some very cool transitions to do time flashbacks and flash forwards. It's very easy. It's like putting slot B into tab A. That's fun when they work, but I also like finding things that fit together just randomly or graphically. I'm not a big fan of dissolves, but on this show we're doing a lot of dissolves because we're finding lots of big beautiful open frames and when you dissolve, something pretty comes through. Typically, I don't have things planned out by the director; they just shoot a lot of film.

HAVE YOU EVER LOOKED AT A SEQUENCE AND SAID, "WHAT THE HELL AM I GOING TO DO WITH THIS?"

In *Natural Born Killers,* there's a scene in the jail with Juliette Lewis and Tom Sizemore, and they'd shot all kinds of great coverage—black and white, blown-out color, normal color—but they'd spent so much effort making all these cool shots that I didn't have any really good performances from any one take. So I did a series of five jump cut close-ups on Tom Sizemore. Each one was in a different format. That turned a problem into a solution.

WITH *NATURAL BORN KILLERS,* HOW CLOSE WAS THE FINAL EDIT TO THE ORIGINAL VISION SET FORTH IN THE SCRIPT?

Well, we worked on that for a little more than a year. It was written in flashback form so we cut it that way. Then at the five-month point, we decided, "Let's try it linear." So we rearranged the whole movie and worked on it that way for a month or so, and then ended up going back to the original flashback form. It was radically different from our first cut because the first cut was about four hours long. But some of the scenes were very similar. That happens a lot.

Sometimes the director, after chasing his tail on a particular scene and problem, will say, "Show me your first cut." And you pop it back in and they prefer it. That happens a lot, and it's not always the best thing. The director is giving up on whatever he was trying to achieve. Quite often, it's the difference between their intentions and what ends up on film. But part of the editor's job is to stay objective and fight for what works best based on what was shot, not based on what was written or intended.

TELL ME ABOUT SOME OF THE EDITING CHALLENGES YOU'VE FACED ON *THE MOTHMAN PROPHECIES*.

Too many shots. This movie has a huge climax action sequence. If I cut it the way it was story-boarded and shot, it would probably be 15 or 20 minutes long. It should be about 5 minutes long. So, sometimes you'll find a point where an action will loop back on itself. Like we have the actress walking to one end of this bridge and she used to do something else, but I skip that whole section and pick her up when she passes back to the bridge again. It's just ways to find *lifts* in a scene to streamline it.

DO YOU LIKE A DIRECTOR SITTING WITH YOU IN THE EDITING ROOM, OR DO YOU PREFER TO BE LEFT ALONE?

I prefer someone who leaves me alone. I like him to get a fresh look when I show it for the first time. If I've completely struck out on a scene, we'll go through the dailies again and get our heads together on what he likes about a particular performance. But then I've got to go back and approach it by myself again. You need to concentrate, and if there's too much back and forth on every little thing, you lose your concentration. Editing to me is more subconscious. It's like sculpting with clay, and as you play with it, it keeps dripping and moving, and you're inspired by the way it drips. But I also like a lot of personal contact. It's tough when I'm working by myself for too long; I can get lost. Then I need the director's input, so it's a balance.

DESCRIBE YOUR EDITING STYLE. IT SEEMS VERY DIVERSE.

I try to just listen to what the film says. As the first audience member, that's your job. The one thing I always listen to is: What do you want to see, and when do you want to see it? You want to give the audience what they're expecting but in a unique and special way.

DO YOU HAVE ANY ADVICE FOR YOUNG EDITORS?

Keep watching movies. Don't turn down any opportunity to cut. Do anything you can to get on a professional film. Being an assistant on a bigger film allows you to be around bigger people. I was the assistant on *Heaven and Earth* with Oliver [Stone]. I was just in the right place at the right time. I'd already been editing before that, and I was willing to take an assistant job again because it was in a bigger pond. Always try to cut scenes off hours and get input from the editor.

HAVE YOU PLAYED WITH FINAL CUT?

I got the program for the beginning of this show. Pretty cool thing to use. We used it on location for a week before I had the Avid out there—pretty funny: Cutting a big motion picture on the laptop at my hotel or on the plane.

CHAPTER TWO
Film Language

Film is a language. And like any language, before you can speak fluently, you need to understand its rules. What are the nouns, what are the verbs? What form does the punctuation take? Most importantly, how do you combine all these "parts of speech" to communicate your meaning?

As with any language, there are those who communicate competently and those for whom expression is an art and a craft. They not only know the grammatical rules and how to apply them, they are also attentive to style and nuance—and they know when to break the rules of syntax.

Of all of those who shape a film, the editor must think like a poet. She must comprehend the director's overall vision and know all the footage the cinematographer has provided so that she may choose the most compressed, economical, and precise expression of the intended theme through all its dimensions.

The most basic component of the film language is the shot, an individual segment of film, and it is the editor who stitches these shots together to form filmic phrases, sentences, and paragraphs, creating meaning and communicating to the audience.

TYPES OF SHOTS

Each shot is capable of performing a number of functions at once. Like a noun, it can define a subject—a house, a river, a man. But because film is a visual, time based medium, that shot can contain information that further describes the subject —an empty house on a crowded street, a river flowing past a chemical plant, a man suddenly chilled with fear. These elements further affect the mood and context of the subject and provide the building blocks of drama and story. As an editor, you need to be able to read shots for this information so you can describe and categorize them, and ultimately combine them into the grammatical structures that will be the scenes and sequences of your film.

Subject Size

I will start with the most common way to characterize a shot: size of subject in the frame. In many ways this is the most important piece of information about a shot. How close you are to the subject directly influences the audience's emotional reaction to that shot. The closer you are to the subject, the more intimately you will relate to it.

Extreme Close-up (ECU, BCU, XCU)

An *extreme close-up,* or ECU (also abbreviated XCU for those who can't spell, or BCU, for *big close-up*), is a shot in which the subject extends beyond the boundaries of the frame. The actual framing may vary: In one instance an ECU might show a single eyeball. In another it might frame a tight shot of a face. An ECU might also show a single chip on a computer circuit board or a finger dialing a telephone. In all these cases, it's understood that the subject is bigger than the particular detail being shown (**Figure 2.1**).

Figure 2.1 An extreme close-up (ECU) is any shot where the subject extends beyond the boundaries of the frame.

When the subject is a person, the ECU creates tension and intensity, since it brings the viewer and the subject closer than we ordinarily get in a real conversation. It is often used to reveal a character's inner psychological space, or sometimes her thoughts and memories. This shot can also focus attention on a particular detail, such as the veins on a leaf. This can be useful in an instructional context, or it can provide a story detail that will be meaningful when combined with other shots.

Close-up (CU)

The *close-up*, sometimes called a *tight shot,* is one of the most frequently used shots. Most often it frames a person's face and cuts off midneck, showing the face or the entire head (**Figure 2.2**). Editors use the close-up for capturing subtle emotional movements of the face. It's a very intimate shot and should be used when you need to establish a personal connection with the subject. Think of this shot as simulating the distance a friend or family member might stand from the subject; a mere acquaintance would rarely get this close.

Figure 2.2 A close-up (CU) is a shot in which the subject fills the frame. In the case of a human, the subject is usually the person's head.

One reason we feel we "know" movie stars so well is that we're used to seeing them so closely—more closely, in fact, than many of the real people in our lives. Sometimes a close-up is intended to force intimacy; some editors use it to make the audience feel connected with, or sympathetic to, a character.

The close-up can also be used to show an inanimate object. In this case, the camera moves close enough so the object fills the frame comfortably.

Medium Close-up (MCU)

As its name suggests, a *medium close-up* is a slightly wider shot than a close-up. Usually it frames the head and upper torso, cutting off mid-chest (**Figure 2.3**). If the close-up suggests familial intimacy, the MCU feels more like the social distance an acquaintance or business associate might enjoy. It gets close enough to read facial expressions, but holds a polite distance from the subject. It is also wide enough to reveal a bit of the environment surrounding the subject.

Figure 2.3 The medium close-up (MCU) simulates the distance we'd stand from someone with whom we're having a casual conversation. The MCU on the right allows us to see both subjects comfortably while focusing mainly on their faces.

Medium Shot (MS)

A *medium shot* frames the subject from the waist up (**Figure 2.4**). It is, as the name implies, a happy medium between a close-up (which emphasizes facial activity) and a long shot (which favors the environment). Since it allows the subject enough room to move around inside the frame, it is ideal for active subjects. Emotionally, as you might expect, the MS is slightly ambivalent. Although it is less intimate than a close-up, it still favors a single subject and clearly directs the viewer's attention.

Figure 2.4 The medium shot (MS) gives us a sense of the subject's environment. In the shot on the left, we can see that Rich's office has big windows overlooking the city. The scene on the right is obviously taking place in a laundromat.

Long Shot (LS, FS)

The *long shot* (sometimes known as a *full shot*) can be framed various ways. When dealing with a human subject, the camera might be set back just far enough to include the whole figure. However, a LS may also place the camera even farther back, so we can see that person walking around. In either case, while the point of focus of the shot is the human being, the environment is clearly visible as well (**Figure 2.5**).

Figure 2.5 The long shot (LS) shows the entire human figure. While it allows us to clearly identify which character we're looking at, the environment is an equally important element.

For the most part the LS is used to show action, not convey emotion. We rarely interact with people from this far away, so this shot suggests a more objective point of view than the closer shots. Since it can't capture the details of facial expression, the LS relies on a broader context, placing the subject in relation to his environment and the people around him. When the subject is an inanimate object, a LS or FS usually frames the object in its entirety, showing it in its environment.

Wide Shot (WS)

The wide shot focuses primarily on the environment. In a WS the camera is far away from the action and captures roughly what might be witnessed with the naked eye (**Figure 2.6**). The human subjects in a WS are no longer the point of the shot, even if their activity is. For example, a WS might show a firehouse with the fire truck exiting. This shot provides information and context we need to make sense of the actions and events occurring in the sequence. Although a WS usually interrupts the story's flow, audiences have become familiar with such shots and stay with the narrative when they occur.

Figure 2.6 The wide shot (WS) shifts our focus from the characters in the shot to their environment.

Extreme Long Shot (ELS, EWS, XLS)

The extreme long shot (sometimes called an extreme wide shot) covers a vast area. Like the LS and WS, this shot supplies context—but not just for a specific action or event. Usually editors use an ELS to provide broad context for the entire story line of the film. It can supply a temporal context as well as a geographical one. For instance, an ELS might show a vast, sandy desert with the hero's caravan seen as a tiny speck of black in one corner. Or it could hover over a cloverleaf on the Los Angeles freeway with the protagonist's car caught in an endless traffic jam (**Figure 2.7**).

Figure 2.7 The extreme long shot (ELS) not only gives the filmmaker an opportunity to show the subject and his environment but also provides a sense of the larger context of the sequence, or even the entire film. The image on the left emphasizes the feeling of loss by placing a tiny figure amid ruins decaying around him. The image on the right, from *Want,* shows Trey futilely throwing rocks at the giant TV billboard, a miniature Don Quixote tilting at the digital windmill.

Camera Angle

Subject size is only one way of organizing shots and understanding their function in film language. Another way to identify a shot is by the camera angle.

By default, the camera is usually placed at or near average human eye level which could be considered a neutral position. Sometimes it may be adjusted to simulate a character's point of view while sitting and so on. When a shot takes an angle that's notably different from average human eye level, that shot is generally identified by that angle, because the point of view has particular significance. These names apply to shots of any subject size.

High-Angle Shot (hi <)

The *high-angle shot* is achieved with the camera above the subject and looking down. A high-angle shot applied to a WS or an ELS suggests a kind of omniscience that may provide context for an event. When used for closer shots, it tends to make the subject appear inferior or weak (**Figure 2.8**).

Choosing this type of shot is one way to guide the audience's opinion of a character. An extremely high angle draws attention to itself, and rather than conveying a subtle emotional judgment, it will suggest a psychological distortion that might, for example, indicate the subject is in dire conflict.

Figure 2.8 A high-angle shot like the one on the left will give the audience an "omniscient" view of an event, especially when the angle is not too extreme. The high angle of the image on the right is much more radical, simulating the giant billboard's POV of Trey. This angle was chosen to reciprocate the angle of Trey's eyeline, as well as to diminish him in size.

Low-Angle Shot (lo <)

A *low-angle shot,* filmed with the camera below the subject and shooting up, has the opposite effect of the high angle (**Figure 2.9**). As with the high angle, the more extreme the low angle, the more exaggerated the effect.

Figure 2.9 Low-angle shots like these can make a character appear more powerful or can simulate a subject's POV.

In tight shots, a lower angle tends to accentuate the feeling of being immersed in the action. It's less common to use a low-angle LS, unless you're looking at the bottom of a boat or standing at the foot of a redwood tree looking up.

Low angles are often used to make an object or person appear intimidating or powerful. Cutting back and forth between slightly high- and low-angle shots in a dialogue sequence is an effective way to guide viewers toward understanding the power relationship between two people.

Both high and low angles should be motivated in some way. Use an extremely low-angle shot without a clear justification, and you run the risk of distracting the viewer.

For instance, if you simply drop in a low-angle shot of your main character and then continue cutting from normal angles, the viewer's attention may be drawn to your technique and away from the story. However, if you follow the low-angle shot with a reverse angle of the character's dog (thereby letting the viewer know that the low-angle shot was from the point of view of the dog), everyone is happy. (For more information on this "shot–reverse shot" technique, as well as point-of-view shots, see "Reverse Shot" and "Point-of-View Shot," later in this chapter.)

Camera Angle and Gender

When you're trying to make subjects look as attractive as possible, it's traditional to photograph women from a slightly high angle and men from a slightly low angle, since men are typically taller than women, and these angles reflect the perspective from which we look at each other. Still, it's interesting to note how this subtle power relationship influences audiences. One of the benefits you'll gain from making a more active analysis of the film and television shows you watch is a sharpened ability to see what filmmakers are trying to communicate to us and how our cultural stereotypes are subliminally reinforced or challenged.

Dutch Angle

The term *Dutch* or *Dutched* refers to a shot in which the horizon is tilted (**Figure 2.10**). A Dutch angle literally puts the audience off balance to create tension and anxiety. If the angle is too extreme (sometimes called *gonked*), the effect can be comical. In *Want* we repeatedly used what's known as a "rolling Dutch," where the camera rocks from left to right, to convey Trey's inability to make a decision.

Figure 2.10 The more you "Dutch" the angle, the more disoriented the subject appears—and the more disoriented the audience feels. We used this shot in *Want* for the moment when Trey finds out his father has died.

Camera Movement

Camera movement adds significant impact to a shot, but it's important to understand when to use moving shots and when to stick to static ones. When the camera moves, the audience feels as if it's moving, too. This produces a definite sense of exhilaration, but it can make the viewer miss details.

Editors must be efficiency experts. If you can get your point across with a fast, simple cut rather than a long, luxurious camera move, it's usually good practice to choose the cut. Using a move may add dynamism to a dull scene, but if you use moving shots gratuitously, you attract the viewer's attention to the shots themselves and break your storytelling flow.

A moving shot must provide new information with every new framing. Famous, elaborate moving shots, such as the opening crane shot in Orson Welles's *Touch of Evil* or the seemingly endless tracking shot through the restaurant in Martin Scorsese's *Goodfellas,* are effective because they continually provide new information, so there is no need for a cut.

It is your job as an editor to make these decisions, and you should make every choice deliberately and consciously. Moving shots should follow the Rule of Motivation: If you don't know why you are choosing a moving shot, don't use it.

Pan and Tilt

A human head can turn(or *pan*) from left to right, and it can *tilt* up and down. That's why shots in which the camera pans (**Figure 2.11**) and tilts (**Figure 2.12**) can feel quite natural to the viewer. You can use a pan or tilt to drive the action of a sequence (and the audience's point of focus) from one place to another. The trick is to use a pan or tilt only when there's something to pan or tilt *to*. In and of itself, a pan across a room is a completely dead shot unless there's something worth seeing at the beginning and the end. These shots are even more effective if there's something to lead our vision across the space—for example, a golf ball rolling towards the cup.

Figure 2.11 This pan follows the barrel of a gun from the shooter to his victim. You can see in the diagram how the camera is pivoting on a single point, as if the viewer were turning his head.

Figure 2.12 This shot tilts up from the proposal Rich is reviewing to show his face as he delivers his first lines. As the diagram illustrates, the camera's pivot simulates the effect of nodding your head.

For example, imagine a shot of a cop standing in an alleyway scratching his head. Then imagine the same shot tilting from the cop up to a jewel thief climbing the fire escape above him. That's a much more compelling editing choice than simply cutting from the cop to the thief. The tilt provides information about the proximity of the two characters, as well as showing us that the thief is escaping at exactly the same time that the cop is looking for him.

The pan and tilt shots can be effective nonfiction storytelling tools too. One example would be a sequence showing an assembly line at an auto factory. Cutting between stations on the line would show the different tasks and might communicate the order in which they occur, but a pan from one station to the next, following the movement of the conveyor belt, will give a much better understanding of how the pieces make up the whole.

Tracking Shot

Tracking shots, dolly shots, crab shots (named after the "crab dolly"), and truck shots are all terms for shots that begin with the camera in one physical location and move along the ground to another. You can use a tracking shot to immerse the viewer in a location in a way that you can't achieve with a static camera, such as when following a politician walking through a crowd. Because humans can walk around, too, simple tracking shots can be very organic and pleasant to watch (**Figure 2.13**). They are also one of the most compelling ways to guide your viewer's point of focus.

Figure 2.13 This shot, from *Want,* is a tracking move straight back from Trey after he identifies his father's body. It begins with a pedestal move that raises the camera from Gene's face to Trey, and then pulls backward until Trey becomes a tiny figure in the frame. To emphasize how Trey withdraws into himself at this moment, we removed the gurney and nurse from the corridor before the track-back could reveal them. In this way they seem to vanish. The camera setup is shown in the diagram.

At the same time, using a moving shot is like taking your viewer on a physical ride—complete with the possibility of motion sickness—so they should be used with discretion. Just like pans and tilts, dolly shots should follow the Rule of Motivation: If you don't have a deliberate reason for choosing a dolly shot, don't use one.

Follow Shot

When a tracking shot is used to move along with a subject (for instance, a car-to-car shot), it is often called a *follow shot*. This is simply a special kind of tracking shot, but it is exempt from the Rule of Motivation. As long as the viewer is moving along with the subject at a constant velocity, you can edit this tracking shot just as you would a static shot. For example a car-to-car shot would appear to the viewer as a static shot, even though the subject is moving. You could safely edit this against a static shot of the baby in the backseat, or of a man standing in his driveway, waiting for the car to arrive.

Crane Shot

A *crane shot* moves freely in three-dimensional space, and since it can make the viewer feel as if she's flying, it's quite exhilarating (**Figure 2.14**). Modern dollies usually have an arm (called a jib) that facilitates some complex camera movements, but the impact of a crane is significantly different from that of a simple dolly shot.

Humans can walk around, but they can't levitate into the air or dip their heads down to ground level while walking the way a camera on a crane can do. The crane shot is one of a category of shots that are outside the range of normal human activity. For this reason, a crane shot is much more likely than any of the previous shots to pull a viewer's attention away from the narrative. On the other hand, the impact and excitement of a successful crane shot is unparalleled. It conveys a god-like omniscience that's often exploited in action flicks or romance films.

Pedestal Shot

Many camera dollies include a hydraulically controlled pedestal that raises or lowers the camera position. If you combine a dolly move with a pedestal move, you end up with something pretty close to a crane shot, only without the complication and expense of a crane. By itself, a pedestal move is a "natural" movement, since humans can kneel and stand up. When you combine it with a dolly move, however, it seems less natural.

Figure 2.14 This crane shot follows Bruce as he approaches a window and sees a woman dancing outside. The camera moves down to a tight close-up on the doorknob as Bruce opens the door. As it swings open, we move back up, revealing that the woman has now become a man drinking tea. Frightened, Bruce slams the door shut and turns away. Using a crane allowed us to create a single fluid shot that elevated the suspense and emphasized the bizarre transformation of the dancer. Also, moving into a tight CU on the doorknob gave the dancer and tea drinker time to switch places. The camera setup is shown in the diagram.

Zoom Shot

It's hard to find a DV camera that doesn't have a zoom lens. A *zoom shot* involves changing the focal length of the lens while the shot is rolling to make the subject seem larger or smaller in the frame. This is similar to moving closer in or farther away with a dolly, but the visual effect is quite different (**Figure 2.15**).

Figure 2.15 The image on the left shows the final frame of a zoom-in. The image on the right shows the final frame of a dolly-in. Notice the difference in the size of the windmill in the background.

When you physically move the camera closer to a subject, the relationship between the subject and the background changes in an organic way—similar to what you'd see in real life if you walked closer to an object. An object ten feet away will get larger, but one 200 feet away will not change size very much. On the other hand, when you zoom in, all the objects in the frame get larger at the same time. This odd visual effect can distract the viewer.

Most instructors lecture on the evils of the zoom shot, but I think it has its place. By pulling the subject out of natural space, a zoom shot can create a psychological connection between the viewer and the subject. This technique is often employed in melodramatic shows like soap operas.

Sometimes a zoom can be combined with a dolly move. If you zoom out and dolly in at the same time (a technique popularized by Alfred Hitchcock in *Vertigo),* you can create a sense of diving into someone's head (or out of it). If the zoom complements the dolly (zoom in/dolly in), it amplifies the dolly movement and disorients the viewer. At times this is desirable.

Hand Held Shot

With new lightweight camcorders, it's easier than ever to shoot while holding a camera in your hand. This means you can take a camera places you could never get to with a bigger, heavier camera and explore nonstandard angles. The disadvantage of hand-holding is the same one I described earlier in terms of crane and zoom shots: the unnatural-movement problem.

Since our eyes are not mounted at the end of our arms, the types of movement our arm can make with a camera do not match up very comfortably with the types of movement we expect to see with our heads stuck on our necks. One of the biggest problems is simply the speed at which your arm can move around. Watching footage that was shot with a wildly swinging camera feels weird and is hard on the eyes.

You may notice that professional DV cameras are still the same size as their older Betacam cousins. This is partly because a professional videographer uses the weight and inertia of the large camera (which still rests comfortably on her shoulder) to restrict her movement—which creates smoother, more pleasing shots. The instability of a hand-held shot invariably puts the audience on edge psychologically. This effect can be felt even in shots that waver only slightly. We can detect movement in the frame at very subtle levels.

Types of Shots: As the Editor Sees Them

Now that we've considered shots in terms of subject size, camera angle, and camera movement, here's another useful way to think of them: by their function to the editor.

Master Shot

A *master shot* is framed to capture all of the action in a scene and usually runs from the beginning of the scene to the end. Typically, a master is a wide shot, but it doesn't have to be. The term is useful to the editor because you know that you can cut back to it at any point during the scene (**Figure 2.16**).

Figure 2.16 These master shots show all of the people who will appear in each scene, as well as placing them in their environment. In both cases, these masters were used as the first shot in the scene.

A master shot is often the simplest way to start a sequence: Tell the audience where the events are happening through a master WS, then move in and use tighter shots to put across the emotional content of the scene. Of course, this convention has been so overused that some modern editors do everything they can to avoid opening a sequence with a master shot. Just remember to learn and understand the rules before you start breaking them.

Single Shot

A *single* is simply any shot of one person (**Figure 2.17**). Most of the time a single will be a close-up, but it could be a medium shot as long as only one character is clearly the subject. Often the term is used to differentiate a shot with one character in it from an *over-the-shoulder* shot or a two-shot. For instance, if you were talking about getting coverage for a dialogue scene, you might call for "a wide master, an MCU over-the-shoulder shot of each player, and a single CU of each player."

Figure 2.17 A single can be as close as the CU on the left or as wide as the high-angle MS on the right. Note that in the shot on the left, even though there is technically more than one person in the shot, it's still considered a single since the figure in the foreground is clearly the focus of the shot.

Over-the-Shoulder Shot (OS, OTS)

Over-the-shoulder, or OS, refers to a shot in which two people are facing one another—one in the foreground with his back to the camera, the other facing the camera (**Figure 2.18**). An OS shot could be an MS, an MCU, or a CU. The tighter the shot, the more obscured and out of focus the foreground character will be.

An OS shot has a very different psychological effect from a single. It shows the two players in relation to one another, whereas a single focuses on the emotional state of the individual subject. Typical syntax for an over-the-shoulder shot would be: CU Trey OS Ben. This means that Trey is the subject of the close-up, shot from over Ben's shoulder.

Figure 2.18 Most often, the over-the-shoulder (OS) shot is a medium close-up (MCU), as in the example on the left. But it can be tighter, or wider like the MS on the right. Typically, the tighter the OS shot, the more obscured and out of focus the foreground figure is.

Note: "OS" is also sometimes used to mean "offscreen," as in "Rich laughs OS." Context will dictate which meaning is implied. Typically, "offscreen" refers to sound, while "over the shoulder" refers to image.

Reverse Shot

A *reverse shot* (or "reverse angle") is a relative term for any shot taken from the opposite angle of the previous shot. It often serves to explain the source of the preceding shot—such as a high-angle shot of a college quad following a low-angle shot of the bell tower. It can also be used in the simple case of reciprocal OS shots (as in "Follow the OS of Trey with a reverse of Dana") (**Figure 2.19**).

Point-of-View (POV) Shot

A *point-of-view shot* lets us look through a character's eyes, so we see exactly what she's seeing. If she's in a conversation with her brother, for instance, a POV shot might show the brother speaking directly into the camera lens.

A POV shot is a common way to justify a strange angle—for instance, a shot peeking out from behind a wall or the extreme high- or low-angle shots described earlier in this chapter. Standard editing technique calls for bracketing a POV shot with a matching reverse single to indicate whose POV it is (**Figure 2.20**). So in the bell tower example above, if you intended the low-angle shot of the tower to be a character's POV, you would follow it with a shot of someone in the quad looking up at the tower.

Figure 2.19 A reverse shot is a reciprocal angle of the shot that preceded it. Here are two examples.

Figure 2.20 The point-of-view (POV) shot is commonly used in conjunction with a reverse shot. Here, the shot on the left is Trey's POV, showing what he sees when he peeks out from behind the curtain. The shot on the right is the reverse, which reveals whose POV it is.

Reaction Shot (RXN)

A *reaction shot* reveals how a character reacts to something that just happened. This term refers less to the content of the shot than to its emotional purpose in terms of editing. This is almost always a shot of a person or a group of people, and it must be close enough to read the emotional response to the previous shot.

Frequently, an RXN will be a single cut right after another single, and most often it's a shot without dialogue (**Figure 2.21**). Alternatively, a reaction shot can be a single following some event. For instance, after an LS of the marketplace in which a bomb goes off, you would cut to an RXN of the mother hearing the explosion and turning to see what happened (**Figure 2.22**).

Two-Shot

A *two-shot* is any shot with two characters in it. It could be an MS, an MCU, or a CU (**Figure 2.23**). An OS shot is a kind of two-shot, although it's rarely identified as such. Often it is more important for the editor to know how many players are in a given shot than to know how large they may be in the frame.

1. WS Rich and Trey in restaurant.

2. CU Rich describing how much money Trey can make.

3. RXN shot of Trey.

4. CU Rich continuing his sales pitch.

Figure 2.21 In this dialogue sequence, shot 3 is the reaction shot.

Figure 2.22 The reaction shot in frame 9 gives the explosion emotional impact.

Figure 2.23 A shot with two people in the frame is called a two-shot.

Group Shot

A group shot is simply any shot that shows a group of people. It could be as wide as a LS or as tight as a MS (**Figure 2.24**). Here again, the content of the shot is often more important to the editor than the size of the characters in the frame. Sometimes people will describe a shot based on the number of people in it. You might hear terms like "three-shot" or even "six-shot," although this is usually relevant only when everyone involved knows specifically *which* three or six people are in the shot.

Figure 2.24 Any shot that shows three or more people is called a group shot. You could also call the picture on the right a three-shot.

Cutaway

A cutaway is a shot of any subject that's *not* part of the current shot but *is* part of the current scene. The editor can use a cutaway to show passage of time or just to break away from alternating shots of the characters without interrupting continuity of place. Cutaways provide atmospheric context and contrast.

In this case, the cutaway indicates the passing of time without breaking continuity of place. A cutaway allows the editor to take the viewer's focus away from the subject at hand or to change focus within the same locale (**Figure 2.25**).

1. MCU Trey sits on beach.

2. LS OS Trey looks at girls on beach.

3. MS girl playing.

4. Cutaway CU seagulls flying.

5. MS Trey walking away.

Figure 2.25 In this 5-shot sequence, shot 4 (the seagulls) is the cutaway. The seagulls are presumably part of the environment of the previous shots but do not necessarily appear in any other shot.

Insert

An insert functions much like a cutaway, but the term refers to a tight shot of a subject or object that's already present in the current shot. By definition, an insert must be tighter than the shot preceding it. In this case, the insert draws attention to the wineglass. Rather than disrupting the action of the scene, it focuses viewers' attention on a particular item. It's typically followed by some kind of RXN shot to give it emotional context (**Figure 2.26**).

1. Master FS Trey, Gene, and Starr in restaurant.

2. Two-shot Gene and Starr as she reaches for wine glass.

3. INSERT wineglass as Starr picks it up.

4. CU Trey RXN shot.

Figure 2.26 In this sequence, shot 3 (the wine glasses) is the insert. Shot 4 is the reaction shot that shows how Trey feels about Gene and Starr getting drunk.

Voice-Over

A *voice-over* is an audio-only shot. It may be narration or speech from another context, overlaid on a scene to provide commentary, context, or a special point of view. Don't forget audio when thinking about the editing options available to you. Often you can perform an audio "insert" or "cutaway" without changing the visual focus. For example, adding a sound of a school bell during a shot of a kid taking a test could indicate that his time is up without ever having to cut away.

Ten Dollar Words

Now and then you may find a single shot that achieves multiple purposes. Sometimes it's a moving shot that changes subject or point of view. Alternatively, it might be a static shot where many things come and go in the frame or happen simultaneously on different planes in three-dimensional space.

But be careful. If a shot is too complex, it will draw attention to itself and may need to be cut into pieces to avoid distracting the viewer.

With even a modest desktop editing system like Final Cut Pro, you have a huge library of options at your fingertips that allow you to modify pre-existing shots or develop new shots from scratch.

Slow Motion and Other Visual Effects

Your editorial lexicon can include a variety of shots that were not achieved in the camera but can be created during post. Digitally enhanced shots range from something as simple as a cropped shot to something as complex as a multilayered composition with elements *rotoscoped* into the scene.

Types of Cuts and Transitions

As I mentioned at the beginning of this chapter, if you think of shots as nouns, the basic building blocks of cinematic sentences, then the transitions the editor uses to move from one shot to the next can be thought of as verbs.

There are really only a few ways to make a transition from one shot (and its point of focus) to another. The simplest way is a straight cut from one shot to the next: Stop the first shot and start the second. But you can accomplish even a simple cut in many different ways. The editor is always drawing the viewer along, guiding the point of focus so skillfully it seems effortless, while carefully maintaining the precise sequence of thoughts, emotions, and reactions the director desires.

Continuity Cut

Most cuts within a scene should be continuous. That means action that begins in one shot should continue in the next with flawless continuity of time, space, and screen direction. (I'll get to screen direction shortly.)

The simplest example of this is a door that starts to open in one shot and finishes opening in the next. This could be a cut from a CU to a WS, or it could be one MS cutting to another MS from a complementary angle. In every case it would be a successful continuity cut only if the door appeared to open with a natural, fluid movement across the boundary between the two shots. Fluid movement between shots is one of the most critical elements in convincing your audience of the reality of the film, and it's deceptively tricky to achieve (**Figure 2.27**).

Figure 2.27 The action in this edit will appear continuous across the cut point.

The more smoothly space and time seem to run across an *edit point,* the more invisibly you can guide the focus of the scene. Of course, most often the shots you are cutting between were not actually shot at the same time, so the action may not match perfectly. For instance, the door may be opening fast in one shot and slowly in another. Compensating for inconsistencies like this is a huge part of the editor's job, and as you read on, you'll learn many ways to accomplish this.

Split Edits

Creating seamless audio continuity across shot boundaries is even more important than maintaining visual continuity. While you see only 25 or 30 frames per second of visual information, you hear 48,000 samples of audio. Even a tiny discontinuity on the soundtrack will be far more jarring than a visual error.

One of the most common techniques editors use to create seamless continuity of sound is to overlap the audio from the shot that's ending with the start of the picture in the following shot. For instance, if Dana is speaking in shot 1, and you want to cut to her companion Lindsey listening in the next shot, you would probably cut to the image of Lindsey before Dana finishes her dialogue. The sound from shot 1 would continue over the image of shot 2.

Generally, any edit where audio and video are cut at different points is called a *split edit.* How many frames of audio you overlap depends on the content of the shots and their length. When the sound of the first clip overlaps the image of the second, it's called an L cut. When the sound of the second overlaps the image of the first, it's called a J cut (**Figure 2.28**). I find myself using the latter ten-to-one over the former, but that may just be a question of personal style.

A typical dialogue scene should be cut entirely with L and J cuts, otherwise it feels jumpy and unnatural. Most action sequences also employ L or J cuts to tie the events together. Sometimes you can even use L or J cuts to take the viewer from the end of one sequence to the beginning of another or to bridge two locations into a single event.

Figure 2.28 In this Timeline, you can see how audio and video clips overlap in time relative to one another. The lower tracks represent the audio, while the V1 channel above represents the video. The selected clip begins with a J cut (where the audio clip begins before its corresponding video clip) and ends with an L cut. In the L cut, the audio extends past the end of the corresponding picture.

If you look at mainstream media, nearly every cut will have overlapping audio except for changes in location or event. Final Cut Pro has a couple of features designed specifically to help you perform split edits (see the section on split edits in Chapter 6, "Advanced Editing").

Jump Cut

A jump cut is any cut or transition that breaks the continuity of time, space, or screen direction—deliberately or accidentally—or where the action doesn't match across the edit point. This is true even if the jump cut is disguised to appear continuous.

Jump cuts used to be considered unacceptable mistakes. Jean-Luc Godard's *Breathless* (1960) was the first time jumpcutting was used extensively in a narrative film. Godard employed it to show the isolation of his two characters, even though they were sharing the same physical space. In recent years, jump cuts have become a fashionable way to draw attention to the act of film creation and celebrate the artifice of the medium.

Since jump cuts force the audience to reconstruct the time or space that has been "jumped," they can be used to disorient or agitate the viewer. Jump cuts are also wonderfully effective, when used selectively amidst a mostly conventional editing palette, to simulate moments of confusion or disconnection.

Jumpcutting is an art. I find that compositional choices become more critical than ever in a jump cut, because while the goal in a continuity cut is to keep the focus on the similarities of the two adjacent shots, a jump cut is designed to highlight their differences. If the shots are only slightly dissimilar, the power of the jump-cut is undermined. To achieve a good jumpcut, contrast two opposite Dutch angles or break screen direction. And take time to experiment: You may find that by rearranging the order of a jump cut sequence, you can achieve very different emotional results (**Figure 2.29**).

Figure 2.29 This is a sequence of jump cuts focusing on Trey as he practices asking his co-worker for a date. The first few images illustrate good contrast in composition, primarily thanks to alternating screen direction. The last few shots rely on the actor's gestures to create contrast across the edit points. Our goal was to show Trey getting more and more frustrated. While the performance conveys most of this, we accentuated the effect by using a telephoto lens for the earlier shots and a wide angle for the latter ones.

Unwanted jump cuts are more troublesome. You will create an unwanted jump cut by cutting between two camera angles that are too similar, even if the action across the cut is entirely continuous. In general, a shot should be 30 percent or 30 degrees different from the previous shot. That means either 30 degrees to the left or right, 30 degrees higher or lower angle, 30 percent tighter or wider, and so on.

Scene Cut

A *scene cut* takes the viewer from the end of one scene to the beginning of another. Traditionally, transitions between scenes were marked by some sort of punctuation, like a dip-to-black. These days, fashion favors "hard cutting" from one scene to the next. The effect is a more forceful transition—especially if the audio is also hard cut rather than overlapped. Using this technique, you don't give the audience quite enough time to digest the final images of the previous scene before they must begin taking in all the new information associated with a new location and a new event, which can be a good way of keeping them focused on the action.

Crosscutting

Crosscutting, also known as intercutting, is one of the oldest editing techniques in film. It's the process of showing two events that are taking place in two different locations at the same time by alternating shots from each of the events. Crosscutting usually depicts events that are taking place at the same time, but it can also be used for other purposes, such as a scene where someone remembering an event is intercut with footage of the event itself.

Crosscutting is essential in editing a chase sequence where you cut between the pursuer and the pursued, usually alternating shots from the two sequences faster and faster until the pursuer converges on the pursued and the crosscutting evolves into a single scene. This is one of the most common editing structures in film language. By showing the audience two events at the same time, you allow viewers to not only observe those events but draw some conclusions about the relationship between them.

Usually, crosscutting involves intercutting two complete sequences. For instance, you might cut a western like this:

1. ELS outlaw in desert.

2. CU outlaw smokes and throws his cigarette butt to the ground.

3. ECU INSERT cigarette butt.

4. LS sheriff riding through desert.

5. CU sheriff's face. He sees something on the ground. He stops his horse.

6. ECU INSERT same cigarette butt.

7. CU sheriff's face lights up.

8. MS outlaw pitching tent near a campfire.

9. ECU cigarette pack as outlaw takes one out.

In this example, the story of the outlaw could have been shown continuously by simply using shots 1 through 3 and shots 8 and 9, but by intercutting the sheriff's story we set up suspense. Now the audience not only knows that the outlaw is being followed but that since the sheriff has spotted the cigarette butt, he will probably catch the outlaw.

Note: The edits between shots 3 and 4 and shots 7 and 8 are scene cuts. All the others are probably continuity cuts.

Cross-Dissolve

A *cross-dissolve* (also known as a dissolve, cross-fade, or mix) is a transition between shots where frames are superimposed, "mixing" the images for the duration of the transition (**Figures 2.30** and **2.31**).

The most common use of a mix is to suggest the passage of time. This is why a cross-dissolve is often a good choice for scene cuts where time passes between the scenes.

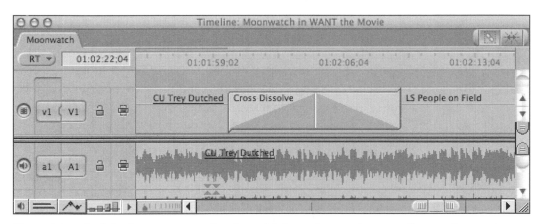

Figure 2.30 Final Cut Pro represents dissolves with icons that overlap two adjacent clips on the same track.

Figure 2.31 Image 1, an ECU of Trey, is dissolved with image 2, a wide overhead shot of a crowd gathering on a field. The frames in the middle show the images overlapping.

Cross-dissolves can be particularly effective when you use them to bridge what would ordinarily seem like a series of jump cuts: shots from the same angle with the subject moving in the frame. If you use cross-dissolves instead of cuts, the viewer will accept that the jump cuts are actually taking place with long periods of time between them. For instance, imagine a sequence in which someone is hiding in a room. A series of high-angle shots shows him washing dishes, then pacing the floor, then reading, then banging his fist against the wall. If you use cuts, they may seem jarring; if you use dissolves, the shots just show that time is passing.

Make Sure You Have Extra Media

An important technical point: If you're considering using a cross-dissolve, remember that both shots need to have extra media on either side of the cut point equal to half the length of the dissolve.

For instance, if you want to place a one-second dissolve between two shots, there must be half a second (15 frames of NTSC video) of good frames before and after the cut point on the incoming clip and the outgoing clip. If a slate or a light-leak appears within those 15 lead-in or lead-out frames in either shot, it will become visible once the effect is applied, making the dissolve unusable.

Cross-dissolves offer the editor an opportunity to create beautiful and powerful filmic images, especially on longer dissolves. When planning a mix, think carefully about composition and how the two images will overlap spatially. You can mix any two images, but when the images work together compositionally, they can have a profound impact.

Soft Cut

A very short dissolve that lasts between three and five frames is often called a *soft cut* because its effect falls halfway between that of a hard cut and a cross- dissolve. You've probably seen soft cuts used in documentaries as an elegant way to disguise the jump cuts that occur when you trim a long interview down to watchable length.

At one time, to bridge those gaps you would have had to cut away to a reaction, a graphic, or an insert in order to avoid a jump cut that might unsettle your audience. But as viewers have gotten more accustomed to seeing jump cuts in creative shows, editors working in more conservative genres have been able to introduce techniques like the soft cut. The soft cut is less gentle than a full-on cutaway but less disorienting than a flat-out jump cut.

Lap Dissolve

At the other end of the spectrum is the *lap dissolve*—a cross-dissolve that lasts longer than two seconds; in fact, it may last 15 or 30 seconds. This effect is more like superimposing the two images and has a very different impact than a shorter dissolve.

A dissolve that lasts this long puts the two images up for some kind of comparison. A resourceful editor might employ this effect as an alternative to a scene cut to show a character moving from one world to another and to illustrate the differences between those worlds. Or she might aim for the same effect as a crosscut sequence. Alternatively, a lap dissolve can lead the viewer to compare two events or perspectives within a scene.

The long duration of a lap dissolve gives the audience time to contemplate the situation or circumstances. Sometimes such dissolves can be used sequentially, with one following another, sometimes leaving three or more images on-screen simultaneously. The opening scene of *Apocalypse Now* is one of the most elegant and elaborate uses of continuous lap dissolves, showing two worlds at once (the outer world of the Vietnam War and the inner world of the protagonist's internal conflict). This creates a correlation between them that captures the essence of the entire film. Simultaneously, the sequence begins unfolding the plot without feeling expository or didactic.

Other Effects

Editing tools like Final Cut place a vast selection of special visual effects at your disposal—effects you can use for transitions between scenes (and occasionally between shots). For the most part, they fall into three categories:

- Wipes (including iris effects).
- 2-D effects, such as pushes or slides.
- 3-D simulations, such as cubes turning or pages peeling.

There are also countless combinations and variations, everything from the famous Toaster wipes to custom-shaped dissolves based on a corporate logo.

Traditionally, editors have scorned these effects, I suspect because they are relatively new, relatively unfamiliar, and break the rule of the invisible edit. In general, wipes and effect transitions make no effort to hide the contrivance of an edit. On the contrary, they draw attention to it. They say in essence, "Hey! You're watching a movie, and movies are *fake,* and by the way, this is a scene change!"

Wipes were initially used in feature films. Nowadays, ironically enough, they are most likely to be found in corporate or educational shows, which are ostensibly more "factual" than fiction films—where they are rarely used anymore.

One notable exception is the *Star Wars* series, where all the scene cuts were made with wipes of various shapes. I suspect this was done as an affectionate nod to the early days of filmmaking and to emphasize the fairytale nature of the story.

Composite Shots

Any time two shots are visible at once—whether it's a picture-in-picture effect used in a news show or a *process shot* of a computer-generated dinosaur chasing real children—that's a *composite* shot. Technically, I wouldn't consider this type of effect a "verbal" transition between shots, but it serves to compare or contrast two or more shots, creating the same effect that transitions do.

Superimposition

The editor creates a superimposition when he displays two or more shots at the same time, each one layered on top of the others. The effect is similar to that of a lap dissolve but lasts for the entire duration of the shots.

Supering two shots does not provide a gradual movement from one event to another but shows a static view of the events together. So while a lap dissolve could be used to show a transition between two different worlds, a superimposition might illustrate two worlds coexisting.

Supering is also frequently used for titles and *lower thirds (the graphic in the lower third of the screen identifying a talking head).*

Split Screen

Split screen effects offer a very different way to show multiple images simultaneously. Although this technique violates the invisible-edit dictum, much like the jump cut, it's finding its way into narrative fiction filmmaking. Even so, split screens can be employed more freely in non-narrative projects (**Figure 2.32**).

It is commonly used in telephone sequences where two characters in different locations are talking to each other. You can also see many creative examples of inventive split screen in Darren Aronofsky's *Requiem for a Dream;* my favorite is where two characters are in the same physical location (lying on a bed together) but emotionally separated by their drug addictions. Director Brian DePalma has often demonstrated his mastery of split-screen storytelling as a form of high-tension crosscutting, particularly in early films like *Sisters* and *Phantom of the Paradise.*

Figure 2.32 Split screens can have a hard edge like the example on the left or a soft edge like the example on the right.

In Mike Figgis's *Timecode,* the entire film was exhibited in a four-up split screen, where four events were going on simultaneously. This was possible because those events were carefully timed so that usually one of the quadrants drew the audience's primary focus. When the events competed for attention, the audio was mixed to let the audience know where to look.

In general, if you're planning to use split screens in your show, you should communicate that fact to the director before the scene is shot. That way she can weight the composition to one side or the other so the joined image will show both subjects.

Split-screen shots can be divided by a hard edge, a soft edge, or even a colored border. This choice further affects the impact of the shot.

> **TIP:** *Any time you put more than one image on the screen simultaneously, arrange your timing so viewers' point of focus is deliberately shifted from one image to the other. One way to accomplish this is by controlling which clip's audio is heard on the soundtrack.*

Rack Focus

Rack focus means the camera operator shifts (or racks) the focus from one character or object to another within a single shot, bringing the audience's point of focus with it (**Figure 2.33**). Since this is a single, self-contained shot, it seems as if it would be a noun rather than a verb. But it does the job of a verb by redirecting the viewer's attention—just as an edit does. Sometimes a camera move can accomplish this same effect.

Figure 2.33 The rack focus effect shifts the viewer's attention without the need for a cut or camera move. Here, focus moves from Trey waiting in the car to the negotiation going on in the office.

Punctuation

There are only a handful of standard ways to begin and end film sequences. Typically, they involve showing some amount of black, which is the film language equivalent of a comma or period.

Fade-to-Black, Dip-to-Black

The most common way to end a sequence is to gradually mix the last shot with black. A dissolve (or fade) is used because it conveys the sense that time continues within the world of the film, even though the viewer is no longer seeing it. Like a cross-dissolve, the duration of the fade-to-black can vary. The most common length is probably between one-half and two seconds (**Figure 2.34**).

Figure 2.34 You can perform a fade-to-black either by *keyframing* a clip's Opacity graph, as shown on the left, or by applying a cross-dissolve at the end of the last clip, effectively dissolving from the clip to nothing, as shown on the right.

Fading to black usually means the show or sequence is over. If the image remains black for only a moment, it's a scene change and is called a dip-to-black. Occasionally you may want to fade or dip to white or some other color, although both alternatives break the rules of the invisible edit.

Why doesn't fading or dipping to black break that rule? Because on the most basic level, a fade-to-black is an organic and familiar transition that exists naturally in our world. We all experience fading to black every day: slowly, as the day turns to night, and more quickly, when we close our eyes.

Fade-Up-From-Black

Matching the fade-to-black is the fade-up. Think of this as a capital letter that marks the beginning of every cinematic sentence. Again, a mix is used to convey the sense that the world you are about to view has been in existence long before you got there (**Figure 2.35**).

Figure 2.35 Fading up from black is the opposite of fading down to black. Use either the transition effect or the *rubber band control* illustrated here.

Cut-to-Black and Punch-Up-From-Black

One alternative to the fade-up-from- and fade-down-to-black is simply to cut. This creates a much more abrupt transition, akin to waking with a start and popping your eyes wide open—or being bopped on the head and knocked unconscious. It's a great way to grab the viewer's attention and demand that she direct her point of focus to the image you're presenting. Because of this, it makes sense to punch to or cut from a close-up; a fade fits more naturally with a wider shot.

Freeze Frame

If you want to contradict the implied consistency of the world within the film, one good way to do that is to end a scene—or the entire film—on a freeze frame. Eventually you will probably fade the freeze frame to black, but in the meantime, halting the flow of images is a very powerful effect, forcing the viewer to stay in that final moment.

This punctuation is best used when trying to leave the characters, and the viewer, in the midst of some kind of dilemma. That's why it often occurs at the end of "Part 1," leaving you anxious to see the completion of the frozen event in "Part 2." You can rarely get away with this in narrative fiction, but it is excellent for training or educational shows because it keeps the viewer psychologically engaged with the conflict, rather than offering the "happily ever after" closure of the more conventional fade-to-black.

Establishing Shot (Locator Shot)

An *establishing shot* (sometimes called a locator shot) shows the environment in which the events to follow take place and indicates to the viewer that a story (or sequence) is beginning. Usually it provides just enough visual context to make sense of the scene.

You'll see this technique employed tirelessly in TV sitcoms. One exterior shot of the *Cheers* pub and you never need to see the outside of the set again. *Third Rock From the Sun* cleverly replaced the standard locator shot with a shot of planet Earth from space. This made fun of the formula by showing a valid locator without actually providing any information.

An establishing shot is not always a wide shot, although that's the standard convention. It might even be an insert, a detail that will later prove critical to the story. In any case, you will rarely create a sequence without using some kind of establishing shot to get your audience's attention and let them know that a new part of the story is about to begin.

Final Frame

Choose your final shot carefully; it's the image viewers will walk away with. It is quite possibly the most important shot in the show, as it is being asked to carry the weight of everything that came before. A powerful ending shot can spin a movie into an entirely new context, or it can summarize and clarify the message your show carries.

RULES OF FILM GRAMMAR

Now that we've gone over the basic elements that make up the language of film, let's consider a few fundamental rules and general guidelines that govern how editors put those elements to use. This is essentially the grammar of film language.

Like any living language, the film language continues to grow and evolve as it's used. Even so, many of the basic rules have remained surprisingly consistent over the years, especially those aimed at maintaining the invisibility of the edit. If you break them, you will create jump cuts or other violations of the invisible edit that will bounce your viewer out of the story you're telling—if only momentarily—and change her point of focus so she's watching the filmmaking process itself.

New Shot = New Information

The most basic question an editor faces day in and day out is when to make an edit. And the basic answer is: Edit only when there's new information to be shown. If there's no new information, don't cut.

This rule also helps you figure out which shot to choose next. Just ask yourself what new information is relevant. It could be as simple as one character's reaction to another character or to an event. It might be as specific as a change of angle that reveals a gun hidden in a character's coat.

This doesn't mean that the new information needs to be revealed exactly at the cut point. As with an L-cut, you can offset the shift in the viewer's point of interest from the cut point itself, thus hiding the edit more effectively.

For example, imagine a scene where a boxer has just lost a match. His wife is begging him to leave the sport, while he's insisting that his injuries are insignificant. In the final shot, we cut to the boxer just before he storms off and leaves the room. After he exits, we see a bloodstain left behind on the wall where he was leaning. The new information is the bloodstain, but we don't see it at the cut point. Revealing this information midshot (after the boxer exits the frame) is more powerful than cutting to it in a new shot.

Screen Direction

A good editor is constantly aware of screen direction, which simply refers to the direction (left or right) that a subject is facing, or moving, within the frame. The simplest way to illustrate this is to consider how a moving object appears as it moves across multiple shots. If the object is moving left to right in shot 1, it must continue to move left to right in shot 2 (**Figure 2.36**).

Figure 2.36 These shots show correct screen direction. If the bicycle in the second image were heading right to left, its motion would not appear continuous in time and space.

This is vitally important in sequences like chase scenes or races, where to follow your story, the audience needs to understand that one party is following another or which horse is ahead (**Figure 2.37**).

Figure 2.37 In this chase sequence, Jane is planning to jump off the Golden Gate Bridge and Anna is determined to stop her. After an establishing shot to set the location (not shown), the scene begins with a CU of Jane walking toward the bridge. The next shot films Anna walking in the same direction (right to left), which makes it clear that she is following Jane. A wider shot of Jane shows that she is now on the bridge, and the next shot captures Anna beginning to run. As long as her legs are moving in the correct direction, we know she's part of the chase. The last shot shows Jane holding the stuffed animal that will prove to be the linchpin of the scene.

Screen direction is equally critical when two or more people are talking to one another (**Figure 2.38**). If one character is shown facing toward the left side of the frame, the person she's talking to should be facing frame-right. This also applies to which side of the frame the character occupies. If the subject is on the right side of the frame in shot 1, then he should *still* be on the right side of the frame in shot 2, even though it's a reverse.

Figure 2.38 In this sequence, Trey remains on the left side of the screen and Dana on the right.

Never Cross the Line (the 180° Rule)

To make sure that all your shots have the correct screen direction, draw an imaginary line between the actors' eyelines (or between an actor's eyes and whatever he's looking at) and take all your shots from the same side of "the line" (or axis) (**Figure 2.39**). A shot made from the other side of the axis will result in the actors appearing to be on the wrong side of the frame. If you violate this rule, a viewer watching the scene will think that the actors have switched places—a hugely disorienting effect.

Figure 2.39 Draw an imaginary line between the eyes of the subjects. All the shots taken from one side will have proper screen direction. If you take a shot from the other side, the characters will appear to switch sides, confusing the audience.

Solving Screen Direction Errors

Regardless of why mistakes happen, it is the editor's job to prevent errors in screen direction from making it into the finished film. Several common solutions can get you across to the other side of the line if necessary.

*One is to use a shot that's directly on the line: one where the eyeline is directly at the camera (**Figure 2.40**). Another is to use a moving shot that crosses the line during the shot (**Figure 2.41**). From that point on, you can use coverage from the other side of the line.*

Figure 2.40 This sequence begins with Pete Peters (at the podium) on the right side of the frame looking left. Shot 2, the reaction shot of Trey, confirms this (since he is looking the opposite direction). In shot 3 we show a neutral angle in which Peters is dead center in the frame. After that we are free to move to the other side of the line, as in the fourth shot, where Pete is looking left to right.

Figure 2.41 In this sequence Kip Ruthburn is addressing the workers of Hot Tot Dot Com. It begins with a shot of him looking right to left and a reverse shot of the workers looking left to right, watching him. The camera dollies around in front of him until he's looking left to right. In order for the workers' reactions to match, they must now be looking right to left, as Tess, the office manager, is doing in shot 5.

continues on next page

Solving Screen Direction Errors   continued

*In desperate cases you can flop (reverse horizontally) a shot (**Figure 2.42**). But this is difficult to pull off, because even if there are no obvious errors (like a sign with the writing backward, or a car with its steering wheel on the wrong side), people usually look "funny" when reversed. We are not symmetrical beings, and although you can often get away with one shot like this, cutting back and forth between a flopped shot and a normal shot of the same subject may not work.*

*In Final Cut, flopping a shot is as easy as choosing the Flop filter from the Effects menu and applying it to a clip (**Figure 2.43**). Fortunately, in Final Cut Pro 4, this is a realtime filter so no rendering is required to view the flopped shot. That means you can make your edit, and even undo it if you find it doesn't work, without losing time to processing. (There's more on filter effects in Chapter 8, "Special Effects.")*

Figure 2.42 Any shot can be flopped to change its screen direction, but beware of things that give the trick away. Who knows, maybe Trey drives a British car?

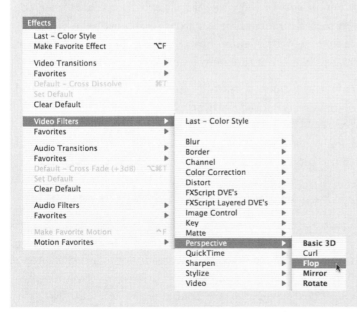

Figure 2.43 To flop a shot in Final Cut Pro, choose the Flop filter from the Perspective submenu of the Video Filters section of the Effects menu.

While it's the production team's responsibility to avoid errors of this sort during shooting, it's not always as clear-cut as the simple case I just described. Sometimes multiple eyelines are going on simultaneously. Sometimes the eyeline shifts during the course of the action. Sometimes one shot is made on Monday and the reverse isn't shot until Thursday.

Sometimes you might intentionally disrupt screen direction to create a specific effect. For instance, if two people in conversation are facing the same direction, one is talking to the other's back. You can use this to show a power relationship (**Figure 2.44**).

Figure 2.44 In this scene, Dawn has picked up her brother from prison. Throughout the long bus ride home, they almost never look at each other.

You can also show two people conversing while facing away from each other, conveying conflict between the characters. This is harder to achieve than you might think, because in an edited sequence, intercutting subjects who are looking in opposite directions usually gives the impression that they're facing each other.

This has to do with the way audiences naturally interpret images and has to do with *noseroom*. If the shots are composed with proper noseroom (see the section on noseroom in Chapter 1, "The Editor's Job"), the people appear to be looking at one another. If, on the other hand, the shots are composed with insufficient noseroom (that is, with the subjects seeming to face directly into the frame edge), intercutting them creates the effect that they are indeed looking away from one another. This also depends on the eyelines not matching (**Figure 2.45**).

Screen direction is not neutral. Subjects moving or facing right to left have a very different psychological effect than those moving (or facing) left to right. In some ways this may be cultural, based on the fact that we read words left to right and tend to read pictures similarly: The left comes before the right. (I've long been curious whether people whose languages are read right to left, like Arabic or Hebrew, have different interpretations of screen direction in our movies.)

Figure 2.45 In the first two images, the characters seem to be looking at one another. In the second two, they don't. Composition and eyeline differentiate the two sequences.

Left-to-right orientation impacts composition in subtle but interesting ways. Things on the left tend to read as though they have a certain amount of cause over the elements (or effects) on the right. This is not an absolute rule, but it tends to be what audiences unconsciously expect.

You can use this effect to your advantage. If you want to show something moving harmoniously in flow with the story, or the universe, use left-to-right movement. If you want to show something creating conflict, or stopping the flow, use right-to-left movement. In static shots, positioning the agent of change on the right side of the frame (opposite to the expectation) can create tension and conflict (**Figure 2.46**).

Figure 2.46 This shot illustrates how the right side of the frame can be used very effectively to show an obstacle facing a character. To emphasize the significance of this barrier for the man, we placed it in bright light and left the subject in dark silhouette.

Cutting on Action

One of the best ways to hide an edit is to place it in the middle of action. If the action is continuous across the two shots, the shot change will go virtually unnoticed. This is why editors are always making mental notes about shots with doors closing or people making hand movements. Any clear action in the frame that pulls the viewer's focus is a potential cut point. Of course, it requires a second shot containing the completion of the same action. This is why it's so critical for actors to match their actions exactly across different shots and multiple takes.

Pay attention to the films you watch, and you'll see that most edits occur on some kind of action. An edit between two static shots will draw unwelcome attention to itself. If you're forced to make such a cut, use audio to bridge the shots.

Matching Your Shots

When cutting back and forth between two shots, as in a dialogue sequence, it's best to use shots that match each other in focal length and frame size. Intercutting between a CU and an MS creates a jarring effect that keeps the viewer from falling into the dramatic flow of the scene.

Take this example from a dialogue scene.

1. Establishing LS, busy restaurant.
2. MS two-shot of couple at table.
3. MCU Max OS Julie.
4. MCU Julie OS Max.
5. MCU Max OS Julie.
6. ECU INSERT engagement ring.
7. CU Julie.
8. CU Max.
9. CU Julie.
10. CU Max.
11. MS two-shot of couple at table as waiter arrives with check.
12. MCU Max OS Julie.
13. MCU Julie OS Max.
14. LS Max and Julie exit restaurant.

Notice that in this sequence I match MCUs to MCUs and CUs to CUs. Using the insert to make the transition from MCUs to CUs isn't strictly required, but it serves to make the transition more subtle. Likewise, when I want to pull back out to the MCUs (after the intimate dialogue is done), I bridge it by cutting back to my master shot, which, in this case, is a two-shot of Max and Julie at the table. That cut is additionally motivated by the new information of the waiter arriving.

It is also critical to choose shots with matching focal length. Ideally, this will be handled in production, but as the editor you're going to have to deal with the results if someone screws up. If one CU was shot from 5 feet away with a wide-angle lens and the other was shot from 25 feet away using a telephoto, the shots will match so poorly that you'll find it hard to maintain the illusion that they were taken in the same place (**Figure 2.47**).

Figure 2.47 These shots are both close-ups, but they were filmed with different focal lengths. Trying to cut back and forth between the two shots would be disruptive to your scene.

In such a situation, if this is the only footage available to you, I suggest using especially long J and L cuts to accentuate the connectedness of the shots. I would also recommend cutting as little as possible. Once you settle on a shot, the audience will forget the rough juxtaposition of the last edit—but every time you cut, you'll reintroduce that disorientation. It may be better to stick with an OS shot even if the subject talking is facing away from the camera than to cut back and forth between mismatched singles. At least the OS is a two-shot and shows the two people in physical proximity.

Cut Moving to Moving, Still to Still

Another mistake that can draw unwelcome attention to your editing is to mix moving and static shots within a sequence. If you use a moving shot of an object and cut to a static shot of the same object, it reads as a sort of unwanted jump cut—even if continuity is maintained. For example, if you had a dolly shot that circled around the outside of a dinner table and a tripod shot of one of the people eating, these shots would not cut well. If instead, the single of the eating person was moving even slightly, it would make for a much smoother transition.

Moving shots can be cut against other moving shots, but before cutting to a static shot you should ideally let a moving shot come to a standstill. If you have no choice because of limited coverage, try to bridge the transition from moving shot to still shot with an extreme angle. For instance, in the dining room scene I just described, you might cut from the dolly shot to an ECU of a plate of food or an extreme high-angle overhead shot. In this way, you are creating a dramatic visual change that overshadows the distraction of the moving-versus-still-shot problem.

This rule has a few exceptions. One occurs when the movement is motivated by the subject. For example, it's OK to cut between the moving POV of a child on a merry-go-round and the static POV of his father watching from the solid ground.

Another exception involves the *follow shot*. As described above, in a follow shot the camera and subject are moving at the same speed, such as a car-to-car shot. Follow shots really function in the same way as static shots and therefore should not be intercut with genuine moving shots.

Finding a Compositional Link

If at all possible, every edit should contain a compositional link between the two shots. Sometimes the shots will give you this automatically: For instance, two OS shots will usually provide reciprocal angles and match compositionally (**Figure 2.48**).

Figure 2.48 Reciprocal shots like these naturally provide a compositional link between shots.

This technique can be used to make scene cuts work. Use this sort of visual continuity to carry the viewer past the cut. For example: If the last shot in scene 1 is a round car tire, a good beginning shot for scene 2 might be a globe of roughly the same size spinning in approximately the same place in the frame. This provides a smooth bridge between the scenes (**Figure 2.49**).

Figure 2.49 A good scene cut matches a graphical element from the ending frame of the outgoing scene with one in the first frame of the incoming scene. In this case, we cut from the park adjoining Kachina's apartment to a CU of her CD collection. The strong vertical lines create a visual bridge between the scenes.

Visual continuity is usually lower priority than contextual continuity, but it really enhances an edit to have a matching visual component to soften the transition. This is particularly critical in scene cuts and dissolves.

Manipulating Time

Sometimes in editing a scene your goal is not to precisely recreate reality, but to *enhance* reality, to create a fictional world that's most appropriate for carrying your themes.

This is particularly true when it comes to conveying a sense of time. Film is a time-based medium, which means that the fluent manipulation of time becomes a critical element for successful editing. There are exceptions, (like the shoot-out at the end of Fred Zinnemann's *High Noon),* but usually film time is far more compressed than real time.

Think about it. Let's say you need to go to a police station to give a deposition about your crazy neighbor who is building a nuclear submarine in his backyard.

You step out your door, turn around, and lock it (which takes five seconds). You walk to your car (:20), get out your keys (:10), open the door (:05), sit down (:05), put on your seat belt (:05), start the car (:05), put it in gear, and pull out of your driveway (:20). You drive to the police station (5:00). Once you arrive, you have to park and walk into the building (1:00). Then, after waiting in line (3:00), you get to talk to the detective and explain about the suspicious periscope peeking over the fence (5:00).

You get the idea.

In real time this sequence could take over 15 minutes, but if you were editing it for a film you would probably cut it down to 90 seconds, maybe less. It's not just that the details are so familiar that they're boring to watch, but that real life simply takes a long time. Even in the so-called reality shows that are so popular on television, gobs of time are edited out to allow viewers to focus on the bits that actually tell a story. This is what makes film more interesting (and more exciting) than real life: It's compressed.

Let's say that the director who is shooting the story about you and your neighbor abridges this sequence to take just 75 seconds. She then shoots three sequences:

1. You leaving your house.

2. You arriving at the station.

3. You greeting the detective and giving the deposition.

She will probably end up shooting at least 7 to 10 minutes of footage. In reality, coverage and multiple takes could triple that total. The editor is responsible for taking that 10 (or 30) minutes and whittling it down to the 75 seconds that will play in the final film. If you are that editor, you will need to decide which individual moments, or beats, best capture the whole event.

Here's just one sample solution:

1. You lock your door at home (:03).

2. Your foot hits the parking lot pavement as you exit your car at the police station. The shot tilts up to show the doorway as you walk toward it (:05).

3. The handshake as the detective greets you (:02).

4. The detective's fingers press the record button on his tape recorder (:02).

5. You take a sip of water before you begin (:03).

6. A sequence of simple two-shots and singles shows you telling your story and the detective listening.

This last sequence (6) probably comprises 12 to 15 shots (1:00). Most of them just show faces (CU or OS shots), but a good editor might include a cutaway to the tape recorder, or the clock on the wall, or your foot tapping nervously. All the cutaways emphasize the emotional undercurrents of the scene and its physical circumstances.

Even within a simple conversation, a good editor will often find himself manipulating time, adding or removing pauses between lines, or removing lines altogether to create a natural-sounding conversation—while keeping the lines clean enough so viewers can follow them. This is a real art. In reality, most conversations have dead spaces where no one is talking—or sometimes, as soon as one person starts talking, several others overlap her. In a crowd everyone might be speaking at once. If your intention is to direct the viewer's attention to the dialogue, you have to make sure that the content of what is being said is audible, even while you maintain enough overlap so the conversation feels natural.

A Word of Caution

Beware: While compressing time can improve the scene's pacing and rhythm, it is generally considered bad form to alter the timing of an actor's performance without the director's approval. Presumably the director would have said something during the shoot if he wanted the actor's pacing to be much faster—or slower.

Respecting Silence

Not every moment should be filled with dialogue. The most powerful moments are often those that occur during silence: reactions, thoughts, emotions. These are the elements that really tell the story. Give them space to work.

Setting the Pace

Pacing makes a huge impact on how a film works—and for the most part the editor is responsible for setting it. Pacing can vary widely. Some stories need to be slow, languid, or contemplative; others want to flash by quickly, packed with dense editing sequences. Pacing is generally determined by the themes and intentions of the entire show, your target audience's attention span, as well as the special dramatic requirements of any given scene.

Slow pacing doesn't mean you're wasting screen time. No matter how hard you look, you probably won't be able to find any "dead time" in a well-edited film—even one with a languid pace. Every frame will be working to tell the story.

Fast pacing doesn't mean overwhelming the viewer, either. No matter how much information you cram into every second, the emotional content of the scene must be paramount.

Most of the time the director will let you know what sort of pacing he expects. However, you will be primarily responsible for bringing that pacing to life, moment to moment, as you tell your story. As an editor, you are perpetually guiding the viewer, and you must feed her new information at just the right pace to keep her engaged. This is why it's critical not only to know the subject and intention of the piece but also to know your audience.

STORYTELLING

Put it all together and…you're telling a story. All films are stories—even documentaries, music videos, and industrial films. According to the classic definition, a story is a sequence of events that follows characters in conflict in context. The typical story also has a beginning, a middle, and an end. But at its most basic level, a story is a vehicle for exchanging information and making sense of the world around us. To be a good editor, you need to become a good storyteller and to become a good storyteller you need to have a strong command of the language you are working in and you also need to understand a few basic attributes of why stories work.

Stuff Happens

A chronicle, an account, a version, a history, a legend, a saga, a myth, a fable, a parable. This is the story of story. Stuff happens, and in order to explain it to someone else, the storyteller breaks it down into smaller chunks and communicates it. The receiver reassembles the chunks and understands the whole. As the story is passed from one source to another, as in a game of telephone, the chunks may be modified, simplified, forgotten, and reinvented—but each time, meaning is derived.

You can break down events into smaller events, and break those down in turn, until you're looking at a single human event, or *therblig*.

> **THERBLIG** *This term was coined by Frank and Lillian Gilbreth, behavioral scientists whose analysis of human behavior made huge contributions to the technological advances of the 20th century. It refers to the most basic mechanical action a human can make. The Gilbreths came up with 17 or so unique therbligs. Note that "therblig" is Gilbreth spelled backward (almost).*
>
> *"Well, I <u>said</u>, 'Walter, you're the one!' And he <u>gasped</u>, and <u>sat</u> down, and <u>looked</u> at me..."*
>
> *That sequence has four therbligs.*

When an editor sits down to cut a film, she is handed an enormous pile of individual therbligs, often shot completely out of natural sequence. What an editor does all day long is to assemble one therblig after another, one element after another, shot by shot by shot. She arranges them one way, and then another way, until finally a coherent story begins to emerge.

Characters in Conflict in Context

Who, what, where, when, why, and how? These are the elements that comprise a story. You know that list by heart, because we all use those questions every day in daily life to understand the world around us: We think in stories. In film, these elements are represented by individual shots. Every shot has a point of focus: one or more vital bits of information it can communicate to the viewer. A good editor must be able to look at a shot and understand which bits of information it contains and which questions it answers.

How you deal with characters, conflict, and context has a huge impact on how you tell your story. It conveys the sense of theme and meaning in your work. And it answers the most important question: *Why?*

Stuff Happens to Characters (Who?)

Humans are most interested in stories about humans. Even a show about animals or objects requires a degree of anthropomorphizing in order to help the viewer make sense of the events. Sequences without a character quickly lose an audience's interest. Which shots in your sequence are about characters?

Event = Conflict (What? How?)

Basic logic dictates that things can only be defined in relationship to other things. This is why conflict is the heart of drama. Without some kind of contrast or opposition, an event does not occur—or at least cannot be depicted or described. Conflict can take many forms, but the editor creates meaning by contrasting ideas or images. What are the opposing or contrasting elements of this event? What shots can you use to represent them?

For example, let's say your story is about a divorcing couple. What are the elements of the conflict? Primarily, you have the two parties: husband and wife. Each time you juxtapose separate singles of each party, you emphasize the conflict. This may be obvious when they are in conversation, but you can make the point even more subtly by contrasting a shot of the wife having coffee with her new lover and the husband at home with their child.

Events Take Place in a Context (Where? When? With Whom?)

To further enhance your understanding of an event, the event must exist within some context. You can't prevent context from affecting the events in the story, but you can shape *how* the context affects events through your editing choices.

For example, let's expand our divorce story and set it in the midst of the Spanish civil war. Your editing choices will determine how the external conflict contrasts with or reflects the domestic story. You might align the husband with the government forces by linking them with similar music or grouping shots together so every time we see the husband, he is preceded by a shot of tanks in the streets.

Another interesting way you might align the two elements is by screen direction. If you make sure that the government forces are always moving left to right, and the revolutionaries are always moving right to left, you can borrow those directions and show the husband and wife moving in similar ways. Although this effect would be subtle, it might be effective in communicating the correlation between the political struggle and the personal one.

On the other hand, sequences that contain too *much* context may seem overly expository and disengage the viewer; just because a scene is set in the Reina Sofía museum in Madrid doesn't mean you have to show every Picasso in its collection.

Ask yourself which shots in your sequence show the context. What would happen if you eliminated those shots or rearranged their order? Perhaps choosing one image of Guernica and inserting it in the midst of the heated argument will serve not only to identify the location as the Reina Sofía, but also to emphasize the conflict between the characters by comparing it to Picasso's rendering of the bloody war.

Don't get stuck thinking that context simply means location. A shot of a Model T Ford or a particular costume can be used to convey a specific time period. A close shot of a child laughing and playing in a playground might serve to flavor the emotional context of a scene.

Rules from the Real

There are two important rules of storytelling, both derived from the rules of the world we live in.

Rule #1 is Cause and Effect, and it comes from physics: For every action, there is an equal and opposite reaction. The order in which you present events to your viewers implies cause and effect. Every good editor must understand this essential insight for arranging shots.

For instance, if you follow a shot of a dead soldier with a shot of his comrade saving a baby, you might be implying that the death of the soldier inspired his comrade's bravery.

On the other hand, if you show the comrade saving the baby followed by a shot of the dead soldier, you might be suggesting that saving the baby required sacrificing the soldier.

In most stories, many events are going on simultaneously. When you tell a story on screen, you instill meaning by the choices you make in arranging how those events will be presented to the viewer. Even a simple conversation contains actions and reactions. Precisely when you choose to cut to a reaction shot indicates what the character is reacting to—right down to the word.

Rule #2 is Timing Is Everything. You probably know people who tell wonderful stories and others who can't tell a joke to save their life. Good storytelling is all about good timing. The difference often lies in knowing how much time to spend telling each piece of the story.

For instance, if you spend too long describing every detail of the heroine's clothing, or go off on a tangent about how she loves horses and raised several when she was a girl, the audience will lose interest in her current escapade. And if you rush past her escape from the castle too quickly, you'll disappoint the audience and lose its interest again.

Timing is the most difficult editing skill to teach, because it's very personal and often unique to each event. The only overall rule is this: Stay on a shot exactly as long as is necessary to communicate the information it contains—not a frame less and not a frame more.

Sharing stories is as vital to us as love, and like love, well-told stories move us in a way that's nearly incomparable and largely indescribable. This is one reason we are drawn to filmmaking, to writing novels, to storytelling. But even if the final effect seems magical, it's worth the exercise of analysis to deconstruct a story and learn what craft went into creating that powerful effect. And almost every time, the secret that's revealed is *structure*. The order in which events occur as a tale unfolds is fundamental to affecting an audience. And since the editor determines the order of events in a film, down to the tiniest detail, she is the one who ultimately tells the story and makes it work.

Sources on Story Structure

You can find some excellent theoretical writing on story construction, notably Joseph Campbell's The Power of Myth *and* The Hero with a Thousand Faces. *If you find those useful, take a look at* The Writer's Journey *by Christopher Vogler, an interesting work that applies Campbell's theories to the art of screenwriting. All three books will help you understand storytelling structure. While these books focus primarily on overall structure, they provide useful insights on how to organize smaller events and even how best to set the specific order and timing of shots.*

INTERVIEW

Curtiss Clayton has edited a wonderful collection of independent films, including many of Gus Van Sant's best pictures. Clayton's credits include *Drugstore Cowboy* and *My Own Private Idaho* (both directed by Van Sant), Vincent Gallo's *Buffalo '66,* Bill Duke's *A Rage in Harlem,* and Jonathan Kaplan's *Brokedown Palace.* At the time of this interview, he had just completed the delightfully stylish *Made,* directed by Jon Favreau. Since then, he cut *Rules of Love* for Bruno Coppola and made his feature directorial debut in 2003 with *Rick,* which he also edited.

MICHAEL WOHL: WHY DID YOU CHOOSE A CAREER IN EDITING?

Curtiss Clayton: When I was in film school I didn't like the fact that as the cameraman, or in some of the other crew positions, you had this intense experience on the set, you finished shooting, and then you were done. Some time later you'd go to see the finished film, and very often it was not what you thought you were working on. I think that's one reason actors are so frustrated in Hollywood, and why so many want to be directors. As the editor, you participate in the ultimate form of the film, deciding what it's finally going to look like. Ultimately, the film becomes whatever it is in post production, and creatively its very satisfying to finish something and know what it is, rather than finishing [your work] in the middle of the process and not knowing what the ultimate project is going to look like.

ARE YOU AWARE OF HAVING A UNIQUE EDITING STYLE?

Generally, a particular aesthetic is already built into the shooting. Style is 80 percent determined by how a film is shot. You're in trouble if you have to impose some sort of style that's not inherent in what the film material already is.

HOW DO YOU START A PROJECT, AND WHAT'S YOUR WORKING PROCESS?

I begin working on the first day of shooting. As soon as the footage comes in, I start cutting it together just based on how it strikes me. Usually you have a chance to sit in dailies with the director and hear what he has to say, although that is becoming increasingly rare because of digital technology; a lot of projects don't even have dailies anymore. But even in the days when it was a standard thing, I found the directors comments were less useful to me then the footage itself; you can never really deal with the requirements of the scene until you start cutting it. You can talk about it and identify takes that you think are the best, but then you start cutting them together and what seems like one of the best takes very often is not the best or the most useful, so you immediately look for an alternative.

AFTER THE SHOOTING'S FINISHED, YOU SHOW THE DIRECTOR AN ASSEMBLY OF THE FOOTAGE. WHAT'S INCLUDED IN THAT?

In the assembly, I include everything because the director wants to see everything he shot in script order—to see what works and what doesn't. So, even if I have a pretty strong hunch something's going to hit the floor, I include it—not wanting to get too ahead of the director. Then we look at it; the way you work depends on the director and what type of chemistry and communication you have with him or her.

THEN, AS PRODUCTION PROCEEDS, YOU START CUTTING SCENES.

That's the most fun. You're looking at the dailies, you're following the lead of the footage, but you're also following your own taste and instincts, putting it together in what you think is most the effective [fashion]. I'm just there; I'm cutting and having a ball.

HOW MANY OF YOUR EDITING DECISIONS ARE MADE THINKING ABOUT YOUR AUDIENCE VERSUS THINKING ABOUT THE FOOTAGE ITSELF?

Everything is done with the audience in mind, the idea that you are going to present this to somebody.

DO YOU MAKE STYLISTIC DECISIONS BASED ON WHAT TYPE OF AUDIENCE IS LIKELY TO SEE THE FILM?

I follow my cue stylistically by what I am given. I feel like you can definitely take that to a higher level if you understand the style that's being used and the language that's being employed to communicate. In a film like *Buffalo '66,* a film of very vivid stylistic strategies, many of the things in it were discovered in the cutting room, but they came as a result of looking at and feeling the style that Vincent Gallo used while shooting. For instance, in the film there is this technique where there are flashbacks, and the flashbacks begin as little squares in the middle of the screen that get bigger and bigger until they fill the whole screen. They were scripted as flashbacks, and they were shot as flashbacks, but given some of the other stylistic choices made during shooting, it just didn't seem satisfying enough to "dissolve to a flashback." So we came up with something that was consistent with the visual language of the film.

TALK ABOUT THE DIFFERENT WAYS DIRECTORS WORK WITH EDITORS.

Some of them like to sit there with you all day long, look at takes with you and go through the process with you, and some, the kind I don't care to work with, just sit there and function with you as if you were an online editor; they tell you when to cut — "Use this take, cut on that frame, cut to the other close up." I'm not interested in working that way because I'm not doing anything.

A less severe director sits there with you all day long, investigating it with you. They aren't really that clear on how to proceed but they're indicating what they like and what they don't like. Very often you have to take the initiative to try something, but without going too far, so they don't feel like you're running away with it. That type of director likes to feel that you're working together, but you have to take the lead in terms of suggesting things. And you have to be emotionally equipped to play the roll of throwing out ideas when whatever the director likes are kept and what he doesn't like are not kept, regardless of how you feel about the ideas or their potential.

The objective is to—through the investigation and questioning—understand what they're trying to do, their taste, what appeals to them. Generally, within a week of that kind of working situation, you have the person pretty well figured out and you can start offering things you know they're going to like; you can see what they're after and start to go to that right away.

Other directors will look at a cut and give you notes or general reactions and then go away and say, "Show it to me when its done." And of course that's more fun for me because then I'm more or less autonomous.

HOW HAS THE NEW TECHNOLOGY CHANGED THE WAY YOU WORK?

It's fantastic. You don't need to spend nearly as much time searching your material; that's the best part about it. You have random access to any shot in the whole library of images, whereas before you'd be thinking of a moment you remembered from the dailies, and you'd have to go to that scene on the shelf, and take down the box, and there would be maybe five takes, and you'd have to wind through all of them looking for what you wanted. It's like, "Roll down through take one, then roll down through take two…" Now, you just click your mouse a couple times and it's instantaneous. That's the most wonderful thing about the new technology. It's like the difference between silent film and talkies.

DO YOU HAVE ANY ADVICE FOR BEGINNING EDITORS?

Anyone who wants to study editing seriously should study the fundamentals and not have an attitude about it, like, "I don't need these rules. These are just hindering my creativity." Concepts of screen direction, matching, the axis, the stage line, creating that illusion of a three-dimensional space…all that stuff is really important.

You also need to know how the sound and image work together, how important the sound is, how to manipulate the sound to create the illusion of continuity and seamlessness, especially applied to a cut that might not work visually. There are a bunch of weapons in your arsenal that you can employ if you take the time. It's like studying your multiplication tables: It's necessary. You can do anything you want. The questions are: Does it look good, is it going to be clear, and can you follow it?

CHAPTER THREE

Editing Patterns

Film editors rely on a library of standard editing patterns that serve them as stylistic guidelines for approaching different kinds of shows. By "patterns" I mean particular sequences of shot types and editing strategies that a good editor can draw upon to produce a desired effect on screen—excitement, suspense, humor, horror—regardless of the specific content of the shots. To extend the grammatical metaphor from the last chapter, think of these patterns as idioms or expressions in the film language, visual shorthand for conveying certain moods and relationships.

Naturally, some turns of phrase become overused and clichéd as time passes, and innovative editors are always creating new ways of presenting even the most familiar stories. In this way the language is continually evolving. Still, its important to understand why certain patterns work. It's important to understand the rules even as you break them.

I know you think that you are a unique snowflake, with a personal vision so fresh and insightful that every editing choice you make will be both original and stunningly beautiful. But remember that an average hour of film contains as many as 1,000 edits, and under that kind of pressure even the most resilient snowflake is likely to melt eventually. There is nothing wrong with standing on the slush pile of editors who have come before you and following the tried-and-true editing patterns they have established.

This chapter is a selection of essential sequence types, such as dialogue, action, comedy, documentary, and so on, along with guidelines for applying traditional editing patterns to cut each one most effectively.

EDITING WITH COMMON PATTERNS

Before diving into editing patterns for specific genres, let's consider patterns that are so basic they cut across genre lines. You'll find yourself using these structures again and again in common editing situations.

Starting a Scene

Every scene has to start somewhere, but getting started is often the hardest part. The most common way to start any scene is with the basic once-upon-a-time film "sentence" that goes, LS, MS, CU—long shot, mid shot, close up. The LS can be any establishing shot that introduces the characters in an environment. Cutting to an MS moves your viewer closer to the subject. Finally, you settle into a close shot to show the details of what's going on (**Figure 3.1**).

Figure 3.1 In this typical scene opening, we begin with a master LS showing Gene and his entourage. Next, we cut to an MS so we can see who's talking; the audio is of Gene reading an astrological chart. Finally, we move into an MCU of Gene, framed so we can see Trey approaching in the background.

This convention is one of the most basic editing patterns. It can be applied at the beginning of a scene, or at the beginning of a new event within a scene. Used in reverse—CU, MS, LS—it's often an appropriate way to end a sequence.

Changing Locations

One of the most common ways editors create smooth transitions between locations is by using the exit-entrance pattern. Here, a shot of someone exiting a frame is cut to match a shot of the same person entering the next frame. This relies on the shots maintaining correct *screen direction,* although in some cases you can flop one of the shots if it doesn't match (**Figure 3.2**).

Figure 3.2 Here, in shot 2, we see Trey exiting frame-right and, in shot 3, entering frame-left. Keeping him partially in frame across the cut point maintains continuity of time even though the location has changed.

To make this transition seamless, cut from the outgoing shot a few frames before the subject actually exits, and cut to the incoming shot a few frames after he enters. Because the subject stays onscreen, his motion appears continuous and provides a smooth transition, even though you may be cutting between two locations.

Showing Time Passing With Location Changes

The exit-entrance technique can be varied to link scenes where you want to show that time has passed during the transition. Let the subject exit the frame completely in the outgoing shot, wait a few frames, then cut to the incoming shot a few frames before the subject arrives. This requires you to decide how many frames should be shown after the exit and before the entrance. If you wait too long, the viewer's focus will change from the character himself to the surroundings the character has just left behind. Typically, you want an equal number of "empty" frames at the end of the first shot and the beginning of the second.

Shot–Reverse Shot

When a scene features a live person, the audience will watch the eyes to see what the character is thinking or feeling. If the subject is looking at something off screen, the audience will want to know what she's looking at. This is the basis for one of the most useful phrases in film language, the shot–reverse shot. "Reverse" refers to any shot that shows the opposite of the previous shot.

Using Shot–Reverse Shot to Cut Between Two Characters

When cutting dialog, you'll often want to cut back and forth between the characters to show not only who's speaking but also the reaction of the listener. That's a classic application of shot-reverse shot. For instance, when actor 1 looks at actor 2, cut to show what he's looking at (actor 2). Then, when actor 2 looks back at actor 1, cut back to actor 1. An actor's look can provide a great clue as to when to make your cut.

Using Shot–Reverse Shot to Show Offscreen Action

Also use the shot–reverse shot pattern to edit a scene where the subject is looking at something offscreen. Again, the viewer will be watching the actor's eyeline and will want to know what he's looking at.

Let's say a man is sitting next to the window in a café, writing in a journal. At some point, he looks up and glances at something going on offscreen, outside the window of the café, then he smiles. If you wait too long to reveal what he's looking at, you will confuse and irritate your audience. You can hint at what's going on with offscreen sound or a CU revealing your character's emotional state, but eventually you've *got* to show what the heck he's looking at.

Narrative patterns and expectations are so powerful that even now, gentle reader, you are probably wondering what that man is looking at. If I wait too long to tell you, you will get frustrated and perhaps forget the point of this lesson. The longer the editor waits to reveal the answer, the more tension he creates in his viewer—which can be effective, if you know when to release the tension. If you wait too long, it just comes across as bad editing. (Oh. The man in the café was looking at Alfred Hitchcock, making his customary personal appearance, carrying a French horn.)

Montage

Although in French, *montage* is the general term for editing, in English, editors often use it to mean an extended sequence of short images that are tied together thematically but break the rules of continuity of time and space.

Montages are used widely across all types of projects. They can often solve the problem of how to show a lengthy, complicated event in the shortest period of time. A well-executed montage has a poem's efficiency, communicating deep feelings with an impressive economy of words. The art of montage is conveying the essence of the entire event with a few meaningful images.

Using Montage to Show Time Passing

Among the most clichéd montages are those used to indicate the passage of time—intercutting pages blowing off a calendar or hands spinning on a clock face with shots of pertinent action involving the characters, such as a prisoner sitting in his cell or snapshots of children growing up.

To avoid repeating the cliché, find a unique way to convey the passing of time: perhaps through your character's hair growing or graying, or by leaves turning gold. Try to find something that fits with the story. In a training video for gas station attendants, I once showed time passing through candy wrappers accumulating in the trash can.

Using Montage to Compress Complex Processes

You can use a montage to simplify complicated procedures. For instance, imagine a story about an auto company designing a new car. Once the drama of the design team's decisions is played out, the actual construction of the cars might be summarized into a montage showing various operations taking place on the assembly line. This way, a process that might take several hours or days in real time can be condensed into a few seconds.

Techniques for Effective Montage

In many ways, building a montage is a lot like creating a sequence for an experimental film or music video. Since the rules of continuity are suspended, creating a memorable montage depends almost exclusively on the visual and emotional contrasts of the images you bring together.

Start by collecting the shots you intend to use. Of course, you will want to choose shots that are appropriate to the subject at hand. Usually, you won't need to include more than one angle of any one scene or detail. For instance, in the assembly line montage I mentioned, one shot of each machine would be enough. Choose shots that best illustrate the procedure or event taking place, and always look for the most visually striking shot.

Next, experiment with ways to assemble the shots. The order of shots in your montage is seldom critical, so try rearranging them in different ways for the best visual effect. Continuity doesn't matter, so what you're left with is the visual effect of bringing together two adjacent shots.

Pay close attention to the composition of the shots, just as you do with jumpcuts and scene changes. How do consecutive shots compare? How do they cut together visually? Look at the positive and negative space of the different shots. Adjacent images should contrast with each other. If the shots are too similar, the cut may be missed or misread as an accidental jump cut.

These issues can affect your shot selection as well as the order in which they're assembled. In the assembly line montage, for instance, you might choose only ECUs of the various moving parts on the machines (assuming they look different enough to be visually engaging). Alternately, you could cut back and forth between ECUs and LSs.

Ideally, you can apply these same rules to the emotional content of the shots in a montage. If a prisoner goes through a range of feelings while in solitary confinement, don't worry about continuity or showing subtle changes from one state to another. Cut from a shot of him crying to one of him calm, then show him screaming, then catatonic. The juxtaposition of contrasting emotional content will heighten the impact of the sequence.

Using Montage to Recap and Review

A montage can be very handy for presenting a recap or review. Typically, if you were cutting an educational or informational video, you would place a montage of memorable frames from the film at the end of a section (or the whole show), joined with dissolves or cuts.

Occasionally, a dramatic film will use this technique to recap key events in a brief montage at the end. This can give the entire film a broader context. A good example is Woody Allen's *Annie Hall*. At the end of the film, Allen's character, Alvy Singer, is reminiscing about his failed relationship with Annie Hall. Allen shows us a montage of the highlights of the relationship. It wouldn't work if he included shots that we had not seen already. The point is to remind us of the emotions associated with each scene in the movie. The montage brings the scenes together to make a larger point about the bittersweet nature of relationships.

WORKING WITH NARRATIVE STRUCTURE

While you might think that narrative editing patterns and storytelling techniques are most pertinent to fictional feature films, you can apply the same insights and strategies to almost all film editing. You will find yourself drawing on storytelling techniques whether you're editing informational corporate communications films or educational projects. Basic storytelling is also essential to good documentary filmmaking. In fact, the only place where narrative conventions go out the window is in abstract cinema, which these days is found mainly in music videos, experimental films, and some advertising.

Some of the most frequently used editing patterns and techniques involve dialogue scenes and action sequences. If you can master dialogue editing and the art of the *continuity cut* in action scenes, you'll find that 80 percent of your editing will be a variation on these techniques.

Editing Dialogue Sequences

The dialogue sequence is the centerpiece of all narrative filmmaking and supplies some of the most common editing patterns. Whenever two or more people are speaking, the editor can fall back on standard patterns for editing the sequence.

The primary goal in almost any dialogue sequence is to allow the content of the dialogue to get across to the viewer. However, there is usually much more going on in a scene than just the words being spoken: the body language of actors, the reactions of the listeners, the environment in which they exist, and all the other elements that contribute to the story.

It's also important to understand dramatic timing to create a naturalistic effect when cutting dialogue that may have been recorded at different times (see the section on manipulating time in Chapter 2, "Film Language").

Cut Audio First

In most dialogue sequences, you will want to create natural, conversational timing. One way to make this a lot easier is to cut your *track* before you start worrying about the picture.

Once you've captured all the clips you need for the dialogue scene, you'll find them in Final Cut's Browser window. Review the shots one by one to find the best ones, and start building the sequence. For starters, don't worry too much about what the images look like. Choose the shots that will allow you to create the most fluid, seamless audio track.

You'll probably need to play with your clips quite a bit, making minute adjustments before you find the right timing to create a natural-sounding conversation. You may have to alter the pacing by adding gaps between words or phrases or editing out fractional seconds of the clip. You'll often need to overlap your audio clips to make the dialogue overlap as it does in actual conversation. Since you're not paying much attention to the images yet, you can concentrate on fine-tuning the audio. Use Final Cut Pro's Timeline tools to move the clips in one direction or another, fade them in and out, and so on, to create just the right overlap (**Figure 3.3**).

Once you've built the audio track, you should be able to close your eyes and hear a natural-sounding conversation. You'll continue to refine the audio as you cut your picture, but the better you build the audio in the first place, the easier it will be to choose visuals.

Figure 3.3 The audio on tracks A3 and A4 is from CU_Trey_29s_04. By overlapping this clip with the audio clips on tracks A1 and A2, the editor can condense time, giving the impression that the characters' dialogue is overlapping.

Sometimes, there may be a mistake in either the picture or the track that threatens to ruin the shot. It's much easier to replace audio (through Foley, ADR, or stealing good audio from another shot) than it is to replace images (which could require a reshoot). You will generally overlook an audio error to use a great-looking shot but will almost never overlook a visual error.

For example, pretend you're editing an imaginary wedding scene in one of *The Godfather* movies. Your goal at this stage is to create the best audio track you can. You have two takes of the CU of Michael Corleone giving a toast to the newly-weds. In take 1, there's a fabulous flash of light refracting through his upraised glass—but the noise of a plane ruined the audio. In the second take, there's no flash but the dialogue is perfect. Make an exception and lay in take 1. You can fix the audio by using the track from take 2 or another take in the sequence; in the worst case, add the shot to the ADR list.

> **TIP:** If the actors turned in good performances, you may be able to use their pauses and phrasing to guide your pacing, but most often, when you're matching shots from various takes and different setups, you'll have to set dialogue pacing on your own. The current fashion is for film editors to create somewhat accelerated speech. What might sound natural in real life or onstage often feels too slow or "stagy" when played on film.

Doing it by the Numbers

*In Final Cut Pro you can move Timeline items forward or backward by specific numbers of frames, simply by selecting the item in the Timeline and typing +5 or –3, or any appropriate figure to indicate the number of frames you want the item to move. It's just the thing for fine-tuning an audio track. You'll quickly get the feel of how long "+5 frames" is onscreen, and learn how many frames to move items to achieve the timing you want (**Figure 3.4**). (I'll elaborate on all these techniques in greater detail in Chapters 4, "Preparing to Edit," and 6, "Advanced Editing.")*

*Items can also be dragged around in the Timeline, but this is less precise than the technique described above. Depending on how far you've zoomed in your view, the same tiny drag might move the clip ten frames or ten seconds (**Figure 3.5**).*

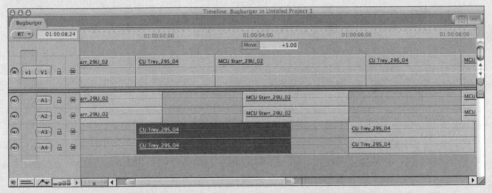

Figure 3.4 Any time an item in the Timeline is selected, simply typing ⊞ or ⊟ initiates the Move function. Hitting ⎣Enter⎦ or ⎣Return⎦ performs the edit. The pop-up window gives visual feedback so you can see what you're typing.

Figure 3.5 Clicking and dragging any Timeline item allows you to move it, but this is less precise than typing in a numerical entry. In a pinch, you can move one frame at a time by holding down ⌘ while you drag.

Dialogue for Two

The simplest dialogue sequence involves two people. It comes with its own set of editing patterns.

Establishing a Physical Relationship

When you cut a dialogue sequence involving two people, it's important to begin with a two-shot to establish the characters' physical relationship. If you can't make it the first shot of the sequence, show it as early as possible. If too much time passes entirely in singles, the audience will lose the sense of connection between the characters.

Your choice for the two-shot can be an establishing shot or long shot that places the characters in their environment, or it might be a tighter MS that shows the characters' proximity to each other. This critical two-shot also provides an opportunity to reveal the physical dynamics of the discussion. Are the protagonists facing away from each other? Across a table? Side by side? Once you establish this in the two-shot, the screen direction in the singles will continue to communicate the relationship. Another common two-shot is the over-the-shoulder shot; sometimes you can edit almost an entire dialogue sequence between two people just using OS shots.

Cutting in Close for Pivotal Moments

Emphasize the key moment of a sequence with an effective editing pattern. Typically, you'll begin a dialogue sequence in wider shots, perhaps MCU over-the-shoulder (OS) shots. Then, at the pivotal moment of the scene, you can switch to close-ups (CUs). This focuses attention on the subjects' emotional state.

Once the key moment is over, you can back out of the CUs in order to close the sequence comfortably. You might switch back to MCUs, jump back out to a MS, or try something even wider. Usually, the scene is pretty much over after its climax, so there won't be too many shots after the CUs.

For instance, in a critical scene from *Want,* Trey goes to his mother to seek help after he's been fired from his job. The sequence opens with a long shot (LS) of her livingroom as Trey sits down. They exchange a line or two of small talk, which is covered in matching MCUs. When Trey tells her about getting fired, the sequence cuts to a CU and matches it with a CU of the mother as she responds. Once Trey realizes that she is unable to comprehend his problem, his delusional defense mechanism kicks in. To convey that, the sequence cuts back to the wider master to show the whole set: Trey looks on, horrified, as stagehands come in and disassemble the set of his mother's living room while she watches TV, oblivious (**Figure 3.6**).

Figure 3.6 The close-ups (shots 4 and 5) focus attention on the key emotional content of the scene. Once the crucial moment is over, we cut back to a long shot.

Following the Reactions

Once you get the hang of it, cutting dialogue scenes is fairly easy. The only trick is understanding when to make the cuts. One good way to figure that out is to follow the characters' reactions.

People's feelings are more important to the audience than moving lips. Your protagonists' reactions to what others say tell a more important story than the words themselves. Rather than cutting back and forth to focus on the character who's speaking, edit to show important reactions.

For example, in the sequence above, as soon as Trey begins his confession about the job, both he and the audience are wondering how Mom is going to take it.

His complete line is: "Mom… I'm not working there any more. I quit… Well, actually I got fired…"

I might have stayed on him for the entire line, but instead, as soon as he says, "Mom…" I cut to her reaction and the rest of his line is heard offscreen. This works nicely because when he calls her name, he elicits her eye contact—which gives us a physical action to cut on (her looking up). Even more important, it allows us to see her reaction as he stumbles through his confession. Because her next line is still part of her reaction, I stay on her until she finishes the line. Then I cut back to Trey to show *his* reaction to *her.*

Using Split Edits

As I've already said several times, successful dialogue editing requires offsetting your audio and video cuts. This technique carries the viewer past dialogue cuts so smoothly she never notices them. Almost every editor uses lots of split edits when editing conversations. Those are edits where the audio and video begin and end at different times. In fact, in most dialogue sequences, *every* cut is an L or J cut (**Figure 3.7**). (See the section on split edits in Chapter 2.)

Figure 3.7 Most dialogue scenes look something like this in Final Cut Pro. Note that nearly every cut is a split edit.

Don't Cut on Pauses

It's tempting to make your cuts exactly on the beginnings or endings of phrases. Resist the temptation. These cuts become painfully apparent, especially when you're taking the audio from different shots. Since your goal is usually to make your cuts invisible, avoid cutting at these natural pauses.

Better yet, you can turn one of these "natural pause" edits into an invisible L or J edit by *rolling* the video edit forward or backward so it doesn't coincide with the audio cut point (see the section on the roll edit in Chapter 6).

Finding the Best Performance

To make your dialogue scenes as effective as possible, use the best performances for every line in the show. This brings sequences to life and keeps the dramatic action at a high level.

A lazy editor cutting a two-person dialogue scene may pick one take of each shot (e.g., two matching CUs) and simply cut back and forth between them for the duration of the scene. This is easy, but it runs the risk of missing a gem hiding in another take. Every time you cut, you have the opportunity to go to a new take (unless continuity problems make that impossible). The only thing to watch out for is that sometimes the energy in a particular take will be so consistent that dropping in a moment from another take can destroy the scene's subtle continuity.

In any case, a skilled editor will look at all the footage and mark every good line reading for possible use.

Three or More People

Editing an effective dialogue sequence with three or more people forces you to vary some of the rules for working with two people.

Using Group Shots

Since group scenes involve more camera angles, it's important to use shots that show more than one person at a time. This reinforces the physical relationships between the participants and keeps the viewer from becoming confused. Using too many singles in a row can destroy the sense of physical space in the room.

Following the Dominant Character's Eyeline

You already know how important it is to stay on the same side of the axis when you're editing (see the section on the 180° rule in Chapter 2). However, group dialogue scenes can be a nightmare in terms of keeping track of the axis. Because eyelines are continually changing as people move and interact, staying on one side of the line can become a major challenge.

One way to solve this puzzle is to identify the character who is dominant and guides the conversation. Then simply follow that person's eyeline and treat it as the axis—until it changes.

Avoiding Confusing Two-Shots

Another thing to watch out for, though, is creating screen direction problems by using two successive two-shots of the same person in different positions (**Figure 3.8**). Imagine a scene of three people talking. Even without crossing the line, it would be easy to make one of the characters switch frame location by cutting the wrong two-shots together.

The way to overcome this is by interjecting a single into the series, or cutting to a wider shot before going to another two-shot (**Figure 3.9**).

Figure 3.8 Notice how player 2 is on the left side of the frame in shot 1 and on the right side of the frame in shot 2. This violates continuity of screen direction even though the camera has not crossed the axis.

Figure 3.9 The sequence can be remedied by inserting a WS or CU between the two offending shots.

Editing a Soliloquy

Editors encounter many film sequences showing a single person talking or thinking. This is almost always a scene illustrating a character's inner conflict.

First, remember that you don't need to make any edits at all unless there is new information to provide. With dialogue between multiple people there is constantly something new to cut to as each person speaks, but with a single character, you may not need to cut at all. When you do need to cut (to cover a moment of bad framing or flubbed performance) it may be hard to identify the best way to assemble the various shots you have.

One of the most commonly used techniques to make this type of scene dramatic and exciting is to cut back and forth from LS to CU of the same subject (**Figure 3.10**). This allows the audience to contrast the subject's thoughts (in CUs) with an objective view of his situation (in LSs), and it has the added benefit of avoiding jump cuts.

Figure 3.10 Alternating tight shots and wider shots is an effective way to cut a scene of one person alone, thinking. Here, Trey is preparing to face his family after his father's death.

On the other hand, if jumpcutting doesn't bother you, try using jump cuts of the subject doing different things or different angles of the same action. These jump cuts might be a series of CUs, a series of LSs, or a mix of both. This has the effect of adding tension to the sequence, forcing the viewer to participate in the subject's conflict.

There may be a voice-over monologue or another audio element that can help you figure out how to cut the sequence. For instance, if an astronaut is describing his ordeal in a crippled landing module, he might list the specific things he did to save his life. In the editing room, you could jump cut between the different actions he describes. This narration then becomes a clear guide for what to show and when to show it.

Editing Action Sequences

Any narrative sequence that is not a dialogue sequence is an action sequence. An action sequence can be as simple as a single person walking down a hallway— or as complex as a huge war scene, with people running in all directions and multiple events going on simultaneously. In either case, the basic rules are relatively straightforward.

At its simplest, action is movement, and, in general, the more movement in a shot, the more exciting it is. This has been taken to an extreme in popular action films, where almost every shot is filled with moving objects; indeed, the basic premise of some films involves a fast-moving vehicle like a helicopter, bus, or train. To raise the excitement level even more, many action films employ shots where the camera seems to fly through the air with dizzying speed, moving along with a bullet, an arrow, or a falling bomb.

Even if you're not editing a high-speed chase, camera movement can add excitement to otherwise boring scenes. For instance, you can raise the suspense level of a shot of a static object simply by employing slow, smooth camera moves around it.

Unfortunately, many filmmakers abuse these concepts and shoot every scene in the movie with moving cameras—even when there isn't any call for it in the story. While this adds drama and tension, it has the cumulative effect of diluting the impact of truly dramatic scenes and numbing audiences into a shallow engagement that evaporates the second the credits begin to roll.

Preserving Continuity

The first thing to think about as you begin editing an action scene is creating a sequence of events that makes sense in a chronological time frame. The key to this is maintaining continuity across cuts: Actions that begin in one shot and continue in the next should feel continuous.

The simplest example is someone walking through a doorway. If the first shot ends with the door one-third open, the next shot should begin with the door one-third open. If instead the second shot begins with the door all the way open, or opened just a crack, there will be an overlap of action and the edit will be a jump cut (**Figure 3.11**).

Figure 3.11 In the first series, continuity is preserved because at the edit point, the door is partially open in both shots.

In the second series, the door has opened too wide in the first shot and creates a jump cut.

To convince the viewer that the action is continuous across the cut, the match in door position and the speed at which the door moves must be fairly precise. Of course, in reality the action is not continuous. The first shot may have been shot on Tuesday at 3 p.m., and the reverse inside the room may have been picked up a week later at 10 a.m., but in the story the action is supposed to be continuous, and your job is to stitch it together so it appears that way.

This is true of any action, no matter how big or small. Someone getting thrown through a plate glass window should be the same percentage of the way through the window across the edits—accounting for momentum.

Preserving Momentum

Creating a smooth, invisible continuity cut in an action sequence requires some understanding of basic physics, particularly the concept of momentum. Fortunately, you don't need to explain the underlying theories mathematically as long as you understand them. A good editor always accounts for the velocity at which an object is moving when she is editing. Since video runs somewhere between 20 and 30 frames per second (fps), you need to allow for how far a fast-moving object will travel in the short time between two frames when you make a cut.

In the plate glass window example, the man being hurled through the window might be just hitting the pane when you cut out of shot 1, but shot 2 must begin at a point where he is already a few inches through the glass. If you were working in PAL (which runs at 25 fps), he would move a bit farther in between frames than he would if you were working in NTSC (30 fps) (**Figure 3.12**).

Frame **1** Frame **45** Frame **46** Frame **90**

00:00 00:10 00:20 01:00 01:10 01:20 02:00 02:10 02:20 03:00

Figure 3.12 As time progresses, the man moves farther through the window. In this example, it takes him three seconds from the beginning of the motion until he lands on the ground. Because he's moving so quickly, you can't cut during this motion without accounting for his momentum.

> **TIP:** When switching video formats, editors who've grown accustomed to one format (PAL, NTSC or 24p) go through an adjustment period during which they are likely to make timing mistakes.

Allowing for one single frame's worth of momentum entails a very subtle adjustment, but if you fail to make it the action won't feel right and the audience will notice.

If you have to cut between shots where the velocity of the movement is inconsistent (in shot 1 the actor slams the door shut, and in shot 2 he closes the door delicately), you will have great difficulty matching the momentum. In this situation, experiment, frame by frame, evaluating what will make the smoothest motion across the cut. In dire circumstances, modify the speed of one clip digitally, or avoid the problem altogether by using a cutaway.

Cutting on Action

This is one of the most basic action-editing rules: If you have the same action in two different shots, and you are trying to cut between them, and you want the cut to be as invisible as possible, hide the cut by doing it while movement is occurring within the frame. In other words, cut on action.

If the viewer's attention is focused on movement within the frame, and you present that movement continuously across the cut, the viewer will pay attention to the moving object and won't notice the cut (or the perspective change it forces). You can also use this technique to shift point of view without drawing attention to the edit.

For example, rather than running shot 1 until the subject has opened the door, stepped through, and closed the door behind her, and then cutting to shot 2 of the subject already inside the room, cut while the door is in motion. Then the audience won't notice that there were two shots, two camera positions, and an editor who joined them together.

Cutting on Action Adds Excitement

In addition to masking the edit point, cutting on action adds dynamism. For instance, in the plate glass window example, it would be much more exciting to cut while the man is in midair than wait until he lands outside.

You can tell the same story many ways. For instance, if you don't want to actually break the plate glass window, you can take one shot from inside (of the subject hurtling toward the window) and another shot from outside (showing him landing on the ground with glass shards falling around him). With proper timing and a sound effect of glass breaking, the audience will think it has just seen the character plunge through a plate glass window—and you will have told your story. Probably more safely and more cheaply, too.

Of course, this version sacrifices the excitement of seeing the violent shattering of glass. In our first example (cutting with the subject in midair), we maximize the impact by showing it twice, from two angles.

Building Tension

Action sequences depend on building tension. A good editor can create tension in a number of ways.

Using Crosscutting

One common method for building tension is through crosscutting—cutting back and forth between multiple events that are occurring simultaneously (see the section on crosscutting in Chapter 2). Each time you cut from one event to the next, as in the outlaw sequence I described in Chapter 2, you force the viewer to try to complete the action of the event left behind, while disorienting them with a whole new scene to compare it to. This keeps the brain busy (thinking of two things at once), which causes a tense mental and emotional state.

Speeding Up the Cutting

Another way to build tension is to speed up the cutting. By shortening each shot, you force the audience to absorb more information in less time. Before viewers can figure out what's going on, you cut to a new shot and compel them to start taking in new information. In real life, when you are forced to take in too much information, your stress level rises. This is why many people turn down their car radios when trying to maneuver in fast-moving traffic. You can evoke a similarly tense state for your viewers through editing. As you overload their ability to keep track, you cause an actual physiological reaction.

Raising Tension With Close-Ups

Editing a sequence using tight close-ups has a similar effect. Just as crosscutting or cutting quickly forces the viewer to construct the surrounding time, using tighter shots makes the viewer construct the surrounding space. Cutting to a tight CU (especially without an establishing shot to let the viewer know what the context is) requires the viewer to construct the environment in order to understand what she is watching. Cutting from ECU to ECU without showing any context makes it even harder for the audience to understand the larger circumstances. This creates stress and serves to heighten the tension of the scene.

Imagine the climax of a movie about a sailing race. Two rivals are in the final leg, and we want to create a tense atmosphere to give the audience a sense of the adrenaline rush the racers are experiencing.

1. WS two sailboats cutting through the bay. One boat suddenly begins to tack.

2. ECU captain's face screaming orders.

3. ECU sailor 1's hands reeling in the main sheet.

4. ECU tell-tales on sail beginning to flop.

5. ECU sailor 3's face grimacing.

6. ECU captain screaming.

7. ECU tell-tales straightening out.

8. MCU several sailors stacked in perspective, all working frantically.

9. ECU sailors' hands.

10. ECU captain's eyes looking toward the other ship.

11. Reverse POV (LS) showing the other vessel rounding the final marker.

Syncing Up On the Easy Spot

One of the best ways to ensure accurate continuity of movement across shots is to first make your cut on a spot that's easy to identify in both shots, such as the moment the door cracks open (**Figure 3.13**). Then roll the edit forward to some point where the door is in the process of opening, and make the actual cut there (**Figure 3.14**). (See the section on the roll edit in Chapter 6.)

If the door is opening at the same speed in the two shots, no matter where you roll the edit to, it will be a successful continuity cut.

Figure 3.13 Find a point that's easy to identify in both shots. The moment the door opens is especially handy because the sound of the door opening is easy to locate.

Figure 3.14 Rolling the edit allows you to move the cut point so it occurs mid-motion. Experiment to find the best place for the cut.

The most straightforward way to cover the scene would involve close-ups of the key personnel, full shots of the crew hard at work, and wide shots showing the two boats and their relative progress. However, in order to raise the tension of the scene, I would cut one close shot after another and limit the number of wide shots that reveal the racers' relative positions. After all, most of the crew members are so engaged in their jobs that they don't have time to look at the competing vessel, and not knowing who's ahead is part of what causes the tension we're seeking to evoke.

The chaos created by cutting tight close-ups back and forth amidst the many actions going on simultaneously is an effective way to keep the viewer engaged—as if she were on the boat herself.

Sex, Violence, and Responsibility

It's amazing (and slightly creepy) that a skillful film editor can create involuntary physical reactions in an audience. This is one reason film is such a powerful medium. Similarly, the simple act of viewing images of sex and violence has a visceral impact on us. I won't enter the battle about whether or not it changes our behavior, but it is inarguable that films can cause a physical reaction in audiences.

By learning which shots to choose, how long to run them, and in what order to arrange them to affect an audience most powerfully, you are acquiring a type of mind control. Never underestimate the power of the film medium or your responsibility in wielding that power.

Using Setup to Create Suspense

The setup is a common pattern that editors use quite often in action or suspense sequences. It creates an expectation in the audience by showing a subject or object that implies some expected result.

Recall our suicide bomber sequence:

1. LS woman and her young son shopping for fruit at a stall in a public market.
2. MS mother walks away to another stall, leaving the boy behind.
3. MCU man carrying a suitcase approaches the marketplace.
4. LS man approaches a shopping cart where the boy is.
5. MCU mother is engaged in a conversation with a vendor.
6. ELS explosion in the square.
7. MCU mother looks to where her son was.

8.   LS (reverse: mother's POV) cart is gone amid debris and chaos.

9.   CU mother screams.

The setup is shots 2 and 3. These shots create most of the tension in the scene.

When the woman walks off, leaving her son behind in shot 2, we become aware of the boy's vulnerability. The next thing we see, in shot 3, is the agent of conflict, the suicide bomber. The fact that the shot is a CU draws our attention to the character and gives him extra significance. If shot 2 had been skipped, we wouldn't know where the bomber is headed when we see him in shots 3 and 4. If shot 3 had been skipped, the impact of the man walking into the market would have no meaning until the bomb went off, and there would be no suspense.

Don't Forget the Payoff

Every setup should have a payoff, or the viewer will feel cheated. The emotional payoff of this scene is in shot 9, when we see the mother's reaction to the bomb blast.

As the editor, you have the ability to guide the emotional dynamics of the scene. For instance, you could have told this event entirely through shots 4 and 6: A man walks into a market and sets off a bomb. But when you include the woman and her son, even if we never see them again, you provide a human point of view that draws in the audience and intensifies the scene's emotional impact.

The Cliffhanger

In the section on storytelling in Chapter 2, I discussed the importance of cause and effect, and how you can manipulate these editing elements to control the flow of your story. One familiar cause and effect technique is the cliffhanger, in which a sequence ends with a "cause" shot, but doesn't reveal the result. Since humans are programmed with a need to know the outcome of uncertain situations, good storytelling (and therefore good editing) can use cliffhangers and payoff shots to powerful effect. If you need to maintain viewers' interest across commercial interruptions (or summer reruns), the cliffhanger is an excellent way to do it.

The cliffhanger is used tirelessly in soap operas and other episodic television programs to keep viewers hooked enough to sit through the commercials, and return to the show from episode to episode. However, this technique is equally effective if you need to interrupt an educational program to summarize a section with graphics, or send your viewers off to their workbooks.

By all means, go ahead and experiment with how long you can separate the cliffhanger and the payoff. The more intensely you have engaged your viewers, the longer you can leave them hanging.

> **TIP:** An adept editor can stack up several "cause" shots before paying off any of them, playing on viewers' anticipation level to keep suspense and interest heightened. Because most humans can keep track of about five things at the same time, you will need to pay off a cliffhanger that's been hanging for a while in order to introduce a new one. Superb editors know how to create a payoff that resolves multiple cliffhangers simultaneously.

Working With the Writer to Accentuate the Cliffhanger

All this may sound like the writer's job to you, but an editor has to understand these techniques, too—which is why editors frequently make good screenwriters.

For instance, imagine a scenario in which a villain plans to take over the world by implanting microchips in people who drink the coffee sold in her ubiquitous chain stores. Our hero walks unsuspectingly into one of the coffee shops and orders a mocha. By ending the scene on the shot where he orders the drink, we create cliffhanger No. 1.

The villain has a deadly allergy to chocolate, alleviated only by a shot of epinephrine she keeps in her purse. In the next scene, she is in an argument with one of her store managers and drops her purse. To create cliffhanger No. 2, we end the scene with a tight shot of the medicine falling out of the purse and rolling under the table.

The writer has created the story elements that generate the cliffhangers, but by ending the scenes on these specific shots, the editor builds the suspense and compels the reaction in the viewers. Best of all, the editor resolves both cliff-hangers in a single shot, as illustrated in the following sequence.

1. LS villain walks out of the back room and orders a latte.
2. MS hero picks up a newspaper.
3. CU coffee jerk making hero's mocha.
4. ECU the chocolate as it's poured in the cup.
5. MS villain pacing, dreaming of world domination.
6. ECU espresso machine inserting microchip into mocha.
7. MCU hero, reading the paper.

8. CU coffee jerk makes latte for villain.

9. ECU newspaper story about chocolate allergies.

10. MCU villain yells at coffee jerk, "I'm late! Hurry up!"

11. MCU coffee jerk puts two identical-looking drinks on the counter.

12. ECU one of the coffees marked as a mocha.

13. MS hero and villain collide as they reach the drink counter.

14. CU villain accidentally takes mocha, leaving clean drink for the hero.

Effective suspense requires holding off, or suspending, the resolution as long as possible without destroying momentum. If you feel confident that the audience will stay involved, stretch the suspense even further by introducing extraneous shots—for instance, the coffee jerk chatting with a co-worker. In any case, the repeated references to chocolate and the microchip remind the audience of what they are anticipating and accentuate the suspense. If those reinforcing shots were left out, the power of the sequence would be reduced.

Finally, shot 14 succeeds in simultaneously resolving both cliffhangers. Alternately, you could cut the scene so it's unclear who got which drink, and you could continue intercutting shots of the two players drinking their coffee, further suspending the resolution.

Manipulating Cause and Effect

Action sequences depend on proper manipulation of cause and effect to create tension and drama. When an editor chooses the order in which shots and sequences appear in a film, she is controlling the chronological flow in which the viewer will experience events. This in turn translates into meaning for the audience (see the section on storytelling in Chapter 2).

For instance, if there is a cause (say, a hand grenade with the pin pulled) with an obvious effect (an explosion), one quick shot of the grenade is all you need to make the audience anticipate the explosion. Thereafter, your viewers will be waiting anxiously for the explosion, and that expectation will flavor every shot in between the CU of the grenade and the eventual explosion.

Consider this cutting sequence:

1. LS soldier outside the enemy barracks.

2. MS enemies inside playing poker.

3. MCU soldier pulls the pin from a grenade and throws it through the barracks window.

4. CU grenade lands softly on a cot, not making a sound.

5. MS the poker players are oblivious.

6. MCU soldier covering his ears, anticipating the explosion.

7. MS poker players.

Even looking at this shot list, you are probably anticipating the coming explosion. But without those preceding shots of the live grenade, the same shots of the poker players would have a completely different meaning. The tension can be increased even further by cutting back to the grenade once more before it explodes.

The impact that any one shot has on the images that follow it is a type of cause and effect. For instance, in the sequence above, you might cut to a framed family picture belonging to one of the poker players. In and of itself, that image is virtually devoid of meaning—but here, combined with the previous grenade shot, it creates sympathy for the doomed men.

Similarly, if you never show the faces of the poker players, your audience will probably feel little sorrow when the grenade goes off. But if you spend just a few seconds showing the soldiers' camaraderie and pleasure in playing the card game, the scene takes on an entirely different emotional meaning. Your director may well have shot both options, leaving this final and critical decision in your hands.

The precise placement of cause and effect shots is critical to building tension. Like other timing issues, this requires a learned ability to judge when, and for how long, to show these shots for maximum effect. As a beginning editor, you can always fall back on trial and error to get it right.

Cutting the Shoot-out

The shoot-out, a familiar element of many action sequences, comes with its own set of standard editing patterns. You can use them with equal success in hand-to-hand combat or a courtroom drama where the subjects are shooting each other with words. Oddly enough, the shoot-out is actually a variant on a dialogue sequence—so the basic rules about matching similar angles, cutting for reactions, and copious use of L and J cuts, remain in effect.

Don't Forget the Witness

One unique element of the shoot-out is the presence of a witness. In fact, you'll rarely run across a shoot-out without a witness. The witness provides an opportunity for cutaways and adds additional tension to the scene.

Consider this sequence:

1. ECU villain draws his gun.

2. CU witness observes the action.

3. MCU sheriff leaves his office, laughing with his partner.

4. LS (witness's POV) of sheriff. Gunshot rings out. Sheriff ducks.

5. CU sheriff pulls out his gun. (Continuous action as he ducks.)

6. MCU villain hides behind a post.

7. MCU sheriff warns villain to drop his gun.

8. MCU villain rejects the sheriff's order and fires his gun.

9. MCU sheriff dodges bullet and shoots back.

10. CU witness watches in horror.

11. CU villain shoots again.

12. ECU sheriff gets hit (in the arm, of course).

continues on next page

13. MS villain runs across the square.

14. CU sheriff fires.

15. CU witness reacts as we hear the villain exclaim.

16. MS villain slain on the ground. Sheriff and crowd gather.

You'll note that this sequence closely resembles the cutting pattern for a conversation between two people. The basic pattern goes like this: We exchange MCUs of the two participants until the scene escalates, then transition to CUs for the key moments, bridged by a cutaway to the witness (shot 10). Once the climax is over, we retreat to a wider shot (16) to put the conflict in a larger perspective.

In this case, I used the witness's reaction to avoid showing the actual moment of death. While most audiences these days seem to have an unquenchable appetite for violence, I feel that the approach taken here will have a more lasting emotional impact. Sure, showing the bullet striking the villain would have a powerful physical effect, but the deeper emotion would be sacrificed for the physical gross-out factor. Rather than dulling the viewer with shock, I chose to show the impact the death has on the witness, which provides a concrete emotional reaction that the viewer can identify and empathize with.

Effective Chase Sequences

Chase sequences are another of the basic building blocks of action films. Like most action sequences, the chase is based on a familiar editing technique: crosscutting.

Building Your Chase by Guiding Screen Direction

The key to crosscutting an effective chase sequence lies in manipulating proper screen direction.

Typically, party A will be chasing party B, and you can crosscut between them indefinitely—as long as they continue traveling left to right, or vice versa (**Figure 3.15**). If you intercut even a single shot that shows one party moving in the opposite direction, you'll destroy the flow of the scene.

Figure 3.15 If you want to show that one party is chasing another, it's vital for both of them to be facing and moving in the same direction.

Indeed, one way you know that the chase sequence is over is when the screen direction changes. If you plan it right, that change can give the audience an important clue about the outcome of the chase.

For example, take a story about an adopted woman searching for her birth mother. Throughout the film, the two have been traveling in the same screen direction. Finally, as the film nears its climax (when the two will meet), the editor might choose to change the mother's screen direction. Although the effect will be subtle, the audience will unconsciously sense a change in the dynamic between the two parties—and know that something important is about to happen.

This same technique (changing a character's screen direction) is often employed to set up the super villain's "one wrong move," which allows the hero to catch him. It's a way to tip off the audience that there's been a change in the flow of events and a confrontation is imminent.

Using Chase Patterns for Romantic Comedy

You can use the same chase-sequence editing patterns in circumstances far beyond the basic car or helicopter chase. Romantic comedies, for instance, frequently turn on a subtle chase of sorts, where screen direction plays just as important a role.

Even though the characters in a romantic comedy may not be chasing one another physically, repeated shots of them traveling or facing in the same direction indicate that an emotional chase is occurring. Editors of romantic comedies often cut conversations in which the romantic duo are facing in the same direction. This is ostensibly motivated by the story or context, but the effect is to let the audience know that one is pursuing the other or that one is avoiding the other.

You can mark the turning point from avoidance to affection in a subtle way by inserting a shot of one of the parties suddenly facing the opposite direction (so she is now looking toward the romantic interest). This indicates an emotional change, and even though the audience isn't consciously aware of the editorial trick, the point will be made.

Editing Fight and Battle Sequences

In action films, fights and battle sequences are almost as common as chases. You can think of a fight or battle sequence as simply a group of simultaneous shoot-outs, but using standard patterns and techniques will help you make them exciting.

> **TIP:** *During a complicated battle scene, it's easy to lose track of who's on which side and exactly what's going on. You can make the sequence play more effectively if you include snippets of dialogue or breaks in the action to give the viewer a chance to catch his breath and make sense of what's occurring.*

Providing Context With Long Shots

To convey a larger context and tie the various melees together, it helps to intercut occasional long shots that contain complex intra-frame action (that is, lots of activity taking place within the frame). This helps the viewer maintain his orientation in the midst of all the confusion.

Or, if you wish to reinforce the sense of mayhem and confusion on the battlefield, deliberately avoid these context shots. This technique was effectively employed throughout Ridley Scott's *Black Hawk Down* and in that unforgettable opening sequence of Spielberg's *Saving Private Ryan*.

Expanding the Duration of Key Action

Creative editors accentuate action by expanding the duration of stunts and impacts (for instance, a blow, a fall, an explosion, or a bullet hitting its target) by duplicating some of the action in both the outgoing and incoming shots. This gives you the opportunity to extend the viewing time of exciting moments. The technique involves making an ordinary continuity cut over the point of action, but rather than placing the edit points so the action appears continuous, you overlap the action so it occurs in both shots. The more time you overlap, the more stylized the effect.

This is commonly employed in explosions. Actual explosions happen in a split second, but to maximize the impact, editors usually show the blast two or more times from different angles. For instance, if an explosion lasts five seconds, you might include the first 4 seconds in your first shot and the last 4 seconds in the second shot. Seconds 2 through 4 would be duplicated and appear in both shots.

Technically this breaks continuity, but it has become widely accepted. This may be because the excitement caused by the violent image distracts the audience, which ignores the temporal discontinuity.

Countdown to Climax: Speed Up the Cutting

As a sequence or a film approaches its climax, the editor will normally want to raise the excitement and tension. The most common way to accomplish this is by increasing the speed of the cutting. Sequences will grow shorter as the film nears its end, and individual shots will get shorter within each sequence. Interrupting this process with a lengthy shot or sequence dissipates the tension and disrupts the audience's anticipation of the climax.

> **TIP:** If you're building excitement by speeding up the cutting, and you need to include a critical event that will take a long time to show, break the long event into smaller pieces and keep those smaller pieces moving along briskly by crosscutting them, thereby compressing time.

As your story reaches its climax and you are crosscutting between two events, typically the crosscutting should get faster, the sequences you are intercutting should get shorter, and you will end by intercutting shot for shot between the two separate events. Finally, the way that's paid off is by making the two events being crosscut converge into a single scene. Like so:

1. MS serial killer prepares to load gun (:10).

2. MCU his victim squirms (:05).

3. MCU killer grins (:05).

4. ELS cop caught in traffic jam (:05).

5. MS cop beats fist on dashboard (:05).

6. CU cop curses (:05).

7. MCU killer loads gun (:05).

8. CU victim cries (:05).

9. WS cop breaks out of traffic (:05).

10. LS cop car screams down the street (:05).

11. CU killer cocks gun (:03).

12. MS cop breaks down door of house (:03).

13. ECU killer's finger tightens on the trigger (:02).

14. CU cop runs down hall (:02).

15. MS cop breaks into room OS killer (:05).

In this example, shots 1 through 3 are from scene 1 and last 20 seconds. Shots 4 through 6 are from scene 2 and last 15 seconds. Shots 7 and 8 return us to scene 1, lasting 10 seconds, and shots 9 and 10 are from scene 2, also lasting only 10 seconds. From here on we begin intercutting the two scenes shot for shot, until, finally, in shot 15, the two scenes are joined by the OS shot. At this point the scene would likely culminate in a typical shoot-out pattern, with the victim acting as the witness (see "Cutting the Shoot-out," earlier in this chapter).

Notice that while the sequences are getting shorter and shorter, the shots themselves also get shorter until shot 15. In addition, the angles of the shots get increasingly tighter, adding another element of tension.

Cooling It Down

After the climax, traditional storytelling calls for a resolution, a relatively quiet moment when the characters and the audience get an opportunity to think about and understand the impact of the preceding events. This is an essential element of narrative structure. Don't fail to provide this period of reflection and resolution or you will leave your audience in an uncomfortable state. While the script probably includes a scene to serve this important purpose, it is your job as the editor to adjust your pacing and cutting style to support this emotional effect. Generally, that will mean slowing the editing, using longer shots, and avoiding moving-camera shots.

In the example of the serial killer, once the killer is apprehended, good structure dictates a scene in which the victim will get a moment to reflect on her ordeal. But even if the writer has neglected to put that scene in the script, you can look for a shot of the victim walking alone, outside. Maybe it was filmed as part of the scene where she was abducted, but placed here it will seem to be taking place after the ordeal and provide the reflection time missing in the script. If a shot like that isn't available, you could try ending the "shoot-out" with a long, static single of the victim, which will again serve to allow some reflection on the events that just took place.

CUTTING FOR COMEDY

An action scene can be cut in many different ways, and the same shots can create tension or comedy depending on how they're arranged. A good editor should be able to manipulate a scene to play either way.

Creating Laughter With Surprise

One of the main elements that makes comedy funny is surprise. In editing surprise is created by setting up expectations and then breaking them—another way of manipulating cause and effect.

In our hand grenade example, once you build up the expectation that the grenade is about to go off, the audience will be anxiously awaiting the explosion. If you cut back to the grenade again and again, and it never explodes, the audience will eventually catch on that it is actually a dud—and laugh.

Sometimes the goal is to let the audience in on the joke, even though one of the characters might not be savvy. By paying attention to the placement of the "cause" shot you can imply whether or not the character knows that the "effect" shot is coming. When the audience knows and the character doesn't, the humor is in watching his surprise. Don't spoil this sort of humor by waiting too long to reveal the secret cause shot. The longer the audience knows what's going to happen, the funnier it is anticipating the surprise.

Funnier the Second Time Around

Repetition is another key element that can be used for great comic effect. Imagine another version of the grenade sequence:

1. LS soldier outside the enemy barracks.

2. MS enemies inside playing poker.

3. MCU soldier pulls the pin from a grenade and throws it through the barracks window.

4. CU grenade rolls under the poker table.

5. MS poker players are oblivious.

6. MCU soldier covers his ears, anticipating the explosion.

7. ECU grenade.

8. MCU soldier.

9. ECU grenade.

10. MS poker players.

11. MCU soldier anticipating explosion.

Now imagine how the audience would react if the soldier pulled out another grenade and went through the whole sequence again, and the second grenade was also a dud. It would be funny. If he did it a third time it would be *really* funny. Eventually, through a little artful editing, there might be 100 grenades piled up under the card table, the poker players would still be oblivious, and the audience would be rolling on the floor. The repetition of the joke is what makes it funny.

Remember the classic comedy maxim: Tell them what you're going to do, do it, and then tell them that you did it. With the right editing, you can get three laughs out of every joke.

There's a great sequence in George Clooney's *Confessions of a Dangerous Mind* where two spies are meeting for coffee and one is intending to poison the other. The editor (Steven Mirrione) uses an overhead tight shot of the coffee tray, which contains two cups of coffee, one marked with a sugar cube on the saucer. The first time we see it, The assassin arranges the tray so the victim will get the poison. When the victim distracts her, the editor returns to the same overhead shot and we see the victim move the sugar cube– foiling the assassin's plot.

In that case, Mirrione was mainly playing for suspense (in fact the whole sequence plays only after we have witnessed the "victim" pretend to be poisoned). But if you wanted to play the same scene for comic effect, you could repeat those two shots, where each of the two characters manipulate the tray to poison the other. The first time, it's suspense. The second time it's amusing and by the third time it's downright hysterical.

TIP: It's generally a bad idea to use the exact same shot more than once in a dramatic film. If the viewer notices, it will pull him out of the narrative and draw attention to the form. In comedy, however, you have tremendous leeway with this rule. Sometimes, reusing the same shot again and again can be terrifically funny.

For example, when the jewel thieves are sneaking through a museum, you might cut to a shot of a guard sitting in front of a bank of security monitors—fast asleep! Each time the thieves penetrate another security barrier, you cut back to the sleeping security guard. Repeating the same shot emphasizes the uselessness of the guard.

Giving it Room to Play

Another way the editor can reinforce a comic tone is to stick to wider shots, especially avoiding close ups. In general, comedy plays better in a wider frame. There are several reasons for this. One is that much of comedy is physical. From pratfalls to a pie in the face it is the physical indignity that makes the joke funny.

Another factor is that most comedy is circumstantial. The basis of most humor is incongruity; a person or thing in an inappropriate place, or a strange or unpredicted contrast between people or things. Wider shots are perfect to emphasize these unexpected relationships.

One of the problems with using close shots when you're trying to be funny is that too much emotion can spoil the humor. The tighter the shot, the more internal and emotional the content. While there are plenty of examples of humor hinging on an unexpected or incongruous emotional reaction, usually a strong personal, emotional moment will undermine the necessary distance that makes things funny.

DOCUMENTARY PATTERNS

While most documentaries follow the basic rules of narrative editing, including cause and effect, chronological passage of time, and other familiar storytelling conventions, some of the editing patterns and techniques you'll see in documentaries differ significantly from those used in narrative or dramatic films.

For one thing, while most film projects begin with a script, often the "script" for a documentary is created after some (or all) of the footage is shot. Sometimes that script creation comes out of a collaboration between the editor and the director. To build the script, the two of you will need to sit down and go through the footage together before you start editing. Otherwise you may waste your time venturing down a path that is ultimately not going to be part of the film.

Documentaries take all forms and shapes. Some contain sequences that might feel like (and be cut like) straightforward action scenes or, at the other extreme, abstract passages that resemble an experimental film.

A great example of a documentary that does both is Errol Morris's *Mr. Death,* a film about Fred A. Leuchter, Jr., a maker of capital punishment devices who became a Nazi apologist and Holocaust denier. One sequence in the film shows how Leuchter designed and built a gallows for the state of Tennessee. The sequence could be a scene from any dramatic film, since it includes extensive coverage and uses traditional narrative editing techniques. But another scene is an abstract vision of Leuchter encased in a huge, weird, bubble-like machine. There is no dialogue in this sequence, and the editing is rhythmic and poetic. No effort is made to explain the "story" of this sequence, nor what the images mean.

Cutting documentaries is a bit like putting together a jigsaw puzzle without looking at the picture on the box. One thing working in your favor is that there's more than one right answer. It's like a treasure hunt. Often the magic moments happen unexpectedly, when image and sound come together to make an emotional impact beyond your expectations.

Beginning, Middle, and End

One of the most critical elements to crafting a successful documentary is transforming subject matter into a story. You may have a collection of fabulous footage about factory farming, stunning tracking shots past endless rows of chicken cages, and moving interviews illustrating both sides of the issue, but how do you put this information together in a way that will make sense to an audience?

The answer is to go back to the ancient rules of storytelling. Start by identifying a beginning, a middle, and an end. Think about how you might explain the subject to a child who has never heard a thing about it. Answer the standard "who, what, where, when, why, and how" questions. Perhaps you tell the factory farming story framed in the chronological life of a chicken, or you might start at a suburban dinner and trace the food on the table back to its origins, only to return to that dining room at the end, wiser from your journey.

The Socratic Method

Another way of presenting nonfiction information is to follow a different ancient model. Begin with a question or thesis and systematically discuss each facet of the subject. In the end you can summarize your conclusions and ultimately prove or disprove your thesis. Although this may sound painfully academic, it doesn't have to be.

Suppose your documentary is about bizarre pet owners. You're handed one hundred hours of footage of people interacting with their pets. The original script idea fell through and you're left holding the football. You might begin with the thesis that people love their pets better than other humans, or perhaps you'll have a narrator ask the question "What is the strangest human-pet relationship imaginable?" Then, you may go through the examples and string together the best ones to make your point. In the end you can reiterate your theory and draw conclusions.

Documenting an Event

One common documentary subject is an event such as a concert, a protest, or a race. With today's low cost digital video cameras, you are likely to have every minute of the event captured, and probably from more than one angle. What techniques can you use to effectively distill an interesting film from all that?

A Unique Perspective

One of the most important editorial goals should be to find a unique point of view from which the audience can identify and experience the event. This might involve a narrator or interviews, or it might be more abstract, such as a specific camera location or visual device. For example to help give structure to an event shot at an amusement park, repeatedly return to a high angle overview shot, or even a graphic of a map illuminating the context for the event. One film that found a way to provide a unique and captivating perspective to document an event was *Confessions of a Burning Man*, a study of the annual Burning Man art festival held in the Nevada desert. There have been dozens of films made about it but few have been particularly interesting or moving. The festival is full of cinematic events such as fire and laser shows, huge art sculptures, and tens of thousands of festively costumed participants. Most of the documentaries capture this spectacular visual feast but lack a coherent point of view that would provide context.

Confessions followed the stories of four disparate people: a taxi driver, a burn victim, an heiress, and an at-risk inner city youth. The film chronicles the festival, but continually returns to interviews with these subjects as they are transformed by the amazing intensity of the event. The result is a film that provides a larger context, which gives it considerably more meaning than could ever be achieved by merely compiling all the beautiful pictures.

Cutting Interviews

Many documentaries use interviews to tell their stories—and cutting interview footage is a very different task than cutting dialogue. Depending on how the project was produced, you may be working with pre-scripted Q&A sequences that have obvious beginning and end points. More often you will have to wade through lengthy interviews hunting for verbal nuggets that summarize or illustrate the points you're looking for. Unlike dramatic footage, where you will have multiple takes to choose from, with rare exceptions you will get only one take of any given "answer" in interview footage.

Usually, the first pass I make on documentary footage is to collect all the interesting bits of the interviews and store them as subclips (see the section on marking subclips in Chapter 5, "Basic Editing"). Once I've collected all the good stuff, I go through it with the director and decide what to use. Then I lay down all those selected chunks end to end, ignoring jump cuts and any visual concerns.

Finally, I fine-tune the timing of the soundtrack, rearranging sections, trimming unneeded bits, finding what sections go best with others, and essentially creating the structure that will serve as the basis for the show. Only when this audio edit is complete do I go back and begin inserting cutaways and other shots to correct visual problems and bridge jump cuts.

Using Ripple Delete to Eliminate Pauses

Time and again you will find yourself working with an interview that includes pauses or mistakes. One quick, easy way to eliminate them is to use the Ripple Delete function in Final Cut Pro. This tool removes clips, or sections of clips, from a sequence without leaving gaps.

First, drop the entire section you want to use into Final Cut Pro's Timeline (**Figure 3.16**).

Then play the sequence, and set your In and Out points at the beginning and end of the section you wish to eliminate (**Figure 3.17**).

Finally, select Ripple Delete from the Sequence menu—or press $\boxed{\text{Shift}}$-$\boxed{\text{D}}$ on the keyboard. The area between the In and Out points is eliminated, and the gap will be closed (**Figure 3.18**).

continues on next page

Figure 3.16 Place the entire clip in the Timeline.

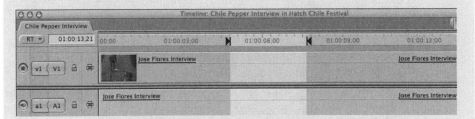

Figure 3.17 Set In and Out points at the beginning and end of the section you want to eliminate.

Figure 3.18 Ripple Delete will remove the section and close the gap automatically.

Using Ripple Delete to Eliminate Pauses continued

Beware! Ripple Delete works first on selected items, so if something in your Timeline is selected, Final Cut Pro will delete the selected item rather than the material between the In and Out points. In general, it's a good idea to get in the habit of hitting Option-D *(deselect all) before you use Ripple Delete. (Note: in Final Cut Express and prior versions of Final Cut Pro, Deselect All is* ⌘-D.)

*In Final Cut Pro 4, Timeline feedback indicates what tracks and items will be affected by your editing operation (**Figure 3.19**). The Auto Select button at the head of each track controls whether a track will be affected or ignored (**Figure 3.20**). If a clip is selected somewhere in the timeline, the area between the in and out point will not be highlighted. This should alert you that your Ripple Delete operation will not delete the area you intended (**Figure 3.21**).*

Figure 3.19 Areas that are to be affected by edits are highlighted, dark areas will be ignored.

Figure 3.20 When Auto Select is disabled, that track will not be included in the edit.

Figure 3.21 As long as a clip is selected somewhere in the timeline, the area between the in and out points will not be illuminated.

Editing Narration

Another element you'll often find in documentary projects is off-camera narration. Narration is usually recorded after the basic picture is complete, so the writer and narrator can adjust the length of the narration to the existing edit. Sometimes it's done as a scripted interview. In that case, you'll have the advantage of multiple takes and different line readings, but you should edit the footage much the same way you'd handle interview footage: Lay down the tracks, cut for audio first, then go back and clean up the picture by incorporating the B-roll elements that illustrate what is being said.

Working With B-roll

B-roll is a catchall term used to describe the footage that is neither interview nor narration. Most commonly, this will be action footage displaying whatever the narrator or interviewee is talking about, but it could be anything from establishing shots of environments relevant to the commentary to dramatic reenactments, photos, or contextual illustrations.

Variety is the Spice

While the talking heads who make up your A-roll deliver most of the information, you will create the flavor of your piece by the B-roll elements you employ. There's no limit to the type of images you can choose to spice up your documentary, and using a variety of elements will be more palatable to the audience than repeating the same images again and again.

For example, *Reason to Fear,* a documentary about a Native American on death row, employed nearly ten types of B-roll elements. The filmmakers went to the location of the alleged crime and filmed all the locations, street signs, and buildings that were described in the courtroom testimony. They also included photographs of the people involved, the alleged murder, and the aftermath of the crime, as well as historical photos, lithographs, and illustrations of Native Americans and their plight during the American expansion. Finally, the filmmakers created maps, diagrams, and charts that provided a factual context for the testimony and helped to explain the specific details of the case. All of these elements were woven together to illustrate and punctuate the interviews that made up the spine of the documentary.

In using a rich variety of B-roll elements, the filmmakers kept the audience interested by continually supplying new types of material to supplement the interviews that otherwise might have come across as dry legalese.

Providing Creative Solutions

Sometimes the B-roll will hold carefully planned shots intended for use with specific interview sequences, but more often it will be a jumble of random shots that you'll have to sift through to discover the usable moments. In many cases, your editorial creativity can find brilliant ways to put the material you find there to work.

For instance, your B-roll will probably become your cutaway footage. You can use it to cover up a jump cut in the interview or break up a long passage of talking heads.

If you're lucky, the B-roll footage will show exactly what the audio is talking about. For example, a documentary on chile peppers might have a section of narration explaining how and where they are grown. Ideally, the B-roll would include shots of fields full of growing chiles, a map depicting regions where chiles are grown, and shots of workers harvesting the fruit in the fields.

In many cases, however, you'll find yourself in a sticky situation where, for instance, the narration refers to the medical benefits of eating chiles, and you don't have any footage of a hospital, or anything even vaguely medical, on the B-roll. Here's your chance to get creative with your interpretation of the script. Look for a shot of a healthy-looking family eating some chile rellenos, or even some shots of food being prepared. In the worst case, you can always just cut back to the talking head or request a pickup shot or a graphic.

Looking for Imaginative Images

Sometimes you can create a thematic link that might not have been present in the narration by choosing the right B-roll clip. For example, if the narrator is talking about how genetic engineering of chiles has reduced the available varieties and potency of the fruit, your first thought might be to show a supermarket shelf with limited choices, a literal illustration of the point in the text. However, by venturing further afield and using a shot of a family farmer selling his farm, you will enrich the subject by illustrating another effect of genetic engineering and mass production: the negative impact on family farming. This is especially powerful because you are increasing the amount of information communicated without making the sequence overly dense.

Using Keywords

*Final Cut Pro has a powerful search engine built into the Browser (**Figure 3.22**). The more information you provide when you name your B-roll clips (or create subclips), the easier it will be for you to find those clips later. Use one of the Comment fields in the Browser window to enter keywords for searching (**Figure 3.23**). It's important to use consistent spelling, though, or when you search for "chile," you won't find the clips where you spelled it "chili" or "chilli."*

Figure 3.22 Final Cut Pro's Find tool (⌘-F) can search on as many as eight criteria.

Figure 3.23 Choose any one of the Comment columns to enter useful information about your shot.

*You can make it easier to enter the same exact text into the Comment field for each subclip by using the Shortcut menu (accessed by pressing Ctrl and clicking on the Comment field), which will let you select an entry from a pop-up list of previous entries in that column (**Figure 3.24**).*

Figure 3.24 Each time you enter text in a given column, it is added to a list you can access via the Shortcut menu. To bring up the Shortcut menu, Ctrl-click on the field you wish to modify.

continues on next page

Using Keywords *continued*

The more information you provide when you're logging clips and subclips, the better. What shot type is it? CU? LS? What's the subject? What details might be helpful when you're searching for just the right clip four months from now? Don't skimp. Remember, you may not be the one doing the search. It might be your assistant, or even the director.

*If you plan to dedicate one of your Comment columns to keywords, you can change the name of the column by using the Shortcut menu on the column header and selecting Edit Heading (**Figure 3.25**).*

Figure 3.25 The Shortcut menu for the column headers allows you to change the name of any of the four Comment fields.

EDITING FOR CORPORATE COMMUNICATIONS

Corporate communications include in-house training videos, video press releases (sometimes called EPKs, short for "electronic press kits"), messages to stockholders, product demonstrations, and similar materials.

In many ways, corporate or industrial video is situated halfway between narrative and documentary work, and sometimes may seem the best of both worlds. Corporate videos are like pre-scripted documentaries. The B-roll footage is usually meticulously planned out, with adequate coverage to ensure that the subject is successfully captured. (No more hunting for just the right shot!) Interviews are usually scripted and may well include multiple takes so you'll have a choice of shots to use. Best of all, corporate videos are frequently well funded. On the downside, they often lack the excitement and soul of true narrative or documentary films.

Corporate videos usually center around a narration or scripted interviews, so building your initial framework is similar to the recipe for documentary cutting described earlier.

Eliminating Graphic Overload

Corporate clients often worry that their points will not be made clearly with moving footage alone and want every point reinforced with a title card or chart. Sometimes you can find a way to incorporate at least some of the graphics the client wants without boring your audience to tears, but other times you'll have to try to talk the client out of it.

If you find yourself faced with a plethora of graphics, such as charts, bulleted text, and logos, which must be incorporated into the video, watch out! Too many interruptions can drive the viewer crazy and make it impossible for her to lose herself in the material.

Still, as the editor it's your job to make everyone—the viewer and the client— happy. Occasionally you can accomplish this as easily as superimposing the graphics on top of your B-roll shots. Beware, though: It's possible to make the screen so dense with information that neither the text nor the video will hold the viewer's interest or keep information flowing.

> **TIP:** *One of the most common problems for beginners working with titles and graphics is not knowing how long to leave them onscreen. Sometimes the script will tell you, but you can always double check by having two or three people watch and raise their hands when they have had adequate time to read the text onscreen. Keeping text onscreen too long runs the risk of making viewers lose interest. The rule of thumb is one second fade up, then hold for three seconds for every line of text and then one1 second fade to black.*

EDITING EXPERIMENTAL VIDEO

The film medium is capable of communicating in much more subtle and stylized ways than what we see in most Hollywood blockbusters or high school sex-education films. Moreover, every editor loves to experiment with variations on how to cut images together, looking for new ways to convey a mood or feeling through a creative arrangement of image and sound. At one time experimental filmmaking was relegated to an obscure, marginalized area categorized as avant-garde or underground cinema. Today it's recognized as a film genre akin to poetry.

Experimental filmmakers like Stan Brakhage, Maya Daren, Andy Warhol, and many others have made countless incredible films that ignore traditional editing structures. Sometimes these experiments work brilliantly, communicating unusual feelings, ideas, and themes with terrific power. Other times they are too obscure or random to make much of a mark on their audience.

Just as the French New Wave of the 1960s introduced jumpcutting as a viable story-telling technique, a new generation of "experimental" editors has introduced countless innovations to contemporary editing that were previously considered bad or wrong. These include *ramping* (changing playback speed during the shot); mixing different types of media, such as film and video, or color and black and white; rapid cutting that sometimes shortens shots until they're just a few frames long; holding shots onscreen for unusually long periods; layering multiple images on top of one another (see the section on composite shots in Chapter 2); and most significantly, a fundamental disregard for continuity of time and space. This last innovation is perhaps the most important, because it flouts most of the basic rules of editing.

Experimentalists Join the Mainstream

Thanks to MTV, so-called experimental filmmaking has moved into the commercial mainstream. As long as you intercut your images with an occasional shot of someone holding a guitar, anything goes in the music video genre. At the same time (perhaps because of the popularity of MTV and its ilk), television commercials are striving to differentiate themselves and appeal to younger audiences by employing some of the most outrageous, experimental cinematic techniques in highly polished (and very expensive) 30-second spots.

As audiences have grown more sophisticated, experimental editing techniques have begun cropping up in mainstream feature films as well. A recent example is Darren Aronofsky's *Requiem for a Dream,* edited by Jay Rabinowitz. *Requiem,* a film about drug addiction, uses a series of ECUs, cut very quickly, each time the characters take drugs. The sequence is repeated almost shot for shot many times throughout the film. These sequences are intensely poetic, unfettered by ordinary limitations of visual cause and effect, continuity of time and space, or traditional narrative structure. The film also uses split screens (both vertical and horizontal), slow motion and fast motion effects, and many other creative techniques seldom seen in narrative drama.

If you have the opportunity, and you're interested in experimenting, there are some useful guidelines to help you decide where to venture.

Emphasizing Mood Over Plot

Going back to music video for a moment, the goal of most of these short films is to complement the emotional tone of the song. To do that, filmmakers are willing to abandon virtually all the traditional rules and grammar of film language—including the basic concept of continuity. Add a three-to-four-minute time limit, and the filmmaker must accelerate the amount of information he delivers and simultaneously loosen the bonds of traditional narrative structure.

This has created a stylistic revolution in film editing, the key to which is mood over plot. Of course, most shows are still based on the rules and techniques described in this book—but exceptions are increasingly common.

Oliver Stone's *Natural Born Killers* and David Lynch's *Lost Highway* are wonderful examples of how these "MTV" techniques can be applied to traditional narrative cinema to create stunning (and disturbing) visual poems. Both films provide amazing insight into the new age of film editing. *Killers* was shot on more than six types of media (video, 8mm, 35mm, and so on), but the shots are intercut with no concern whatsoever for the dislocation such editing forces on the audience. *Highway* makes seemingly random jumps in time and space that are so disorienting they can only be compared to waking up in someone else's dream world. The striking similarity between both of these films, and others like them, is that they emphasize the emotional tone of the scene at the expense of the basic continuity that is the spine of traditional editing.

Rhythm

Another key to successful "experimental" film is to find a sense of rhythm that serves as a structural guide. This will help to give your piece some sort of coherence and flow. The music video format provides a literal rhythm that will often serve as such a guide, and you can incorporate a musical score with any experimental piece, but you don't need music playing for the film to have it's own sense of rhythm. Your film still has a beginning a middle and an end, and you need to find a timing device to illuminate the way from one passage to the next.

Films like *Baraka* and *Koyaanisqatsi* are feature length experimental productions that illustrate the systems of the earth in breathtaking and fascinating ways. And though both are entirely non-narrative and include no obvious structural boundaries, they have attracted audiences of millions. I think that in lieu of the traditional storytelling forms, their careful attention to rhythm has resonated with a deeper cosmic harmony that entranced viewers.

Consistency of Style

One of the few rules that can be applied to this unfettered approach to editing is to try to maintain a consistency of style. No matter how abstract a film is, success is derived from clarity of vision. You must understand what you are trying to say or to do with a piece. Good style is consistent style. Even if you break all the traditional rules, break them in a deliberate and consistent way. No matter how abstract the visual logic of the world you create, it should have rules. If you're going to incorporate jumpcuts or distortions in the linearity of events, think about what those devices are meant to imply or the feeling they're meant to evoke. If you find a logic for what they mean to you, then you can better convey that sense to your viewer.

Editing Hints

Given the intrinsically radical nature of experimental filmmaking, there are fewer rules and patterns to worry about. Still, here are some general editing guidelines you may find useful.

Ask yourself: What is the emotional tone of the scene? What images can I use to convey that tone? What special effect might help to communicate it to my audience? Because the palette of effects at your fingertips is so incredibly broad, part of the challenge is deciding which ones are appropriate.

If you're interested in distorting the linearity of time, try rearranging cause and effect, as editor Dody Dorn did with Christopher Nolan's film *Memento*. In that film the entire movie is told backward, reversed sequence for sequence from ordinary chronology.

If you want to draw attention to the filmmaking process itself, use visual devices like *wipes* for transitions, or paint on the frames themselves. Alternatively, you can try a minimalist approach, like the Dogme 95 filmmakers who shoot everything hand-held, refuse to use any music that wasn't played when shooting, and strive to create a rawer film experience in reaction to the controlled nature of mainstream cinema.

Whatever approach you take, don't try to put all the effects available to you into the same scene. Just as with mixing paint in kindergarten, if you combine too many elements, it becomes a dull brown mess.

INTERVIEW

Hervé Schneid is responsible for editing some of the most striking films to come out of France over the last ten years, including *Delicatessen* and *The City of Lost Children* (both co-directed by Jean-Pierre Jeunet and Marc Caro). In addition, he has cut films for directors Mike Figgis (*The Browning Version*) and Sally Potter (*The Tango Lesson, The Man Who Cried*). At the time of this interview he had just completed Jeunet's *Le Fabuleux Destin d'Amélie Poulain,* released in the United States as *Amelie.* Since then, he has cut *Michel Vaillant* and *Sansa.*

MICHAEL WOHL: HOW DO YOU DECIDE WHICH FILMS TO WORK ON?

Hervé Schneid: By reading the script or knowing the director. With some directors, I don't even need to read the script. It takes such a long time to work on a film, and if you don't make a good decision you're stuck for half a year or even a whole year.

WHAT IS YOUR FAVORITE PART OF EDITING?

It is not exactly the editing part of the work that is very interesting and important to me. What I really like is to get in connection with the director. The human bond of the work is interesting; the discussion, understanding a director's universe. It opens your mind, opens little drawers in your head, and you can fill them with new and interesting things.

HOW MUCH INTERACTION DO YOU HAVE WITH THE DIRECTOR?

We have a lot of interaction, but it obviously depends on the director. Each time is a different adventure. I think when you're an editor you have to be a chameleon in some ways. You have to try to understand the director's vision, but dive into that vision with your own experience. Then you can bring out things that you might not have even imagined.

YOU'VE WORKED WITH A VARIETY OF DIRECTORS: JEAN-PAUL JEUNET, SALLY POTTER, AND LARS VON TRIER, AMONG OTHERS. CAN YOU TALK ABOUT SOME OF THE DIFFERENCES?

Jean-Paul Jeunet works everything out very much in advance. Everything is prepared. He does storyboards, he makes trials of the framing with his DV camera, rehearsing all the time—really preparing everything ahead. Then you have other directors who don't. For example the one I'm working with right now, when he arrives in a place, he knows what kind of scene he is going to shoot, but he just feels the place out and goes with the wind. So he is not prepared in the same way. During editing, both are very much with me all the time. And we're having a wonderful time with it.

DO MOST OF THE FILMS YOU WORK ON START THE EDITING AFTER THE FILMING IS FINISHED?

In France, you normally start about two to three weeks into the shoot. You have your assistant start at the beginning of the shoot—synchronizing everything and preparing the work for you. Then, after two or three weeks, I come in and start working. But some films and some directors prefer to start after principal photography.

I like both approaches. It depends on the mood, the director and the film. It's wonderful when you work with a director like Jean-Pierre [Jeunet] who loves editing; then it's very good to start after principal photography. He's available all the time and you can spend a lot of time with him. That way you get what the director really wants, and what he was wishing to say. If you have the director with you, you can compare the power of each take, the power of each shot, the direction of a scene; you can change it on the spot. I really like to start with the director, but it is also interesting to have to do it by yourself, because then it is more of a challenge.

WHAT DO YOU DO ON AN AVERAGE WORKING DAY?

It depends on the day. I split the editing of a film into three or four stages. The first would be choosing shots, and then making the first cut scene by scene. I like to take a day for choosing, then I let it rest in my head without even thinking about it, then I cut it a day or two later.

When the first cut is finished, you can look at the film as a whole and discover the internal life that it has taken without asking you. It's alive, so it goes in directions that you didn't think of, and you discover this when you look at the complete project. It's a very interesting moment, very depressing sometimes, but I feel reassured to know that at least the film exists already.

HAVE YOU EVER LOOKED AT A SCENE AND HAD NO IDEA HOW TO CUT IT, HOW TO MAKE IT WORK?

When you have problems with a scene it's quite interesting because problems have to be solved, and if you have to solve a problem you'd better find a creative solution, so it pushes you further. Very often when you have problems on a scene, you are more creative and the scene is better than if you didn't have all the problems.

CAN YOU TALK ABOUT THE DIFFERENCE BETWEEN FILMMAKING IN FRANCE AND ELSEWHERE? AS AN EDITOR, DO YOU MAKE FILMS DIFFERENTLY IN FRANCE THAN IN ENGLAND OR THE U.S.?

I did a few films in England, one in America, one in Denmark. I try to do the films how I would do them—adapting to the director's style, the script, and the film. I'm not working for an American product or a French product.

WHAT DO YOU LIKE ABOUT WORKING ON THE COMPUTER?

A movie has no physical existence, so I love the idea that now, with this tool, everything is digital. It's ones and zeros and it's the same as the final result: You can't really define it. It's something in the air you can't touch.

DID YOU START EDITING ON FILM?

I did a lot of film, 35mm. Each time I see one I ask myself how I could have done it—because it seems impossible to me now to cut a film on 35mm. [Digital technology] hasn't changed my work, cause the tool is not cutting the film, I am cutting the film, but it does give me so much more freedom. You can try things, things that you might not have tried on film because it's quite heavy [a lot of trouble], changing a scene from one place to another. You have to wait while you change the reel, pick the scene, take it out, put the new reel on the Steenbeck, then run to the place, reposition the shot, then go back and look at it. You know, it takes a long time.

DO HAVE ANY ADVICE FOR AN EDITOR WHO'S JUST STARTING OUT?

First, you should be brave. Each film is a challenge, and you have to look for perfection each time. So you should make sure that you are trying everything that you can, finding all options, finding the right line and not deviating. Also, listen to the unsaid. The interesting part of making a film is to listen to what is not said, to see what is in the frames, what is said without saying it.

WHAT'S YOUR LEAST FAVORITE PART OF EDITING?

I hate that it's so tough not to smoke while cutting a film.

THAT'S A VERY FRENCH ANSWER. AT LEAST IT'S NOT DANGEROUS LIKE IT WAS WHEN THE FILM WAS FLAMMABLE...

Well, it is dangerous. After all, the film is not important; it's your health that's important. The film is just a film at the end of the day. My philosophy is not to make films which are going to be important, or even which are going to be successful. The important thing is to have pleasure doing the films you've chosen. I think that is very important. That's your life you are spending in the cutting room.

CHAPTER FOUR

Preparing to Edit

I know you're eager to get started. You're sick of all the theories and patterns and definitions and tips. You're ready to start cutting film. Well, hang on we're almost there.

Before we can get into the nitty-gritty of editing, you have to get some footage into your computer. And in order to do that you must first prepare your workspace and learn how to catalog and organize your media.

Much of this chapter details how to use various features of Final Cut, but I'm not just rewriting the manual. I'll explain the most effective, efficient, and powerful ways to apply these features, and tell you which ones you can ignore for now.

THE ASSISTANT EDITOR'S GUIDE TO FINAL CUT PRO

Traditionally, editors start out as assistant editors—and it's assistant editors who usually transfer the raw footage into, and the final program out of, the editing system. If you're going to be working as an assistant editor on a Final Cut Pro project, you'll need to learn every detail in this chapter.

If you are a high-powered editor who always has an assistant by your side, rip this chapter out of the book and hand it to him. But if you are your own assistant editor, as is the case with many Final Cut Pro editors, you'll want to read this chapter yourself.

PREPARING YOUR WORKSPACE

No two editors are identical and there's no reason to expect that you're going to use your editing tool in exactly the same way that I use mine. This is why Final Cut Pro offers so many ways to customize the interface. Although this introduces a significant level of complication in the initial setup, once it's done, you can work more efficiently; with your most commonly used tools, functions, and data where you want them.

For example, let's say you do most of your editing by dragging things around in the timeline, and the show you're working on requires a variety of wipe transitions for all the scene cuts. You might layout your windows so that the timeline gets most of the real estate, and then add a few effects buttons to the button bar (**Figure 4.1**).

Figure 4.1 This layout features an enlarged timeline and several transition buttons on the button bar.

You can also store these settings so that more than one user can share a single workstation. If you are a freelance editor, working on different systems for each job, bring your favorite settings along with you and load them up, making that windowless new editing suite feel a little more like home. Or you may prefer a different layout or setup when working on the flashy title sequence for your documentary than you do when cutting the body of the show. Final Cut Pro lets you easily switch between various settings.

Window Layouts

The most significant way to customize your workspace is to arrange the windows on the screen. As you work on different aspects of your show, you're likely to want different windows enlarged at different times. While you're searching through your browser and organizing your clips, you might dedicate half your screen to the browser window. Later, however, when you're doing color correction, you may want the browser as small as possible to make room for filter control windows, preview windows, and scopes.

Final Cut comes with a handful of preset window layouts to help accommodate common editing situations. Choose one from the Window Layouts submenu (**Figure 4.2**). The presets vary depending on the resolution and number of the monitors you're using, and certain layouts only appear if your monitor is large enought to display them.

Figure 4.2 Presets are in the middle, custom layouts are listed at the bottom.

Custom Layouts

No matter how many presets are included, you invariably will want your own personal layouts, and there are two ways to store layouts. First you need to manually arrange the windows to your liking. Final Cut's windows stick together. This helps eliminate wasted space between windows and keeps the desktop tidy.

No matter how many presets are included, you invariably will want your own personal layouts, and there are two ways to store layouts. First you need to manually arrange the windows to your liking. Final Cut's windows stick together. This helps eliminate wasted space between windows and keeps the desktop tidy. Also, if you're using Final Cut Pro 4, once your windows are directly adjacent to one another, you can drag the seam and resize all the windows simultaneously (**Figure 4.3**).

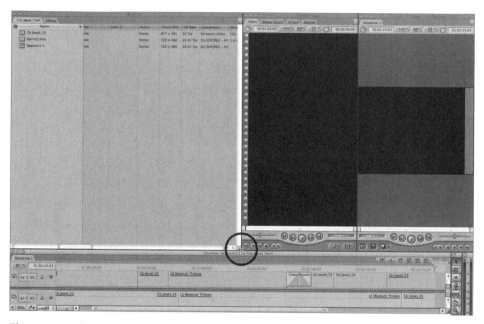

Figure 4.3 When you're in a hurry, drag the seam between the windows to resize them all simultaneously.

Once you're satisfied with the arrangement of the windows, you're ready to store that state. Hold the option key down when opening the Windows menu, and the Set Custom Layout commands will appear. By choosing this option your layout is stored in one of the two custom slots at the top of the menu (**Figure 4.4**).

Figure 4.4 The Custom Layouts are only active after you've stored one by pressing Option as you open the menu.

Alternately, you can choose Save Window Layout from the same menu (no option key is required for this function) and a dialog box will ask you to name and save the custom layout as a file on your disk (**Figure 4.5**). You will be prompted to save it in a folder called "Window Layouts" which is inside your Final Cut Pro User Data in your Preferences Folder. It's important to save the custom layout in this particular folder because the first 10 layouts stored in it will appear at the bottom of the menu. (See Figure 4.4 above.)

If you want to load a layout from another folder, or if you have more than 10 custom layouts, choose Restore Custom Layout and a dialog box will prompt you to identify the desired layout.

Figure 4.5 The first 10 layouts stored in the Window Layouts folder will appear in the Layouts Submenu.

An Odd Aspect

Window Layouts can either be stored with Fixed Aspect Ratio or Auto Aspect Ratio. (See Fig 4.5 above). This is to accommodate situations where you may be switching between 4 X 3 projects and widescreen projects. When you restore an Auto Aspect layout the Viewer and Canvas windows will appear at the aspect ratio of the current sequence. If the ratio is Fixed, the windows will appear at the aspect ratio that was current when you saved it.

In general, for layouts that feature the Viewer and Canvas windows you should set the Aspect Ratio to Auto, but for layouts where your focus is on the Timeline or Browser, set it to Fixed.

Complex Layouts

Custom layouts can contain more than the four main windows. When setting up layouts for some tasks, such as audio mixing or color correction, you will want other windows visible. There is no limit to how many of the windows that can be open—as long as you can fit them on your screen (**Figure 4.6**). Your saved layouts will store windows accross all of your monitors.

Figure 4.6 In this layout, there are four frame viewers and four scopes windows. This is ideal for complex color correction tasks.

Getting Rid of Old Layouts

Although you can store as many layouts as you wish, only the first 10 (alphabetically) appear in the menu. If you want to rename or delete one of these layouts to change the list, you must do so in the finder. Unfortunately, you are advised to quit Final Cut Pro before you make this sort of change. Go to the Window Layouts folder (inside the Final Cut Pro User Data folder, inside your Preferences). When you add layouts to this folder in the Finder, they will appear in the Final Cut Pro menu upon relaunch.

Customizing the Timeline

The Final Cut Pro Timeline itself is also highly customizable. Because there are so many different tasks that are done in the timeline, one layout is not appropriate in all cases. When doing rough assemblies you may leave your tracks small and hide all filter controls. You may even hide several audio or video tracks using the splitter (**Figure 4.7**).

When trimming, you may want the primary video track larger and show the Opacity graph for doing fades (**Figure 4.8**).

For audio mixing, you will want to give most of the space to audio tracks, making them large enough to see the Level graph and waveforms (**Figure 4.9**).

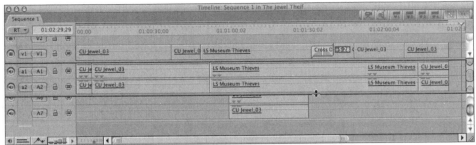

Figure 4.7 This layout is good for quickly assembling and arranging clips in a sequence.

Figure 4.8 This layout is good for trimming video clips.

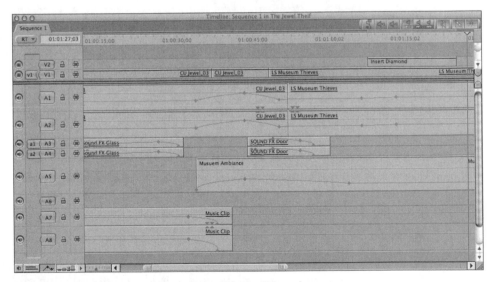

Figure 4.9 This layout accommodates eight audio tracks.

Compositing is just the opposite; more room is needed for multiple video tracks (**Figure 4.10**). You might also turn on the filter and motion bars. Speed effects can now be done in the timeline by turning on the Speed Indicator (**Figure 4.11**).

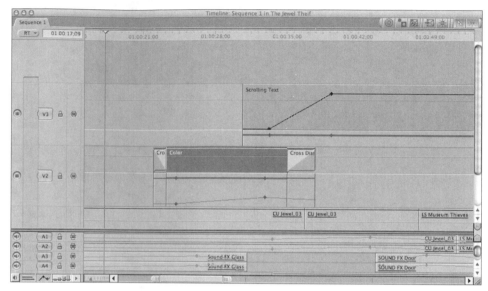

Figure 4.10 For compositing you need more room for video tracks.

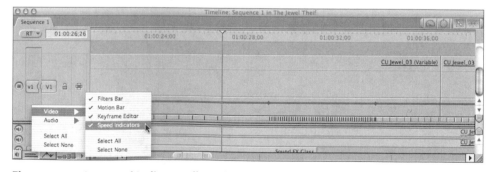

Figure 4.11 The Speed Indicator allows for complete time manipulation in the timeline. Choose Speed Indicator from the Shortcut menu on the Filter and Motion Bar.

Track Heights

Track heights can be changed uniformly by using the Track Height Control (**Figure 4.12**). To manipulate track heights individually, drag the top of the track header (**Figure 4.13**). This is an enormous benefit when you're trying to fine tune an edit, adjust an audio level, or line up a filter keyframe with a marker in another clip. Once you get used to the idea that this is possible you will start using it constantly. I find that I use this "vertical zoom" almost as frequently as I use the temporal zoom controls when editing in the timeline.

Figure 4.12 Choose Large, Medium, Small or Itsy Bitsy.

Figure 4.13 Each track height can be manipulated individually.

Storing Track Heights

Timeline track heights can also be stored. You can save custom track configurations in the pop-up next to the track height indicator (**Figure 4.14**). Like window layouts, the first ten you store appear in the menu for quick access. These saved presets, however, only apply to timeline track heights. The current state of the filter/motion bars, audio controls, audio waveforms and all the other timeline settings are not stored. Because of this, I find these presets only moderately useful.

Figure 4.14 Save and restore custom track height settings via the track height popup.

Audio Controls

There is a new control in the lower left corner of the timeline that toggles the visibility of the audio mute and solo buttons (**Figure 4.15**). This is primarily useful when doing audio mixing (see "Audio Mixing," Chapter 7).

Figure 4.15 Make the Audio Controls visible when doing audio mixing.

Filter/Motion Controls

The Filter and Motion Bar Controls have been given a major reworking in version 4, but you wouldn't know it unless you opened the shortcut menu on that button (**Figure 4.16**). By default, turning on this button adds an array of new controls beneath each track. Filter and Motion Bars indicate whether a clip has any filters or motion effects applied, and show an overview of keyframes for

Figure 4.16 The shortcut menu contains all the customization controls for the Filter and Motion Bars.

selected parameters. The Keyframe Editor is a resizable keyframe graph for a single selected parameter, and the Speed Indicator displays a clips playback rate including variable speed and reverse effects (**Figure 4.17**). Though you'll almost always leave the entire control turned off while editing, for special effects and compositing work, having direct access to these controls is a time-saver.

Choose one parameter to be displayed.

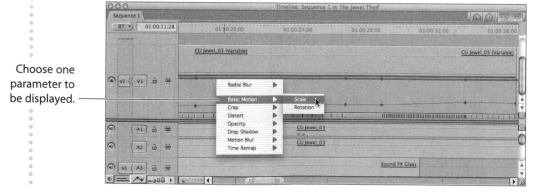

Figure 4.17 This clip has all settings applied.

You can resize the keyframe graph almost the same way you resize a whole track. Rather than dragging the top edge of the track, drag anywhere in the tiny column at the far right edge of the track header controls (**Figure 4.18**).

Figure 4.18 The grey line indicates the height of the Keyframe Editor.

Other Timeline Controls

There are several other important ways to customize your Timeline. To access these customization options, open the Sequence Settings dialog and select the Timeline Options tab (**Figure 4.19**) to choose whether or not to have thumbnails in your video tracks and waveforms in your audio tracks, as well as other options. In Final Cut Pro 4, you can also control some of these functions through the Track Height shortcut menu (**Figure 4.20**). Prior to version 4, defaults for these options were stored in the Sequence Presets, but now they are stored in the User Preferences. Changes you make to any sequence after it's been created will only affect that individual sequence.

Figure 4.19 Further Timeline customization can be done in the Timeline Options tab.

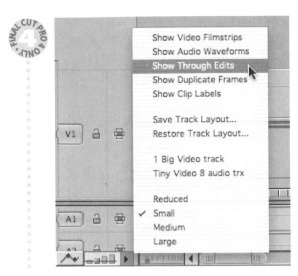

Figure 4.20 Several important timeline controls are hidden in the Track Height shortcut menu.

Customizing the Browser

Just as different editing jobs require specific timeline layouts and settings, different projects and styles benefit from customizing the Browser. On large projects, where you've got hundreds or even thousands of clips, it's essential to organize them in bins and sub-bins and to populate them with searchable keywords and comments. For smaller projects, or for shorter sequences within a larger project, you might choose to arrange the clips into a *storyboard* by using a large icon view (**Figure 4.21**).

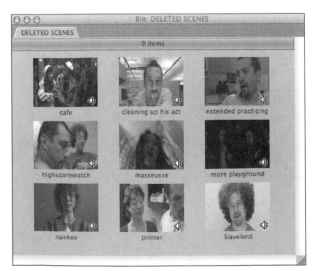

Figure 4.21 Icon view allows you to arrange clips into a storyboard in the bin window before you edit them into the sequence.

Column Lists

In list view you can choose which columns are visible and the order in which they appear in the window. Once you create a set that serves your project, save the layout and apply it to other bins or projects. For example, on many shows editors name their clips based on arcane numbering schemes. This might make sense in terms of identifying the scene number, camera used and date, but it may not be helpful in terms of identifying the subject of the shot or the camera angle. This additional information can be stored in comment fields (**Figure 4.22**). On the other hand, if your clip names only indicate the subject of the shot, you may want to add more information to clearly associate it with the correct scene or location. Different columns can be shuffled to the front to help you grab the correct shot (**Figure 4.23**).

Name	Shot/Take	Who What Where	camera log notes	Location	Con
07_6b_01	01	Gary Laughs twice	Good take		
14_02MS_01	01	Suzanne & Gary		Dog park Scene	
16_03CU_02	02	Harriet upside down	airplane noise		
21-22(a)_18b_02	02	Gary loses everthing	Pick-up at "I'm mad"	Westside Deli	
21-22_18b_02	02	Gary loses everything	whole scene	Westside Deli	
21_06a_01	01	Suzanne springs for it		Westside Deli	
21_06_01	01	Suzanne RXN	Good		
43_1aa_04	04	Harriet in ecstacy			
43_1aa_05	05	Harriet in ecstacy	n/g		

Figure 4.22 If the clip name isn't adequately descriptive, use comment fields to provide additional information about the clip's subject.

Name	Good	Scene	g Note	Label	Who What Where	Description	Shot/
CU Julie		28a	sparkling eyes	None	Julie Dog Pound	Julie laughs	01
CU Julie_02		4	n/g	None	Julie	RXN dog	02
CU Julie		110v	Good take	None	Julie, Max restaurant		01

Figure 4.23 There may be three shots called "CU Julie." The scene column can help you decide which one you want.

Managing Your Columns

Rearrange the order of the columns by clicking on a column header and dragging the column left or right. There are many columns visible in the default view, but most of them are so far to the right that you may not notice them. If there's a column you want to see, such as a comment field or the Last Modified column (very helpful in determining which sequence you recently changed), drag it to the left so it will be visible without scrolling.

With so many columns available to you, one of the first things you may be inclined to do is hide the ones you're not going to use. There is a lot of technical information that you may not need to see once all your clips are successfully captured. For example, you're not likely to look at the Audio Rate, Pixel Aspect Ratio, Alpha Channel, Frame Size and Compressor fields unless you're having a problem. I say hide 'em — too many visible columns make the Browser more complex and complicated to use. I've long believed that most of these fields should be hidden by default as they confuse new users and provide rarely needed information. While you can't make your own default column set, you can save a set and load it up each time you begin a project. Each new bin you create will automatically inherit the column list of its parent.

The only way to control which columns are visible is by opening the shortcut menu in the column header area. This reveals a list of all the hidden columns and provides options for saving or restoring custom sets of column lists (**Figure 4.24**).

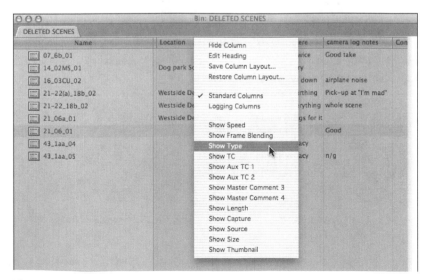

Figure 4.24 The shortcut menu for the track headers is the only place to turn on or off the columns visible in your current browser window.

You may notice that the shortcut contains an option for switching between the "Standard Columns" and the "Logging Columns." This functionality is left over from the first two versions of Final Cut Pro which didn't save custom sets. Since you are typically going to be interested in different columns when logging your footage than when you're later editing, this allows you to quickly switch between the two sets. Like the other customization features, in Final Cut Pro 4 your first ten custom layout sets will appear in the shortcut menu for quick access (**Figure 4.25**).

Figure 4.25 Custom layouts appear in the menu beneath the [obsolete] Standard and Logging sets.

The Thumbnail Column

The Thumbnail column is one of the most interesting features not visible in the program's default layout. This column adds a mini-preview of your clips in the browser list view (**Figure 4.26**). I find that this column is most useful if it is arranged as the first column in the browser, to the right of the clip name. The image visible in the Thumbnail column is the current poster frame for the clip. If you haven't set a poster frame, this will default to the first frame of the clip.

Figure 4.26 Activating the Thumbnail column simultaneously gives you the best of List view and Icon view.

You can *scrub* through the entire clip by clicking on top of the thumbnail and dragging left or right. I find this scrubbing ability extremely useful on projects such as documentaries where there may be a variety of different bits of footage within a single shot. For dramatic shows where each shot is usually a single angle, this seems less useful.

To set a new poster frame, scrub to the frame you want and hold the Control key down as you release the mouse button.

The downside to turning on the Thumbnail column is that it spreads out all of your clips vertically; so far fewer clips are visible without scrolling. However this provides one very interesting (if unexpected) benefit. Because all of the columns are enlarged to make space for the thumbnail, there's more room for multiple lines of text in your Comment and other columns. This can be very helpful when using these columns for transcriptions or other text-heavy notes (**Figure 4.27**).

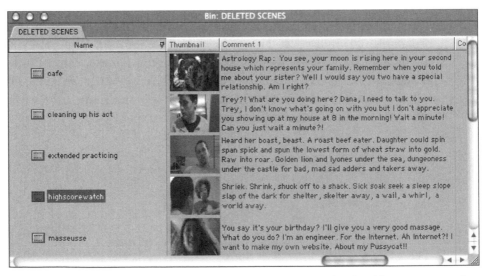

Figure 4.27 The Thumbnail column has the unintended benefit of making more room for longer notes, such as these transcriptions. Beware, though, this feature was broken in Final Cut Pro 4.0.

Storyboarding in Icon View

If you like the visual information the Thumbnail column provides, you may want to switch your browser to Icon view (**Figure 4.28**). There are three sizes to choose from, either in the View menu or in the Shortcut menu in the Browser. Icon view allows you to group your clips into piles, or arrange them into a pictorial list serving as a type of storyboard.

Figure 4.28 Icon View turns your Browser into a Storyboard editor.

A storyboard is a *pre-visualization* tool that has been used in filmmaking for many years. It's a way to look at a film in comic book fashion, as a series of sequential images, each of which represents a shot, and which can be rearranged. The storyboard enables you to put timing issues aside while choosing the best order of the shots. Traditionally, storyboards were made from drawings on paper, but now you can create them with thumbnail images of the actual shots from your show. This isn't going to apply to all editing situations, but imagine that you are choosing the b-roll shots for a documentary about commercial bread baking. The exact timing of the shots will be determined based on the interview or narration. All you need to think about is the selection and order of the shots. Arrange and rearrange the shots in the browser window until you find the best combination and then edit the entire sequence into your timeline all at once. Final Cut will add the shots consecutively; left to right, then top to bottom.

Figure 4.29 The Scrub tool allows you to shuttle around and set new poster frames in clips while in Icon view.

Scrubbing and Poster Frames

To scrub through the video of the individual shots in Icon view, and to set new poster frames for your shots, use the Scrub tool (**Figure 4.29**). To set a new poster frame, use the Scrub tool to find the desired frame and hold the Control Key down as you release the mouse.

Choosing Good Poster Frames

When choosing poster frames, remember that the single frame you choose is meant to represent the entire shot. Try to find the frame that will help you remember the shot and distinguish it from similar ones. For example, if I have two close-ups of the same woman, but in the middle of one shot, she puts her arms behind her head for a moment, I might set the poster frame to show that. Then, when looking at the two clips side by side, I immediately know which is which. Some editors prefer to set the poster frames to show the slate at the head of each shot. This lets the editor quickly know what shot and take he's working with. Personally, I prefer to leave that information in the Shot and Take fields in the browser and use the thumbnail to provide a more specific visual cue. If you have a shot that includes several sections that cannot be represented by a single poster frame, consider breaking up the shot into multiple subclips. That way each one can have its own representative poster frame.

Customizing the Keyboard

For years, Avid aficionados claimed that one of the most important features differentiating the Media Composer from Final Cut Pro was Avid's level of customizability. They repeatedly cited Avid's customizable keyboard layout, which Final Cut Pro lacked. Now, in Version 4, Final Cut Pro has finally implemented this fundamental feature.

Since advanced editors rely heavily on keyboard shortcuts to work quickly and efficiently, extensive keyboard control is essential to accommodate fast workflow. Final Cut Pro has always allowed hundreds of different functions to be accessed through keyboard combinations, but now Version 4 enables users to map any command to any key.

This is powerful, but can also be dangerous. Good editors learn to rely on certain shortcuts. If you are used to a specific set of controls and then sit down at a system loaded with another editor's preferred layout, it can feel like sitting in a car with the steering wheel on the wrong side. If you move around from one editing system to another, make your own custom set and load it whenever you begin a new job.

I find the default keyboard shortcuts well arranged and efficient (of course I helped to choose them). There is consistency among sets (previous edit, next edit, previous marker, next marker, previous keyframe, next keyframe, etc.) and the main transport and edit controls (J, K, L, $;$, $'$, I, O). The main trimming controls (U, $<$ and $>$) are well thought out, allowing one hand to perform many of the most common commands without leaving the keyboard (these were directly based on Avid's keyboard shortcuts.).

Still, because Final Cut Pro does so many things, there are some shortcuts that are reserved for features that you may never use. Or if you are using Final Cut Pro after spending a lot of time using Adobe After Effects, you may find yourself repeatedly hitting the wrong key combo.

For example, one of the most frustrating keyboard inconsistencies I've found when switching between Final Cut Pro and tools such as Adobe Photoshop or Adobe After Effects is the difference in shortcuts to move an object in space. The Adobe products consistently use the arrow keys to move an object up, down, left, or right. In Final Cut Pro, the left and right arrow keys are reserved for moving the playhead back and forth in time, one frame at a time. The up and down arrows move the playhead forward or backwards one clip at a time. (To do a nudge, you must hold down the Option key when hitting any of the arrow keys.) Finally, I can remap the Final Cut Pro keys to match those other programs. Of course I only want this functionality in Final Cut Pro when I'm doing compositing. For general editing, I prefer the default behaviors. This is why I have two sets of custom keyboard layouts, one for editing and one for compositing. You may find you want an entirely different keyboard layout for audio mixing or color correcting.

Making your own keyboard layout is easy. Choose Customize from the Keyboard Layout submenu in the Tools menu (**Figure 4.30**). Then drag and drop your desired command onto the corresponding key (**Figure 4.31**). If you want to use a key with a modifier, such as Shift or Control, click on the picture of that modifier or choose from the tabs atop the keyboard image. Some keys cannot be remapped like ⌘Q or ⌘Option Esc because they're reserved by the system. These keys are marked in pink to indicate they're unavailable.

To find the commands in the list on the right, you can either search through the menus and sections in the hierarchal list or use the search field at the top of the right side. Once you begin typing, the list automatically converts to an alphabetical list of every command available (**Figure 4.32**). Search on either the name of the function (i.e. nudge) or type a keystroke (i.e. ↑) and see all the commands currently assigned to that key. To return to the hierarchical menu based list, clear the search field by clicking the x.

You can even set keyboard shortcuts to switch between custom keyboard shortcut sets. To do so, under the Tools section assign the first five custom layouts to a key of your liking. This is how I switch between my custom Editing set and my custom Compositing set.

Figure 4.30 Open the Keyboard Layout window in order to customize your keyboard.

Figure 4.31 Assigning new keyboard shortcuts is as simple as drag and drop.

Figure 4.32 You can search across all the commands available in the program, clear your search by clicking here.

Play Options

Final Cut Pro offers useful options for playing your clip or sequence in different ways, though up until now some have been underused by many editors because they have been hidden under relatively obscure keyboard shortcuts. For example, if you have an in and out point set, you can play between the in and out by pressing Shift-\. *If you want to play from the current position to the out point (very useful for confirming your out point without having to play a large part of the sequence), press* Shift-F. *If you want to play from the current position to the next marker, the default shortcut is* Ctrl-Opt-1. *Now that you can customize your keyboard, you can assign these very useful functions to keys you can more easily remember (such as* P, Shift-P, Option-P, *etc.) You would be giving up the single-key access to the Pen tool, but how often do you use that?*

Assigning Special Effects to Keyboard Shortcuts

Among the few things you cannot automatically assign to a shortcut are the plethora of Final Cut Pro filters, transitions, and effects. However, there is a workaround that will probably satisfy most users.

Imagine you're editing a music video that incorporates several different effects again and again. One is a blur effect that starts clear and quickly smears into mush. Another is a white flash transition. By making favorites out of the effects you want to use repeatedly, you can assign a shortcut key to the first nine favorite transitions, filters and motion effects. By setting up a blur filter with the desired parameters and storing it as a favorite, and building the white flash transition by making a five frame additive dissolve, you can assign each of them to keyboard shortcuts. Then as you go through your program you can quickly assign the effects and wow your client.

*Beware: The list sorts alphabetically, so if you wind up with 10 or more different favorite effects, you may need to rename them so that the ones that you want keyboard access to fall within the first nine. You can always add numbers or spaces to the beginning of names to promote them in the sort order (**Figure 4.33**). Note, however, that you must restart the application for the re-ordering to take effect.*

Once you have your desired effect in that magical first nine, assign it to a keyboard shortcut. Find the commands in the Favorites section of the Keyboard Layout List.

Figure 4.33
In this list, White Flash appears before Additive Dissolve because of the space before the name.

Saving Shortcut Lists

As you probably expect by now, the first ten Keyboard Layout Sets that you save will appear in the Keyboard Layout submenu of the Tools menu. (Just note that you must choose "Export Layout" instead of "Save Layout" like the other features.) This affords another quick way to switch between layouts (**Figure 4.34**). When working on a single machine that is shared by multiple editors, this is a good way to store the different custom layouts used by each editor.

Figure 4.34 Custom Keyboard Layout sets appear in the Keyboard Layout submenu.

Adding Buttons to the Button Bars

Another of the new customization features in Final Cut Pro version 4 are the Button Bars at the top of each of the main windows and the Tool Bench (**Figure 4.35**). Any command that can be assigned to a keyboard shortcut can be assigned to a button, which can be put on any of the Button Bars.

Figure 4.35 Button Bars give another level of customization.

If the Button List window (found in the Tools menu) looks familiar, it should, it's the same as the right half of the Keyboard Layout menu (**Figure 4.36**). Access commands in Button List window in the same two ways as in the Keyboard Layout window: Either choose from the hierarchical list of menus and sets, or use the search field at the top and sift through the full alphabetical list.

Figure 4.36 Drag commands from the Button List window to Button Bars anywhere on your screen.

Once you've located your desired command, drag it into the Button Bar of your choice. Feel free to put one command in more than one place. While you can position as many buttons as you can fit into each of the windows, I recommend restraint. Too many buttons mean that each time you want to access one, you have to scan through all of them, and the icons are often not intuitive or obvious. Also, remember to save some space—as you work you may come across other commands that might be better suited for that prime real estate.

Customizing the Button Bars

Once the buttons are in place, it's time to have fun. Using the shortcut menu on the button bar (**Figure 4.37**), group the buttons by rearranging, adding color, and inserting spacers between groups. Save and restore your set of buttons (a set applies to all windows). You might expect the first ten sets you save to appear in the menu for super-quick access, but in this case you'd be wrong. The only way to restore the button set is by choosing Restore Master Button Set and selecting the saved set.

Figure 4.37 Add color, spacers, and store and restore button sets in the shortcut menu.

Other User Preferences

There are many other customization settings found in the User Preferences window (or General Preferences window for Final Cut Express users). These include operational features such as Undo levels, Autosave frequency, Labels, and other features that may vary from user to user (**Figure 4.38**). While these settings are not savable and restorable as the other settings are, they are recorded in the Final Cut Pro Version 4 Preferences file in the Final Cut Pro User Data folder, or in the Final Cut Express 1.0 Prefs file in the Final Cut Express User Data Folder.

Figure 4.38
User Preferences contains all the settings that might vary from user to user on a given machine.

The Final Cut Pro User Data Folder

Inside your Preferences Folder (in your Home Library folder) the Final Cut Pro User Data folder is where all of the customization settings are stored. If more than one editor is working on a single machine, it is best for each user to have her own OS X log in identity. That way, each user will have their own Final Cut Pro User Data folder containing all their custom settings.

If you share the same login identity, you will share a single User Data folder. You can still combine all of your individual customization settings by dragging the individual files into the appropriate folders (Browser column layouts in the Column Layouts folder, Button Bar settings in the Button Bars folder, etc.) Remember, you will share the settings stored in the preferences file.

If you travel from machine to machine, carry your User Data folder with you and place it into the Preferences folder on the new machine. In this way your familiar settings will be automatically loaded and ready as soon as you launch the program.

Logging With Final Cut Pro

Editing begins with *logging:* the process of cataloging footage and preparing your original source tapes for *capture.*

Logging is the first opportunity to review your footage. It's when you'll make your first decisions about what stays in and what's left out of your show. If you think of editing as a process of eliminating all but the most essential frames, then logging is the first, coarsest pass. At the logging stage, eliminate aborted takes, wasted tape before and after the action of the take, and any shots or scenes that just don't work.

Why Bother?

Logging can be tedious. It usually takes two to three times as long as the running time of the footage you're logging. That doesn't include the capturing time, either, which takes an additional 1.2 to 1.5 times the length of the footage. For instance, we shot roughly 60 hours of footage for *Want.* Logging it took about 150 hours, capturing it took another 75 hours.

Because logging involves looking at (and eliminating) a lot of footage you won't use, it may feel like a waste of your time. It's common to let an assistant editor complete the process. This has advantages and disadvantages. The main advantage is that by dividing the work, it's completed faster; you can begin editing captured scenes while additional footage is still being cataloged.

The disadvantage is that you lose a great opportunity to get better acquainted with your footage. Familiarity with every frame of the film is one of the keys to good editing. The more you view the footage, the better. That minute of "garbage" recorded when the camera operator was *rolling out the tape* might hold the key to a problematic transition or sequence somewhere else in the film.

One nice thing about logging is that you don't have to do it in the studio. Since you aren't actually capturing footage yet, you don't need access to the hard disk space required for your editing station. You can log footage on a laptop while in an airplane, or at the beach (**Figure 4.39**).

Figure 4.39 Does anyone really bring his laptop to the beach?

Collect All the Information You Can

The more information you collect during the logging process, the easier your job will be when you edit the film. Final Cut Pro is designed to help you compile a great deal of information while logging and recall it efficiently during the editing process.

What Information Should You Collect?

Ask yourself: What kind of information will help me recall the contents of a clip six months from now?

Start with the categories described in Chapter 2 ("Film Language"). Who or what is the subject of the shot? What is the shot type (CU, MS, LS)? Is it a moving shot? How long does it run? What scene is the shot associated with? When was it shot? What take number is it? Is there anything technically wrong with it (focus problems, audio noise, lens flares)? What were the director's comments about the shot? If you like, you can even include a transcription of the shot's dialogue.

Different footage requires different kinds of logging information. For instance, footage for a dramatic show typically needs the scene and take number, any comments the director made on the set, and any problems recorded at the time of production (such as the sound of an airplane overhead). A short description of the shot might be nice, but if the editor is working from storyboards or a detailed shot list, it may be unnecessary. B-roll footage from a documentary may benefit from much more detailed descriptions of the shots, but information like a take number wouldn't apply.

TIP: *Avoid cryptic descriptions or abbreviations when logging footage. This kind of shorthand can be especially awkward if an assistant is logging footage that the editor hasn't seen. If the editor has to spend hours scouring through the original footage before she can figure out that "L-CTrkTrukDrvTckt_03" means "Long shot to close-up tracking shot of truck driver getting a ticket, take 3," the assistant who came up with the clever abbreviation isn't likely to be working for that editor again.*

Unfortunately, Final Cut Pro limits the length of filenames, so some abbreviation is inevitable. But you have many comment fields and description columns to use in addition to the clip name.

Checking the Camera Log

Ideally, you have access to a camera log or *continuity report* that identifies exactly what was recorded on the tape: timecode numbers, shot names or numbers, take numbers, and some comments about each shot. The log may include additional information as well, such as the focal length and exposure setting of the camera (useful if something needs to be reshot). Transfer all of these details into Final Cut Pro.

You may also have access to a shot list, a breakdown of how a scene is supposed to be filmed, shot by shot. Though some crews may deviate from the plan, this is still valuable information to have.

These documents are the only clues you'll get to understanding what is on the tapes—aside from information gathered via your eyes and ears.

Logging it All

I strongly recommend cataloging every inch of tape on your source reels. You don't have to capture it all; in fact, if you have limited disk space, you won't want to capture more than you absolutely need. But you should log all of it. You never know what you'll want to use.

For instance, if you logged only the *circle takes* of a particular scene, and it later turns out that one of those shots is problematic, going back to find another take will mean relogging the tape. Since you don't want to have to log a tape more than once, do yourself a favor and log everything the first time.

You should even log the junk *between* takes. When you look at the clip list later, you should be able to account for every minute on the tape.

For example, let's say at some point the camera was accidentally turned on between two shots, wasting two minutes of tape. Obviously, the editor won't be using this footage, but if months later he's looking at the takes from that particular scene and discovers a two-minute gap in the timecode, he may suspect that a take or shot is missing—and send you back to the source tapes to check it out. If you logged that segment of tape as an unusable shot in the first place, you'll be able to avoid wasting everyone's time.

Scenes, Shots, and Takes

The terms "scene," "shot," and "take" can be confusing when you're new to filmmaking. Let's see if I can straighten out the jargon.

In the most generic sense, scene refers to an edited series of shots of related events taking place in a single location—for instance, "the bank robbery scene." During production, a scene is usually identified by a number based on the order in which it appears in the script or occasionally by the order in which it is shot.

Shot refers to each of the individual camera angles used in the scene. Every time the camera frames a different angle or image of the events being filmed, it is a new shot.

Take refers to a single iteration of any given shot—take 1, take 2, and so on.

Figure 4.40 A typical slate has one slot for the scene number and one for the take number, and that's that.

*To further confuse matters, most Hollywood productions identify shots by referring to the scene number. For example, successive shots in scene 5 would be called scene 5a, 5b, 5c, and so on. Furthermore, takes are sometimes referred to as shots. This is why a typical film slate has only two blank slots: one for a scene number (which is actually the shot name) and another for a take number (**Figure 4.40**).*

Log and Capture Window

At first glance, the Log and Capture window can be intimidating; it seems to require a lot of information (**Figure 4.41**). Once you learn to use this tool, however, it will considerably speed-up your logging process.

Prompt for Name checkbox

Auto-naming controls

Marker controls

Mark In button   Play button   Mark Out button   Log Clip button

Figure 4.41 The Log and Capture window is accessible by selecting **Log and Capture** from the File menu or typing ⌘-⑧. Use this window when you want to move footage from your tape to your computer.

The Basics

Like most features in Final Cut Pro, the Log and Capture window includes many options you don't need right away. You can get by just fine with a limited subset of logging capabilities.

At the most basic level, you can log a clip if you can tell Final Cut Pro just three things:

- The clip's starting time (its In point).

- The clip's ending time (its Out point).

- The clip's name.

> **IN AND OUT POINTS** *When you're working with a clip, Final Cut Pro allows you to set special markers identifying the frames that begin and end each shot. These markers are known as In and Out points.*

When it comes time to log, four basic steps will do the job:

1. Play your tape, using the [Spacebar] to start and stop playback, until you find the clip you want to log.

2. Use [I] and [O] to mark the In and Out points, thus identifying the precise segment of the tape you wish to log.

3. Hit [F2], or click the Log Clip button to enter the clip into the database.

4. Type in a name for the clip in the dialog box that appears, or accept the name generated by Final Cut Pro's auto-naming feature.

That's it! Once you've learned those steps, you're ready to log and capture your footage. You can forget about all the other controls.

I find the on-screen controls too small to use effectively, especially since you need them so often—so I recommend memorizing and using these four keyboard shortcuts.

Required Fields

As you can see, the Log and Capture window contains more than ten fields waiting for input. How do you know which fields to use for each clip?

Only four fields are required: Reel, Clip In and Out points, and Name.

Providing Meaningful Reel Numbers

It's critically important to enter a reel number (or name) when you log shows with source footage that spans more than one tape. In fact, Final Cut Pro won't allow you to log a clip without entering something in the Reel field.

Be sure to enter meaningful information in the Reel field. It doesn't matter whether you enter text or a number, but whatever you enter into that field is the only thing that will tell you which tape to put into the deck when you later do the capture.

Always include something that's actually written on the outside of the tape. While you may remember which tape is which over the first few weeks of a project, who knows what you'll remember when you need to revisit the film months or years down the road?

It's equally important to be sure that all clips from the same tape are entered with exactly the same reel name. Final Cut Pro will treat Tape 2 and Tape 002 as different tapes. To assist you in making the names identical, the Shortcut menu will pop up a list of all the reel names you've already used in a given project. Rather than retyping a reel name from memory, select it from the pop-up menu to ensure that syntax and capitalization are identical (**Figure 4.42**).

Figure 4.42 The Shortcut menu provides a list of all the reel names used in the current project. Access it by Ctrl-clicking the Reel field.

Setting In and Out Points

I've already described how to set the In and Out points. But how do you know *where* to set them?

Breathing Room

Always overestimate. Set your In early and set your Out late. Once your clip is captured, you don't want to have to go back and look at the tape again. If an assistant is logging, the editor won't know that something exists on the tape if it was cut off during logging.

Also, transitions and other effects sometimes require additional frames beyond the footage you mark between your In and Out points—another reason to provide a little slop on either side of each clip.

When to Add Handles

When you capture the logged footage, you have the option of adding *handles* (extra slop at the beginning and end of each shot) to extend the shots slightly. This is one way of ensuring you capture enough extra footage before and after each shot to allow room for transitions and other effects.

Set the default length for your handles in the Batch Capture dialog box (**Figure 4.43**). Handle length will be applied uniformly to the beginning and end of every captured clip. Usually editors set this value to one or two seconds.

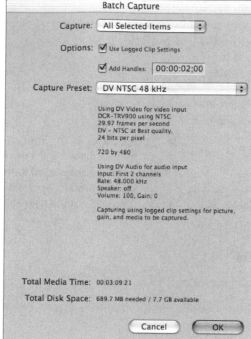

Figure 4.43 The Batch Capture dialog box appears when you click the Batch Capture button in the Log and Capture window. Here you can set how much time you want to add as a handle before and after every clip to be captured.

Using handles ensures that you get a little room to maneuver within each clip, but it's a generalized way to address this problem. If you set your In and Out points properly in the first place, you can customize the amount of elbow room you leave yourself shot by shot—and may not need to add handles at the time of capture.

It's a good idea to decide whether or not you intend to use handles before you begin logging. If you do plan to use them, then you can set In and Out points for the beginning and end of the action in each shot. For example, set the In just as the director calls "Action!" and the Out right as she says "Cut!" The handles will provide the extra frames you may require later. If you don't intend to use handles, set your In point earlier (perhaps as soon as the camera begins rolling) and your out point later (when the camera stops rolling).

The only problem with using handles is that Final Cut Pro requires at least three to five seconds of *pre- and post-roll* before and after each clip it attempts to capture. This means that you cannot safely set an In point earlier than five seconds into the tape or an Out point later than five seconds before the end of the timecode on the tape. Since most people log a tape right up to the last frame, adding a handle may reset the Out point for your last clip off the end of the tape—which will generate an error when you attempt to capture the clip.

PRE- AND POST-ROLL *In order for Final Cut Pro to capture clips accurately, the deck needs at least a few seconds before the clip gets up to speed—and a few seconds after the clip ends so Final Cut Pro can close the file properly. Different decks require different amounts of pre- and post-roll. Set the values in the Device Control Preset Editor. In the Audio/Video Settings dialog box.*

Avoiding Duplicate Filenames

It's very important to avoid creating duplicate names when logging clips. Final Cut Pro allows you to have multiple items with the same name in the Browser, but because clip names will become filenames, they must all be unique.

This may sound easy, but when you start logging shots for a long project, you'll often be tempted to use the same clip name, such as CU Trey_01 or LS Sailboat. Fortunately, Final Cut Pro has a screening mechanism that warns you during capture if you attempt to create a duplicate filename. But at that point you won't know which clip is which, so it's much better to avoid the problem in the first place. Use some piece of information unique to the shot, such as a description of the scene it was in (CU Trey Hockey Game_01) or, with more generically named footage, the date or some other detail to help differentiate the clip (Feb2 LS Sailboat-BootWaves).

When to Use Auto-naming

For certain types of footage, where the names of clips are going to be repetitive or follow numerical patterns based on scene and shot names, use Final Cut Pro's auto-naming features to generate clip names. This capability is designed to name and number your clips automatically, based on the information you type into the fields below the Name field (**Figure 4.44**). The tiny check boxes beside each field indicate whether that field will become part of the clip name. If you leave a box unchecked, that information is still recorded with the clip but will not become part of the clip name.

In the simplest case, use the Description field to name your clips. Every time you log a clip, the field is incremented with a number or letter. This prevents the logging of clips with duplicate filenames.

For instance, let's say you're logging a tape of nature footage taken in Yosemite National Park. The first thing on the tape is a long shot of Yosemite Falls from the valley floor. The shot runs for 20 seconds, and then zooms into a CU of three struggling hikers climbing an adjacent trail. You type Waterfall Hikers Zoom into the Description field and log the clip by pressing F2.

Figure 4.44 The clip name is based on the text in the fields below. Check the boxes next to the fields you wish to include. You cannot type directly into the Name field.

Include check boxes

Once the clip has been logged, the Description field automatically increments to Waterfall Hikers Zoom1 (**Figure 4.45**). Assuming the next shot on the tape is another take of the zoom, all you need to do is set new In and Out points and press F2 again—and the second shot will be automatically logged as Waterfall Hikers Zoom1. No retyping required.

Figure 4.45 The Description field becomes the name of the clip. Each time you log another clip, this field automatically increments the previous shot's name so the current one has a unique name or number.

Using Multiple Fields

If you check any boxes to include additional fields in the clip name, the information will be separated with an underscore. Use the Description and Shot/Take fields when you plan to have multiple takes of each shot.

For example, imagine the next section of the Yosemite tape shows a series of CU shots of the hikers. Since you know ahead of time that this series exists (from the camera log, or from having been at the location), go ahead and type CU Hikers into the Description field and 01 into the Shot/Take field (**Figure 4.46**). After you log the first clip by pressing F2, the Description field remains unchanged, but the Shot/Take field changes to 02. Each time you log a clip, the last-used field will be incremented; the others are left alone.

Figure 4.46 The checked fields make up the name of the clip separated by an underscore. Each time you log the clip, the last-used field is incremented.

If you're working with footage that was shot using the traditional Hollywood naming scheme, you will have scene numbers and take numbers for each shot. In this case, you can ignore the Description field and use the Scene and Shot/Take fields (**Figure 4.47**). Or use all three fields to provide a description with the scene and take information (**Figure 4.48**).

Figure 4.47 Footage named in traditional Hollywood style has only a scene number and a take number. In this case, use just those two fields. Be sure to check the correct Include check boxes to reflect the fields you are using.

Figure 4.48 You can add a description to the shot to help the editor identify the subject.

Alternately, if you have distinct scene, shot, and take numbers, use the Description field for your scene number, the Scene field for the shot number, and the Shot/Take field for the take number (**Figure 4.49**). This is great for footage coming from corporate or industrial shoots, where scene names tend to be discrete from shot numbers.

Figure 4.49 If your shots have unique scene names, shot numbers, and take numbers, use all three fields to hold the different bits of information.

Using Manual Incrementing

All these auto-naming and auto-incrementing features really come in handy. Even a small reduction in steps will save you loads of time and hassle, given the huge number of shots you have to log in any project. Using the auto-naming utilities also assures that your clips are uniformly named, which makes them easier to sort on and search for.

But wait, there's more! You may have noticed a little button, the one with a picture of a slate on it, next to each of these naming fields. This is the Manual Increment button (called the Slate button in the documentation). Clicking the Manual Increment button next to a field adds a number (or letter) to the end of that field.

This is great if you want to increment the scene number. Let's say you're working in the Hollywood naming scheme and the last shot you logged was scene 44a, take 4. The next shot is take 1 of scene 44b. You can increment the scene number from 44a to 44b by clicking the Manual Increment button once (**Figure 4.50**). This not only changes the value in the Scene field, but it resets the Shot/Take field back to 01! It's an enormous time-saver when you're working with clips that are constantly incrementing, such as footage from dramatic or scripted shows.

Figure 4.50 Clicking the Manual Increment button increases the number or letter in the corresponding field and automatically resets the fields below it.

TIP: If you Option-click the Manual Increment button, it clears the entire field.

Why All These Fields?

There's no reason you can't type the scene, shot, and take numbers right into the Description field. But by breaking down the information into individual fields, you will be able to sort and search on any one of the fields later.

For instance, if you want to find all the shots from scene 21, you can perform a Find All in the Browser, search only in the Scene column, and look only for clips with the number 21. Once you do that, you can collect all those clips into a single bin, and sort them based on shot number or take number. For simple projects with only a hundred or so clips, this degree of control may not be necessary. But on a larger project, such as a feature film, with thousands of individual shots, file management at this level is fundamental to the editing process.

How to Log Short Clips

Ideally, you will be able to log your clips without stopping the tape—but when you find yourself logging clips that are less than 30 seconds long, it will be difficult, if not impossible, to name them and enter your comments before they've passed and the next clip has begun. You may find yourself racing against the tape or constantly stopping and starting playback to give yourself a chance to fill in the fields in the Logging tab.

This is the time to turn on the Prompt for Name feature by checking the Prompt check box on the Logging tab (**Figure 4.51**). When this option is enabled, clicking the Log Clip button (or hitting F2) automatically pauses the tape and opens the Log Clip dialog box, which will prompt you for a name (**Figure 4.52**). Once you dismiss the dialog, the tape will begin playing again, and you can move on to setting the next clip's In and Out points.

Figure 4.51 If the Prompt box is checked, every time you click the Log Clip button (or type F2), the Log Clip dialog box will open, asking you to name the clip you are about to log.

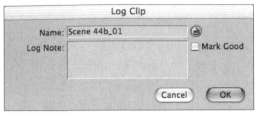

Figure 4.52 The Log Clip dialog box includes the Log Note field and the Mark Good check box to allow you to provide additional information about each shot.

TIP: The Log Clip dialog contains a Manual Increment button (the one with the little slate). If you want to increment the shot name (trees, trees1, trees2) click that button, and the clip name will be updated without any further typing on your part.

How to Log Long Clips

Logging longer shots allows you plenty of time to type in a name, comments, and other information you require while the tape is rolling. If most of your shots are longer than 30 seconds, you may be able to log the entire tape without ever stopping it.

To work this way, uncheck the Prompt check box (see Figure 4.51). Then, while the tape rolls, set your desired In point and enter the name and any other information you want to supply in the fields in the Logging tab. When the shot ends, mark the Out point on the fly and log the clip. The fields you've chosen to fill in are captured and stored with the clip. Playback will not be interrupted, and you can begin logging the next clip immediately.

TIP: Back up your project file! All the information you enter during logging is stored in that file. (It is not stored with the media files when you capture.) With a copy of the project file (and your source tapes), you can recreate your whole project—any time, anywhere.

Entering Additional Information

Experienced editors have learned the hard way that the more information you record during logging, the happier you will be later. Final Cut Pro makes it easy to add all types of additional information while logging.

Using the Log Note Field for Longer Notes

Now that you have the clip-naming process figured out, you will see that you can't put all of the information into the name. If you want to record more detailed or elaborate information, the Log Note field is your best bet.

You can comfortably view two lines of notes in this field (and type as much text as you wish for searching purposes). Be sure to enter the log note *before* logging the clip. Unlike the other fields, the Log Note field is cleared every time you log a clip.

If you want to use the same note repeatedly, access previous notes from the Shortcut menu by Ctrl-clicking the Log Note field. You might use this to enter frequent comments like "Director liked this take," "Aborted take," or "Traffic noise." Using the Shortcut menu minimizes repetitive typing and assures the uniformity of your log notes (**Figure 4.53**).

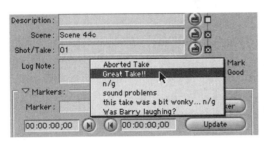

Figure 4.53 The Shortcut menu on the Log Note field pops up a list of the other log notes used in the current project. This way you can reuse comments that occur frequently.

Setting Markers While Logging

Final Cut Pro provides yet another clever feature to make logging easier: the ability to set *markers* while logging.

Markers are among the most valuable tools available to you as a digital editor (see the section on working with markers in Chapter 5, "Basic Editing"). The ability to set them while logging is unique to Final Cut Pro.

It's too time-consuming to bother setting markers for short clips while you're logging, but placing markers in longer clips is a fine way to point out both positive and negative things that occur during the clip. For instance, you might identify a lens flare, a flaw in the performance, a mic boom in the shot, or the duration of an airplane sound that interferes with your audio. Use markers to identify the frames where a character is speaking in a clip that includes long portions of silence, or note a good performance of a particular line.

Here's how to set markers while logging: Twiddle open the Markers revealer in the Logging tab (**Figure 4.54**). (If you're not going to be using markers, you can close this to avoid clutter and distraction.) Set marker In and marker Out points using the buttons you'll find there (shortcuts are ⌷ for In and Option-⌷ for Out). Name the marker by typing in the Marker field. Out points are required only if you want the marker to have duration; if you don't set one, the marker will identify a single frame in the clip.

Figure 4.54 The Logging tab contains a set of controls for adding markers to your clips. These controls can be hidden or shown depending on the state of the revealer widget.

Once you've set your desired marker In and Out point and typed in a name, clicking the Set Marker button adds the marker to the list box. You can stack up as many markers as you want to in the list or delete existing ones. Change markers any time you like by selecting them in the list; making changes to the In point, Out point, or name, and clicking the Update button.

Creating Subclips on the Fly

Because markers turn into subclips, you can easily create subclips from longer clips, on the fly, while logging. Let's say the script calls for an insert of a hand opening a door. When the crew shot the scene, rather than stopping and starting the camera for different takes, they simply ran the action four or five times during one shot. When you log this footage, keep the clip all together as one shot, and use markers to set In and Out points for each door opening. Once you capture the clip, your markers can be accessed directly as subclips in the Browser (see "Subclips in Disguise" in Chapter 5) (**Figure 4.55**).

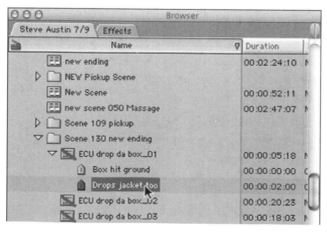

Figure 4.55 Double-clicking a marker in the Browser opens it up as a subclip.

Good, Better, Best

The Mark Good check box in the Log and Capture window (**Figure 4.56**) is another piece of information to store with a clip you're logging. The original idea was that this would be akin to marking a circle take. Check this box to identify good clips you may want to find later. Once all your clips are logged, perform a search to find all clips that have the Mark Good check box checked, and use that list to decide which clips to capture—or to jog your memory on which takes you liked while logging.

Figure 4.56 The Mark Good check box can be used to mark clips you like. Later you can search on the Good column in the Browser to find them.

Of course, you don't *have* to use this check box just to mark good takes. I always wanted this feature to pop up a menu that would let me choose Good, Better, or Best—since most of the time I don't know which is the circle take until I've seen them all.

So, weirdly enough, I generally use the Mark Good check box to mark shots that are unquestionably *bad*. For example, I use it to mark the junk in between shots, or takes that were aborted, or footage of the crew goofing around. Then I know what I *don't* want to capture.

Apple finally addressed the Good-Better-Best concept, but in a somewhat awkward way. The Label Category is an option for every item in the Browser, allowing you to assign a label to each clip that you can later search and sort on.

The default labels are Good Take, Best Take, Interview, B-Roll, and Junk—but the label names are fully customizable in the User Preferences window (or the General Preferences in Final Cut Express). Each label has a color associated with it (also customizable). Once you get used to the colors, you can quickly distinguish clips in the Browser by the color of their icons. This color also shows up on the clip when it's edited in the Timeline, which can be helpful when you're glancing at a long show and trying to identify a particular clip to which you previously assigned a label.

The only problem is that you can't actually apply any of these labels in the Log and Capture window (where you really want to). To use the labels, you must first log the clip, then bring the Browser window forward, select the clip, and change the value in the Label column (**Figure 4.57**).

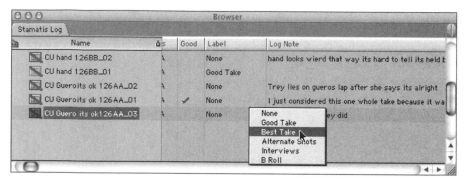

Figure 4.57 You can set a label for each clip you log, but you can only do it in the Browser window after the clip is logged. Ctrl-click the Label column and assign the label of your choice.

Adding Additional Information in Browser Columns

You can use other Browser columns to add additional information to your clips— but as with the Label Category option, you have to log the clip first.

There are four comment fields for cataloging information such as shot type, day/night, script day, shooting day, camera focal length, f-stop, and so on. To use any of these columns, first log the clip, then open the Browser and type directly into the column you want to use. All of the columns support the Recent Items pop-up list I described for the Reel and Log Note fields; Ctrl-clicking a column opens up a list of all the values previously used in that column (**Figure 4.58**).

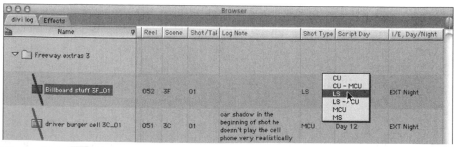

Figure 4.58 Ctrl-clicking any of the comment fields in the Browser will pop up a list of all the comments previously entered in that field for the current project.

Speed Logging

I've already described a number of things that Final Cut Pro does automatically to assist you in naming the clips you're logging, but it gets even better. Check this out:

If you log a clip by pressing F2 without setting an Out point, Final Cut Pro sets the Out point at the exact moment you press the key. And whenever you log a clip, Final Cut Pro resets the In point for the *next* clip immediately following the Out point for the clip you just logged.

These two features make it possible for you to log clips with a single keystroke.

Here's how:

1. Insert a tape, and enter a reel number and name for the first clip.

2. Set your first In point at the beginning of the first shot, and let the tape roll.

3. When you get to the point where you'd like to end the first clip, instead of setting an Out point, hit F2. That sets the Out point and logs the clip.

4. Final Cut Pro automatically increments the clip name, resets the In point, and the tape continues to play. At the next scene break, just hit F2 again.

5. Continue this process until you reach the end of the tape.

If the takes are long enough, you should even have time to enter comments in the Log Note field, change the clip name, and so on. When we developed this method of one-key logging, we informally dubbed it "speed logging." It's a bit too complicated to explain on a marketing sheet, but it's a great feature for the serious user to know about, as it can save lots of time.

Auto Scene Detection

If you still hate the idea of spending hours and hours logging your tapes, you may be curious about a feature called Auto Scene Detection. To use it, capture your entire tape as one single clip, then select the clip and choose Auto Scene Detection from the Tools menu.

Final Cut then goes through the clip and adds a marker at each point the camera stopped and started while recording. (This works on any tape shot with any DV camera. The memory chip included on the more expensive DV tapes is not required.) Each marker can be double-clicked in the Browser and opened as a subclip.

This feature will only identify moments when the camera stopped and started. This may or may not have much relation to where your clip boundaries should actually be. It certainly won't tell you when the director called "Action!" or "Cut!" And it's not going to name your clips in any useful way (unless Marker 31 makes your heart beat faster). For professionally shot footage, you will probably not find Auto Scene Detection terribly useful.

One additional disadvantage is that working this way assumes you are going to capture every second of footage on all your tapes, which will eat up huge amounts of unnecessary disk space.

That said, for certain applications it may be great. For instance, if you're logging footage shot by an amateur videographer on a safari in Africa, just knowing where the camera started and stopped may be useful.

Working With Timecode

One of our goals when designing Final Cut Pro was to make migration from older tools as painless as possible. We wanted people familiar with Avid, Media 100, or even traditional linear editing systems to feel comfortable with Final Cut Pro right away. This had a major influence on our decisions about what to name various features and what keyboard shortcuts to implement.

One important example is the way we designed Final Cut Pro to work with timecode. Linear video editing systems were operated almost entirely from a numeric keypad. Editors became adept at typing in timecode numbers and learning to add and subtract frames in base 30 (for NTSC) or 25 (for PAL).

Although it seems tricky at first, once you learn to think in timecode, you will be able to edit more quickly and more accurately. The more advanced you get, the more you will think only in terms of frames and timecode, and you will probably find yourself editing by typing numbers into your keyboard just as the editors on those older systems did—and less by dragging things around or clicking buttons.

To start you on the path toward timecode enlightenment, here are some of the basic rules and concepts about how to use timecode in Final Cut Pro. Don't panic—it may initially seem mind-boggling, but you'll get it eventually.

Timecode contains eight digits, separated by colons: 00:00:00:00 (hours:minutes:seconds:frames).

If you're going to enter all eight digits, you can forget the punctuation: 18102118 will be interpreted as 18:10:21:18.

OK, but this is real life, and most of the time you aren't interested in the hours column, or even the minutes column. Most of the edits you'll be making will involve a few seconds or a few frames. That's why we arranged for Final Cut Pro to accept less than eight digits. In fact, it will read right to left in two-digit increments.

For example, if you enter 01:23, Final Cut Pro will interpret it as 00:00:01:23.

A colon with no number after it is interpreted as a placeholder for 00. So...

If you enter 11:, Final Cut Pro will interpret it as 00:00:11:00.

If you enter 11::05, Final Cut Pro will interpret it as 00:11:00:05.

Similarly, you can enter math commands such as –5 or +10. These apply to the current timecode following the same conventions:

If the current timecode is 02:20:55:10...

-5 subtracts 5 frames, and the current timecode becomes 02:20:55:05.

Or

+10: adds 10 seconds, and the current timecode becomes 02.21:05:10.

You can use a period or a comma instead of the colon, and you can also omit leading zeros.

So you might type +10.5. which would be read as 00:10:05:00 and bring our timecode from 02:20:55:10 to 02:31:00:10.

In case all that isn't enough, you can also enter simple frame values like +125, which means "add 125 frames." In NTSC timebase, that would equal 4 seconds and 5 frames. This is an easier way for some editors to think. You can even combine these methods:

-2.50 would subtract 3 seconds and 20 frames. The -2. means subtract 2 seconds, and the 50 is interpreted as 50 frames, or 1 second, 20 frames.

At any point while working in Final Cut Pro, you can simply type in a timecode number, even without clicking a field. Final Cut Pro will recognize what it is and apply it to the most likely place based on the current context.

*If the Viewer is active, timecode entry will move the playhead forward or backward. You do not need to actually click the Current Position field, although doing so accomplishes the same thing. Typing an absolute timecode number (01:21:10:15 or just 10:15) will move the playhead to that absolute position. Typing in a mathematical statement (+16, -200, and so on) will move the playhead forward or backward as requested (**Figure 4.59**). The Log and Capture window works the same way: Changing the value modifies the Current Position field to shuttle the tape and cue it up to the requested timecode frame.*

continues on next page

Figure 4.59 Direct timecode entry in either the Viewer or Log and Capture window will apply the timecode to the Current Position field and move the playhead (in the Viewer) or the tape itself (in the Log and Capture window).

Working With Timecode   *continued*

*If you wish to change a clip's duration in either the Viewer or the Log and Capture window, hit t before entering your timecode. This will highlight the Duration field in the upper left corner of the window. You can type in a new absolute value or use math in this field, too. For example, if the current clip duration is 00:10:00:05, entering t–10. would highlight the Duration field and shave off 10 seconds by changing the Out point to make the new duration 00:09:50:05 (**Figure 4.60**).*

Entering timecode numbers when the Timeline or Canvas is active initiates a wide variety of editing operations depending on the current state (see the sidebar "Just Type a Number" in Chapter 6, "Advanced Editing").

If the timecode value you want is sitting in a nearby window, you can actually drag it from one timecode field to another by holding down Option *as you drag (**Figure 4.61**). You might do this while logging to move the tape to the In point. By dragging the timecode from the In point into the Current Position field, you will make the tape shuttle to that timecode, lining your tape up on the current In point.*

Figure 4.60
You can modify a clip's duration by clicking the Duration field (also accessible by hitting Tab). Making changes there will modify the Out point to result in the desired duration.

Figure 4.61 You can drag a timecode value from one field to another by holding down Option when you begin to drag.

Drop Frame vs. Non-Drop Frame

NTSC timecode comes in two flavors: drop frame (DF) and non-drop frame (NDF). Don't be fooled by the name. No frames are ever dropped. These are just different ways of counting the frames. Non-drop frame timecode counts every frame consecutively, and every 30th frame marks a new second. Because NTSC video actually plays at only 29.97 frames per second, this method of counting is not a very good way to tell how long a program will be.

For example, if you ran a stopwatch, a show measuring exactly 1 hour in NDF timecode would actually last 1 hour, 3 seconds, and 18 frames!

So who cares? Broadcasters. Problems arise when television stations are creating broadcast schedules that must be precise lengths. That's why they invented drop frame timecode.

With drop frame, every so often frame numbers are skipped so when the edit machine says the program is 01:00:00:00, it is actually 1 hour long on the clock. No frames are dropped, but some numbers are skipped so the count remains true to real time. It's exactly the same concept as leap year, only instead of skipping the 29th of February 3 out of every 4 years (except every 100 years), DF timecode skips frames 00 and 01 every minute (except every 10 minutes). That means if you want to look at frame 1800 (1 minute), the counter would read 00:01:00:02 even though in NDF, it would read 01:00:00:00. You can tell DF and NDF apart by the punctuation used. DF is always identified with a semicolon instead of a colon between the seconds and frames: 00:00:00;00.

NTSC DV is always recorded in drop frame timecode.

Logging Outside of Final Cut Pro

Logging doesn't require having the hard disk space to capture the logged footage. A logging station can be a minimally configured iMac or laptop. As long as it runs Final Cut and connects to your source deck, you can record all of the logging information you need. Then, you can transfer your information to a computer with big hard drives and capture to your heart's content.

Logging From a Window Dub

Because timecode is not program specific, you can actually log your tapes using any software program, on any system, and transfer that data to Final Cut Pro for capturing. Sometimes tapes will even be logged by hand, perhaps by watching a *window dub*. In that case, all you'll have will be a handwritten list of In points, Out points, clip names, and comments.

WINDOW DUB *Some video decks can display timecode numbers in a window on top of the video image, so you can see the exact timecode number for any given frame on the TV monitor. This is known as BITC—short for burned-in time-code, and pronounced "bit-see." A dub made with that window visible is called a window dub. This makes it possible to record timecode values even from a nonprofessional tape format like VHS* (**Figure 4.62**).

Figure 4.62 When timecode is printed on top of a video image, it's called BITC

Importing Batch Lists

Final Cut Pro can import and process batch lists of logging information from any program as long as it's stored as tab-delimited text. You can even type the details from a hand-written list into a spreadsheet if you know what you're doing. You can use as many or as few of the Browser columns as you choose.

To enable Final Cut Pro to read the file, you must take one additional step. Before importing the file, you must modify it in a text editor, or a spreadsheet program like Excel, and add one new record at the beginning of the file with the exact Browser column headers that correspond with the fields in the data file (**Figure 4.63**). At the beginning of the file add the text "* * drop=on" to ensure that the clips are imported as drop frame timecode, which is required for DV footage.

	A	B	C	D	E	F	G	H
1	**Drop=on							
2	**In**	**Out**	**Name**	**Take**	**Reel**	**Comment 1**		
3	01:18:24:02	01:20:14:28	CU Reggie_01	01	001	Good perf, bad audio		
4	01:21:42:10	01:22:10:20	CU Reggie_02	02	001	n/g		
5	01:22:31:05	01:22:55:13	CU Reggie_03	03	001	Good		
6	01:22:59:10	01:23:30:10	Lions in cage		001	Roar!		
7	01:25:10:23	01:26:29:21	Baby Gorilla	01	001	swings for a few minutes and then climbs		
8	02:02:19:17	02:03:01:18	Momma Rilla	01	002	Kids in background		
9	02:04:10:19	02:05:04:23	Momma Rilla2	02	002	No Kids, good		
10	02:48:18:01	02:49:01:21	Killer Koala		002	draws blood, at end of shot he		
11	02:50:00:02	02:55:28:14	Meerkats	01	002	Spot on		

Figure 4.63 Add one record at the head of the list identifying the Browser columns you want the corresponding data to go into. You can use as many or as few columns as you like. Final Cut Pro will use that first record to identify which data goes into what column.

You can also work the other way around. If you prefer to log your footage in Final Cut Pro and edit on some other system, go wild. Final Cut Pro exports batch lists that you can import into an Avid or another system and use to capture and edit on that system. Beware, though: You are probably limited to essential information: reel number, In point, Out point, clip name, and possibly one comment.

Incidentally, making a batch list is also a great way to create a fail-safe backup of your Final Cut Pro project file. Even if those files are corrupted somehow, or it's ten years from now and Final Cut Pro is so antiquated you've moved on to some new editing program, you will still have a reliable way to access the data gained during that long, painful logging process. Add an *EDL* (Edit Decision List) of your finished show, and you can rebuild it on any system at all.

THE OFFLINE/ONLINE WORKFLOW

There are many instances where you may not want to make all of your editing decisions while working with the full resolution clips from your source tapes. For example, if you want to do your editing on a laptop and you don't want to lug around several external hard disks to hold all of your huge video files, convert your source footage to a lower resolution format and do all of your editing with those files. Once you're done and ready to lay off your finished show to tape, you must recapture the footage you used at the full resolution. At that point, rather than needing to capture all 8 hours of source footage, you only need to recapture the 30 minutes that went into the final show. There are quite a few advantages to working this way and some formats such as HD or film more or less require it. Final Cut Pro has specific tools for working exactly in this way.

This process is called Offline/Online because it's based on traditional tape to tape editing systems found in places like newsrooms, where the editor makes all her decisions on a small, cheap editing system not connected to the whole video network. When the show is ready to go, she reassembles it on the fancier, more expensive edit suite where final graphics, titles and effects are added. Because this system is "online" (connected to the overall video network and uplink facility), the polished show can be output directly from the decks of the editing suite onto the air.

Offline RT

One of the main advantages to working with lower resolution files in Final Cut Pro is added machine power. Because these files are smaller and less demanding on the system, you can typically do more types of effects and manipulations without requiring a render. This saves you time and allows you to experiment with additional special effects and transitions.

It also reduces your reliance on expensive, fast hard disks and allows you to store many times more video in less space. The lowest resolution files commonly used are rendered in the Photo-JPEG codec and are 1/4 the frame size of standard video. Despite their tremendous compression, they are still remarkably useful for making most editing decisions.

(There are even more powerful compressions schemes such as the ones typically used for Web video playback [MPEG1, 2 & 4, Sorenson, etc.], but these files are not suitable for editing.)

Final Cut Pro calls Photo-JPEG compressed files "Offline RT." Photo-JPEG is a wonderful type of compression that can convert a 30 minute video clip into less than 1 GB on disk. By comparison, uncompressed, that same video would take nearly 50 GBs and with the DV compression, it would take about 6GB. This is how several hours of footage can fit on a modest laptop editing system.

IMPORTANT: You can make Photo JPEG versions of any video, no matter what the original source format is. The one vital detail you must keep in mind is that the clips must have the same Reel and Timecode information that is on the original master tapes. As long as you've got that information associated with the clip, you can recapture the files at full resolution in preparation for your final output.

A Note About Audio Compression

Although squeezing video into smaller files is a great benefit while you're making most of your editing decisions, you cannot do the same with your audio. There are many different ways you can compress audio and potentially save disk space, but most of these techniques modify the data in a way that prevents the ability to edit the files. So while your file is smaller, you will get errors when trying to use only a piece of it in your sequence. Fortunately audio is tiny compared to video, so even the uncompressed audio files won't take up nearly as much space as your video will. If you have some audio that is already compressed (such as an MP3 file) you will get much better results if you convert it into an uncompressed format before editing it into your sequence.

Making Low-Res Files

There are two ways of creating offline versions of your video without losing the essential Reel and timecode information. (1) Capture all of your source files as you normally would, then convert them after the fact. (2) Capture directly to the offline format.

Batch Converting Files

Assuming you've already captured your footage at full resolution and you want to switch into an offline mode to take your project on the road with you, you'll need to make a wholesale conversion. The easiest no-mess way to convert a whole project full of files is to use Final Cut Pro's Media Manager tool, which is found in the File Menu near Log and Capture (**Figure 4.64**). It's important to select all of the items in your browser window that you want to convert before activating the Media Manager tool, since it works exclusively on the current selection. When in doubt select everything. If there is more than one instance of a single clip, Final Cut Pro is smart enough not to convert it more than once.

Figure 4.64 The Media Manager has a variety of uses. One is to batch-convert all of your files into an offline format.

The summary at the top of the Media Manager window tells you exactly how much disk space your conversion is going to require. Although you can safely throw away the big original files after the conversion is done, you'll need enough space for both the original and the new files at least temporarily.

When you select Recompress from the pop-up menu in the Media section, you are given the choice of recompressing to any of the sequence presets currently in your A/V Settings. Offline RT is one of the options pre-installed by Apple (**Figure 4.65**).

Figure 4.65 Choose Recompress from the Media pop-up and choose Offline RT in the next menu.

If your goal is to recompress all of your source footage, be sure to leave the Delete Unused Media checkbox unchecked. Next, select a destination disk for your new files and let her rip! Once the operation is done you can safely delete the original media files.

Finalizing the Show

After you've finished editing the low-res shots, roughing in titles and any special effects, you're ready to do the same operation in reverse. Select your edited sequence and open the Media Manager again. This time you want to Create Offline media which will generate a new project ready for capture (**Figure 4.66**). If you select Delete Unused Media, you can avoid recapturing pieces of clips that you didn't use. This way no matter how much source footage you originally had, you'll only need to recapture that footage which is the actual duration of your edited sequence.

If you plan to make any minor adjustments to the edits or add any transitions, be sure to Add Handles so that the recaptured full resolution footage contains a little maneuvering space.

Once you've recaptured the media from the sequence at full resolution, finalize any special effects and color correction and lay off the finished sequence to tape, compress it for DVD or the Web and collect your paycheck.

Figure 4.66 To prepare for recapture, create an offline version of your sequence with the Delete Unused Media checkbox checked.

Capturing Directly to Photo-JPEG

If you were clever enough that you planned to go through this offline/online process before you captured your footage the first time, you can actually capture directly to the offline format. This is as simple as choosing the correct Capture Preset (**Figure 4.67**). By doing this, you eliminate the Batch Compressing step listed above. To finish your show, you'll still need to go through with recapturing your edited sequence at full resolution.

Figure 4.67 The Capture Preset determines the format in which the clips are captured.

Uncompressed Video

While DV is a great format for many purposes, plenty of jobs continue to be done on other formats. These include projects such as shows with heavy special effects components, projects intended for blow up to 35mm or HD, or shows relying on footage from news or industrial sources that are still using non-digital formats. To capture footage from other tape formats such as Betacam SP, Digital Betacam, DV-50, or IDX you will need specialized hardware such as the AJA Kona or Pinnacle CinéWave PCI cards. These are specifically designed to work with Final Cut Pro and capture video at higher qualities than traditional DV.

The downside to working with this kind of higher resolution video is that the video files are bigger and require faster hard drives. This is all the more reason to work in an offline/online model. Your offline format could be Photo-JPEG like the earlier example, or alternately you could use DV. This will give you the added benefit of watching your program on an interlaced TV monitor (through the Video Out component of your DV deck) as you make your editing decisions. When working in Photo-JPEG you are restricted to watching your video on the computer screen.

Regardless of what you use for your offline format, you will need to go through the same process of recapturing the edited sequence in the final full resolution format before you call it a day.

High Def

More and more jobs are being acquired on High Definition video and there's no reason you can't edit them on a Final Cut Pro system just as easily as any other format. Like the *Standard Definition* formats described above, you will need special hardware such as the CinéWave or Digital VooDoo HD card.

> **VIDEO DEFINITIONS** When the High Definition standard was established, all video at "standard" NTSC or PAL frame sizes was deemed "Standard Definition"(SD). This includes Betacam SP, VHS, D1, Digital Betacam, and others. DV is technically not considered SD because it is 480 lines tall instead of 486. Further, in digital terms, SD is often used to refer to uncompressed video compared to DV's built in 7:1 compression.

If you think SD video takes up a lot of space, you'll fall over when trying to calculate how much HD video your spiffy new 400 GB disk array can hold (40-50 minutes). And don't even bother trying to capture HD to a measly IDE hard drive. For now, only super fast SCSI and Fibre Channel arrays are capable of playing back such high-bandwidth video. For these reasons, anyone working in HD will find the offline/online model is the only practical way to work.

Some of the capture cards, such as the Pinnacle CinéWave can automatically down-sample HD to SD as it's capturing, or capture the HD at a reduced quality. These options are other "offline" formats since eventually you will need to recapture at full resolution. Alternately, you can use the Final Cut Pro Capture Presets to capture directly to uncompressed SD, DV, or even Photo-JPEG.

Working with Film and Cinema Tools

The offline/online process is fundamental to projects originating and finishing on film. Regardless of the resolution at which you capture and edit your video version, the negative still needs to be conformed (physically cut and spliced together to match the video edit) before the film is ready to be printed and exhibited.

To work with film based materials in Final Cut Pro, you need additional Apple software called Cinema Tools. (Cinema Tools is bundled with Final Cut Pro 4.) When you *Telecine* film onto video, a log is generated that corresponds to the Keycode printed on the film with the timecode recorded on the tape. Cinema Tools reads these telecine logs (sometimes referred to as Flex files) and converts them into capture logs. This enables you to capture and edit your video, knowing that when it comes time to go back to film, you'll be ready. When you're done with your offline edit, use Cinema Tools again to generate the Cut Lists and Change Lists so the film negative can be edited to match the digital cut (**Figure 4.68**).

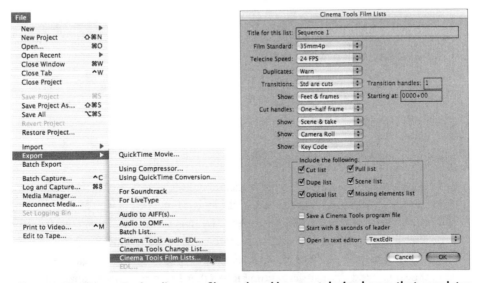

Figure 4.68 Cinema Tools relies on a file produced by your telecine house that correlates your clip timecode values with the keycode numbers on the actual fim.

I N T E R V I E W

Steven Mirrione has cut an interesting variety of projects, alternating big-budget studio pictures with smaller independent films. There's an arresting intensity to all of his work, from Doug Liman's *Swingers* to Steven Soderbergh's *Traffic* and Jill Sprecher's *Thirteen Conversations About One Thing*. At the time of this interview he was just finishing Soderbergh's *Oceans Eleven*. Since then, he cut George Clooney's overly stylized directorial debut, *Confessions of a Dangerous Mind* and *21 Grams* for director Alejandro González Iñárritu (*Amores Perros*).

MICHAEL WOHL: WOULD YOU DESCRIBE YOUR EDITING PROCESS?

Steven Mirrione: I begin with watching the dailies. I don't take very detailed notes, but when I'm watching, if there's a particularly interesting moment, or something I think I might forget, I'll write it down. "Look what that actor did there," or "Look how the camera reveals that." And then, maybe there's a moment where I know, "OK, this is a pivotal part of the scene." And so I'll either go forward or backward from there, and shape the whole scene around that moment.

HOW DO YOU PICK THAT MOMENT?

It's something that maybe caught my eye during dailies, something that happened within the scene— maybe a really important line that an actor got just perfectly and that touched me or moved me while I was watching—something that I want to preserve. So, I'll take that moment and build the scene from there, rather than starting right at the beginning and plowing through it. Because, that way I know where I'm supposed to land in the scene.

Another thing I'll often do is go through and cut the scene without any sound, without listening to the dialogue. Sometimes the dialogue can get in the way of focusing on how I'm cutting in terms of the emotions. It's very easy to get into a trap where you're cutting based on the dialogue rather than based on expressions or body movements or things like that. Obviously, I have a general sense of what the dialogue is, and I can read lips, but I'll turn off all the sound and I'll just start cutting it together based on what's happening in the actors' faces. And the rhythm of that will sometimes be a lot different than if you've got all that other stuff going on. Then, of course, I turn the sound back on, and I make slight adjustments to make sure that everything works well.

When you're dealing with a feature film, it's this huge thing, and if you start thinking about it as a huge thing, you'll get blocked and you'll never get past that first moment or that first cut or choosing that one performance. You've got so many decisions to make that you really have to start whittling it down to: "Okay, this moment here. OK, now I'm going to do this other moment here"— focusing yourself, trying to build that base, then build on top of that and on top of that.

WHAT HAPPENS AFTER THE ROUGH CUT?

After it's all put together, then you work through from the beginning and get to the end. A film gets created in layers, and you're always building on them. It's always becoming a bigger and bigger thing. First you're dealing with the arcs of the individual scenes, then the arc of three scenes together, then the arc of the entire movie. That's why it takes so long to edit a movie. It's not because it takes six months to get it to where you can see it from beginning to end, it's because once it's all together, that's when you can finally start to do the work of the movie instead of the individual scenes.

HOW LONG DOES IT TAKE YOU TO CUT A SCENE?

I might work on two or three scenes a day. Most scenes are about two to three minutes long. After I've screened the dailies, I'll get into the room, turn off all the lights, close the door and start looking for those pieces that I really like, start building the scene. Maybe there'll be a moment that I'll want to keep working on, or I'll finish the whole thing and go back and watch it over and over again and wait for something to strike me—"Oh, I should try that" or "I never noticed that before." There may be one line where I think I can find something better, I'll go through all the dailies of just that one line and try to find an alternate.

DO YOU ALWAYS READ THE SCRIPT BEFORE YOU START EDITING?

Absolutely, otherwise I would be completely lost. But scripts have a tendency to be slightly overwritten. It's the nature of the beast. A writer has to communicate what's going on in people's heads somehow. And a lot of times that comes out through dialogue. When it gets performed, however, you add the element of a human being who can portray things non-verbally, suddenly words are coming out of their mouth that don't seem natural because you can see so much in a look or an expression.

That's exactly what happened at the end of *Traffic*, when Michael Douglas is giving that speech. That speech was twice as long as what's in the movie, but the way he delivered it, you could feel all the things that the script had him saying in the second half of the speech. A lot of times you end up cutting lines of dialogue, or huge sections of stuff, because an actor did something more efficiently with the way he raised his eyebrows or moved his head. Something as simple as that can make three paragraphs of dialogue completely unnecessary.

CAN YOU GIVE AN EXAMPLE OF A PROBLEM WHERE YOU WERE PARTICULARLY PLEASED WITH THE SOLUTION?

One of the things that I had done a few times in *Traffic*, in the interest of getting across a lot of information in an interesting way, was having big chunk of a scene play over somebody just sitting there. In *Thirteen Conversations*, there would be a scene, but I'd love just two lines out of the scene. It would be a master, so how do you edit it so that you're hearing only those two lines of the scene? So I would come up with a way that I could play those two lines over the previous scene. For example, there's a character played by Matthew McConaughey, who's been involved in a hit-and-run accident and he's feeling all this guilt about it. They had shot all these long takes of him just sitting there looking at things or just thinking, I was able to play huge sections of scenes over just his face. That way I was able to focus in on the best bits of dialogue in the movie.

I'm drawn to dialogue-driven movies and character-driven movies. Every word that is spoken is so important. You don't always know from the script which words are going to be the good ones and which ones aren't, or what's going to be redundant because the point is expressed in a character's face.

HOW DOES THE BUDGET AFFECT YOUR EDITING STYLE?

Well, on a movie like *Oceans Eleven*, we shoot it, we cut it, we do a preview screening. There's money in the budget to say, "Okay, there's this whole section here that we really can't fix editorially; let's go back and do some reshooting." You can't do that with an indie film. You either get it or you don't and you just have to make everything work. It becomes so important that while I'm putting [an indie film] together I start to think, "OK, now there are three scenes that we need to get," and I communicate that to the director while they still have a crew and actors and they can actually go out and get that stuff. At the same time, you have to be so careful because it's very easy to jump the gun and say, "Oh, this is a disaster! We need a reshoot" You really have to be careful that you don't create problems that don't exist. It is definitely a balance.

IN TERMS OF LOGISTICS, WORKING ON SMALLER INDEPENDENT FILMS IS VERY DIFFERENT THAN WORKING ON THE LARGER BUDGET PICTURES.

They're completely different. Imagine trying to shoot everything you need in a period of three to four weeks versus five months. Obviously, it changes the style, and hopefully the style of the film you're making matches the way you're trying to make it.

WHAT'S YOUR FAVORITE PART OF BEING AN EDITOR?

Getting to be alone with the film. I'm probably one of the only people on the whole movie, other than the writer when they're first putting it together, who actually gets to just be alone with it and do anything I want to it for a period. That's definitely my favorite part.

YOUR LEAST FAVORITE PART?

After the film has been locked and before it actually comes out in the theater, because that's the time when I really can't do anything else to affect it. It's that time of letting go, letting the film become whatever it's going to become. And there's nothing I can do about it. That's definitely a weird time.

SOMEONE ONCE SAID, "A FILM IS NEVER FINISHED, IT'S ABANDONED."

Right. That's absolutely how I feel.

CHAPTER FIVE

Basic Editing

All right. You're ready. You've committed to memory all the definitions, theories, patterns, and procedures in Chapters 1, 2, 3, and 4. You've looked at every frame of your footage and logged all the good stuff. There's plenty of fresh coffee. You've already spent your first paycheck.

Let's do it.

IF IT WERE EASY, EVERYONE WOULD DO IT

If I haven't made it clear by now that editing is a very complex task, let me state that fact explicitly. When you sit down at the editing console, you have to bear in mind all of the rules and ideas presented in the earlier chapters—more or less simultaneously. For every shot you look at, you must pay close attention to the visual content, the audio content, the emotional and thematic content, and the compositional characteristics. What's worse, you must be acutely aware of all these things not just for one clip but for *two* clips: the ones on both sides of each edit point.

Is your brain tired yet? Sorry, there's more. Don't forget to think about the juxtaposition of the images and the sounds, and the impact it will have. For continuity cuts you must be aware of the three-dimensional space and time within the frame and how the edit maintains or destroys that seeming reality. Remember to maintain screen direction, continuity of motion and action within the frame, and... The list goes on and on.

Most important, film is a time-based medium—and to edit successfully, you need to find the flow of the show. You can't possibly do any of this (let alone *all* of this) if you're constantly being interrupted by your software.

The Disappearing Software

As a matter of fact, the most important thing your video-editing software can do is stay the hell out of the way so you can focus on the complex business of editing your project. Anything that interferes with the process of translating ideas from your brain into your show is an obstacle, not a tool.

Novices at digital video editing often have a hard time understanding the critical differences between various editing platforms. In a magazine ad, the bullet lists of features offered by Adobe Premiere, Avid Media Composer, Discreet Edit, and Final Cut look very similar. But real life in the editing room is more than bullet points, and as far as I'm concerned, Final Cut is the best editing software you can use. Why? Good workflow.

Software should be an extension of your body—in much the same way a musical instrument is to a musician. Once that musician's learned how to hold the bow or vibrate the reed, he can translate his thoughts and feelings directly into music. Eventually, he isn't even thinking about the individual steps required to produce the sound. The instrument disappears.

Similarly, once you master the basic controls of Final Cut Pro, you will be able to groove with the software in such a way that the user interface seems to disappear, enabling you to translate your thoughts and ideas into sequences of images and sounds on the screen. We've all heard of musicians with a favorite guitar, trumpet, or violin. Our goal in building Final Cut Pro was to earn the love of the editors who use it.

Some of the features that make Final Cut stand out become apparent only after you've worked with it for a while. For one thing, it has very few dialog boxes to slow you down. In general, software hits you with a dialog box when it doesn't know what to do next. ("Excuse me, where should I save this file?") This interrupts the workflow. Some disruptions are inevitable, but as much as possible Final Cut avoids unnecessarily interrupting your work.

Modal software is another obstacle to smooth workflow. In order to perform a specific task, modal software forces you to stop working and switch into a different mode—usually via a menu or keyboard shortcut. For instance, many video-editing applications force users to switch modes from working with clips to working with sequences, or from making an edit to applying a filter. Final Cut avoids this distracting process.

Nonetheless, for all its elegant simplicity, Final Cut is a sophisticated tool that offers so many choices about how to perform basic editing functions, it can be daunting to a new user. For instance, the software lets you perform your basic edit (putting a clip in a sequence) in almost any way imaginable. You can drag a clip from the Browser to the Timeline or the Canvas. You can open a clip in the Viewer and drag it from there. You can use a keyboard shortcut, or you can click a button on the screen. And then, for each of those methods, you have seven additional permutations to choose from to determine exactly *how* you want the edit to be executed (Insert, Overwrite, and so on). And while there is no right way or wrong way, there *are* reasons to make different choices depending on the circumstances of the edit.

Now the good news: Final Cut was designed in a way that enables you to use the simpler features without knowing anything about the advanced ones. However, this requires some discipline.

So here's some important advice: Don't go poking around in all the menus or clicking around all the different tabs in each window. Stick to a few basic operations as shown in this chapter, and learn them before you try to absorb everything that the software can do. The key to working successfully with whatever tool you choose is to figure out which of its features you'll be using the most—learn them well, and ignore the rest of the bells and whistles. You'll have plenty of time to learn about them later.

In this chapter, I'll highlight the most important controls, give you a few hints about the ones you should ignore, and offer tips about when to choose one particular editing method over another.

Working with Clips

Once you've captured and cataloged all your clips, you're ready to begin editing—and at this stage, that means assembling sequences. Depending on the type of show you're building, you may go about this in different ways. But the first thing you need to know is how to select and extract the precise parts of those clips you want to include in your sequence.

Marking Clips

Every clip should have some "slop"—unnecessary frames surrounding the section you'll eventually select to use in the show. Before you move a clip from the Browser into a sequence, open it in the Viewer and mark the exact section you want to use (**Figure 5.1**). Identify this section by setting In and Out points at the beginning and end.

Figure 5.1 View your clips in the Viewer before editing them into a sequence.

 The left side of this pill-shaped button will set your In point, and the right side will set your Out point.

Use the Keyboard, Not the Mouse

Software designers don't always get everything they want. One of my biggest complaints about the user interface for Final Cut Pro is that the most commonly used buttons are too small. Using the mouse to place the pointer right on top of small controls requires fine motor skill movements and lots of repetition. This can be very tiring.

Luckily, Final Cut has keyboard shortcuts for almost every command in the program. To avoid fatigue, learn them and use them. (See the Keyboard Shortcuts table later in this chapter for a list of the ones you'll use most.) If you don't like the default shortcut keys, in Final Cut Pro 4, you can change them to your liking. (See "Customizing your Keyboard," Chapter 4).

The first controls to learn are the basic playback and marking controls you'll use to move around inside the clip and mark the In and Out points. Fortunately, these are easy to remember.

The spacebar starts and stops playback; to play backward, hold down (Shift) while pressing the spacebar

Set your In point by hitting (I). Set your Out point by hitting (O).

For more precise playback control, you can use (J), (K), and (L). The arrangement of these keys is not accidental. By placing your hand over this area of your keyboard, you'll have one-finger access to all the most important controls (**Figure 5.2**).

Figure 5.2 **The keyboard layout is designed so you can move around inside a clip and set markers without having to take your hand off the keyboard. The most common controls are at your fingertips.**

(J) plays backward, (K) pauses playback, and (L) plays forward. Tapping (J) or (L) multiple times causes faster and faster play. Holding down both (J) and (K), or (K) and (L), will play at half speed.

(I) sets your In point and (O) sets your Out point. (Option)-(I) or (Option)-(O) will clear those points. (Shift)-(I) or (Shift)-(O) moves your playhead to that point.

Hitting (M) adds a marker at the current position.

If you're left handed (and you're using Final Cut Pro 4), remap the same key arrangement onto the left side of the keyboard. Instead of (J), (K), and (L), program the same functionality onto the (S), (D), and (F) keys. (E) and (R) can serve as Set In and Set Out, and so on.

Marking While Playing

To make accurate decisions about where your In and Out points should be placed, set them while the video is playing at regular speed—as opposed to *jogging* (**Figure 5.3**) or *shuttling* (**Figure 5.4**) through the clip. This is critical if you want to understand the proper timing of the clip.

Figure 5.3 The Jog wheel plays the clip forward or backward, frame by frame, when you roll it left or right. ⊞ and ⊞ on your keyboard do the same thing.

Figure 5.4 The Shuttle control plays the clip forward and backward at variable speeds. The farther you drag the handle from center, the faster the clip plays.

Set the In and Out points as many times as you like while you're working on a clip, but since there can be only one In and one Out point in any given clip, only the last one sticks.

Marking at its Best: Fast and Smooth

With hundreds (or thousands) of In and Out points to set in a show, the faster and more smoothly you place them, the better off you'll be. Here's how a professional editor marks a clip:

1. Double-click the clip in the Browser to open it in the Viewer window.

2. Hit ⊡ to begin playback.

3. Hold your finger over ⊡, and keep tapping it until the action is just about to begin.

4. Stop tapping it when the section you want to use begins.

The last tap sets the In point for the clip.

The better you know the footage, the better you'll know when to start the shot. Even so, it's easy to wait too long. It's best to set the In and Out points while playing backward, too. If you miss the beginning of the action, tap ⊡ for backward play and reset your In point to the correct spot. Then resume forward play and prepare to set your Out point.

Many editors will tap ⊡ constantly as the clip plays, especially as it nears the anticipated end point. That way, when the right spot rolls by, they just stop tapping and the point is marked.

Finding the Rhythm

Pay attention to the pace of your tapping for an early clue about the editing rhythm and pacing of a scene. I try to tap in a regular, rhythmic pattern. If I find myself tapping in a dance club groove of 180 beats per minute (bpm), I know the scene is going to require fast cutting to match the rhythm inherent in the shot. If I'm tapping at a leisurely 30 bpm (about the rhythm of a Frank Sinatra standard), I can prepare for longer shots and less frequent edits.

Typically, action shots inspire faster tapping, and dialogue shots call for slower tapping, but sometimes you'll be surprised. On a show about occupational safety that I was cutting, I was so bored by the narrator that I found myself tapping ⓞ faster and faster while listening to his droning instructions. Although a slow and conservative editing pace seemed most appropriate for the show, I realized that my viewers would probably find the narrator's voice just as mind-numbing as I did— so I sped up the editing pace to offset that soporific narration.

Tapping has the added benefit of working off the effects of drinking too much coffee during the editing session, but if you want to preserve your fingertips and the springiness of your keyboard, simply hold down ⓘ or ⓞ and release it at the spot you want to mark.

Parents, Children, and Masters

Once you've set your In and Out marks, you will edit that section into your working sequence. In doing so, you make a copy of that clip, which is a second pointer to the actual file on disk. Internally, that copy also points back to the originally captured clip. Once this happens the original parent clip is now called a *Master Clip*.

Most of the time, you don't need to think about this Master/Child relationship, but there are times where modifying one instance of a clip will affect other instances of that clip and there are times it won't. To make the most of Final Cut, It's important to understand your clip's family tree.

For example, let's say you are working with a clip in the timeline and you have applied a filter to it. You want to use another instance of the same clip, but without the filter. In this case, you want to return to the Master Clip and generate a new child. Or perhaps you have made several child clips and given some of them unique names. If you ever lose track of where they came from, the inherent master/child relationship will help you find your way back to the original clip.

At any point, a clip can be selected in the timeline and Reveal Master Clip chosen from the View menu. This will highlight the Master Clip in the browser window. Alternately use the Match Frame command; Match Frame works based on the current frame visible in the Canvas. Final Cut finds the Master Clip in the browser and loads it into the Viewer, parked on the identical frame (**Figure 5.5**). You can then edit a new, clean version into your sequence.

Figure 5.5 Match Frame finds the original version of the frame on which you're parked.

Declaring a Clip's Independence

There are occasions when you want your child clip to lose it's reference to the Master Clip, such as when you want to rename a clip. In Final Cut Pro 4, renaming one instance of a clip automatically renames any master, child or sibling clips. If you want to rename two different instances of a clip, you will need to declare its independence. Select the clip and choose Make Independent Clip from the Modify menu.

Creating Merged Clips

Until Version 4 of Final Cut Pro, there was no good way to combine audio from one file with video from another. This was a common problem, encountered by anyone who recorded audio and picture on separate decks. This includes anyone who shoots film, and many video productions that chose to record audio on DAT.

Furthermore, a Final Cut clip could only contain one video track and two audio tracks. This was a limitation that affected music video editors who commonly have two production tracks in addition to a stereo music track linked to every clip. Not to mention anyone who used a DV camera with four audio channels, or someone like director Robert Altman who frequently mics each of his actors individually, resulting in half a dozen or more individual tracks for each shot.

Both of these issues are addressed with the Merge Clip function in Final Cut Pro 4. A clip may now contain as many as 24 audio tracks and one video track. You can merge any clips by selecting them in the browser and choosing Merge Clips from the Modify Menu. Merging clips has no effect whatsoever on the files on disk, but it allows you to create a single clip for editing that references more than one file on disk (**Figure 5.6**).

If you attempt to merge clips of differing lengths, the longest clip will be used and black video or silent audio will be filled in on any shorter tracks. When you load up a merged clip in the viewer, you will get as many Audio tabs as there are audio tracks. You can set level and pan keyframes and add filters for each of them individually (**Figure 5.7**).

Figure 5.6 Finally! Merge Clips allows you to sync up audio from your DAT and picture from a videotape and create a single Final Cut Pro Clip to edit.

Figure 5.7 Merged Clips may contain multiple Audio Tabs.

Keeping Track of Your Tracks

Final Cut can display the Timecode for each track in use as an overlay in the Viewer or Canvas windows. (**Figure 5.8**) This can be especially helpful if you are working with merged clips and you want to see the Timecode numbers from the audio source instead of the video, which appears in the Current Timecode field. You may need to do this if your camera or continuity logs reflect this alternate timecode. If so, turn on Timecode Overlays in the View Options menu of the Viewer or Canvas to see this information (**Figure 5.9**). It will not appear while playing, but whenever you are parked, the overlay will appear. Show Overlays, in the same menu, must also be turned on.

Figure 5.8
The Timecode Overlay shows information for every track in the clip or sequence you're viewing. Timecode from different clips appears in different colors.

Figure 5.9 To view Timecode Overlays, you must select both Show Overlays and Show Timecode Overlays in the View Options menu.

Marking Subclips

Sometimes a clip will contain more than one section you want to use. In those cases, you can create subclips and have access to all the good sections.

For example, you may have several shots combined in one captured clip. This happens frequently with documentary B-roll. Let's say you were working on a documentary about high schools, and the camera crew captured many quick shots of kids in the hallway between classes. When logging the footage, you grabbed big chunks of the reel to sort out later, rather than chopping them up into loads of tiny clips. Now it's time to sort them out.

Or maybe you have several takes of the same shot all wrapped into one clip. This happens frequently when the camera crew is shooting a short action, such as a button being pushed or a handshake. They'll film the action several times in one take, and the series of actions winds up getting logged as one clip.

Or sometimes lazy assistant editors (with access to unlimited disk space) will log and capture the whole tape as one huge clip. I don't recommend this. It saves time during logging, but you'll just have that much more junk to wade through and eliminate once you begin editing. It also means that you're not watching the footage very closely. However, if you end up having to work with one of these huge clips, you can use the subclip controls to break it up into bite-size pieces.

You could skip this step and sort through the whole long clip every time you want to pull out a section, but it is more difficult to set precise In and Out points within a very long clip (each pixel of your scrubber bar may represent many seconds). With a shorter subclip, each pixel may represent a few frames. This makes it much easier to manipulate the clip (**Figure 5.10**).

1 inch = 3 minutes   1 inch = 3 seconds

Figure 5.10 Making subclips means not having to wade through the whole clip each time you open it.

How to Mark Subclips

Marking subclips is much like logging footage, except it happens after the clips have already been captured. Begin by setting an In and Out point as described above. Then, select Make Subclip from the Modify menu (**Figure 5.11**) or hit ⌘-Ⓤ. As soon as you do this, a new item with a new icon appears in the Browser at the same location as the parent clip.

Figure 5.11 Make Subclip is found under the Modify menu. The keyboard shortcut is ⌘-Ⓤ.

Final Cut assumes that the first thing you want to do with your new subclip is rename it, and it brings the Browser window forward with the Name field automatically selected so you can type a descriptive name for your subclip (**Figure 5.12**). The contents of the various Browser columns such as Comment fields and Log Notes are copied from the master clip to the new subclip. Once the subclip is created, you can change the contents of any column without affecting the master clip. This enables you to search and sort your subclips more easily throughout the editing process.

Figure 5.12 When a new subclip is created, the Browser window comes forward so you can name your new clip. Note that a subclip has a special icon.

Creating a subclip does not make a new file on your hard disk; it merely makes a new reference to the file from which the master clip came. Once created, subclips become new Master Clips and can be treated exactly like any other clip—including using them to generate more subclips.

Using the Go To Master Clip Command

Just like ordinary children, you can find a subclip's master clip by using the Reveal Master Clip command from the Mark menu or by pressing [Shift]-[F] on the keyboard. The Master Clip will be selected in the Browser. This is helpful if you're editing a subclip and realize you need it to be a few frames longer to allow room for a transition or speed effect. With the Go To Master Clip command, you can jump back to the master clip and have access to all the original frames right in the Viewer.

> **TIP:** Another way to add frames to the subclip is to use the Remove Subclip Limits command from the Modify menu. This resets the In and Out points of the subclip to those of the parent clip. Beware, though: This change is permanent.

WORKING WITH MARKERS

As I mentioned in Chapter 4, "Preparing to Edit," markers are one of the most valuable and versatile tools available to you as an editor. Final Cut Pro's markers are very robust, and once you begin working with them, you will continually find new uses for them.

Marking a Moment in Time

At its simplest, a marker is just a placeholder or bookmark that can be attached to a given frame of your clip or sequence. When a clip has a marker attached to it, that marker sticks around even when the clip is edited into a sequence. Although there is no functional difference, markers attached to a clip are called clip markers and markers attached to a sequence are called sequence markers. You can place as many markers as you like in any clip or sequence.

Set a marker by clicking the Add Marker button on the Viewer or Canvas (**Figure 5.13**), selecting Add from the Markers submenu of the Mark menu (**Figure 5.14**), or using a keyboard shortcut. The default shortcuts are either [M] or [`] (the key on the upper left corner of your keyboard next to [1]). All markers can be set while the video is playing forward, backward, and at high or slow speeds (as is true for In and Out points, which are just special kinds of markers).

Markers will be applied to the current selection. If you have a clip selected in the Timeline, and you set a marker over that clip, the marker will go into the clip (**Figure 5.15**). If the clip isn't selected, the marker will go into the Timeline itself (**Figure 5.16**).

If you're trying to set a timeline marker and it doesn't seem to be working, check that there is not a selection somewhere else in the sequence. Any selected clip prevents sequence markers from being set. Use the Deselect All command to remedy the problem without going hunting for the culprit clip. In Final Cut Express and in prior versions of Final Cut Pro, the keyboard shortcut is CMD-D. In Version 4, the default shortcut is Shift-Command-A. (Of course, if you want to make it work the old way see the "Customizing your Keyboard" section in Ch 4.)

Add Marker

Figure 5.13 Clicking the Add Marker button adds a marker at the current position. The keyboard equivalent is to type Ⓜ or Ⓐ. If you are already parked on a marker, this button will open the Edit Marker dialog box.

Figure 5.14 Another way to create a marker is by choosing Add from the Marker submenu of the Mark menu.

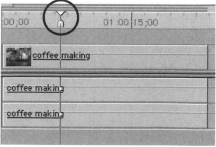

Figure 5.15 If a clip is selected in the Timeline, adding a marker will place it in the selected clip.

Figure 5.16 If no clip is selected, the marker will be applied to the sequence.

What do Markers Look Like?

Markers are visible in every window in the program. In the Viewer and Canvas *Scrubber areas,* markers appear as little pink flags (**Figure 5.17**). When the playhead parks on a frame identified by a marker, the flag turns yellow and the Viewer or Canvas displays the name of the marker overlaid on the video image.

Figure 5.17 In the Viewer or Canvas windows, markers show up as small flags. Names and comments do not appear while footage is playing.

In the Timeline, clip markers appear as flags on the clips themselves, and sequence markers appear in the ruler at the top of the window (see Figures 5.15 and 5.16). The Canvas will display the marker name only when parked on a sequence marker.

Even the Browser shows markers. A clip with a marker attached will appear in the Browser with a revealer (or "twiddle"). Activating the twiddle will display a list of markers and their names (**Figure 5.18**).

Figure 5.18 If a clip has markers attached to it, the Browser will display a revealer next to the Clip icon. Expanding or "twiddling" it reveals a list of all the markers in the clip.

TIP: Clips move around in the Timeline while you're editing. If you want to mark an important moment, think twice about whether you want to use a clip marker or a sequence marker. A sequence marker will stick to an exact location in time, regardless of which clip it happens to land on. A clip marker will stick with the clip and move with it as you edit the sequence.

What's Worth Marking? And When?

I use markers to identify many different things: stuff I like; stuff I don't like; areas that need further work; areas that are complete; sound cues I want to use as sync or snap points. And sometimes I just use them to make notes to myself or my assistant.

Setting Markers While Logging Clips

You'll save lots of time if you set markers while you're logging clips (see the section on setting markers in Chapter 4). I use them to mark areas that are probable cut points or areas that are clearly unusable in the midst of a good clip.

For example, if I were logging footage of highway traffic filmed from the back of a truck, I might make one long clip for the entire time the camera was rolling. But then I'd use markers to identify when the camera zoomed in or out to frame specific cars, a section where the camera went out of focus for a few moments, a spot where a passing driver's face was recognizable (which I couldn't use, since I wouldn't have a release from the driver), and a particularly great moment when a motorcycle split the lanes of traffic and screamed past the lens. Once the clip was logged and captured, all of these important moments would be identified and visible whenever I viewed the clip.

Using Markers as Reminders

There's a limit to how many things you can hold in your mind at the same time. Use markers to leave little reminders for yourself.

I often use markers to hold my place in a sequence or make a note about something I need to fix while I go off and tweak something else. Many times when I'm playing a sequence after making an adjustment, I'll be struck with new ideas, or I'll see edit points that need work. Since I can do only one thing at a time, I usually drop a few markers in at the trouble spots so I'll be able to remember the things I want to work on.

Using Markers as a Third Hand

Working solely with In and Out points is like having only two hands. And while two hands are good enough most of the time, sometimes we all wish we had a third one. Markers give us that advantage.

For example, one sequence in *Want* features Ben and Trey dreaming about ideas for start-up businesses while driving along the highway. At one point Ben looks out the window and sees a billboard that gives him an idea.

Whenever I edit a sequence, I'm constantly using my In and Out points to identify where my next edit is going to be (see the section on three-point editing later in this chapter). In this case, I wanted to drop in the cutaway of the billboard at exactly the right moment to match Ben's eyeline when he looks out the car window, and I wanted to cut back to the car on a specific line of Trey's dialog. (There are my In and Out points.)

Since the billboard was a moving shot, and the words on the ad would be most legible at a particular instant, I used a marker in the cutaway clip to flag the sweet spot for reading the billboard. I wanted that spot to hit the Timeline at just the instant when Ben's eyes light up as he gets his idea, so I used another marker to identify *that* point in the Timeline (**Figure 5.19**). Lining up the two markers in the Timeline enabled me to create the perfect effect.

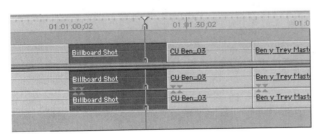

Figure 5.19 In this example I used a marker in the clip to identify the best frame of the cutaway, and a second marker in the sequence itself to highlight where the cutaway should go.

Using Markers for Making Split Edits

Markers can be very helpful when planning L or J cuts (see the section on split edits in Chapter 2, "Film Language"). You can mark the spot where you want audio or video to begin or end separately from the primary In and Out points.

Naming Markers Wisely

Three weeks from now, you probably won't remember what "Marker 27" or "Here" means. Use a name that will remind you why you marked this spot in the first place. Good marker names should be very specific: "License plate visible," "Good match for Trey's POV," or "Soft focus" will be much more useful than "qwkdsl2df."

To name a marker, park on the frame where the marker is located and open the Edit Marker dialog box (**Figure 5.20**). Access this dialog box by clicking on the Add Marker button again (the first click sets the marker; the second click opens the Edit Marker window) or typing Ⓜ or ⌐ on the keyboard. Note that a marker can have both a name and a comment. Both will be displayed in the Viewer or Canvas overlay.

Figure 5.20 The Edit Marker dialog box lets you modify all the parameters of a marker or simply delete it.

Marking a Range of Time

You may have noticed the Duration field in the Edit Marker dialog box and wondered what it was for. Few beginners realize that markers can have duration, but this is a feature that professional editors use all the time.

Not only can you mark a moment of time, you can use a single marker to denote a range of time. Rather than merely indicating when the motorcyclist begins his ride between the lanes, mark the entire ride, from the moment you first see him until he passes the lens.

This compounds the usefulness of markers because now each one has its own In and Out point. Not only can the marker serve as your third hand, one marker can actually be a second *pair* of hands.

Deleting Markers

Once a marker has served its purpose, delete it. Having a bunch of markers that are no longer relevant will clutter up your workspace and may confuse you the next time you want to create a new marker. Even if you're certain you can tell the new ones from the old ones (and if you didn't give them all descriptive, custom names you'll be regretting it now!), sorting out extraneous markers will distract you and slow you down.

There are three ways to delete a marker:

- Park on it and choose Delete from the Marker section of the Mark menu.

- Option-click the Set Marker button.

- Press ⌘-`.

You can also delete all the markers in a clip or sequence by choosing Delete All from the Markers submenu of the Mark menu or pressing Ctrl-`.

Navigating with Markers

Once you begin using markers, you'll want to find them quickly.

Using the Previous and Next Marker Controls

Your playhead can be moved quickly from marker to marker within a clip or sequence using the Previous and Next Marker controls in the Mark menu, or use the keyboard shortcuts Shift-M (next marker) and Option-M (previous marker).

A third technique is to use ↑ and ↓ while holding down Shift; this stops at all markers. (Ordinarily, you can use ↑ and ↓ to navigate through your sequence, but unless you hold down Shift, you will stop only at edit points and the In and Out markers.)

> **TIP:** *Make sure to check your selection before trying to navigate to markers in the Timeline. If a clip is selected, markers in that clip will be included when you go to the next or previous marker. If the clip isn't selected, those markers will be ignored.*

Jumping to Markers

Another handy way to navigate between markers is by using the Shortcut menu on the Current Position field in the Viewer or Canvas (**Figure 5.21**). All the markers in the clip or sequence will be listed at the bottom of the menu. Clicking a marker name will take your playhead directly to that spot. This shortcut is also available on the ruler in the Timeline and on the rulers in the Filter and Motion tabs.

Figure 5.21 All the markers in a clip or sequence are listed in the Shortcut menu, which can be accessed by Ctrl-clicking on the Current Position field in the upper right corner of the window. Selecting one of the marker names will jump your playhead to that spot.

To access clip markers within a sequence, open the Shortcut menu on any clip in the Timeline. All visible markers will be listed at the bottom of that menu as well (**Figure 5.22**).

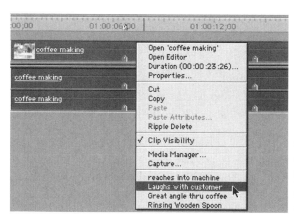

Figure 5.22 Within a sequence, clip markers can be accessed via the Shortcut menu on the clip itself. Selecting one of the marker names will move the playhead to the marker.

I find these features especially helpful when I'm cleaning up the rough cut of a long show. First, I watch the whole show and set markers where I know I want to make changes. Then, using one of these navigation shortcuts, I can jump right to the spots I want to fix. Once each spot is clean, I delete the marker and go on to the next one.

Searching for Markers

Although Final Cut Pro's Search feature is robust in the Browser, searching for something in a sequence is less flexible. You can look only for clip names, timecode values, and, yes, markers (**Figure 5.23**). You can search for text in both the Name and Comment field of the marker, and the Find dialog will take you right to that spot.

Figure 5.23 The Sequence Find tool allows you to search for clip names, timecode values, marker names, and comments.

TIP: *Final Cut's Sequence Find tool only searches forward from the playhead and doesn't wrap around to the beginning of the sequence when it's through. Therefore, it's usually a good idea to press* Home *to bring you to the beginning of the sequence before performing a Timeline find.*

Snapping to Markers

One of the most useful things about markers is that they can be sticky. When you enable *snapping* in the Timeline, both clip and sequence markers will act as snap points.

Snapping is a Timeline state. When snapping is turned on, certain items attract and grab other objects (such as clip edges, edit points, In and Out points, the playhead, keyframes, and markers) that are dragged nearby.

You can toggle snapping on and off by hitting N or clicking the Snapping indicator in the Timeline window (**Figure 5.24**). When you drag a clip with markers into a sequence, the markers are visible for use as snap points during the drag (**Figure 5.25**).

When you drag a clip from within the Timeline, you must click exactly on the marker itself in order to activate it as a snapping point.

Final Cut Pro 4

Final Cut Express

Figure 5.24 The Snapping indicator is depressed and lights up green when snapping is enabled and dims to gray when disabled. Clicking on the button will toggle the snapping state, but it's much easier to use the keyboard shortcut by typing Ⓝ. This shortcut works even while the mouse button is pressed, so you can toggle snapping on and off while you are dragging to help you complete your drag.

Figure 5.25 Dragging a clip with markers attached will display those markers as the clip is dragged into a sequence. This can be very helpful for lining up important frames in your shots.

Reposition Marker

Since markers behave much like In or Out points, you would expect to be able to set a marker by tapping a key until just the right moment, as I described setting In and Out points earlier. And you'd be right, except the default shortcut requires an extra key.

For example, if you notice an audio glitch in a clip, you might want to identify it with a marker to be cleaned up later. So you play the sequence, and (just as if you were setting an In or Out point), you begin tapping Ⓜ as you approach the spot where the glitch should be. You stop when you hear the glitch expecting the last marker to identify the problem spot. Unfortunately, since markers work slightly differently than In and Out points, you have just set 30 or 40 new markers, one for each time you tapped the key.

But hey, don't worry. Final Cut Pro has a special feature just for this situation. It's called Reposition Marker. You access it by holding down ⟨Shift⟩ while you tap the ⟨`⟩ key. Then, instead of setting a new marker each time you tap, it sets just one marker and moves it along until you stop tapping. If this becomes a feature you use regularly, Final Cut Pro 4 allows you to map your own, single-key shortcut to this function.

Extend Marker

Because markers can have duration, In and Out points can be set for a marker that are separate from the In and Out points for an entire clip. And you're probably going to want to set them on the fly. You already know how to set the marker start point (⟨M⟩ or ⟨`⟩). Use the Extend Marker command to set a marker's Out point; the keyboard shortcut ⟨Option⟩-⟨`⟩ lets you set it on the fly. For example, imagine you're making a video about earthquake safety. You've shot a reenactment of an earthquake, during which all the actors reacted to an imaginary temblor. The camera operator even shook the camera to accentuate the effect, but now you need to add a rumbling sound to really sell it.

You've already set In and Out points for the clip identifying the whole scene and dropped it into a sequence. Now you play the sequence back, and at the first frame of camera shake, you type ⟨`⟩ or ⟨M⟩ to set the marker. It will be stamped wherever the playhead is at the moment you hit the key. When the shaking has finished, type ⟨Option⟩-⟨`⟩, and the marker will be extended to that point, covering the entire duration of the earthquake. Now, when you lay in your sound effect, you know exactly where it should go (**Figure 5.26**).

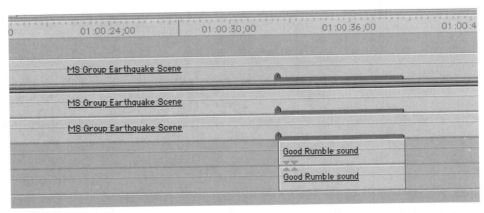

Figure 5.26 When you've set duration for a marker, its flag grows a tail that extends the length of the marker. Both ends will act as snap points. In this case, I can use the extended marker to help me lay in a sound effect for the earthquake safety video.

Subclips in Disguise

One interesting, and little-known, fact about markers is that they are actually subclips in disguise. When you "spill" or twiddle open a clip in the Browser, the markers will be listed below the clip. If you double-click on one of the markers, it will open in the Viewer as a subclip. (If the marker has no specified duration, the subclip will begin at the marker point and extend until the end of the master clip.) If you drag the marker and drop it right into a sequence, or even another bin, it will act exactly like a subclip.

Thanks to this feature, if you understand how to set extended markers (markers with duration) as explained previously, you can use markers as an alternate way of creating subclips.

This is one reason for setting your markers while logging; you get the benefit of a single large file, but the subclips you need for editing are right there when you open up the clip.

Marking Music Beats

Here's another nifty trick you can do with markers. Often when editors are cutting a program to music, they need to arrange the edits to fall right on the beat. Someday, I hope, Final Cut will have a feature that automatically detects the beats in the music, but until then, you can use markers to make a close approximation.

Play back the music clip, rest your finger above $\boxed{\cdot}$, and tap along with the beat. If your rhythm is poor, you may need to delete all the markers ($\boxed{\text{Ctrl}}$-$\boxed{\cdot}$) once or twice, but eventually your markers will hit right on the beat. Now, drop this clip into your sequence and voilà! You've got automatic snap points to help you decide where to make your edits (**Figure 5.27**).

Figure 5.27 By tapping $\boxed{\cdot}$ in time to the music, you can add markers on every beat. These are helpful when you are trying to make your cuts to the beat of a song. Remember, every marker is a snap point you can use to align your edits.

Interacting with Other Applications

Just in case I haven't yet convinced you that Markers are one of the best resources in your Final Cut toolbox, there's one more thing. Final Cut Pro 4 allows you to use markers as a way of communicating between applications. You can apply special tags to your markers that will remain with your clips after you export them. You make a marker exportable by clicking the appropriate button in the Marker Settings dialog box (**Figure 5.28**).

Figure 5.28 Make your markers special so they can be read by other applications.

Chapter Markers

DVD Studio Pro (and some other DVD authoring packages) can read Final Cut Chapter Markers. When you play back the DVD you can automatically skip between these points in your movie. Adding these in Final Cut is infinitely easier than trying to do it in DVD Studio Pro, especially for a long program.

Compression Markers

When preparing your movie for alternate formats for the Web or DVD, there may be certain points where your compression software can use a little help. To better understand this, you'll have to tolerate a little techno babble about how compression works. Among other ways of shrinking your file's size, the compressor stores whole frames only when absolutely necessary. It takes significantly less space to say, "Frame 2 is the same as frame 1 except for this," and "Frame 3 is the same as Frame 1 except for this other thing," and so on. When a certain percentage of the frame is different, a new keyframe is set and the process begins again. If there are too many keyframes, the file size can get too large, and if there are too few keyframes, the picture can get muddy or distorted during the long sections between keyframes.

Final Cut Pro automatically exports an invisible compression marker at every edit point. This gives the compressor a tip for a good place to add a keyframe. But sometimes you want to force a new keyframe even if the compression software doesn't automatically think it's necessary. For example, when you have a title appear on screen, it may only be affecting a small percentage of the overall frame, so the compressor might not deem to add a new keyframe. But you want to ensure that your text is as crisp and legible as possible, so this is a good place to add a special Compression Marker using Final Cut Pro's marker controls. That way, the compressor knows to automatically generate a new keyframe at that point, and voilá: Crisp sharp text, even in a heavily compressed web movie.

Scoring Markers

Scoring Markers are special language that Final Cut Pro uses to communicate with Soundtrack, the music composition software bundled with Final Cut Pro 4. Scoring Markers are helpful when you want to identify a special moment in your sequence that will affect your score. For example if there is a precise moment of tension when a character discovers a friend's betrayal, or you want to have a sound cue occur as a chart appears on the screen, set a scoring marker. This marker will appear in your Soundtrack timeline so you can introduce the cello track at just the right moment.

Don't Forget to Include Them

These cross-application markers will only exist outside of Final Cut Pro if you explicitly include them when exporting your movie. In the Export QuickTime Movie (in Final Cut Pro) or Export Movie (in Final Cut Express) dialog boxes, you can choose which types of markers to include (**Figure 5.29**).

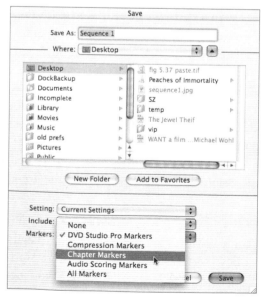

Figure 5.29 Add compression markers for Compressor, Scoring markers for Soundtrack, and Chapter markers for DVD Studio Pro.

For some reason, you are not allowed to export more than one type of marker unless you export all of them. The main disadvantage to adding extra markers is that when watching your movie in QuickTime Viewer, the markers appear as text on top of the video. Another drawback is that other software may not know what to make of the extra data in the file and act unexpectedly.

BUILDING SEQUENCES

Assembling clips into sequences is the most primal act of editing—and Final Cut provides nearly 20 ways to do it. While this might seem overwhelming, once you understand when to use each method (and which ones to forget altogether), this level of versatility will prove invaluable.

Final Cut is a *source/record* style editor. Clips to be edited are "loaded" into the Viewer the way traditional tapes were loaded into a source deck to be played back. Then, bit by bit, sections of the clips are copied from the Viewer to the Canvas (Final Cut's version of the record deck).

Just as with the tape-based systems, Final Cut is nondestructive. On the old systems, content was copied from the source tapes to the master, leaving the source tapes unmodified. Similarly, in Final Cut, the clips you load into the Viewer are not modified when you copy them into the Canvas.

Three-Point Editing

Before I take you too deeply into the nuances of different types of edits, and when you should choose one over another, I need to discuss the nature of *three-point editing*.

Every edit you make has four points (**Figure 5.30**):

- The starting point of the source clip (the Viewer In point).
- The ending point of the source clip (the Viewer Out point).
- Where the clip will begin in the sequence (the Canvas In point).
- Where the clip will end in the sequence (the Canvas Out point).

If you supply three of the four points, the computer can figure out the fourth. (No rocket science required: If a clip starts at 0:00 and ends at 4:00, it's four seconds long—and no matter where you drop it into the sequence, it's still going to last four seconds. Therefore, if you begin it at 5:00 into the sequence, the computer can calculate that it will end at 9:00.)

Figure 5.30 You can set In and Out points in both the Viewer and Canvas windows. The Scrubber area indicates how much media is available outside of the In and Out points.

TIP: If no In or Out point is specified in the sequence, the current playhead position is considered to be the In point. Because of this, if you're laying down clips one after another no In point is required in the sequence.

Which Points Should You Provide?

You will want to choose different sets of three points for different circumstances.

Assembling Clips End to End

If you're assembling a number of clips end to end, as you might for a montage or a rough assembly, you are not going to be too worried about the sequence Out point. You will choose the clips you want to use, set In and Out points in the Viewer, and lay them into the sequence one by one (**Figure 5.31**). The three points you provide will be source In, source Out, and record In.

Figure 5.31 If you're assembling one clip after another, you don't need to worry about In or Out points in the sequence. Each clip will begin where the last one ended by default.

B-roll Editing

After laying down a long clip, such as an interview, you'll probably want to go back and lay in bits of other clips to illustrate what's being said.

Find a section where you want to use a B-roll shot and mark a record In and Out point in the sequence (**Figure 5.32**). Let's say you mark an area five seconds long. When you find the B-roll shot and load it into the Viewer, you need only choose either a source In or a source Out point for the new clip. Either way, Final Cut already knows it's going to be five seconds long. You'll know whether to set the In or the Out depending on the footage. If the narrator is describing how to tie a ristra (an ornamental display of dried chiles) and your B-roll footage shows a man tying one, you may want to find the exact frame where he finishes and holds the ristra up to the camera. If you mark this as your source Out point, the shot will automatically begin five seconds earlier.

Figure 5.32 Set an In and Out point in the sequence where you would like the B-roll shot to appear when you perform your next edit.

If it's more important for the B-roll shot to show how to start the ristra, then, rather than defining the Out point, you should identify the In point and let the computer calculate when the shot should end.

If you must show the entire B-roll shot from beginning to end, from first twist to final knot, you can define both the source In and Out points—but then you'll have to give up one of the record points defined in the Canvas. You cannot stuff a 20-second source clip into a 5-second slot in your sequence. (Unless you speed up the clip, but we'll get to that later. See the section on fit to fill in Chapter 8, "Special Effects").

If you provide all four points, Final Cut Pro will ignore the source Out point.

> **TIP:** If no In or Out point is specified in the source clip, the first frame of the clip will be used as the In point. And if no Out point is specified in the Canvas (so there's no fixed duration), the entire source clip will be used.

Picking the Right Editing Style

When you drag an item to the Canvas, the semi-transparent Edit Overlay appears. It provides targets for the seven different types of available edits (**Figure 5.33**).

Figure 5.33 The Edit Overlay lets you make a decision about which edit type you want to apply *after* you've started dragging your clip.

Overwrite Edits

Most edits you perform will be overwrite edits. This means that the footage you drag to the sequence will replace the shots that were there before, just like pasting text onto a selection in a word processor. Since this is the most common type of edit, if you drag and drop a clip to the Canvas without using the Edit Overlay, the edit type defaults to overwrite. On the old videotape editing systems, all edits were overwrites.

Track Targeting

*If you want to overwrite only the video or just the audio, you must target the tracks to which you want the edit to apply (**Figure 5.34**). The source bud (left side) can be dragged to the destination nub (right side) of your choice (**Figure 5.35**).*

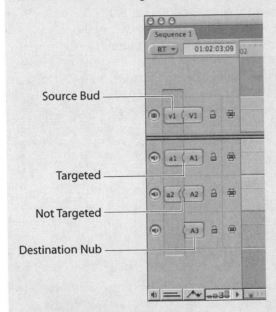

Source Bud

Targeted

Not Targeted

Destination Nub

Figure 5.34 You'll find several important controls at the head of every track in the Timeline. The source targeting controls (Buds and Nubs) determine what source tracks will be edited onto each destination track in your sequence. If a track is not targeted for a given edit, the edit will ignore that track. This is one way of performing an audio-only or a video-only edit. Clicking the Lock control prevents all editing on the locked track. Locking a targeted track serves a similar purpose as turning off targeting, because locked tracks cannot receive edits.

Figure 5.35 In Final Cut Express, and earlier versions of Final Cut Pro, the track targeting looks a little different. Click on the highlighted yellow filmstrip icon or the speaker icon to turn that track off. Turning the video track off will make an audio-only edit and vice-versa.

To perform a video only edit, drag all of the audio source buds away from the destination nubs so that they are disconnected (See figure 5.36 below). Alternately, you can click the Lock icon to lock those tracks, which prevents edits from affecting them.

continues on next page

Track Targeting continued

You can also use track targeting to help arrange your clips on multiple tracks. For example, if you designated timeline tracks A5 and A6 exclusively for sound effects elements, you would target those tracks every time you were about to edit a sound effect into the sequence.

When you have a source clip with more than two audio tracks, each source track is represented by its own targeting bud (**Figure 5.37**). You can drag any source track to any timeline track. For example, imagine a music video project. Before you begin editing, your assistant should have linked the album version of the song in addition to the live recording from the video shoot (For more about how to link multiple audio tracks to a single clip, see "Creating Merged Clips" earlier in this chapter.) This would mean each clip has four audio tracks. When you edit, disregard the targets for the live recording and target Source tracks 3 and 4 into sequence tracks 1 and 2 (**Figure 5.38**).

Figure 5.36 The overwrite edit "writes over" clips where the edit is applied. This is a video-only edit, so the interview can still be heard even while the B-roll image is displayed.

Figure 5.37
Each source track has it's own control bud. These appear and disappear depending on what clip is loaded into the Viewer.

Figure 5.38
Here, source tracks 3 and 4 are the only ones we want to use, so they have been targeted to sequence tracks 1 and 2.

Insert Edits

The second most common edit type is the insert edit. You perform an insert edit by dragging your clip to the Insert target on the Edit Overlay or by pressing F9. An insert edit will *ripple* everything in the sequence forward in time (**Figure 5.39**).

REMEMBER: When you perform an insert edit, your show gets longer.

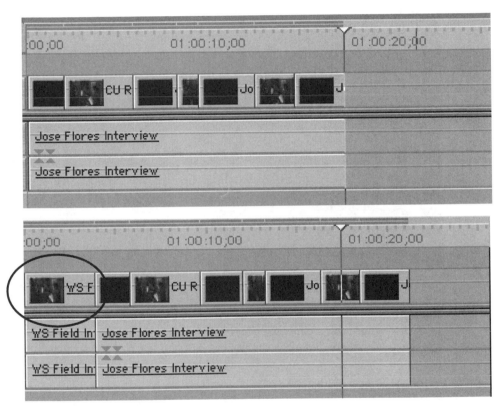

Figure 5.39 The act of pushing all the items in a sequence forward or backward in time to make room for new material is called Rippling. However long the new material is, that duration ripples through the entire sequence like a wave traveling down a rope. Here, a shot was Inserted at the head of the sequence.

Insert edits aren't possible on videotape-based editing systems, since you can't slide the entire contents of a sequence down the length of the videotape. However, when editors are physically cutting film, the insert edit is the only type of edit available. Every time you splice in a new piece of film, the reel gets longer.

Using Insert Edit for Adding a New Opening

The insert is an excellent edit to use when you're adding a clip to the head of a sequence. For instance, if you decide to add an establishing shot in front of shots you've already edited together (as shown in Figure 5.39 above).

Not for Video-Only or Audio-Only Edits

Don't use an insert edit if you plan to do a video-only or audio-only edit. The insert edit can knock clips out of sync *downstream* (**Figure 5.40**). Although Final Cut Pro will alert you that clips are out of sync and provides tools to fix the problem, it's easier to avoid the situation in the first place.

Figure 5.40 Any rippling operation has the potential to knock downstream clips out of sync. Final Cut Pro will usually warn you before allowing you to proceed with operations that will do this. Whenever a clip is out of sync, a bright red Out of Sync indicator appears and tells you how many frames the clip is out of sync. To display options for resolving the problem, Ctrl-click the Out of Sync indicator.

When to Use Overwrite or Insert Edits with Transition

Both the overwrite edit and the insert edit can be performed with an automatic transition effect (such as a dissolve or wipe) built in. Final Cut Pro will apply whatever default transition you have previously selected from the Effects menu.

Although you won't use this function often, in some cases it will be helpful. For instance, it's perfect for building a montage where you want every shot to be mixed together with a 50-frame dissolve.

To use the automatic transition feature, drag each shot onto the Insert or Overwrite with Transition target in the Edit Overlay. If you prefer to use a keyboard shortcut, hold down Shift when pressing the corresponding Function key (Shift-F9 or Shift-F10).

Deleting Clips

Getting clips out of a sequence is just as important as putting them in. You may want to remove a clip or two to shorten a montage sequence that's running too long, or speed up a dialogue scene by getting rid of the last exchange. Or perhaps you want to remove a small section of a clip to create a better continuity cut or slice out a piece of audio or video.

As with everything else in Final Cut Pro, there are many ways to delete clips. The key is knowing when to use which method.

Lift

The lift is the default type of deletion. To execute a lift press Delete. Like an overwrite edit, a lift doesn't change the position of any surrounding clips; it simply removes the selected item and leaves a *gap* in its place. The length of the sequence will not be affected.

I use the Lift command to remove a section of a sequence when I'm not quite sure what to do next. Eventually I'll fill the gap with another clip, or remove it altogether, but lifting a section of the sequence allows me the luxury of delaying that decision.

> **TIP:** Final Cut will let you jump from gap to gap by hitting Shift-G to move to the next gap and Option-G to move to the previous gap.

Lift is also a good way to remove an item from only one track of a particular sequence. For example, when you have a dialog shot where the audio was recorded on channel 2 only, but for some reason it was captured with both audio tracks (see the section on audio shapes in Chapter 7, "Cutting the Track"). When you edit this clip into a sequence, you're carrying around an unnecessary audio track. To delete that single audio track, select it (using Option to temporarily override *linking*) and lift it from the sequence (**Figure 5.41**).

Another common use for the Lift command is to remove a clip on track V2 (such as a lower third graphic) without affecting the clips on the other tracks.

Figure 5.41 To remove a single track of audio, select it and choose Lift from the Sequence menu.

Linked Selection

*Final Cut Pro links clips that should normally remain in sync (such as stereo audio tracks or clips originating from the same file). If you edit a linked clip, the other clips to which it is linked are affected, too. A Timeline state called Linked Selection (**Figure 5.42**) controls whether selecting items in the Timeline observes linking or ignores it. Deactivating Linked Selection makes it easier for clips to get out of sync but permits finer control of individual elements. Whatever the current state,* Shift-L *toggles it and holding down* Option *temporarily overrides it.*

Final Cut Pro 4   Final Cut Express

Figure 5.42 The Linked Selection control lights up green when it is active and dims to gray when it's disabled. The shortcut Shift-L toggles the state.

Ripple Delete

Ripple Delete (in Avid parlance: extract) is the reverse of an insert edit. To execute a ripple delete, type Shift-Delete on the keyboard. This removes the selected elements from the sequence and automatically closes the gap. It's similar to removing a piece of film from a reel and splicing together the remaining pieces; the entire sequence gets shorter. However, Final Cut Pro will not be able to close the gap if edits on another track will be affected (**Figure 5.43**).

Figure 5.43 Ripple Delete will not be able to close gaps if there are clips on other tracks that are in the way. Here, although I deleted the clip from V1, A1, and A2, the edits on A3 and A4 prevented the gap from closing.

I use Ripple Delete when I've got a sequence with several clips stacked end to end and I want to remove one or more of them to shorten the show. In this case—since my intention is to make the program shorter—I know before I start that I intend to close the gap. Ripple Delete is the perfect tool: It deletes the clip, selects the resulting gap, and deletes that, too, all in one step.

Remember that this operation, like all the delete functions, is not limited to clip boundaries. You can delete an area from within a single clip or across the borders of multiple clips. This is perfect for removing passages of dead space in an interview or dialogue sequence.

For example: Recently, I began editing a scene from a Bare Witness project called *Telephone,* and I saw that the dialogue between two characters, Bruce and Rain, was a little redundant:

Rain: I've got this weird condition called hammertoe.

Bruce: Hammertoe? I've never heard of such a thing. Are you making this up?

Rain: No. It's serious, too. I've got to go to Mexico to get it treated. There's a clinic that specializes in holistic medicine. So I need to borrow some money to treat my hammertoe.

Bruce: Are you kidding me? It's called hammertoe? And you need to borrow money from me?

Rain: It's just fifteen hundred dollars...

During production we thought that the more times the actors said "hammertoe" the funnier the scene would be, but in the editing room the repetition seemed to slow the scene down. So I decided to remove the end of Rain's second line and the beginning of Bruce's second line to condense the sequence (**Figure 5.44**).

Figure 5.44 In this scene I wanted to remove the end of clip 3 and the beginning of clip 4, so I set my In and Out points to mark that area.

I set my In and Out points to mark the section I wanted to remove and used the Ripple Delete function to execute the edit (**Figure 5.45**).

Figure 5.45 If nothing is selected, Ripple Delete will apply to the current In and Out points. In one step I eliminated parts of each clip and tightened the scene.

> **TIP:** The In and Out points can be used to identify a particular section of a sequence, but for some operations you may need an actual selection. Convert an area between the In and Out points (called the marked area) to a selection using the Select In to Out control located in the Mark menu, or through the keyboard shortcut Option-A. Do the reverse (convert a selection to an In and Out) via the reverse control: Mark Selection (also under the Mark menu) or by hitting Shift-A.

Ordinarily, when you're dragging items around in the Timeline, Final Cut Pro defaults to selecting whole clips. If you want to select a section of a clip, use the Range Selection tool, which allows you to grab areas not confined by edit points (**Figure 5.46**).

Ripple Delete is best used on simple sequences. When you're working with many tracks, it can become confusing, and you may end up knocking clips out of sync. Still, in straightforward cases it's a handy way to perform several operations in one step.

Figure 5.46 The Range Selection tool allows you to select any area of the Timeline regardless of clip boundaries.

Copy/Paste

Another common type of edit is the cut/copy/paste edit. These familiar commands will work on any selection you make in your Timeline. By default, Cut performs a lift, but it stores the selection on the clipboard until you paste it somewhere else. Paste performs an overwrite edit on the target tracks at the current playhead position.

When would you use Cut and Paste instead of more customized editing tools? Sometimes you know a clip isn't working in its current location, and you want to find a new home for it in the sequence. For instance, say you're doing a show for the History Channel about Galileo, and you've got a great lithograph of a young Galileo with a filter applied. You tried laying it into the introduction, but it just didn't fit—and you aren't sure where it should go. Rather than deleting it, cut it—so it will hang out on the clipboard until you find a new place to put it. Then, when you find that perfect spot, rather than searching for your original clip, just perform a standard Paste (CMD-V) and there it is.

> **TIP:** You can choose to paste clips as an insert edit by pressing Shift-V. This works exactly like a normal paste, but instead of performing an overwrite edit, it does an insert.

Replace, Fit to Fill, Superimpose

Ninety percent of your edits will be a combination of the styles we've just discussed. However, Final Cut Pro offers three other edit types: replace, fit to fill, and superimpose. I'll cover the replace edit in Chapter 6, "Advanced Editing." The other two will be described in Chapter 8, "Special Effects." As a beginner, you should ignore all of them. You will be able to edit successfully using only Overwrite and Insert.

Drag and Drop vs. Keyboard Entry

Any of the edits we've discussed can be performed by dragging a clip onto the Canvas and dropping it onto the corresponding target in the Edit Overlay. You'll also find buttons on the Canvas (**Figure 5.47**) that will perform the corresponding edit on the clip currently in the Viewer—and for every button, there is a keyboard equivalent.

Figure 5.47 Another way to perform edits is by pressing one of the buttons on the Canvas. Holding down the arrow on the third button will bring up a pop-up with the remaining edit styles.

When dragging clips directly into the Timeline, choose between executing an insert or an overwrite edit depending on where you drop the selection. Each Timeline track has a top and a bottom section (**Figure 5.48**). Dropping the clip in the top third will perform an insert edit, and dropping it in the bottom two-thirds will perform an overwrite edit.

Figure 5.48 The top third of the track is for Insert, and when your mouse rolls over this area, the cursor turns into a right-facing arrow indicating that you will be pushing everything downstream. When you roll over the larger bottom section, the cursor turns into a downward-facing arrow, indicating that the edit operation will place the clips right here (Overwrite). The clip highlight also changes from a hollow shadow for Insert to a solid shadow for Overwrite.

I am a big proponent of learning keyboard shortcuts. Repetitive mouse movements can be tiring and even detrimental to your health, but another, equally convincing reason is that it's much faster to hit a key on the keyboard than it is to click on an onscreen object and drag it around. The faster you can work, the more editing will feel like playing a musical instrument—and the less it will feel like filling out a tax form. Now that you know how to customize your keyboard in Final Cut Pro, simplify the memory process by setting your most frequently used commands to your favorite keys.

As a beginner, you can start out applying all of these editing techniques with your mouse. As you discover which tasks you repeat thousands of times, you'll begin to learn the shortcuts that will make your editing experience easier, quicker, and healthier.

Keyboard Shortcuts

Below is a select list of the shortcuts you'll likely use most often (particularly those listed in this chapter), plus a few bonus ones you may find helpful:

PLAYBACK/NAVIGATION

Play Forward	Spacebar or L
Reverse Play	Shift-Spacebar or J
Slow Forward Play	L-K
Slow Backward Play	J-K
Fast Forward Play	LL, LLL, LLLL
Fast Backward Play	JJ, JJJ, JJJJ
Stop/Pause	Spacebar or K
1 Frame Forward	→
1 Second Forward	Shift-→
1 Frame Backward	←
1 Second Backward	Shift-←
Next Edit	↓ or Shift-E
Previous Edit	↑ or Option-E
Go to Beginning of Clip or Sequence	Home
Go to End of Clip or Sequence	End or Shift-Home
Play Around Current Position	\
Play In to Out	Shift-\
Play From Current to Out	Shift-P

SUBCLIPS

Make Subclip	⌘-U
Reveal Master Clip	Shift-F
Match Frame	F

TIMELINE STATES

Snapping Toggle	N
Linked Selection Toggle	Shift-L
Zoom In on Timeline	Option-+
Zoom Out on Timeline	Option-− (minus sign)
Zoom Fit to Window	Shift-Z

MARKING CLIPS

Mark In	⬚I
Mark Out	⬚O
Clear In	⬚Option⬚-⬚I
Clear Out	⬚Option⬚-⬚O
Clear In and Out	⬚Option⬚-⬚X
Go to In	⬚Shift⬚-⬚I
Go to Out	⬚Shift⬚-⬚O
Select In to Out	⬚Option⬚-⬚A
Mark Selection	⬚Shift⬚-⬚A

MARKERS

Set Marker	⬚M or ⬚`
Edit Marker	⬚M or ⬚` (when parked on marker)
Delete Marker	⬚⌘-⬚`
Delete All Markers	⬚Ctrl⬚-⬚`
Reposition Marker	⬚Shift⬚-⬚`
Extend Marker	⬚Option⬚-⬚`
Go to Next Marker	⬚Shift⬚-⬚M
Go to Previous Marker	⬚Option⬚-⬚M

COMMON TOOLS

Arrow/Selection Tool	⬚A
Razor Blade Tool	⬚B
Track Select Tool	⬚T
Range Selection Tool	⬚G⬚G⬚G

TRANSITIONS

Apply Default Transition	⬚⌘-⬚T
Set Alignment to Begin On	⬚Option⬚-⬚1
Set Alignment to Center On	⬚Option⬚-⬚2
Set Alignment to End On	⬚Option⬚-⬚3

PERFORMING COMMON EDITS

Insert Edit	[F9]
Insert Edit With Transition	[Shift]-[F9]
Overwrite Edit	[F10]
Overwrite Edit With Transition	[Shift]-[F10]
Lift	[Delete]
Ripple Delete	[Shift]-[Delete]
Cut	[⌘]-[X]
Copy	[⌘]-[C]
Paste	[⌘]-[V]
Paste Insert	[Shift]-[V]

TIMELINE EDITING

Getting your clips into the sequence isn't the end of the editing process, it's the beginning. Most of your time will be spent fine-tuning the clips and edits in the Timeline. Remember the 80/20 rule: The last 20 percent of the editing process invariably takes 80 percent of the time.

Like everything else, you can manipulate your Timeline clips in countless ways. There is no right or wrong method, and as you gain proficiency in the program, you'll probably experiment with some of the more advanced features.

In this chapter, I'll show you how to do what I call "no-trim editing," an approach in which most of your edits will be done by dragging clips around in the Timeline, using a simplified set of tools and avoiding the complex trim operations that I'll introduce in Chapter 6.

By nature, no-trim editing is slow. If you want to make an adjustment to a particular edit point, such as shortening one clip and lengthening a second, many steps are involved. But, strangely, I like no-trim editing precisely because of its slow nature. Every step is broken up, and it's easy to keep track of exactly what's happening.

Minimizing Your Video Track Count

You can stack up as many as 99 layers of video in a Final Cut Pro Timeline—but it's not always a good idea to do it. In fact, when you're doing basic editing, strive to keep your edits on as few tracks as possible. (The time you'll need all those tracks is when you're doing compositing, where you may want to layer many tracks together to create complex collages.)

> **TIP:** *Final Cut Pro Timeline displays tracks in top-down order, just like the layers in Photoshop. Clips with higher track numbers will obscure clips on lower tracks.*

Ideally, you should put all of your edits on video track 1. This makes it easier to work with transitions (see the section on transitions, later in this chapter) as well as simplifying media-management tasks like recapturing, reconnecting, and working with EDLs.

Swap Edit

One advantage to putting all of your clips on a single track is the swap edit. This edit will rearrange the order of your clips without leaving a gap in the Timeline.

For instance, if you're editing a dialogue sequence, and you want to show an insert of a stolen watch on a player's wrist, your first thought may be to put it right after shot 6, when the opposite player (a cop) mentions the theft (**Figure 5.49**).

Figure 5.49 **The watch insert begins between shots 6 and 7.**

After reviewing the sequence a few times, however, it occurs to you that it will heighten the suspense if the audience is thinking about the stolen watch before the cop mentions it. So you decide to move the insert earlier in time, between shots 4 and 5.

Using the Swap tool makes this operation simple. Select the watch shot and drag it to its new position between shots 4 and 5. Before you drop it, press and hold Option. Notice that the cursor changes to a curved arrow. This is the Swap cursor. When you release the mouse button, the shot will be inserted in that new position, and the gap that would have been left where the shot used to be is automatically closed (**Figure 5.50**).

Figure 5.50 The Swap tool allows you to drag a clip to a different point in the sequence without generating gaps. The Swap tool is activated by hitting Option when dropping the clip.

TIP: Dragging in the Timeline while using Option *has far too many functions associated with it. If you press the key, or let go of it, at the wrong time, you'll get an unexpected result. If you hold down* Option *before you select something, it overrides the current linked selection state. Once the selection is made, you can let go of* Option. *If you begin dragging a clip with* Option *down, you create a copy of that item instead of moving the original item. Finally, if you hold down* Option *right before releasing the mouse button, it will force an insert edit (as opposed to overwrite). Or in the case above, it will perform a swap edit.*

Editing on Two Tracks

There are exceptions to the one-video-track rule. Some editors find it easier to "read" the Timeline if they alternate clips in checkerboard fashion between video tracks 1 and 2 (**Figure 5.51**). This allows you to see that each clip has more media available beyond the In and Out point. However, sometimes it's hard to find the exact edit point.

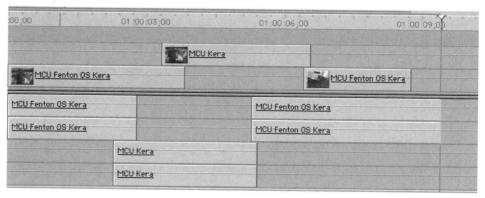

Figure 5.51 When you use multiple tracks, the visual representation of the clips' overlap can be useful.

Another benefit of placing alternating clips on multiple tracks is that it lets you try out a second shot, such as a cutaway, without committing yourself to chopping up the main clip (**Figure 5.52**). If you don't like the positioning of the shot, move it back and forth on V2 until you're happy with its placement.

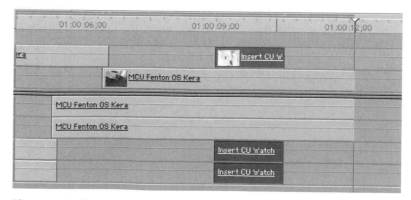

Figure 5.52 You can put a cutaway on V2 and move it around to decide the proper placement without having to modify the underlying clip.

Using the Razor Blade Tool

Beginning editors seem to take an immediate liking to the Razor Blade tool, which splits a clip into two pieces. For instance, you might use the tool to cut a hole in a clip on track 2 to let a clip on track 1 show through (**Figure 5.53**).

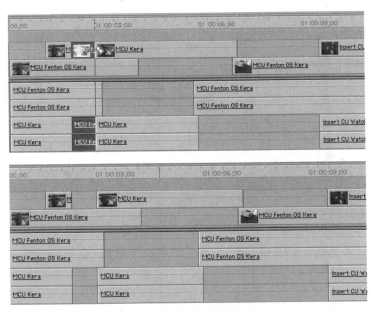

Figure 5.53 Using the Razor Blade tool, you can remove an area from V2 to allow clips on V1 to show through. This is a way of creating two edits (from V2 to V1, and then back from V1 to V2) at one time.

Assume you're cutting a dialogue scene and you want to trim a little space at the end of the first clip to tighten up the edit (**Figure 5.54**).

Figure 5.54 Making a simple edit in the no-trim model can take several steps. Here's the starting point. In this example, we want to shorten MCU Kera.

1. Select the Razor Blade tool by clicking on the Tool palette or hitting B on the keyboard.

2. Place the cursor over the end of clip 1 and click to break clip 1 into two pieces (**Figure 5.55**).

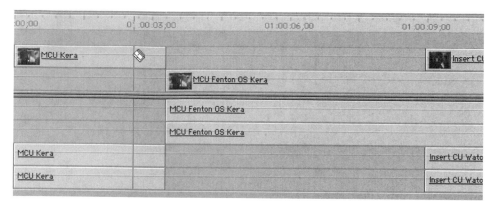

Figure 5.55 Start by using the Razor Blade tool to split the MCU Kera clip into two pieces.

3. Change back to the Arrow tool (click on the Tool palette or type A on the keyboard).

4. Select the chopped piece of clip 1 and lift it by hitting Delete (**Figure 5.56**).

5. Select clip 2 and drag it upstream until it lines up with clip 1 (**Figure 5.57**).

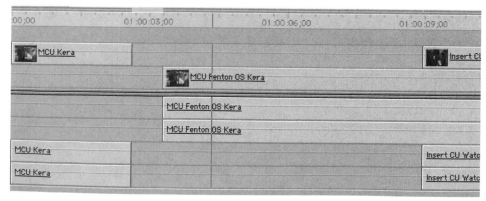

Figure 5.56 By selecting the trimmed section and then lifting it, we leave a gap that will show up as a black section of video and silent audio.

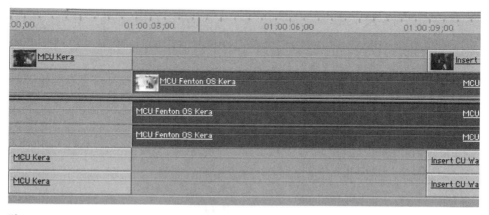

Figure 5.57 Finally, we select the second clip (MCU Fenton OS Kera) and drag it left until it aligns with the new Out point of MCU Kera.

Resizing by Dragging

Instead of using the Razor Blade tool, you could grab the edge of clip 1 and drag it to shorten it. When you grab a clip edge to change its duration, your cursor changes to the Resize tool (**Figure 5.58**). It's tempting to drag clip edges to resize them, since it's so fast and easy, but it's not a very precise way to work.

Also, remember that you should try to make as many editing decisions as possible while playing the sequence. If you want to use the Resize tool to change a clip's length, first play through the sequence and identify the new edit point with a marker. Then use the Resize tool to drag one of the clip edges toward that specific location.

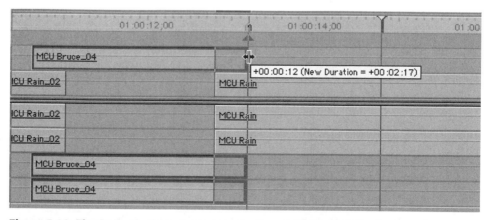

Figure 5.58 The Resize tool appears when you drag the edges of clips in the Timeline to change their duration. Use a marker as a snapping guide when resizing a clip.

Select Track Tools

Another set of tools you'll find handy when working with clips on multiple tracks is the Select Track tools (**Figure 5.59**). They allow you to select all clips on a single track downstream from the current playhead position, all clips upstream, or all clips on multiple tracks. If, in the dialogue example discussed earlier, there were several clips beyond clip 2, dragging clip 2 upstream to align it with the new ending of clip 1 would leave a gap after clip 2 (**Figure 5.60**). If instead you selected all clips downstream by using the Select Track Forward tool, when you dragged them to the left, no gap would remain (**Figure 5.61**).

Figure 5.59 The Select Track tools are extremely helpful in the no-trim model. Once a track is selected, you can add tracks to the selection by holding ⌈Shift⌋.

Figure 5.60 If only one clip at a time is moved, it can leave a gap later in the sequence.

Figure 5.61 The Select Track tool enables you to select all the clips forward and move them all at once. This way you eliminate any gaps.

Editing on the Fast Track

The disadvantage to the no-trim model is that besides requiring many steps, it is not precise. It's easy to leave gaps when you are dragging clips around in the Timeline. This produces little black flashes or moments of silence between your edits. The Snapping control helps to prevent this, but it is still common to create such errors when working this way.

Of course, once you learn some of Final Cut Pro's advanced tools, you can perform these same operations in fewer steps. For example, if the clips in the previous example were on one track instead of two, you could break clip 1 in two with the Razor Blade tool, and ripple-delete the extra piece (**Figure 5.62**). And the Ripple tool can perform that same edit in only one step (see the section on the ripple edit in Chapter 6).

Figure 5.62 When all the clips are on one track, you can perform more complex operations with fewer steps.

TRANSITIONS

Every edit point is a transition from one shot to another, so you can think of every cut as a transition. If you want to create a special transition, such as a dissolve or a wipe, you must apply it to the edit point as an effect.

Transitions can be applied in a number of ways. If you like to drag and drop, you can select a transition from the Effects tab in the Browser (**Figure 5.63**) and drag it to any edit point in your Timeline (**Figure 5.64**). If you're parked on an edit point, you can also drag and drop the effect onto the Canvas. Alternately, you can use the Effects menu and choose an effect from the Video Transitions submenu. The Effects menu and the Effects tab in the Browser are duplicates of one another. If you add or modify something in the Browser tab, it will be reflected in the menu.

Figure 5.63 The Effects tab in the Browser lists all the effects available to you.

Figure 5.64 Drag a transition from the Effects tab to the Timeline and drop it on an edit point. You can also drag directly to the Canvas if the playhead is parked on an edit point.

A video transition from the Effects menu can be applied only when you are parked on an edit point. Otherwise, the effect names will be grayed out. Transitions can only be applied to clips that are on the same track. If you're editing in the checker-board pattern described earlier and you want to add a transition effect, you will first need to put the two clips together on the same track (**Figure 5.65**).

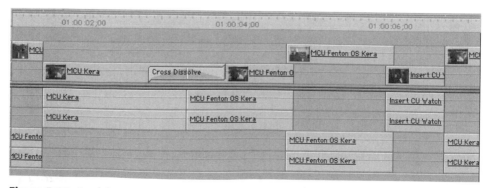

Figure 5.65 Applying a transition requires both clips to be on the same track. Even if you prefer to alternate clips between V1 and V2, when it comes time to add transitions, you'll need to move them onto the same track.

Transitions can be applied from the keyboard by pressing ⌘-T. This will apply the default transition to the edit point at the current playhead position. The default transition can be set by highlighting a transition in the Effects tab of the Browser and choosing Set Default from the Effects menu.

Finally, the shortcut menu for each edit point (accessed by Ctrl-clicking on the edit point) will offer you the option of applying the default transition. I find this shortcut especially helpful for applying audio transitions.

Make Sure You Have Enough Room

*Transitions take place over time, so check to ensure that you've got adequate elbowroom to apply the transition. All transitions default to one second in length. That means that there must be at least half a second of extra footage on either side of the edit point, in both shots, to accommodate the effect (**Figure 5.66**). Once a transition is applied, you can change the duration of the effect either by dragging one edge of the Effect icon (**Figure 5.67**) or via the Shortcut menu (**Figure 5.68**). You are only able to extend the duration to the length of extra frames available in both of the underlying clips.*

Figure 5.66 Every transition requires adequate "extra" media on both sides of the edit point in both clips to cover the entire duration of the effect. And those frames need to be free of obvious mistakes, such as a slate or a shaky camera move.

Figure 5.67 Transitions extend equally on both sides of the cut and require additional frames from both clips. You can extend the length of a transition by dragging one edge of it.

Figure 5.68 You can enter a duration for your transition numerically by selecting Duration from the Shortcut menu. To access the Shortcut menu, Ctrl-click the Transition icon.

Deciding Where Transitions Begin and End

There is a cut hiding underneath every transition, and that cut can fall in one of three places:

- At the beginning of the transition.

- At the center of the transition.

- At the end of the transition.

This is important to understand because it affects how the clips move around if you change the duration of the transition or if you trim the edit point underneath the transition.

Final Cut Pro's Transition icons give graphic feedback to indicate in which of the three locations the actual cut lies (**Figure 5.69**). You can choose which type to apply when you drag a transition from the Effects tab to the Timeline. The transition will snap to these three points, suggesting where to drop it. After you drop it, change the alignment via the Shortcut menu for the transition, or from the Transition Alignment submenu of the Sequence menu.

Figure 5.69 Transition icons show you whether they're set to begin on, center on, or end on the edit point. This state can be changed via the Shortcut menu.

If you have a centered transition and you change its duration from one second to two seconds, the transition will extend equally into both clips (as seen in Figure 5.69). In the case of a transition that ends on the cut, the transition will extend upstream only into the preceding clip. You still need to have an additional second of media in the second clip, but the new frames needed from the first clip are already there, so you don't have to worry about running out of media (**Figure 5.70**).

Once you understand this concept, it can suggest how to use a transition when you don't have enough room in one of the clips. It will also help you construct well-composed dissolves as recommended in Chapter 2.

For example, in a music video I cut for Steve Lucky and the Rhumba Bums, there was a lap dissolve between the guitarist onstage and the dancers swinging on the dance floor. The clip of the dancers I wanted to use started at the beginning of the shot, so I didn't have any extra frames before the action to accommodate the dissolve (**Figure 5.71**).

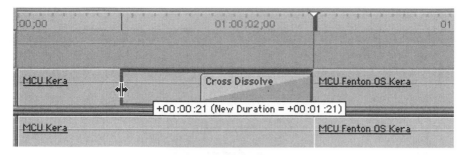

Figure 5.70 When you extend an end-on transition, it extends only in one direction.

Figure 5.71 In this shot of the dancers, I set my In point very close to the beginning of the media, as you can see in the Scrubber area.

I wanted to line up the movement of the guitarist (who was bopping up and down as she played) with the beat of the dancers on the floor to make the dissolve match nicely.

First I made a *straight edit* lining up the guitarist's movement with those of the dancers (**Figure 5.72**). Then I dragged a one-second dissolve onto the edit and set it as a begin-on edit (**Figure 5.73**). This set the effect to begin on the edit point and extend into the clip of the dancers. I wasn't sure exactly how long I wanted the transition to last, so I dragged the edge of the transition downstream into the dancers clip, extending it by ten frames (**Figure 5.74**). Since there was plenty of room in the guitarist clip, I could comfortably extend it—even though there were no spare frames at the start of the dancers clip. I was adding frames only to the transition *after* the edit point.

Figure 5.72 First I create a cut between the guitar shot and the dancers shot. Then I move the edit point to a place that reinforces the continuity of the music's rhythm.

Figure 5.73 When I apply the transition, I set it to begin on the edit point. That way no additional frames are needed before the In point of the dancers shot.

Figure 5.74 As I extend the transition, it moves only to the right (downstream), adding more frames from the guitar shot. Since my edit point was timed correctly, the guitarist's bopping will line up with the dancers' movements throughout the dissolve.

Changing Effect Parameters

Use the Transition Editor to change the parameters of an effect that has options—such as the number of bands in a band wipe, or the center point of an iris (**Figure 5.75**). Double-click the Transition icon in the Timeline to open the Transition Editor. You'll also find controls that let you adjust the start and end point of the transition and reverse the direction of the effect.

You can see that there aren't many spare frames in the second clip.

This unassuming widget allows you to reverse the direction of the transition.

Name of effect

Alignment (set here to Begin On)

These controls enable you to set the starting and ending percentage of the effect. If you set this to start at 50 percent, the iris effect will begin half open.

Figure 5.75 The Transition Editor gives you a view of the transition in which you can see how the clips overlap and view the transition as a separate element. You can also set parameter controls like a border or the center point of this Oval Iris effect.

For example, you could set the iris wipe to begin one-third open by adjusting the starting percentage control. Or by using the Reverse control, you can create an effect in which the transition starts as a point and expands to fill the screen. (Ordinarily, an iris begins full screen and reduces to a point.) The Transition Editor can also be used to trim the contents of the clips underneath the transition (see the section on trimming under transitions in Chapter 6).

More Than Just Dissolves

Any transition other than a basic cross-dissolve draws attention to itself and will usually disrupt the narrative flow. But if your goal is to wake up your audience from the movie dream, by all means use some of the wackier effects.

For example, suppose you're making an educational video about bicycle safety that includes a mix of dramatic scenes, graphic charts, and narration. It's often a great idea to use a wipe or some other flashy effect to highlight the transitions in the dramatic sections, because it lets the viewer know he should disengage from the story and prepare to view a different type of information.

Which type of effect should you choose? Think compositionally. In this case I'd look for a wipe effect that resembled the shape of a bicycle, or maybe a clock wipe that simulates a rolling bicycle wheel. Possibly I would find something suited to the particular images onscreen at the time of the effect. For instance, if the final shot of the dramatic sequence was a bicyclist cruising down a road and vanishing into the distance, I'd amplify the effect by applying a zoom transition where the video image starts moving towards the vanishing point (**Figure 5.76**).

One warning, though: As with fonts on a poster, it's best if you limit yourself to one or two effects and use them consistently throughout your show. Mixing dozens of effects dilutes the impact of any one of them. Also, flashy transitions are similar to exclamation points! If every sentence ends with an exclamation point, no one can understand which bits are more important than others! The more sparingly you use effects like these, the more powerful they will be.

Figure 5.76 This zoom effect complements the footage of the biker riding off into the distance. I use it here to transition from the dramatic section of the video to a title card describing safety rules. During the dramatic section, all the edits were cuts.

Different Types of Dissolves

Even among basic dissolves you've got a lot to choose from (**Figure 5.77**). Your basic cross-dissolve will have highly varied effects depending upon how long it lasts (**Figure 5.78**).

Also, try alternatives, such as an additive dissolve that adds the numerical color values of the images together, making bright areas that overlap become white. This works well for shorter transitions (less than a half second) and creates an organic bright flash effect, but it may look decidedly inorganic on some images. Alternately, try a non-additive dissolve, which has the effect of dissolving the brighter areas of the frame before the darker areas (**Figure 5.79**). Both additive and non-additive dissolves are highly dependent on the specific composition of the shots being dissolved.

Figure 5.77 Final Cut Pro has many dissolves to choose from.

Figure 5.78 This image shows a normal cross-dissolve.

Figure 5.79 These images show an additive dissolve (left) and a non-additive dissolve (right). The results vary widely depending on the lightness and darkness values of the images being mixed.

Another dissolve to try is a dip-to-color, in which, instead of the two images being cross-dissolved together, the first image fades out before the second one fades in. This allows you to create the common dip-to-black scene change with a single effect, rather than fading out one image and fading in the second with two effects.

NOTE: The default one-second duration is usually too quick for the dip-to-color effect, since it results in a half-second fade-out and a half-second fade-in.

Also, try experimenting with changing the color that's dipped to from the default black. Changing it to white is a nice way to create white flashes between shots (sometimes employed to simulate a flash camera going off, or for dramatic psychological impact). In this case, you're better off shortening the transition so the white frames look more like flashes than gradual lightening of the frame.

Choose any color you like to dip to—maybe blood red for a vampire thriller or the royal blue of your favorite corporate logo. If you are going to fade to a color other than black or white, try to pick a color that exists in the outgoing shot. If your subject is standing in front of a green chalkboard, and you set up the dissolve to dip to that exact color, it will make for a much more organic effect than if you choose a color that doesn't exist anywhere in the frame. (Final Cut Pro provides an Eyedropper control that lets you pick a color from your video image.)

Custom Transitions

By default, all transitions in Final Cut are one second long. This is a good length for many occasions, but some effects and some situations may require you to modify this default. Once you apply a transition, you can change the duration by dragging the edge of the transition, using the Shortcut menu, or opening the Transition Editor.

If you want to change the duration of the transition *before* you apply the effect, it's a little trickier. To do this you need to create a copy of the transition and place it in the Favorites folder (**Figure 5.80**).

Figure 5.80 The Favorites folder is where you store any custom transitions that you create. These will stick around across editing sessions.

Suppose you want to make a soft cut transition that will be a five-frame dissolve. First drag the cross-dissolve transition into the Favorites folder, thereby making a copy of it (**Figure 5.81**). Now, modify the Length column and set the value to be 00:00:00:05. Then rename the effect "Soft Cut" (**Figure 5.82**). This effect is now available to you whenever you want it from the Favorites section of the Effects menu (**Figure 5.83**). This can be done with as many effects as you wish, and you can change much more than the length of the effect. Any parameter of the effect can be modified and stored as a favorite. Go ahead and create a Venetian blind wipe with ten bands, or a star iris with seven points and a three-pixel purple border.

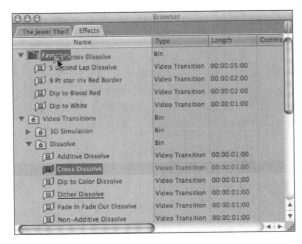

Figure 5.81 Create a new favorite by dragging a transition from another bin in the Effects window. You can also drag a transition from the Timeline to the Favorites bin.

Figure 5.82 Make any changes you wish to the effect in the Favorites folder. Change its duration, change its name, or change parameters in the Transition Editor. All the changes will be saved with the item in the Favorites bin.

Figure 5.83 Any effects you move to the Favorites bin will also show up in the Favorites submenu of the Effects menu.

Making a Custom Default Transition

One of these effects can even be designated as your default transition if you like—which makes it the effect applied automatically when you choose Overwrite with Transition or use the ⌘-T shortcut. The factory default transition is a one-second cross-dissolve. But you can set any effect as your default by selecting the icon in the Browser and choosing Set Default from the Effects menu. If you were doing a nature montage where all the transitions were two-second non-additive dissolves, you could make that your default. Then, rather than having to wade through the submenus to get to the effect you use all the time, it would be available instantly from the keyboard shortcut.

Making a Custom Transition Button

The button bars at the top of each window in Final Cut Pro can hold more than tools and menu commands. You can add buttons for your favorite effects such as transitions. This can be especially helpful if you regularly use more than one type of transition. For example, let's say you edit wedding videos and you have created a set of custom heart shaped wipes. One is fast and has a glowing red border, another is slow and appears to fade from the center point, and there are several others. Buttons can be put into your timeline for each transition. You can then apply them by clicking the appropriate button when you are parked on an edit point.

First create the custom transitions by adding them to your Favorites folder and modifying the parameters (**Figure 5.84**). You are only allowed nine buttons for transitions (as well as nine each for filters, audio transitions, and so forth). You may have to rename the transitions to ensure your desired ones are in the first nine alphabetically. Once you have your transitions set up, open the Button List window from the Tools menu and expand the Favorites section (**Figure 5.85**). Drag the corresponding item from the Button List to the Button Bar in the timeline or any other window. You now have instant access (**Figure 5.86**).

Figure 5.84 Only effects in the favorites folder can be used as buttons in the button bar. Note that any effect in Boldface will not require rendering.

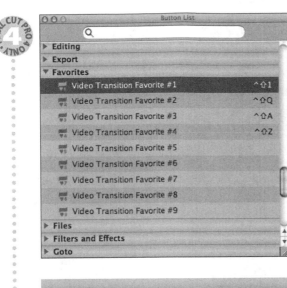

Figure 5.85 The favorites section of the Button List gives you access to the first nine favorite effects in each category.

Figure 5.86 Use spacers and colors, which are accessible in the shortcut menu, to help identify effects.

Transitions as Fades

Transitions can be applied to the beginning or end of a sequence, creating the effect of transitioning to or from black (**Figure 5.87**). This is a quick and easy way to perform a fade-out or fade-in. As with any transition, if you apply it at the default center-on position, you are using frames from the clip that were previously hidden (before the In point or after the Out point). I recommend setting the Out point of the clip to be the very last frame you want seen (as it will have nearly faded out) and applying the transition at the end-on position. (Reverse the process for a fade-in.)

Effects applied to clips on Timeline tracks V2 or higher create a transition between the clip and transparency rather than to black. This means if you're working in the no-trim model with two clips stacked up at the end of your sequence, and you apply a cross-dissolve to the clip on V2 to create a fade-out effect (**Figure 5.88**), you're going to be revealing the clip on V1 as the effect progresses.

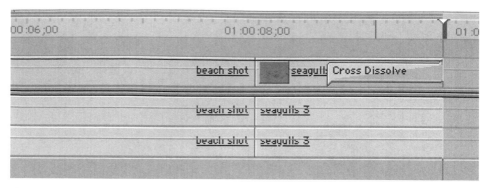

Figure 5.87 A dissolve applied to a clip at the end of a sequence is the same as a fade-out.

Figure 5.88 Applying an effect to a clip on a track above V1 will dissolve to transparent (not black). This means that if a clip exists on a lower track, it will show through as the clip above becomes transparent. Sometimes this is desirable; other times it may not be.

If you line up everything properly, this is another way to create a dissolve between two clips, but it's less precise than doing it as instructed at the beginning of the section on transitions—and with many effects (such as pushes, stretches, or slides), the second clip won't move along with the effect as intended.

Still, this does present interesting opportunities. You could create multiple transitions on multiple tracks that would all combine to create a whacked-out visual layering effect. Or, more likely, a big visual mess. Final Cut places few limitations on what you can or cannot do, but just because something is possible doesn't mean you need to do it. In most cases, simple is elegant and elegant is better.

Let the content of your film speak to the audience without bombarding them with elements that distract them from that content. You can't save a show by adding too many effects.

INTERVIEW

Valdís Óskarsdóttir is an Icelandic film editor who's been responsible for editing many of the Dogme 95 films, beginning with *The Celebration*. She also cut Harmony Korine's Dogme-like *Julien Donkey-Boy*, and brought that same sense of immediacy to Gus Van Sant's *Finding Forrester*. In 2003 she cut Thomas Vinterberg's *It's All About Love* with Sean Penn and Claire Danes, *The Eternal Sunshine of the Spotless Mind* (written by Charlie Kaufman and starring Jim Carey and Kate Winslet), and the Sweedish film *Skagerrak* (*Sweet Dreams*).

MICHAEL WOHL: WHAT HAPPENS AFTER YOU FINISH YOUR FIRST CUT?

Valdís Óskarsdóttir: After the first cut, you start all over again. You watch the film, and usually the director gets depressed. I think I've never met any director who doesn't get kind of depressed or disappointed at that stage.

SO WHAT DO YOU DO?

You go home and watch TV, or you go and see a movie, or whatever. And then you come back, and you watch some scenes, and maybe there's a shot in there that you liked so much, and you know deep inside that you have to take it out, but you just have to keep it as long as you possibly can. It might take you five weeks to throw it out, but once you get a week off, you come back to the computer and say, "Eeek, what was I thinking about?"

HOW DO YOU KNOW THE BEST WAY TO TELL THE STORY?

I don't know. I watch the tape before I go home in the evening, and then when I get back in the morning, I have it. I always have the feeling that the film itself, it is itself. It's your job to find that. And I don't think you can force things on stuff that isn't there. You always have to be true to your characters, to the story, and to the film. Those are the three obligations that you have.

DO YOU TAKE A DIFFERENT APPROACH TO WORKING ON SOMETHING LIKE *THE CELEBRATION* THAN YOU TAKE WHEN WORKING ON A FILM LIKE *FINDING FORRESTER*?

It makes no difference if it's DV or film. You do always the same stuff. You watch the film or you watch the scene and then you start editing.

DO YOU THINK AT ALL ABOUT THE AUDIENCE? DO YOU THINK THAT YOU HAVE TO DO ANYTHING DIFFERENTLY FOR AN AMERICAN AUDIENCE?

No. I always think of the film. Is the story clear? Do we repeat something too much? Is this too much or is this too little? Never think of the audience. I think it's like writing a book. I don't think writers think of the people that are going to read the book while they are writing. I think that they are just telling a story. And this is the same thing. It's just visual storytelling.

DO YOU DO SCREENINGS? IN HOLLYWOOD, THEY'LL SCREEN FILMS AGAIN AND AGAIN FOR AUDIENCES.

Not like test screenings you do in America, but we have small screenings. I had a screening tonight. It was just me and my son. I've never seen a screening with so few people. It was great. We just sat there and talked about the film while we were watching it and that was nice. It can be the producers, the writers, the composer, the soundman, and then some friends—because you need someone who can say some nice things.

WHAT WAS IT LIKE WORKING ON *THE CELEBRATION*?

Well, with all the camera movements and everything, it was like playing because I could do whatever I wanted to do. There was no one who could come and say, "You can't do that. That's not allowed," or, "You can't cross the line, because people will get confused." We had 56 hours of material, and sometimes they had two, three, even four cameras on the same scene. And we had to put everything in order. So, after working for three weeks, we realized that if we were going to sit together and watch all the takes we would never finish the film. So we got a big room, and [director] Thomas [Vinterberg] would sit on the sofa with headphones and watch the raw material, and he'd write down which takes to use, and I was sitting at the computer and editing. It was kind of fun because if he had some doubts about something he could ask me, and if I had a question I could ask him.

HAVE YOU EVER WORKED ON SOMETHING WHERE YOU DIDN'T LIKE THE CHARACTERS?

Yes.

WHAT DID YOU DO THEN?

I did as well as I could with the material that I had. It's mostly if I see bad acting.

HAVE YOU EVER SAT IN FRONT OF A SCENE AND SAID "I DON'T KNOW WHAT TO DO. HOW CAN I POSSIBLY CUT THIS?"

Lots of times. Sometimes it happens day after day after day. Sometimes I think "I don't know what to do with this." And sometimes I think "I don't know what they mean by this" or "I can't do that, I don't know how to put this together, I will never make it. Maybe I should find some other job."

THEN WHAT HAPPENS?

Sometimes I take day off, or two days, or a long weekend, and figure out if I should just give up, you know? Sometimes you also watch the scene you've been editing and know that there's a similar dialogue scene and you think, "OK, again, what can I do different from what I did last time?" And that's what was so great with *The Celebration.* I thought it was like play. It was fun, because I could do whatever I wanted to do. There was no one who could come and say, "You can't do that. That's not allowed" or "You can't cross the line, because people will get confused."

THAT DIDN'T MATTER?

No, I think that you can always go over the line, but you have to be sure that you are not confusing people. And you don't have to take notice of any rules. You just use the material that you have.

BUT DON'T YOU THINK THAT IT WILL CONFUSE THE AUDIENCE IF YOU START BREAKING THOSE RULES?

No, I think people today, all audiences today, are getting so used to fast editing by watching MTV and all the TV series. They have very fast edits, and I think people getting used to it. And you can always cross the line and not confuse the people. It's just a matter of how you do it. If you want to confuse them, then you can do it. But if you want to cross the line and not confuse the people, then you can do that as well.

WHAT INFLUENCES YOUR EDITING STYLE?

I learn something new with each film I edit. But I'm just as affected by what's outside—all the movies and music and books that I've read and paintings I've seen. I take all of that with me into the editing room and use it.

DO YOU HAVE ANY ADVICE FOR YOUNG EDITORS JUST GETTING STARTED IN THIS FIELD?

Well, I think that if you want to become an editor, you have to be very patient, because you have to do things over and over and over and over again. You always have to look and say, "OK, what's wrong here?" Even though there's nothing wrong, ask yourself, "Can I do it faster? Can I do it a little bit better than this?" Also, always push your limits. I know that it's very hard to get into the business in the States. You have to be an assistant for many years before you can do something.

CERTAINLY IN HOLLYWOOD.

I think in New York as well. If you know someone is looking for an editor and can't pay you, if you can afford to, say "Yes." Work for nothing, because the experience is so important.

HOW DID YOU GET STARTED?

In Iceland, in those days, there was very little filmmaking and I didn't know anything about editing. I wanted to be an editor, but I haven't the faintest idea where I got it from. I worked as a photographer for many, many years and then I made radio programs, with music and dialogue and interviews. I went to a film school in Stockholm called the Dramatist Institute for two months and we did everything. We shot and took sound and acted and edited, and after those two months I decided there was something in life that I wanted to do. I remember my teacher at the school, when we had finished our last five-minute film, he asked me, "How many years have you been editing?" And I said, "I've never edited anything." And he didn't believe me. I told him that I used my eyes. I listened to music and then I used my eyes, and then I closed my eyes when I was cutting and opened them again. That's how I trained myself on editing.

CHAPTER SIX

Advanced Editing

I previously likened film editing to solving a jigsaw puzzle, but a more accurate analogy might be playing a chess game in which every move is an edit point. You have dozens of possible choices, but the one you pick will affect all the decisions available from that moment onward. As you consider each move, you have to play out the consequent scenario at least a few moves ahead in order to make the best choice. And at all times, you must be able to take in the whole board to keep track of the big picture.

Fortunately, in editing, you have no opponent (except time, or perhaps your producer). Furthermore, Final Cut Pro provides you with up to 99 undos, so you can try out an idea and let it play for a few steps before you're stuck with it. And since Final Cut is nondestructive, you can even save different versions of your sequences (or your entire show) and let the director make the final choice.

IN THE GROOVE

Once you find the heart of the scene, the edits flow like a surging stream of water. You're swept up by the current of the action, and your hands can hardly keep up with your ideas. These magical moments are what editors live for. When you're in that groove, you want to be able to work as quickly as possible—and Final Cut Pro is endowed with advanced tools to enable that seemingly effortless workflow.

Sure, you can use Final Cut to create successful pieces without understanding more than a few of its capabilities. But the longer you work with it, the more familiar it becomes, and the more you learn how to take advantage of some of its esoteric features. This chapter is just a sampling of Final Cut's advanced capabilities—and how professional editors make use of them.

TRIMMING

The no-trim method I explained in the last chapter works fine to get your scenes assembled, but it's too slow to accommodate the rapid-fire, high- powered editing that I just described. The trimming tools are the key to fast editing. They enable you to control both sides of one edit point at the same time, or even modify two or more edits at once. And working fast is not only efficient, it's exhilarating.

Some editors define trimming as anything done to your sequence after the initial clips have been laid down. While that's an accurate definition, under its terms, plenty of the slowpoke techniques I described in Chapter 5, "Basic Editing," would qualify as trimming. For our purposes, I'll refine the meaning to refer specifically to the advanced techniques experienced editors use to edit quickly and confidently with Final Cut Pro's trim tools: *Roll, Ripple, Slip,* and *Slide.*

Roll Edit

The simplest trim operation is the roll edit. Rolling an edit shortens one clip while lengthening the other (**Figure 6.1**). It doesn't matter whether it's the outgoing clip (clip 1) getting shorter and the incoming clip (clip 2) getting longer or the other way around; the overall sequence length doesn't change.

Figure 6.1 A roll edit moves the edit point, shortening one clip while lengthening the adjacent one. It doesn't disturb the rest of the sequence.

I've already described some practical uses for this tool, such as syncing continuity edits and creating split edits (see the sidebar "Syncing Up on the Easy Spot" and the section on using split edits in Chapter 3, "Editing Patterns"), but the Roll tool has infinite applications.

Access the Roll tool by choosing it from the Tool palette (**Figure 6.2**) or typing ⓡ on your keyboard. The Roll tool operates only on edit points. If you pass your cursor over the middle of a clip, you'll see an "x" next to the cursor (**Figure 6.3**). This helps you understand where and how to use the tool.

Figure 6.2 The Roll tool looks like a pair of film reels. The two reels are a reminder that you're changing both sides of the edit when you apply this tool. The Ripple tool (discussed later) has only one reel and correspondingly affects only one side of the edit.

Figure 6.3 The Roll tool works only on edit points. If your cursor is over an area where the tool won't work, a tiny "x" appears next to the Roll icon.

Once the Roll tool is activated, the simplest way to execute a roll is to click the tool on an edit point and drag (see Figure 6.2). A Tip window will appear indicating how many frames you're moving the edit. If you are zoomed out, dragging can be imprecise. Holding down ⌘ helps in this situation by "gearing down" the effect of your drag and limiting movement to one frame at a time.

If you roll both the audio and video tracks of a particular edit point, you move the whole edit point, but if you roll either the audio or the video independently, you will create a split edit (**Figure 6.4**). If you are rolling an edit that includes sync sound elements, such as lips moving or a car door slamming, you need to roll both the audio and video to keep the picture and sound lined up.

I roll almost every edit point in every sequence back and forth a few times until I like the feel of the transition, sometimes creating splits, sometimes just fine tuning the cut. I can't stress how often you'll use this tool once you get familiar with it.

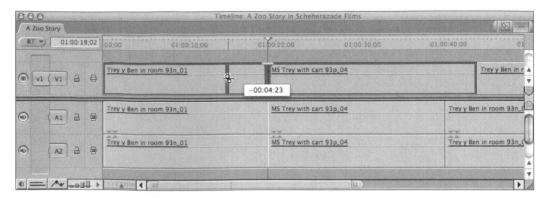

Figure 6.4 By rolling only the video clip, I can create a J cut that smoothes out the transition across the two clips.

TIP: When you're making tiny frame-by-frame adjustments to an edit to create seamless continuity, keep moving the edit one frame at a time until it's clear that you've passed the sweet spot. Then back it off a frame or two until it feels just right.

Canvas Feedback

When you roll an edit in the Timeline, the Canvas temporarily turns into a special two-up display showing the two frames getting modified (**Figure 6.5**). This can be extremely helpful in deciding where to make your edit. As you drag the edit point back and forth, you can make decisions based on the content and the composition of the frames on either side of the edit point.

Figure 6.5 When rolling a clip, watch the Canvas window to see the frames that will become your new edit point.

Extend Edit

Because editors use the roll edit so frequently, there's a way to do it in one step. The Extend Edit command will roll the currently selected edit point to the playhead position (**Figure 6.6**).

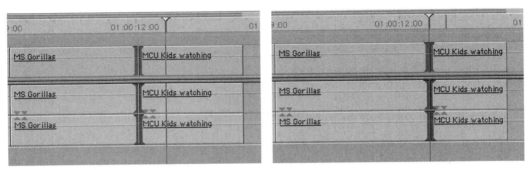

Figure 6.6 Roll an edit without using the Roll tool by using the Extend Edit command.

This has essentially the same effect as selecting the edit point with the Roll tool and dragging it to the new position, but it can be done from the keyboard by hitting E. Professional editors tend to use this feature while playing the sequence.

For example, suppose you've got a sequence of kids in a zoo looking at gorillas. You rough in a couple of edits:

1. LS kids looking at gorillas

2. MS gorillas

3. MCU kids' faces

But there's a problem with shot 3: The MCU of the kids is supposed to show them looking interested in the gorillas, but in the beginning of the shot one kid is staring at the ground, bored as a stick. After a moment he glances up and gets mildly interested to the point where he might pass as engaged, especially surrounded by the other excited kids.

You decide to fix the problem by extending the gorilla shot to cover up the undesirable frames of shot 3. (Who could complain about a few extra frames of gorillas?) Here's how you might use Extend Edit to accomplish that very quickly.

1. Select the edit point between shots 2 and 3.

2. Play the sequence.

3. At the moment where the kid stops looking bored, hit E.

That's it! No setting markers, no dragging, no calculating how many frames you want to trim. If you do this while playing, Final Cut will even extend you the courtesy of backing up a few seconds and play over the new edit point—all before you can say "Stop."

Extend Edit works in reverse, too, either by letting you extend the edit while playing backward, or by allowing you to position the playhead upstream from the selected edit and pressing E.

Deleting Shots With Extend Edit

You can even extend your edit right past another edit point, completely eliminating a clip. This is another efficient, high-speed strategy.

Perhaps you'd like to try the zoo scene without gorillas—you want to extend shot 1 (the LS of the kids looking) right past shot 2 (the gorilla shot) and past the bored kid in shot 3, so you'll end up with two shots of kids, no gorillas, and no bored kid.

Select the edit between shots 1 and 2, place the playhead at the right spot in shot 3, and perform an extend edit (**Figure 6.7**). This will eliminate the gorilla shot from the sequence entirely, along with the bored brat.

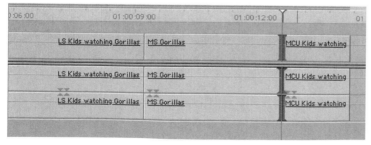

Figure 6.7 As long as there's enough media in the underlying clips, you can extend an edit as far as you like. In this example we completely overwrite the second shot.

Ripple Edit

The ripple edit modifies an edit point by changing the duration of only one of the clips involved. This changes the duration of your entire sequence. While you can roll in only two directions (forward and backward), you can ripple in four different ways (**Figure 6.8**). Rippling is one of the most powerful tools in Final Cut Pro, but it can wreak havoc by affecting clips on other tracks.

Figure 6.8 You can ripple either side of an edit point in either direction.

Even though a ripple edit modifies only one clip and a roll modifies two, the ripple is much tougher to keep track of in your head, since it actually modifies the whole sequence. Consequently, you should be more careful with it than with a roll. Part of the problem is that some ripples create results that are the exact opposite of what you expected.

In general, changes to the outgoing clip are more straightforward than changes to the incoming clip. To make the outgoing clip longer, you drag it to the right; to make it shorter, you drag it to the left—just as you would with a roll edit.

For example, let's go back to the kids and gorillas. Suppose you wanted to make shot 2 (the gorilla shot in the middle) longer without changing the duration of shot 3. Type RR to bring up the Ripple tool, select the outgoing side of the edit, and drag it to the right. Shot 2 would get longer, shot 3 would remain the same, and everyone would be happy because you'd have more gorilla footage in your movie (**Figure 6.9**). However, you would not have solved the bored kid problem.

Figure 6.9 Everyone loves gorillas. To make shot 2 longer, select that side of the edit point and drag to the right. The duration of shot 3 will not be affected, but your overall sequence will be lengthened.

To do that, we must shorten shot 3. Select the incoming side of the edit with the Ripple tool, and drag it to the right. This is exactly what you would do if it were the only clip in the sequence, but the result can be confusing because it's the opposite of how the Roll tool works (**Figure 6.10**). Watch the highlight on the back end of the clip to see how long the clip will be after the trim is done.

If you want to make the incoming clip longer, drag it to the left (**Figure 6.11**). Watch the highlight to see the length of the resulting clip.

Figure 6.10 To shorten the incoming side of the edit, grab the right side of the edit point with the Ripple tool and drag to the right. Note the highlight around the back end of the clip, which indicates its new ending point.

Figure 6.11 If you drag the incoming clip to the left, it gets longer—but the edit stays in the same position. The highlight on the back end of the clip indicates how long the clip will be following the edit.

Checking the Canvas

As with a roll, the Canvas provides feedback about your ripple edit. Since rippling an edit modifies only one frame, only one of the two frames in the Canvas changes. Use this to help determine which frame you want to set as your new edit point.

Selecting Edits

*An edit point can be selected in one of three ways: as a roll, where operations will affect both sides of the edit; a ripple outgoing, where the outgoing clip will be affected, but the incoming clip is left alone; or a ripple incoming, the opposite of a ripple outgoing (**Figure 6.12**).*

continues on next page

Ripple outgoing   Roll   Ripple incoming

Figure 6.12 The Timeline indicates which way an edit point is selected by displaying one of these three states.

Selecting Edits *continued*

Final Cut includes so many different ways to select edits, it can make your head swim. The simplest method is to click on the edit with the Arrow tool or press ⓥ, which selects the nearest edit point to the playhead backward or forward. (If you're exactly halfway between two, it will select the one downstream.)

Selecting an edit with the Arrow tool will select both sides of the edit (making it a roll edit). You can also click on an edit with the Roll tool itself. If you click on an edit point with the Ripple tool, you must choose which side of the edit you wish to select, incoming or outgoing. The shortcut key ⓥ will select an edit as a roll—unless the Ripple tool is active, in which case it will select either incoming or outgoing, depending on which clip the playhead is currently parked on.

Once an edit is selected, toggle between the three types of selections (roll, ripple outgoing, ripple incoming) by using ⓤ.

*As if this weren't complicated enough, Final Cut provides one more way to select edits: a special tool called Edit Selection (**Figure 6.13**). Armed with this tool, you can select edits either by clicking on them or by dragging a marquee around a group of edits (**Figure 6.14**). Once edits are selected with the Edit Selection tool, the Trim Edit window will open automatically. This methodology exists primarily to accommodate migrating Avid users who are used to this exact behavior.*

Figure 6.13 The Edits Selection tool can be accessed by pressing G.

Figure 6.14 Use this tool to select edits by dragging a marquee or lasso around them. This allows you to select different edits on different tracks.

Just Type a Number

The more you edit, the more you'll find yourself thinking in frames. You'll be able to look at an edit and estimate just how many frames it needs to be adjusted. An experienced editor can easily identify even two- or three-frame errors. Does the edit feel smooth? If not, is the first clip too long? Too short? And by how many frames? How about the second clip? Or maybe the continuity seems fluid but the edit point occurs at the wrong instant in the action: after the door closes completely instead of midway through its motion.

Once you begin thinking in frame numbers, you will want to be able to tell the software precisely how to make these fine adjustments. Final Cut easily permits numerical edits like these.

Any time you type a number on the keyboard, or press ⊞ or ⊟, Final Cut Pro understands that you want to perform a numerical edit. All you need to do is tell it what kind of trim you want to perform: a roll, ripple outgoing, or ripple incoming edit. The current selection defines which edit will be applied.

For example, if you want to shorten the clip of the gorilla at the edit point where it begins, select the edit point as a ripple incoming (**Figure 6.15**) and type ⊞ 1.15. This will perform a ripple edit, shortening the clip by one and one half seconds. (The ⊞ is optional.) Why does entering a positive value make the incoming clip shorter? Because you are moving the edit point forward in time by that amount.

continues on next page

Figure 6.15 Select the edit you want to adjust numerically. The type of edit you select determines how the numerical entry will be applied. In this case, the edit is a ripple incoming. The pop-up window in the middle of the Timeline confirms what type of edit is being made.

Just Type a Number *continued*

*When you begin a numerical edit, Final Cut pops up a tiny window in the middle of the Timeline indicating what type of edit you are performing (see previous figure). If you want to perform a roll edit to make the adjacent shot longer while making this one shorter, select the edit as a roll (**Figure 6.16**).*

*If a clip is selected instead of an edit point, typing in numbers will move the clip by the number of frames entered. In this case, the pop-up will identify the operation as a move (**Figure 6.17**).*

Figure 6.16 If the edit is selected as a roll, the numerical entry will be applied as a roll edit.

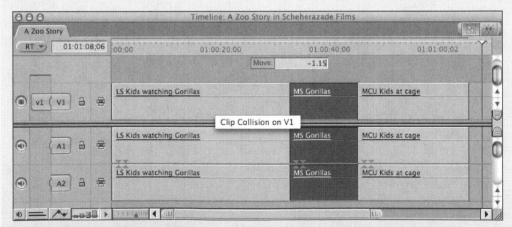

Figure 6.17 If you select a clip rather than an edit point, numerical entry will attempt to move the item by the timecode value you specify. If other clips are in the way, you will get an error; a numerical move operation will not overwrite clips.

Just Type a Number *continued*

*If no clips or edits are selected, and you begin typing in timecode numbers, Final Cut Pro will direct the entry into the Current Position field and move the playhead by the desired amount (**Figure 6.18**).*

Whenever you make a direct numerical entry, Final Cut Pro translates your entry into timecode values. If you type in more than two digits without a separator (colon, semicolon, period, or comma), the program will assume you are entering a total number of frames and will calculate how many seconds or minutes it equals depending on the current timebase (frames per second). (See the sidebar "Working With Timecode" in Chapter 4, "Preparing to Edit.")

Current Position field

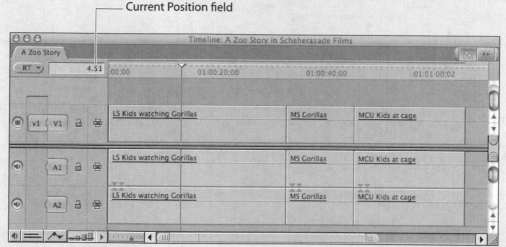

Figure 6.18 If nothing is selected in the Timeline, entering a timecode doesn't pop up a window; the numerical entry goes directly into the Current Position field and moves the playhead. If you omit the ⊞ or ⊟, Final Cut Pro assumes you are typing in the destination timecode.

Adjusting Two Edits at Once

It won't take long until you're seeing your way several moves down the chessboard—and you may spot places where you want to adjust two edit points in one operation. I don't mean two sides of one edit point (as with the roll edit just discussed); I mean two entirely different edit points.

Final Cut provides two editing tools specifically for this case: Slip and Slide (**Figure 6.19**). Both tools limit you to adjusting adjacent edits only—and only by the same amount. Nonetheless, you'll encounter many cases where one of these tools is just right for the job.

Slip Item - S

Figure 6.19 The Slip and Slide tools are connected in the Tool palette. The keyboard shortcut for Slip is Ⓢ, and the shortcut for Slide is ⓈⒸ.

Slip Edit

A slip edit simultaneously changes both the In and Out points of a single clip. Essentially, it changes which section of the clip you are using by trimming frames off the front of the clip and adding them to the back—or vice versa. It does not change the duration of the overall sequence, and it has no effect whatsoever on the surrounding clips. Performing a slip is equivalent to doing a ripple incoming and a ripple outgoing on the same clip at the same time.

When to Slip

Here are several situations when the Slip tool is precisely what you need.

Fine-Tuning Problem Clips in Finished Sequences

If just one clip in a nearly finished sequence needs adjusting, the Slip function can fix it without messing up your sequence. Imagine we're still working on that zoo video, and you're using a shot of a koala lashing out with her claws right at the camera lens to show why kids shouldn't feed the animals. Unfortunately, the shot begins too early: There's nearly a full second of dead space before the vicious koala strikes. Since the rest of the sequence is locked down, you can't just ripple or roll the edit, because that will modify the other clips. But if you slip the clip about 20 frames to the left, thereby setting a new In point a few frames before the paw swings toward the lens, you're in business (**Figure 6.20**).

Figure 6.20 You can slip one clip to modify an edit without disturbing the surrounding clips. The marker indicates the frame where the wild beast strikes.

Finessing Continuity Cuts

If you're building a sequence from footage shot with multiple cameras and cutting back and forth between them, sometimes one clip will get slightly out of sync with the shots around it. Use a slip edit to fix a clip where both sides contain a continuity edit.

For example, one sequence in the zoo video contains a series of shots of penguins playing. The setup involved one camera on land and another underwater, shooting simultaneously. As you're editing, you notice a misalignment in a continuity cut from above water to underwater just as one penguin breaks the water's surface. Correspondingly, the next edit will also be out of sync, when you cut back to the above-water camera. Using the Slip tool, adjust the In and Out points of the underwater clip to match continuity across the first edit point—and the edit point on the other side of the clip will be adjusted automatically at the same time (**Figure 6.21**).

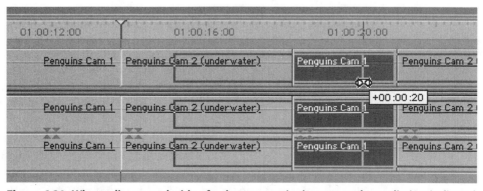

Figure 6.21 When edits on each side of a shot are continuity cuts, and one clip is misaligned on both sides, slipping can fix both edits at once.

How to Slip

Performing a slip edit is as simple as selecting the Slip tool and clicking and dragging a clip in the Timeline (**Figure 6.22**). While you drag, the Canvas window switches to a two-up display showing you the new In and Out points you are selecting. The Timeline feedback tells you how much media is available to you, based on how long the clip is.

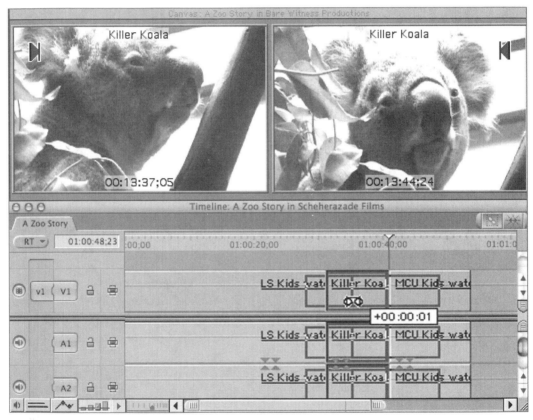

Figure 6.22 Slip a clip by dragging it in the Timeline with the Slip tool. The feedback in the Canvas shows the new In and Out points, and the highlight in the Timeline displays all of the media in the clip to show you what part of the clip you are using and how much spare media exists around it.

Dragging the clip left sets the new In and Out points *later* in the clip, and dragging it to the right sets the new In and Out points *earlier* in the clip. If this seems backward, try to see it like this: Rather than thinking about rippling two edit points, remember that you're simply selecting a different part of the clip—without disturbing the sequence.

Slip With Markers

You can enhance the functionality of the slip edit by using a marker as a midclip guide.

For instance, in another scene in our zoo video, there's a shot of a flock of flamingos taking flight all at once. The narration explains that zoo animals possess a natural urge for freedom. Here you want to adjust the timing of the clip so the flock takes off right on the word "freedom." In this case, you can use markers along with a slip edit to align the two events.

First set a marker on the frame where the flamingos fly and another one on the frame where the narrator says the word "freedom," using the marker controls described in Chapter 5 (**Figure 6.23**).

Figure 6.23 First we set markers on the points of interest. One goes on the frame where the birds fly, and another goes in the audio clip on the word "freedom."

Now select the Slip tool, click on the flamingos clip, and drag it until the two markers line up. You must click precisely on the marker in the flamingos clip to make the other marker act as a snap point. If the markers are not snapping, double-check to make sure that snapping is turned on and that you selected the clip by clicking directly on the marker (**Figure 6.24**).

Now the flamingos erupt into flight at the very moment the narrator says "freedom," creating a provocative combination of visual and aural elements.

Figure 6.24 By selecting the clip directly on the marker, you can use that point to snap to other points in the Timeline.

Slip in the Viewer

If you want to perform a slip before you drop the clip into a sequence, you can perform that edit in the Viewer. Hold down (Shift) while you drag either the In or Out point in the Viewer, and the other point will move along with you (**Figure 6.25**).

Figure 6.25 You can slip in the Viewer window by holding down (Shift) while you drag the In or Out point. The Viewer and the Canvas become a two-up display to assist you in setting your new points.

The duration of the clip remains the same, but the section of the clip you're using changes.

When you slip a clip this way, the Viewer window and the Canvas window become a giant two-up display, showing you the In and Out points you are selecting as you drag.

Now the hard question: Why in the world would you want to perform a slip edit before you drop the clip into a sequence?

Imagine you have just enough room in your show for a four-second cutaway of seagulls at the beach. The shot you choose is a minute and a half long and includes many different framings of seagulls. Sometimes the gulls are flying; sometimes they're walking around on the sand. Occasionally the shot is zoomed in to show one or two birds; other times it's an ELS of the beach with the gulls as tiny specks in the sky.

The section you pick must be only four seconds long, but you haven't yet decided which part of the clip to use. For now, just set an In and Out point anywhere in the clip (as long as they're four seconds apart), and slip around the clip looking for the best four seconds. Preview this by using the Play In to Out shortcut ((Shift)-(\)), which plays the clip exactly from the In point to the Out. Once you find the section that fits the sequence best, perform the edit and you're done.

Slip by the Numbers

When you look at a problem edit, you may instantly say to yourself something like, "Hmm, that clip probably needs to be slipped by seven frames."

To slip a clip by a precise number of frames, type in timecode numbers while the Slip tool is active. Unfortunately, this isn't quite as straightforward as doing it with a ripple or a roll edit, since you also need a clip to be selected, and the Slip tool doesn't exactly *select* clips. Normally, when you click on a clip with the Slip tool, you drag to perform the edit—and when you let go, the clip is no longer selected.

To slip a clip numerically, you must first select it using the Selection tool by pressing A, then choose the Slip tool by pressing S. Only then can you begin typing numbers.

If you've already selected the Slip tool before you decide to do a numeric operation, you can temporarily select clips in the Timeline by holding down Shift. Once the clip is selected, entering a numeric value will perform a slip edit on it (**Figure 6.26**).

Figure 6.26 If a clip is already selected, and the current tool is the Slip tool, typing in timecode values will perform a slip. To select a clip with the Slip tool, hold down Shift.

Slide Edit

The slide edit is sort of a reverse slip. Rather than adjusting the In and Out points of the selected clip, the slide edit changes the In and Out points of the *surrounding* clips, allowing you to slide a clip around within a sequence (**Figure 6.27**). Like Slip, Slide will not alter the overall duration of your sequence. Performing a slide is equivalent to making two roll edits in a single step.

Figure 6.27 The slide edit moves your clip around within the surrounding clips. Here I'm sliding the Pygmy Hippo clip, making the previous clip (Reggie in Gift Shop_01) shorter and the following clip (Orangutan1) longer.

When to Slide

Slide is a more specialized tool than Slip, but for the right situation it's perfect. For instance, in Chapter 5, I described a situation where I put a cutaway on track V2 so I could move it back and forth to decide the best placement without disturbing the clip on track V1. Sliding is a way of performing the same operation when all your clips are on a single track.

How to Slide

Sliding a clip is done exactly the way you slip one: Select it with the Slide tool (see Figure 6.20) and drag the clip—or enter numeric values while the Slide tool is active.

Let's take a scene from *The H Tour,* a short supernatural thriller created by the Bare Witness ensemble. During a confrontation in the toolshed between Jesse and the Entity, I used an insert of a chain saw to remind the audience of the danger Jesse faced, but I didn't bother finding the perfect spot for it. Later, while fine-tuning the sequence, I used the Slide tool to find the best placement for the shot.

The clip leading into the chain-saw shot was an MCU of Jesse, and the clip following the chain saw was a CU of the Entity. (I was also using the insert to bridge my move from MCUs to CUs.)

When I played back the sequence, my first idea was to slide the chainsaw shot earlier and have it begin just after Jesse shivers with fear (**Figure 6.28**). This made a good cut point at the head, but it had the added effect of lengthening the shot of the Entity that followed the chainsaw shot. Because all the shots of the Entity required digital effects (we painted a glow on the shots to enhance his ethereal nature),

I knew that adding extra frames to that shot meant more effects work, so I slid the chain-saw shot to a later spot, setting it to begin after Jesse begins his line, and cutting to the Entity just as he laughs.

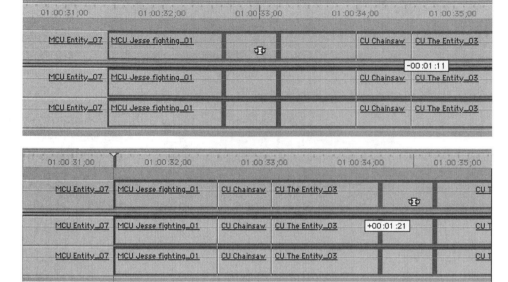

Figure 6.28 Using the Slide tool, I can experiment with different positions for the chain-saw shot.

Slide won't let you move beyond the clip boundaries of the surrounding clips, so you must choose a new location for your cutaway somewhere within the two adjacent clips. If you want to move a shot entirely out of its current position, consider the swap edit (see the section on the swap edit in Chapter 5).

Play Around Your Edit

I've already emphasized how important it is to make your editing decisions while playing your film in real time. You can't judge the nuances of proper timing any other way, so while you're trimming, get in the habit of watching your edit repeatedly as you make adjustments. The best tool for this is the Play Around Current control, which plays from a few seconds before the current playhead position to a few seconds after it (**Figure 6.29**). To activate it from the keyboard, just press ⌐\⌐ after each editing operation.

Figure 6.29 The Play Around Current control is a valuable tool to learn about. Although it sits close to the center of both Viewer and Canvas windows, it is surprisingly underused. If you find the button too small to hit easily, use ⟍ on your keyboard.

— Play Around Current control

The Trim Edit Window

Fine-tuning your edits is such a critical part of the editing process that Final Cut Pro provides a way to focus your entire desktop on a single edit point. The Trim Edit window (**Figure 6.30**) shows you a zoomed-in view of a single edit point. The left frame (where the Viewer normally is) displays the last frame of the outgoing clip, and the right frame (where the Canvas usually sits) displays the first frame of the incoming clip. The Scrubber areas below the frames provide valuable information about how much media is available to you while you trim, and you'll find a few other unique controls such as the Play Around Edit Loop button.

The truth is, though, that only a few of the cool features in the Trim Edit window are not available when trimming in the Timeline, and I find that the speed and seamlessness of trimming in the Timeline outweighs the value of calling up the Trim Edit window.

Then why did we include it? Well, early versions of Avid Media Composer didn't let you do trim operations like ripple, roll, slip, and slide in the Timeline—as you can in Final Cut Pro. As a result, Avid users learned to love its Big Trim mode (which is essentially the model for Final Cut Pro's Trim Edit window), and many of them refused to work any other way. To accommodate those users, we included this feature in Final Cut. No doubt some editors are grateful, and perhaps you will be one of them.

Outgoing frame   Incoming frame

Additional frames available ⌐   └─ Play Around Edit Loop button

Figure 6.30 The Trim Edit window is a good way to view a single edit point.

Play Around Edit Loop

The Trim Edit window *does* include several excellent tools, though. For instance, the Play Around Edit Loop button.

If you press the ⟨Spacebar⟩ while the Trim Edit window is active, rather than just playing forward, Final Cut plays from five seconds before the current edit point to two seconds after. (These values can be set by the user in the User Preferences window, which is accessible from the Application menu.)

As the name implies, this feature loops the area around your edit—which is helpful, since you can watch the edit again and again. Not only that, while it's playing, you can enter numeric trim commands (such as ⟨+⟩⟨3⟩, ⟨-⟩⟨8⟩, ⟨+⟩⟨1⟩⟨1⟩). The next time the edit loops around, the new trim will be applied, so you can keep making tiny adjustments until you're satisfied.

> **TIP:** *You can create a similar effect while trimming in the Timeline by turning on the Loop Playback switch found in the View menu and using the Play Around Current control described in the previous section. However, unlike when using the Play Around Edit Loop button in the Trim Edit window, each time you trim, playback will be interrupted.*

The Trim Viewer

Another handy feature in the Trim Edit window is the ability to set a new edit point by using the Clip Playback controls. Since you can see the whole clip on either side of the edit point, you can play into the unused area and choose a new spot for the edit.

For example, imagine you've got a dialogue sequence like this one:

Car dealer: My friend, you've got to tell me how much you're willing to spend.

Trey: Well, I really wanted to get it for under sixty...

Trey (continued): There's all those fees and stuff...

Car dealer: My friend. Say no more. Wait right here...

Car dealer (continued): I'll be right back.

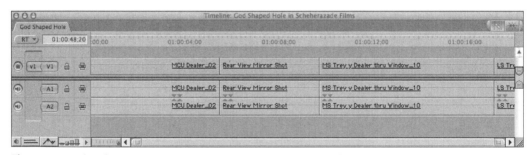

Figure 6.31 The clips are arranged in the Timeline as illustrated.

The dialogue is continuous across the edit points. But let's say you want to roll the edit between shots 2 and 3 backward so we cut to the MS just before the dealer says, "Wait right here."

You could roll the edit in the Timeline, but then you wouldn't know exactly where the car dealer begins that line in shot 3—since the media isn't visible. You could make an estimate based on where the line begins in shot 2, but because they're different shots, there's no certainty that the edit will line up properly (**Figure 6.32**).

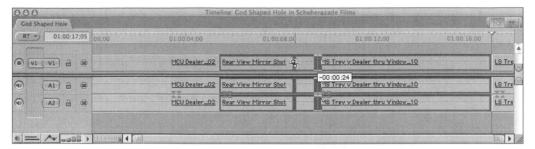

Figure 6.32 You can roll the edit in the Timeline, but you can't hear the section of shot 3 you've just added before committing to the edit.

If you work in the Trim Edit window, play clip 3 from beginning to end, find the exact spot the line begins, and stamp down a new In point for the clip. If you select the edit as a roll, this will automatically move the Out point of clip 2 back, and your new edit will be complete (**Figure 6.33**).

└─ New In point

Figure 6.33 By trimming in the Trim Edit window, you can see all the media in shot 3 and find the exact spot where you want to set the new edit point.

Dynamic Trimming

As you get handy with the Trim Edit window, try turning on Dynamic Trimming, which allows you to work even faster. When the Dynamic Checkbox is activated (**Figure 6.34**) the edit point will follow your playhead, so whenever you stop playback the edit point is automatically moved to the exact frame where you stopped.

Figure 6.34 Check this box to Trim on the fly.

This is designed to work with the J, K, and L keys. Ordinarily, if you use those controls to navigate in your sequence while the trim window is open (as you might do to evaluate an edit), every time you stop the playhead, it jumps back to the edit point. When Dynamic Trimming is active, rather than the playhead jumping to the edit point, the edit point jumps to the new playhead position. If, while playing you don't want the edit point changed, hit Escape instead of K to stop playback. This will stop playback and reset the playhead to the existing edit point.

Making edits while stepping through the video one frame at a time is useful when you are lining up a visual continuity cut such as a door closing or a handshake, but even in those cases you will want to review the edit in real time to ensure that the action is smooth and the momentum is correct (See "Cutting On Action," Chapter 3).

Dynamic trimming is most useful for cuts where perfect continuity isn't critical but perfect timing is—such as a common dialogue passage. When cutting back and forth between matching OS MCUs, the cut point depends on the nuance of the lines being spoken and the subtlety of the reactions in the actors' faces. While watching your sequence play you can judge the most natural and appropriate edit points. The edit applied will be a ripple or a roll depending on the current selection (just like all trimming operations).

Toggling the Dynamic State

Once you get the hang of it, Dynamic Trimming is an extremely helpful tool to add to your trimming arsenal. However, sometimes you'll want to navigate the trim window using J, K, and L without performing edits. If you're like me, you'll want to avoid having to point your mouse at the itty-bitty checkbox every time you want to change the state, but there's no keyboard shortcut assigned. What can you do?

Assign your own shortcut. In the Customize Keyboard layout window, find the Dynamic Trimming control listed in the Editing section or by searching (**Figure 6.35**). I recommend assigning this to either the [P] or the [Y] key. By default, the [P] key activates the Pen tool. I find that I use this shortcut very rarely, and if I want a shortcut for the Pen tool I can always use [⌘]-[P] (Since Final Cut Pro has no "Print" function, that shortcut is unassigned). The reason [P] is such a good choice for Trimming is that the [[ ] and [ ]] keys beside it also perform Trim operations (they trim the edit forward or backward 1 frame) and it is easily in reach of the [J], [K], and [L] keys where you'll be controlling your dynamic trimming in the first place.

Figure 6.35 Drag the control name to the key of your choice.

If you don't want to give up your Pen key shortcut, the [Y] key is also unassigned (in previous versions it toggled the now-obsolete Render Qualities). That key is also in close proximity to the [J], [K], and [L] controls.

Trimming Under Transitions

In Chapter 5, I discussed how to edit a transition effect, including the length of the transition, its alignment on the edit point, and its parameters. But since every transition sits on an edit point, you can also trim the edit underneath the transition.

This means you can do all of the trimming operations previously discussed even on an edit where a transition effect has been applied. And you can do it in three places: in the Timeline, in the Trim Edit window, or in the Transition Editor.

Using the Timeline or Trim Edit Window for Edit Decisions

Using the Timeline or the Trim Edit window to trim an edit point with a transition on top of it is a breeze: Just pretend the transition isn't there. Select the edit point with any of the trim tools and ripple, roll, slip, or slide the edit right underneath the transition (**Figure 6.36**). Because the transition requires additional frames beyond the edit point, the trim tools are smart enough to keep you from editing away the frames required for the transition, but otherwise you don't have to know the effect is there.

Figure 6.36 You can select an edit (in this case, a roll) right underneath a transition effect and trim it like any other edit point.

If your purpose in making the trim is to adjust overall timing or fine-tune the edit point regardless of the effect, this is the way to go. For example, if you've got a wipe that occurs across an edit that's also a continuity cut, and you want to fine-tune the edit to ensure flawless continuity, trim it just like any other edit.

Using the Transition Editor to Custom-Fit Effects

If your reason for trimming the edit-with-transition is to make the clips fit the transition better, do it in the Transition Editor. For example, suppose that the narrator of our zoo video delivers his lines facing the camera. Then, when he's finished speaking, he turns and walks offscreen-left. A push transition will move the frame of the outgoing clip offscreen from right to left while replacing it with the new clip (**Figure 6.37**). Let's further suppose that we used a push to replace the shot of the narrator with a shot of a kangaroo that's hopping right to left as well (**Figure 6.38**).

Figure 6.37 During a push, the incoming clip shoves the outgoing clip out of the way.

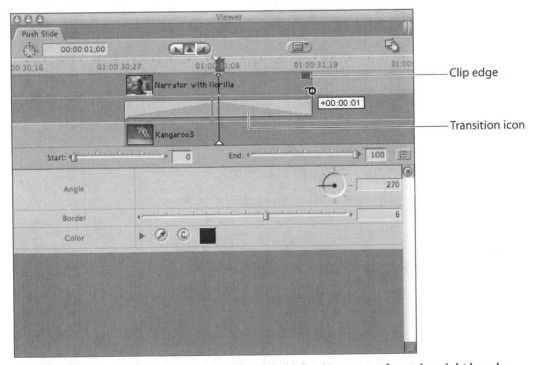

Figure 6.38 In the Transition Editor, you can see both clips. You can perform trims right here by grabbing the edge of a clip (to ripple) or by moving the Transition icon itself right or left (to roll).

There's only one problem: When we play back the sequence, the effect doesn't work because the narrator starts his walk offscreen too late (**Figure 6.39**).

Figure 6.39 The effect doesn't work because the timing is wrong on the outgoing clip.

The way to fix the edit is to ripple the outgoing clip, making it a little bit shorter so the narrator begins walking off just as the transition begins. While we could perform this trim in the Timeline, doing it in the Transition Editor allows us to see how it will line up with the transition effect as we trim (**Figure 6.40**).

Figure 6.40 The effect is fixed so that Reggie walks off just as the image is wiped off the screen.

Trimming in the Transition Editor

You can roll the edit point in the Transition Editor by dragging the Transition icon itself. (When you move your mouse over it, your cursor automatically becomes the Roll tool.) To ripple either the outgoing clip (above) or the incoming clip (below), click on the clip edge you want to change. Your cursor automatically changes to the Ripple tool, and you can trim the clip. The transition moves along with it (see Figure 6.38).

Canvas Provides the Feedback

As with ordinary trimming, the Canvas provides feedback while you're dragging in the Transition Editor. If you're rolling, it shows you a two-up display, but the frames you're seeing are not the ones on either side of the edit point. What you're seeing is the last-used frame of the outgoing clip and the first-used frame of the incoming clip (**Figure 6.41**).

If you're rippling, you'll see a one-up display in the Canvas showing the frame that will become the first or last frame used in the transition (**Figure 6.42**).

Figure 6.41 When you roll an edit in the Transition Editor, the Canvas displays a two-up showing you the frames on either side of the transition. Note that the icons in the Transition Editor illustrate which frames are being displayed.

Figure 6.42 When you ripple an edit in the Transition Editor, the Canvas displays a single frame indicating the frame that's changing. The Display Frame indicator in the Transition Editor shows which frame it is.

Trimming Multiple Tracks

The trim tools are immensely powerful, and usually only advanced editors are brave enough to experiment with some of their more esoteric features. For example, many editors shy away from multitrack trimming. In fact, some don't even know it's possible. But if you understand exactly what you're trying to accomplish with a particular edit, this feature makes perfect sense—and will let you move really fast.

Whenever you trim, you can modify one edit on each track in your Timeline. The edits don't need to be lined up or come from the same clips. They don't even need to be the same *type* of edit. One track can be set to ripple and another to roll. However, all of the edits will move by the same number of frames if they're selected together.

A Simple Multitrack Trim

Here's a simple example: Suppose we've got an interview with a lower third title card laid on top of it (**Figure 6.43**). We want the lower third to begin three seconds after the interview starts and stay on-screen for five seconds.

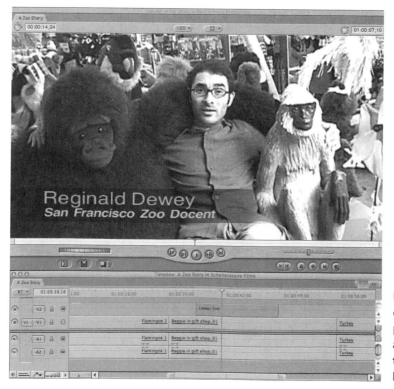

Figure 6.43 The graphic on track V2 appears precisely three seconds after the beginning of the shot below it, and lasts five seconds.

As we trim the beginning of the interview shot, we want the graphic to move along with the clip so it always begins exactly three seconds after the edit. To do this, in addition to selecting the interview clip and its corresponding audio, I add the lower third title card to the selection. Now as I roll or ripple the interview clip, the title moves along with it, always beginning exactly three seconds after the primary edit point (**Figure 6.44**).

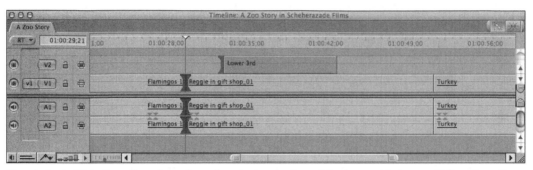

Figure 6.44 With the edit point selected at the beginning of the lower third, any edit I make will move both clips at once. Since I don't want to change the length of the lower third, I select the edit as a ripple outgoing. This ripples the gap exactly as if it were a clip. The result is that the lower third keeps its relative position to the clip below but never changes duration.

Selecting Edits, Part Two

Final Cut Pro will let you create very complex trim operations that roll one track while rippling another, or simultaneously modify one picture edit and an unrelated audio edit. It all depends on what edits are selected and how they are selected when you begin trimming. You already know how to select an individual edit, but how do you add additional edits to that selection?

This is a little tricky, so pay attention.

Figure 6.45 With linked selection active, selecting the video edit automatically selects corresponding edits on linked clips.

*If linked selection is turned on, selecting one edit will automatically include edits on linked clips on other tracks (**Figure 6.45**). If you want to select one part of a linked clip as a roll, and the other as a ripple, disable linked selection or temporarily override it by holding down* Option.

continues on next page

Selecting Edits, Part Two *continued*

Pressing ⌘ *as you click will add edits to the current selection. If you click with the Arrow tool or the Roll tool (while holding down* ⌘*), you will add the edit to the selection as a roll. If you select the Ripple tool, and* ⌘*-click on the edit, it will add that edit to the selection as a ripple (incoming or outgoing, depending on which side of the edit you click on). If you are using either the Ripple or Roll tools, you can temporarily toggle to the other by holding down* Shift*.*

Once an edit is selected, you can toggle which type of edit it is by clicking on it with the Ripple or Roll tool while holding down both ⌘ *and* Shift *as you click. This will allow you to set any individual edit point to any of the three states (ripple outgoing, roll, or ripple incoming) without deselecting any of the surrounding edits.*

One edit can be selected on each track in your timeline. All selected edits will move each time you perform a trim operation, each according to its selection type.

A More Complicated Multitrack Trim

Now that you get the concept, let's look at a more complex multitrack trim. Suppose you've got a number of tracks lined up together and you need to fine-tune one of the elements. In this example, you've got a sequence with a picture edit on track V1, synced audio on track A1, sound effects on track A2, and stereo music clips on tracks A3 and A4 (**Figure 6.46**). You want to make an adjustment to the picture by trimming nine frames off the end of the outgoing clip. But a sound effect on A2 is lined up with a particular frame in the picture. Likewise, on the music track, the transition from Marrow.aif to Gray.aif is set up to happen at a particular moment in the sequence.

Figure 6.46 In this complex situation, you've got synced elements on five different tracks that should all be trimmed together.

Since your plan is to trim nine frames from the outgoing clip, select that edit and the corresponding audio edit as ripple outgoing edits. Next, also select the sound effect as a ripple outgoing. This ensures that it will stay in sync, no matter what changes are made to the primary edit.

Now, select the audio edit underneath the transition between the clips on A3 and A4. Since the transition can safely occur anywhere in the two songs, we can choose a roll edit here (**Figure 6.47**).

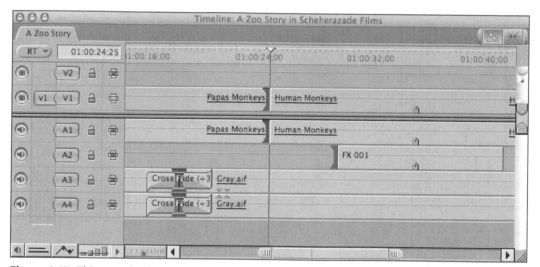

Figure 6.47 This complex edit selection makes perfect sense if you go through it step by step: You want the sound effect to stay at the same position relative to the video and main audio (just like the lower third in the previous example), and you want the music to transition from one clip to the next in sync with the picture edit.

With all your edits selected, trim the nine frames by dragging any of the edits, or by typing ⊝9 on the keyboard. Best of all, if it turns out that nine frames isn't quite right, you can keep adjusting the edit frame by frame, as easily as dragging or typing in numbers. As long as all the edits are properly selected, they'll all move accordingly.

You can do this in separate operations, of course, but then you won't be able to play back the finished edit until you've completed all three separate trims. More important, once your complex trim is properly selected, you can experiment all you like, checking the result each time. If you were doing this via a bunch of individual edits, you would have to reselect and retrim each edit point for every new frame count you try—opening the possibility of making a mistake and losing the critical timing you previously set up.

Snap and Trim

Once you know where you want an edit to go, if there's a snap point there, drag your mouse anywhere nearby and let go. The Snapping function will take over, performing the precise alignment that's almost impossible with a mouse. This makes the Snapping feature one of the most useful tools in Final Cut Pro. Trying to make fine adjustments to an edit point during a trim edit is one of the places you'll appreciate it most.

The Snapping feature can also be one of the most *annoying* tools in Final Cut Pro: If you're not sure where you want to drop your edit, or you're trying to drop it close to a snap target but not right on it, snapping will constantly pull your mouse around, disrupting what you're trying to do and causing you major frustration.

Here's how to use snapping when it's behaving itself:

Most of the time, before you begin a trim operation, you should play your sequence and figure out (while playing) where you want the new edit point to be. Every edit point is a timing decision, and proper timing can best be gauged while playing at normal speed. For example, you're looking at an edit of someone walking down some stairs. Shot 1 is a LS of the stairway and shot 2 is a CU on the character's foot. Let's presume you've already synced up the shots so wherever you edit will have continuous motion (see the section on the continuity cut in Chapter 2, "Film Language"). Now you want to move the edit so the CU starts as soon as the guy's feet hit a certain step in the LS (**Figure 6.48**).

Play the sequence until the feet in the LS are about to hit the step, and stop playback. Set a marker at this point, or just park the playhead there. You can also use the In or Out point if you're not already using it for something else.

> **TIP:** Using the playhead for marking an edit point is not usually a great idea, since it's easy to forget you were using it as a placeholder and pick it up and move it accidentally.

Once you've marked the desired edit point, drag the edit to the new position and use the Snapping feature to ensure precise alignment (**Figure 6.49**).

Figure 6.48 In this sequence, we want to line up the edit on the frame where the feet are about to hit the step.

Figure 6.49 Once your destination is marked, you can roll the edit right to it and snap it into place.

Turning Off Snapping

In Chapter 5, I mentioned a keyboard shortcut that allows you to toggle snapping, but it's worth pointing out again here, since it's one of the most important controls in the program, and one you'll use a lot while trimming.

One problem with snapping is that most of the time you never know if it's on or off when you begin dragging something. And too often the only way you find out is the hard way: When you get near your desired end point, suddenly your mouse is pulled over to some nearby marker or edit point you don't care about.

The magic fix for this potential frustration is N, the keyboard shortcut for turning snapping on and off. Best of all, tapping N to toggle the snapping state works even while you're in the middle of a drag operation.

THE REPLACE EDIT

The replace edit is one of the most powerful tools in Final Cut Pro, but for a beginning editor, it can be confusing since it breaks some of the general rules about three-point editing. A replace edit can be applied as easily as an insert or overwrite: It is one of the options on the Edit Overlay and is also available via F11. However, you need to understand when and why to use it before it will do you much good.

Replace is a variation on the overwrite edit, but rather than relying only on In and Out points, it allows you to define an additional point somewhere in the middle of the clip to use as the basis for the edit. This is wonderful, because often the element that drives the cut doesn't happen exactly at the edit point. For instance, although a good edit always provides new information, a great edit doesn't necessarily provide it right at the edit point. It's often more effective to make the audience wait for it to appear sometime during the shot (see "New Shot = New Information" in Chapter 2).

The replace edit works based on the current playhead position in both the Viewer and the sequence. It lines up those two points, and then it overwrites the new clip into the sequence, replacing the clip that was previously there.

A replace edit ignores the In and Out points set in the Viewer. And if no In and Out points are specified in the sequence, Final Cut uses the In and Out points of the clip currently under the playhead in the Timeline (on the target tracks). These rules make it work very differently than the basic edits described in Chapter 5.

Showing Different Angles of the Same Event

Editors often use a replace edit to choose a different angle of the same event. For example, imagine that you're editing a movie about a jewelry heist. At the climax of the heist scene, security doors begin to close around the thieves, cornering them.

Since this is a big-budget picture, you've got lots of coverage to choose from. In your rough cut you used wide shots to show the doors closing, but after a sneak preview you decide to replace one of the wide shots with a CU of the door latching shut.

First, in the sequence, park your playhead on the frame where the door shuts completely.

Next, in the new source clip (the CU), find the frame where the door shuts completely and position your playhead there.

Finally, drag the source clip onto the Replace target on the Edit Overlay (**Figure 6.50**).

Figure 6.50 By lining up the playhead in both shots to the frame where the door shuts completely, we create a sync point that will enable the entire duration of the shots to sync up. We perform the replace edit by dragging onto the Edit Overlay.

Not only will this replace the WS with the CU, but the timing will be exactly the same. The door in the new clip will shut at precisely the same moment as it did in the old clip.

It's helpful to have some clear point on which to sync up your replace edit, but it's not required. For instance, if you want to replace a cutaway of a security camera with a cutaway of a clock ticking, place your playhead anywhere in the clip—and as long as the clock shot has enough room to match the length of the security camera shot, you can successfully replace one shot with the other.

Syncing a Clip With a Cue Point (Using Match Frame)

A replace edit can also be used to sync up one clip with a cue point on another track. In this case, rather than replacing one clip with another, we're going to reuse the exact same clip, but with different timing. That may sound confusing, but I'll take you through it step by step.

For example, let's stay with the jewelry heist show. In the rough cut, you covered the moment when the thieves grab the 500-carat diamond in a CU that shows the überthief lifting the stone in front of her face and gazing at it rapturously. A moment later, the security alarm goes off, and you cut to an LS showing the thieves huddling together to plan their escape.

However, test audiences are lukewarm on this sequence. According to the comment sheets, there's no suspense: Viewers don't worry about the thieves getting caught, since the robbers have already snatched the diamond seconds before the security alarm goes off.

So...back to the editing room, where you decide to change the timing so the security alarm goes off just at the instant the thief lifts the diamond. Here's how you would use a replace edit to do it.

First, open the Timeline, find the first frame of the thief lifting the jewel, and park your playhead there (**Figure 6.51**).

Next, use the Match Frame command (found in the Go To section of the Mark menu or by hitting F on the keyboard). Match Frame opens a copy of the currently viewed clip in the Viewer. Match Frame also matches the exact frame you are looking at, so the clip in the Viewer is now parked on that exact frame where the thief is about to lift the diamond.

Next, go back to the Timeline and place your playhead at the exact moment the bells go off (**Figure 6.52**).

Figure 6.51 Park your playhead on the frame you want to use as a sync point.

Figure 6.52 After using Match Frame to put your first sync point in the Viewer, find the spot in your sequence that's going to be the second sync point and park your playhead there.

Finally, perform a replace edit. This will line up the frame in the Viewer (the thief about to lift the jewel) with the frame in the sequence (the sound of the alarm going off), and re-edit the same shot with the slightly altered timing (**Figure 6.53**).

The studio loves the new version, the producer signs you on to do *The Jewel Heist II,* and when you test the show again, the audience decides it liked the original sequence better.

Figure 6.53 Using the Match Frame command and the replace edit together allows us to line up two spots in a few simple steps. I've used markers to show you that the two points are now lined up, but the markers aren't required.

Replace With In and Out Points

The replace edit doesn't require any In and Out points, but you can use sequence Ins and Outs to give you additional control over how the edit works.

For example, go back to the shot of the doors closing where we replaced a WS with a CU. Suppose that rather than replacing the whole shot, we just wanted to cut to the CU one second before the door closes. We can do that using an In point and a replace edit.

You would begin the same way, by opening the CU in the Viewer and parking the playhead on the frame where the door closes.

Next, in the Timeline, find the frame where the door closes in the WS and mark an In point one second earlier. Be sure that the playhead is still parked on the sync point, which is the door closing (**Figure 6.54**).

The area between the In point and the end of the clip will be replaced.

Figure 6.54 The replace edit will always line up the playhead in the sequence and in the Viewer, but if there's an In or Out point in the Timeline, the edit will observe it.

When you perform the replace edit, only the area between the defined In point and the end of the clip is replaced, not the whole clip. Now the WS cuts to the CU one second before the door closes. Continuity flows across the edit point, since the door was closing at the same speed in both shots, and we know that they are synced because Replace lined up the two frames of the door closing.

Syncing to a Playhead Position Outside the In/Out Mark

This can be taken one step further by syncing to a point *even if it's outside the area being replaced.* If you define an In and Out point in the sequence, and place the playhead outside of that area, the playhead location will still serve as a sync point.

This may seem pretty advanced, but there are some situations where it's the most straightforward way to edit and it can be quick too! For example, in a common dialogue scene, you may have several shots cutting back and forth between CUs (**Figure 6.55**). If you wanted to add a CU later in the scene, you can use this Replace edit technique to insure that the shots all line up and maintain sync, and it only takes three steps.

Figure 6.55 In this basic dialogue scene, you want to cut back to "CU Trey_02" without having to manually line up the edit.

First, set an In and Out point in the sequence to mark where the new shot is to be edited (**Figure 6.56**). Then, park your playhead anywhere over the CU you want to use and select Match Frame > Master Clip from the View menu (**Figure 6.57**). Finally, perform a Replace edit. Although the playhead is outside of the In and Out points, it serves to insure that the new clip is in perfect sync with the rest of the sequence (**Figure 6.58**).

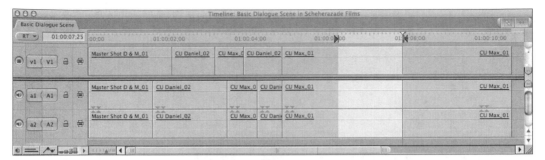

Figure 6.56 Set up the Replace edit by first identifying where you want the new shot to go.

Figure 6.57 Put your playhead anywhere over the clip to be replaced and perform a Match Frame. The In and Out points in the Viewer will be ignored when using the Replace edit style.

Figure 6.58 The new clip will automatically be in sync because the duration from the playhead to the In point is the same in both the Viewer and the Canvas.

Make Sure You Have Enough Media in the Viewer

The most common problem editors experience when using a replace edit comes from having insufficient room on one side or the other of the playhead in the Viewer. For example, if you are trying to replace a ten second clip in the Timeline, and your playhead is parked seven seconds in, your source clip in the Viewer will need to have at least seven seconds before and three seconds after the current playhead position. If your playhead in the Viewer is only one second into the clip (even if the clip is 30 seconds long), the edit will fail and give you an error message saying you have insufficient content for the edit (**Figure 6.59**). To perform this edit, your playhead in the Viewer must be at least seven seconds into the clip, and there must be at least three seconds remaining after (**Figure 6.60**).

Figure 6.59 To execute a successful replace edit, you must have sufficient media in your source clip. Here, the playhead in the Viewer is parked at 1:00, but the playhead in the sequence is parked seven seconds into the clip. Attempting a replace edit at this point gives an error message.

Figure 6.60 By moving the Viewer playhead farther into the clip, you get plenty of room before and after the playhead to replace the target clip in the Timeline.

GANG SYNC

Traditional film editors kept their sequences in sync by locking all of the strips of film and soundtrack together into a device called a sync block. Sometimes, when performing an edit, the editor would line up a separate piece of film into the sync block and run it alongside the main show. This was called "ganging." This way he could see how various bits of the shot might cut with the existing scene. For example, he might have the Master Shot cut into the main show and a CU shot running along side it. Because the two shots were of the same scene, and because the actors performed exactly the same each time, the two pieces of film would remain in sync throughout the scene. He could then cut many small pieces out of the new shot and splice them into the main scene. The sync block ensured that all the bits would remain in sync.

Final Cut Pro 4 added a simulated Sync Block to your editing toolbox, which you can use in much the same way that the traditional film editor employed the real thing. Of course, because digital technology offers much more versatility than the old film tools, Final Cut Pro's Sync Block has several different modes to accommodate a variety of editing situations. The Sync Block appears as a pop-up in both the Canvas and Viewer windows (**Figure 6.61**). The four options are, Off, Follow, Open, and Gang.

Figure 6.61 The Sync Block menus in the Viewer and Canvas are tied together. Setting one automatically sets the other.

Follow Mode

The Follow mode is the simplest case. Follow only gangs together shots that are already in the sequence. To make use of it you must first double-click one of the clips in your sequence and set the Sync Block to Follow. Once you open any other clip into the viewer, the Sync Block will be reset to Off.

This mode is useful for judging timing differences between two shots already in your sequence or for re-editing a single shot back into your sequence. For example, in one scene, I intend to cut back and forth between a CU of Trey and a MCU of Gene & Starr (**Figure 6.62**). Because I know I want to return to the CU shot for his next line, I double-click that shot to open it into the Viewer and set the Gang mode to Follow. Now as I move my playhead in the sequence, the Viewer will move along with me. Next, I play forward into the second clip and mark an In and Out point where I want the CU to go (**Figure 6.63**). I can assume that both shots are the same length (since they were from the same scene) so I can trust that the CU will be in sync when I edit it into the sequence. I perform a Replace edit to insure that the Viewer In and Out points will be ignored (**Figure 6.64**).

Figure 6.62 This sequence cuts back and forth between different shots from the same scene.

Figure 6.63 Mark the area where you want to use the first clip again.

Figure 6.64 Since your playheads are sure to be in sync, you can perform a Replace Edit which will ignore the In and Out points in the Viewer.

Open Mode

The Open Mode works similarly to the Follow Mode, except that as you play across different edits in your sequence, each new clip is loaded into the viewer. This is not useful for the type of editing I just described, but it's great for doing color correction, or other effects where you want to modify the various clips in your sequence without repeatedly double-clicking them in the Timeline. (For more on this mode, see "Color Correction" in Chapter 8.)

Gang Mode

The Gang Mode is the most similar to my earlier description of the film editor working with a sync block, and is the mode I use most often. The Gang mode will link together the playheads of the sequence and any clip you load into the Viewer, not just ones already in the sequence. This can be used to compare the timing of two different takes of the same shot, or to compare different angles on a single action. Because the Viewer stays in sync with the Canvas, as you move along you are always just one Replace edit away from a new shot that's guaranteed to be in sync.

Use this mode in a similar way to the Follow Mode steps, but instead of re-editing the same shot, use Match Frame to load the Master Clip into the Viewer and edit from there. This is essential if you've applied a filter or level adjustments to the clip already in the sequence. Also, rather than depending on the Replace edit (which won't work if there's not a clip in the sequence to replace), this enables you to do simple Overwrite edits from the Master clips.

Imagine the same sequence as above, but rather than extending the last clip, you just lay in the bit you know you want to use (**Figure 6.65**). Park anywhere over the first clip, Match Frame (shortcut: f) to load the master clip into the Viewer and set the Sync Block to Gang. Then play forward in the Viewer and set an In an Out point. Use the Playhead to determine the sequence In point and you're ready to edit the clip into the sequence (**Figure 6.66**). Move on to Clip 2 and do the same thing. You can repeat this again and again, building up your sequence bit by bit. If the shots are both of the same action, all of your edits will always, almost magically, line right up in sync creating smooth edits that require very little trimming or tweaking.

The only disadvantage to this is that each time you load a new clip into the Viewer, the Sync Block is reset to Off, so you need to set the menu each time you do the Match Frame. This is inconvenient but of course there is an elegant solution—make yourself a keyboard shortcut to set the Sync Block to Gang.

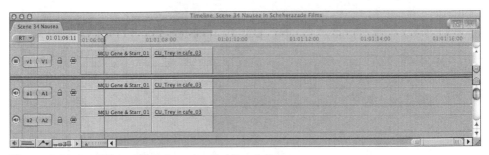

Figure 6.65 **Begin by editing in a couple bits of dialogue.**

Figure 6.66 Set three points and perform an Overwrite edit.

Open the Keyboard Layout window and type "Gang" or "Sync" into the Button List on the right side of the window (**Figure 6.67**). Drag the command to the key combo of your choice.

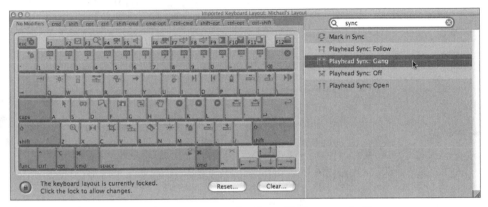

Figure 6.67 Set your own shortcut to turn the Gang Mode on and off.

SPLIT EDITS

I've already discussed why and when you'll find yourself using split edits. By separating audio edits from picture edits, you can smooth over the inevitable interruption any edit creates. Split edits are essential for almost every dialogue scene and many action scenes as well.

Most editors split their edits after the clips are already in the sequence by rolling the video edit separately from the audio edit, or vice versa (**Figure 6.68**). This works fine, but frequently you need to adjust the new edit point a bit to finish the job.

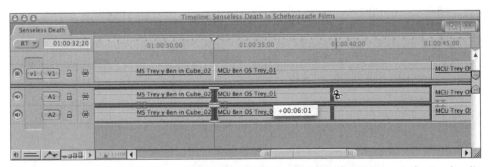

Fig 6.68 The simplest way to create a split edit is to roll either the picture or the track edit point without the other.

Fine-Tuning a Split Edit

Different cases may require different amounts of fine tuning, but a potent combination of rolling and rippling enables you to create and polish the split edits that make transitions smoother, overlap your dialogue to sound natural, and sync up various material across different shots.

I'll use a typical dialogue sequence as an example.

Ben: It's a new video game!
I want to call it Senseless Death.

Trey: Ben, that's sick!

Ben: (nods excitedly)

Trey (continued): How do they get away with sending guns through the mail?

Ben: I don't know, dude! It's Thailand. They don't know what the hell's going on!

Figure 6.69 The sequence begins with the three clips, all with straight edits.

As is almost always the case, the dialogue runs continuously across the edit points. And so far, all the edits in this sequence line up on dialogue breaks. There are no split edits yet.

In order to split the last edit, so the beginning of Ben's line, "I don't know, dude..." is heard over shot 2, follow these steps:

1. Play the sequence and stop at the point where you want the new edit. Set the In point or a marker to identify the spot.

2. Roll the video edit forward until it reaches the marker (**Figure 6.70**).

Figure 6.70 Once the marker is set, use the Roll tool to line up the edit point with the desired spot.

In some cases, this may be all you need to do. But sometimes after you roll the edit, you'll spot footage in the first shot that doesn't sync up with the audio underneath it. In this case, even though shot 2 is an OS, where Ben is facing away, his movements don't match the timing of the audio from shot 3. To solve this, we can further trim the edit using the Ripple tool (**Figure 6.71**).

Figure 6.71 In many cases, to make a seamless split edit you must adjust the edit point after the initial roll. Here I ripple the clip back to compress the time in between the lines and tidy up the timing of the edit.

Now, when we play the sequence, the offset of the split hasn't changed, but we've trimmed the end of shot 2. This tightens the edit, allowing less dead space between lines, and more important, it syncs up Ben's movements in shot 2 with the lines heard in shot 3.

Split Marks

Because split edits are such a fundamental part of professional editing, Final Cut has a special feature designed to make creating them easier: split marks. When you're setting your In and Out points in either the Viewer or the Canvas, this feature enables you to set different points for your audio and video (**Figure 6.72**). It allows you to define the split edits before you edit the clips into the sequence.

Why would you bother? It's useful for cases when you already know from watching the source clip where you want to split the edit. For instance, often when I'm cutting dialogue I'll hear a line or see a gesture that I know will precipitate an edit. I can mark a video only or audio only In point right there in the Viewer and figure out the other point later.

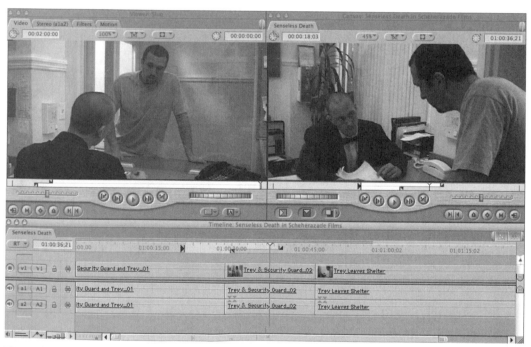

Figure 6.72 Split marks let you set individual In and Out points for your audio and video. Video marks are on the top half and audio, the lower. To drag one of the points individually, hold down Option.

How to Set Split Marks

Split marks can be set (and cleared) by using the commands in the Mark menu, or by accessing the Shortcut menu in the Scrubber area of the Viewer and Canvas or the ruler in the Timeline. Of course, as good editors, I know you want to learn how to set them on the fly, and while the key combos are a little convoluted, Final Cut provides one for each case:

Mark Video In	Ctrl - I
Mark Video Out	Ctrl - O
Mark Audio In	⌘ - Option - I
Mark Audio Out	⌘ - Option - O

While splitting marks provides impressive power in terms of allowing you to perform a very complex edit in a single step, it also requires more presence of mind in the planning of the edit. You must be able to hold twice as much information in your head as you do with an ordinary edit. Where do you want the picture to begin in the source clip? Where does the audio begin? Do they end at the same point, or is the backside of the clip going to be a split edit as well? And in the sequence, where do you want the split to begin and end? Finally, once you've sorted all that out, you have to decide which of the various points you have to define.

Four-, Five-, and Six-Point Editing

With three-point editing, you need to provide only three of the four necessary points in order to complete the edit. But when you're working with split edits, the number of points you need to define varies. And inexplicably, only some combinations work.

One Split

The simplest arrangement is to split only one of the four points. For example, define separate source video In and source audio In points and leave the Out point undefined. Then set unsplit (normal) In and Out points in the Canvas (**Figure 6.73**).

When you apply the edit, the split source In points (audio or video) that come first will line up with the sequence In point (**Figure 6.74**).

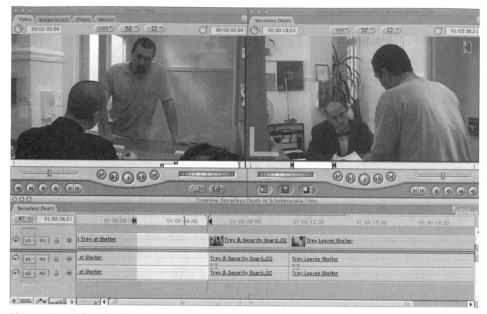

Figure 6.73 The simplest use of split marks is to split only one of the four marks. As with three-point editing, you can leave one of the points undefined. In this example, the Viewer Outpoint is not defined.

Figure 6.74 When you edit this clip into the sequence, the sequence In point lines up with the earlier of the two source In marks in the Viewer.

This is the most common way to use split marks—but you need to be aware that the reverse case doesn't work. If you split the source Out point and provide a record Out, Final Cut ignores the audio Out point and treats the video Out as if it were an unsplit Out. This is a bug, and unless you know about it, it might drive you nuts. Unfortunately, you may run into a few cases like this, even in version 4 (**Figure 6.75**).

Figure 6.75 One case that doesn't work (for no good reason) is where you split the source Out and don't set a record In.

Two Splits

Often you want to exactly define where the edits land in the sequence. As I explained, the program default causes the sequence In point to sync with the earlier of the two points in the Viewer. If you want to override that default so the sequence In point lines up with the *later* of the two points, you can make that happen by setting a single split mark in the sequence (**Figure 6.76**).

Why would you want to do this? Well, once you've begun a sequence, each clip you add must match one that's already there. If you're editing with many splits, you're going to have to sync up either the audio or the video as a continuity cut.

For example, let's say you have a sequence of two people talking. You're cutting back and forth between MCUs, and you know that you want to create an L cut so the incoming picture hits before the incoming track arrives.

You can split the respective starting points for audio and video in the Viewer, but when you go to edit it into the sequence, you're primarily concerned about lining up the audio so the dialogue seems continuous; you don't care exactly where the picture edit happens (**Figure 6.77**). To accomplish this, mark an audio In at the desired point in the Timeline and the dialogue will line up perfectly. The picture edit may need some fine tuning, but the L edit will be accomplished in a single operation.

> **TIP:** You can't set two pairs of splits that don't match. If you attempt to set a source split where the audio precedes the video by 20 frames, and at the same time you set a split in the sequence where the audio precedes the video by ten frames (or the video precedes the audio at all), you'll get an Invalid Edit error.

Banana Split

As you gain confidence and experience, you can get creative, setting a wide variety of split marks to perform complex edits with a single stroke. (Imagine a shot that's an L edit at the head and a J edit at the tail and gets laid into the sequence at a precise location you've defined with a split mark.) Unfortunately, you're likely to encounter some arrangements of split marks (in addition to the one I identified previously) that don't work—even though they should. If you run into one, you've probably hit a bug. Call Apple.

While I do recommend fooling around with split marks, I find that if I'm trying to do anything more complicated than what I described in previous sections, I spend more time *preparing* the edit than I save by doing it in one step. In many cases, it's faster to perform a basic edit (or a simple split) and tweak it in the Timeline after the fact.

Figure 6.76 If you want to override Final Cut's default (which puts the earlier split source point at the sequence In), set a split sequence In. This will put the edit exactly where you want it.

Figure 6.77 In this example I want to specify exactly where the audio In point begins in the sequence, and then create an L edit in one step by using the split marks in the Viewer.

USING SUBSEQUENCES TO MANAGE LARGE PROJECTS

Final Cut allows you to *nest* one sequence inside of another. This is a tool that's essential for some types of special effects techniques (see Chapter 8) but it's also exactly the tool for managing long-form shows.

Construct each scene in its own sequence, then create a master sequence and drop in your subsequences one after another to playback or output the whole show at once (**Figure 6.78**). If you do this, swapping scene order is just as easy as swapping individual clips. Simply pick up a scene, drag it to its new location, hold down Option, and release.

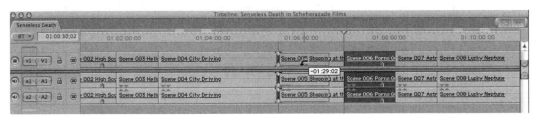

Figure 6.78 You can arrange each scene as a single sequence in a master sequence. This allows you to rearrange sequences just as you would clips.

A Live Link

If, after you've stitched all the subsequences together, you want to go back and modify the contents within one of the scenes, no problem! Any edits or changes you make in any of the nested items will automatically update in the master sequence. If you change the duration, making the subsequence a bit longer or shorter, the master sequence will ripple to accommodate the change. Beware: If you have an In or Out point set in the master sequence, no automatic rippling will occur.

No EDL Support

One drawback to this technique is that the contents of the subsequences will not be included in an *EDL* (Edit Decision List) from the master sequence. This will affect you if you are planning to do a preliminary edit in Final Cut and then reproduce the sequence in another program. EDL's are also a reliable failsafe backup format for your sequence, since their simplistic format will enable you to automatically recreate your show from your source tapes on any editing system long after Final Cut Pro is obsolete. Also, because they are merely text files, they are extremely small and editable in any word processor.

Edit Sequence Contents

There is a solution to this problem, but it requires Final Cut Pro 4. When dragging one sequence into another, the CMD modifier key will alter the edit so that instead of the sequence being treated as one item, its contents is used instead (**Figure 6.79**). This applies whether you perform the edit by drag and drop, keyboard shortcut, or on-screen edit button.

Fig 6.79 You can edit the contents of a sequence by holding down CMD when performing the edit.

In this case, there is no live link back to the subsequence, so you should only perform this sort of edit after all of your decisions have been made inside the subsequence.

Once you have edited the contents of each of your subsequences into your master, you can export a single EDL to cover your entire show.

Workaround for Final Cut Express Users

For Final Cut Express users, there are two suitable workarounds:

- Export individual EDLs for each subsequence.

- Copy and paste all the clips from each subsequence into the master sequence.

Neither of these is a terribly elegant solution. If you choose to copy and paste, you must be very careful to avoid any accidental overlaps and ensure that the correct tracks are selected. This also can take an inordinate amount of time. (Final Cut's Copy and Paste tools are notoriously slow.)

THE BIG PICTURE

All these advanced editing techniques tend to focus our attention on the minute details of every edit, and that's important because you'll be employing many of these techniques for thousands of edits in your show.

But don't forget to step back at some point and look at the entire chessboard. The worst editing mistake you can make, far more dangerous than losing track of an edit point or using a roll when you need a ripple, is losing sight of the big picture.

What Makes a Sequence Work?

When you play back a sequence, ask yourself whether it works.

At the very least, the narrative flow should be smooth: No edit points should jar the viewer and disturb the story. Also, the pacing should be right: no "dead" sections where nothing is happening; no areas so dense that viewers can't make sense of what's going on. Finally, the sequence should be free of blatant continuity errors caused by editing or production mistakes. (For instance, if the hero's hat was on in the CU, it should be on in the next LS.) If you see any of these problems, dive back in and fix them.

But that's just for openers. After you've worked out your various scenes, look at the overall movie and decide how it makes you feel. How does the show *play?* Here are some important things to watch out for.

Awkward Bridges Between Scenes

Pay attention to scene cuts (see the section on scene cuts in Chapter 2). How well do the scenes transition from one to the next? If they don't flow, can you create bridges with sound or compositional elements to help smooth out the scene changes? Sometimes simply rearranging the order of scenes (like swapping shots in an individual sequence) makes a big difference.

The Overall Story

In most cases, the film embodies thematic elements you are trying to convey or theses you want to prove or disprove. Does the film accomplish those goals? If it's intended to be informative or educational, does it convey the relevant information effectively, economically, and efficiently? If it's a dramatic feature, is it exciting? Is it unique? Is it moving?

Put Away the Script

Sometimes problems are inherent in the script. This may give you a scapegoat, but it won't make your picture better. At some point in the production process, the script becomes irrelevant. You must find a way to make the best movie you can make with the footage available to you.

If the film is in serious trouble, you may have to cut important subplots, or even turn a subplot into the main plot while you downgrade what was supposed to be the main plot to a background event. Obviously, in a drastic revision like this, you'll need to work closely with the director and the writer to decide how to proceed.

Honesty is the Best Policy

Everyone on the production team must be brutally honest about what works, what doesn't work, and what can be done to improve the film. While I certainly recommend being diplomatic and constructive in offering criticism, you're not doing anyone any favors by pretending something is good when it isn't. You need to be just as honest about your show as you'd be about any show you come across on TV, in a film festival, or at your local theater.

Put Up and Shut Up

Of course, you want to make the best show you can, but if you're editing a film for a corporate client or a government agency, all that matters is whether or not your client likes the finished piece. It doesn't really matter whether you like it or your husband likes it or you want to include it on your sample reel. Your job is to give the client what he wants.

Show it to Somebody

On the other hand, if you're cutting a film for public consumption, part of your obligation to the producer and the director is to make it as effective as possible for the audience. This means getting outside input. At some point, you need to show the program to someone completely disconnected from the project (and, ideally, representative of your target audience) to provide real-world perspective.

Make it Shorter

If a film is too long, it doesn't matter how good it is: Fatigue and impatience will alienate your audience. It's a given in the film biz that you can make almost any film shorter—and nine times out of ten it will be better. But it can be a bloody affair. If you're looking at a show that isn't working, start by identifying what can be cut.

Recently I watched a rough cut of a friend's film. She intended it to be a theatrical feature, and the rough cut was 96 minutes, but it had problems and she wanted advice about how to resolve them. While many of the scenes were terrific—funny, poignant, and honest—a handful of scenes were heavy-handed, poorly acted, even slightly untruthful. On top of which *all* of the scenes went on too long. I decided that about one third of the film was great, one third was mediocre, and one third was poor.

So I suggested that my friend consider turning her feature into a short. At 30 minutes, it could have been a terrific film: entertaining, meaningful, and funny. Sure, she'd have a significant amount of work to do to tie together the great moments, but a good 30-minute film is a lot better than an uneven one that runs 90 minutes.

The length of a show has a broader impact on your audience than you may realize. Some of it's purely physical. For instance, how long can your audience sit still comfortably? (Movie theater seats are cushioned, but the seats in most classrooms or corporate auditoriums are not.) Will people need a bathroom break? These may sound like silly questions, but for longer projects you must take them seriously.

I remember an early review of *Titanic* in which the reviewer went on and on about how, as the show moved into its third hour, with shot after shot featuring torrents of rushing water, pouring water, dripping water, spilling water, crashing water, all he could think about was how desperately he needed to pee! At the end of the film, he said, the line outside the men's bathroom was out the door.

Unless you have stars like Leonardo DiCaprio and Kate Winslet (and a director like James Cameron) to keep your viewers in their seats, consider how distracting that sort of physical discomfort can be and how it can interfere with your audience's appreciation of your film.

Anyone can cut bad footage from a film. The mark of a great editor is knowing how to cut *good* footage to make what's left even better.

Keep Cutting

No matter how many times I've polished it, every time I sit down in front of a scene I'm working on, I see ways to trim a few more seconds. Trust your audience to read your shots quickly, and keep feeding them new ideas and fresh information to hold their interest. I'm not talking about spoon-feeding eye candy to impatient channel surfers; I'm talking about engaging your viewers with meaningful material.

My first rough cut of *Want* was 190 minutes long! My target length was 90 to 110 minutes. I had to find a way to cut at least half the film. Upon discussing this with other professional editors, I was reassured. A three hour rough cut is a guarantee of a good 90 minute film. You're only in trouble if your rough cut is exactly 90 minutes already.

Before I went crazy cutting whole scenes, I reviewed each scene and tightened it up. I removed dead spaces between lines. I cut some lines altogether. I eliminated transitional shots that seemed extraneous. And before I had to cut one single scene, I'd eliminated more than 20 minutes—ten seconds here, twenty seconds there, and not only did the film become shorter, it played faster and better. Later, on another tightening pass, I managed to wring out 12 more minutes.

Kill Your Darlings

Even if you are enthralled with the composition at the end of the shot, when two women are walking off of the bridge silhouetted against the sunset, that doesn't justify 15 seconds of dead time between the last line of dialogue and that wonderful image.

Unless you've made a very bad decision about your chosen profession, any film you edit will be packed with moments—sometimes as brief as a single reaction shot, sometimes as long as a whole scene—that fill you with pride when they go by. Maybe you're particularly happy with one continuity edit that took two hours to match, or a serendipitous cut that makes a statement about the entire film. Perhaps it's a scene that cost a fortune to produce, or a performance that gave the director chills on set.

Whatever it is, if it doesn't work in the finished film, it's got to go. And you're the one who has to kill it.

I'll tell you a story. In my film *Want,* there was an interesting character, an old woman named Señora Guero. I wanted to draw a subtle connection between Guero and the younger woman Trey is infatuated with, so I asked the same actor to play both roles. We used latex makeup to age her for the scenes where she portrayed the old woman.

The actor hated sitting through the tedious makeup sessions. Applying the latex took more than five hours, and it was quite uncomfortable. To make matters worse, after watching the dailies I decided I didn't like the way the makeup looked anyway, and I wanted to reshoot all of her scenes using a different type of latex. This meant that a series of scenes that was supposed to take two days wound up taking more than six. Hiring the special effects makeup artist was very expensive, and all of the scenes involving Guero were technically complicated and emotionally intense. Those six days were unquestionably the most costly and grueling ones of our whole production.

I'm sure you know where this story is going. Late in the editing process, unhappy with the way the film was coming together, I made a drastic decision and cut the entire subplot involving Señora Guero. It was an agonizing decision, but it changed everything—for the better. Not only did it allow me to trim 10 minutes off the total running time, it opened up new opportunities for ways to bring the scenes together. My crew and I grieved for Guero, but in the end killing her scenes was what needed to be done.

Finding Redundancies

A certain amount of repetition can be artful, as in comedy or suspense (see "Funnier the Second Time Around" in Chapter 3). But invariably you'll find scenes or shots in your show that are redundant. Perhaps the same point is being made twice, two scenes may communicate the same emotion, or maybe a significant gesture or shot is repeated too many times. You must eliminate these elements. Find the one that does the job best, and cut the others. Repetition usually slows down the story with unnecessary information.

Intercutting Scenes

One trick to help you shorten your show is to intercut scenes. You may find that two four-minute scenes can be intercut to make one six-minute sequence, with virtually no loss of impact. Even if you don't stick with the intercut version, I guarantee the exercise will help you find at least one minute from each scene that's expendable.

Apply this technique to other redundant elements as a way to boil them down to the essentials. If you have three scenes that all accomplish essentially the same goal thematically or plot-wise, try intercutting them. You may find that one shot from each scene is all you need.

A Game of Inches

I used to race sailboats, and someone once described the sport to me as a game of inches. Not only because the winning boat might cross the finish line inches in front of its competitor, but because in a tight race, boats can maneuver mere inches apart, nearly colliding and damaging one another. Also, the stiffer the sail, the more precisely you can control the wind, and pulling the main sheet three inches tighter will make a measurable difference that could determine whether you win or lose the race.

In the same ways, editing can also be a game of inches. Tiny changes can have a dramatic impact on the overall show. An edit point that's off by only three or four frames will make a transition look terrible. One poor edit can make a whole scene play badly. Eliminating just one shot that doesn't fit perfectly will change the entire dynamic of a sequence. And one slow sequence can make the whole show seem too long.

While we're talking about inches, be careful not to oversteer. Make very small changes and see how they impact the whole before you do something drastic. The more experience you get, the more you'll understand how a few subtle changes can have a significant influence on the whole.

Early in my career, I found myself editing a short film about a hotel clerk—and when I showed my first cut to the director, he hated it. He couldn't tell me exactly what was wrong, but he felt I hadn't captured the best performances from the actors.

I spent days going back through bins of outtakes (I was editing 16mm film), desperately watching all the footage and trying to find new shots that would save the film. Then I began to doubt myself and started making broad changes to the cut. After a while, when I detested the way it was coming out, I went back in deep despair and restored the film to a close approximation of my first rough cut. However, in all my reshuffling I had managed to lose a piece of film (easy to do when you're cutting 16mm), and I had to cut the scene together without it.

As soon as I watched the film, I felt different about it. The shot I'd lost was a reaction shot in which the main character had been hamming it up a little. When I showed the new cut to the director, he didn't realize exactly what the difference was, but he agreed that I had made a big improvement over the last edit.

The moral is: Don't despair, make changes judiciously, and trust the process. You may discover that the scene or sequence you thought was unsalvageable simply needed two shots switched around.

INTERVIEW

Chris Tellefsen began editing professionally in 1990 on Whit Stillman's *Metropolitan*. Since then he's worked on an amazing variety of projects, everything from Wayne Wang's improvisational *Blue in the Face* and *Chinese Box* to Milos Forman's controversial *The People vs. Larry Flynt*. His credits also include comedies like Harold Ramis' *Analyze This* and David O. Russell's *Flirting with Disaster*. When we spoke, he was in the middle of cutting *Changing Lanes* for British director Roger Michell. Most recently he edited *The Human Stain* featuring Anthony Hopkins and Nicole Kidman.

MICHAEL WOHL: WHAT DO YOU LOVE MOST ABOUT YOUR JOB?

Chris Tellefsen: What I love more than anything is creating and constructing scenes and carving out performances. Making performances really shine and bringing them forward.

WHAT HAPPENS ONCE PRINCIPAL PHOTOGRAPHY IS DONE?

Within a week, I have to have a script cut, except I'll cut some things that I think are truly extraneous. Then it's time to shape. Then I'm going from something that's, like, two hours and 15 minutes down to 90 minutes.

AND THEN?

Well, you don't immediately get to 90. It takes a long time to get that hour out. Because you really feel out where the strengths lie and the weaknesses are, where things feel repetitive. You do that with repeated viewings and by studying it. Once it's all together, you get more of a sense of overall style and things that feel right. You can get more of an idea of how to keep something rhythmically more interesting, and also pacing the rhythm, keeping it in hills and valleys. Making sure that it doesn't have too even a pace, or finding out what scenes that are together that have too similar a rhythm, or too similar a look.

DO YOU EVER VISIT THE SET?

On occasion. I don't like visiting the set that much on a film that I'm editing. I don't find it that helpful or even that interesting, to tell you the truth. I like to keep somewhat of an illusion, especially when there's an elaborate set, because I like the illusion of it. Sometimes seeing too much of the artifice bugs me or makes me think about it when I'm editing, and I have to erase it from my mind.

CAN YOU TALK A BIT ABOUT CUTTING COMEDY?

Comedy has its form: You have to get a laugh. It's very clear what you're trying to achieve. It's a matter of sharpening it and making it really, really razor-sharp funny. That's where the preview process is fun. You really feel the laughs. You feel what's coming off the audience, and in your head you're checking out when those responses are not quite there. With drama it's less well-defined, it's a little more a searching process to get it absolutely right.

WHAT ARE YOU LOOKING FOR IN THE PREVIEW AUDIENCE FOR A DRAMA?

Engagement. You're looking for them to be engaged with the characters. To be engaged with the story, to have a satisfying experience. You have to feel their presence, feel their response. Whereas with comedy, you know they've had a satisfying experience if they're laughing.

YOU EDITED WAYNE WANG'S *CHINESE BOX*. HOW WAS THAT?

Really interesting because there was a script, but it was almost completely thrown away. I was working in New York and they were shooting in Hong Kong. My daughter was only a year old; I didn't want to be away for four months. So, we would communicate by fax and by tape; the scenes were changing constantly. It was really funny, because I would cut stuff and send it, and then Wayne would send a new order of scenes. Then I would change those and we'd fax them back and forth. It evolved a lot. There was a lot of change. We had an interesting time with that. There was also a lot of footage that was shot on DV, because the main character was a journalist who was dying, and who was shooting all over town—for preservation before the changeover [from British to Chinese government administration].

TELL ME ABOUT A SCENE YOU'VE BEEN WORKING ON RECENTLY, AND SOME OF THE SPECIFIC CHALLENGES YOU'RE FACING.

Sure, today I'm working on a film [*Changing Lanes*] that's made up of two days in its original form, and it's been a real trial to get the first day, which is basically an introduction, to work properly. So, we made a very drastic leap of having it all take place in one day. Time-wise, it's very problematic, but it does cut to the chase. So, what I've been dealing with is to boil down the end of that first day to make it feel as brisk as possible, but still have the transition. That's something I've been grappling with today, and I think I'm getting somewhere with it, getting somewhere very positive and good.

DOES THE STYLE OF CINEMATOGRAPHY AFFECT YOUR EDITING?

Yes, I had a nice time with Sal Totino [director of photography on *Changing Lanes*]. We talked a lot during dailies and I got very excited about some of the things he was doing. And I would show him cuts and we'd talk about it. [The cinematography] is very naturalistic. It's very aggressive camera work for an urban story about two men. It's not a flashy thing, but it's very immediate; not "wild swinging pans, hand-held" but "camera breath hand-held." It has some life to it. There's a lot of wonderful short focus that makes you feel very close to the characters.

ARE THERE SPECIFIC WAYS THAT IT AFFECTED OR CHANGED YOUR EDITING?

Oh, yeah. I know that Roger [Michell, director of *Changing Lanes*] was really interested in the short focus and little moves, things that were a little odd. I would get the footage and look at it for all of the details that could work dramatically. Within one scene, I found we got a little too carried away with style and distanced the emotional impact of the scene, so we changed that rather drastically away from the stylistic to something that cuts to the chase more in terms of the emotional content. In that case, there were all these layers of glass. It was kind of exciting—the idea of all these reflections—but it was just a little too cool, a little too stylistic. So, I used more of the tight coverage, rather than the stuff that was shot through the layers of glass. I haven't completely changed it, but I had to beef it up for emotional purposes, for the audience to really connect with the characters.

HAS EDITING ON THE COMPUTER CHANGED THE WAY YOU WORK?

Sometimes the most thoughtful cut is a spontaneous cut. That's something I love about digital: You can be very spontaneous. You can suddenly have a thought and go with it. And even if it's the totally wrong way, you can just undo it. It's so flexible. I find it very liberating. I loved film editing, but you can do so much more with digital. It's made me more able to experiment.

HOW WAS WORKING WITH MILOS FORMAN?

We were on location in Memphis where [*The People vs. Larry Flynt*] was shot. The first two scenes that were shot were Courtney Love's dance—Althea's strip— and Larry and Althea's first meeting in the office, and they were wonderful scenes. I was so excited. There was so much chemistry between them. It was really, really exciting and I really dug in. Milos was very excited. He was very happy and all. But then, when there was a simpler, not as exciting a scene, he was all grumpy: "Why can't you make it sing?" So the next time I met with him, I had cut a scene four different ways, because it was the second digital film I had done. (My first digital film was *Flirting with Disaster*.) And he said, "Oh, this is better, but not four versions, ten versions!" And it was insanity; I was making 11 cuts of every scene. It was like boot camp. And when we worked together it was like, no joke, we were in the cutting room from 9:30 in the morning till 11:00 at night. We'd never look away. It was insane.

WHAT IS YOUR LEAST FAVORITE PART OF YOUR JOB?

Sometimes the preview process can be very painful. But, it can be painful and you can learn a great deal from it as well. It can be both constructive and destructive. The hardest thing is to keep your head when you know there needs to be drastic changes, and you don't want to lose the balance of what you have. I think that's the toughest, the most difficult thing. But I think I do well, because I can keep that balance.

DO YOU HAVE ANY ADVICE FOR YOUNG EDITORS?

Cut. If you want to cut, cut. You've got to get experience. Assisting is great, but assisting is a very specific thing. It's a very specific procedure, but if you're going to cut, you've got to cut. First, get your feet wet and feel loose about cutting. Don't be afraid. Look to discover something. Have a good time with it. Once you've gotten experience, be discerning about what you do. Don't waste your time on crap. Look towards good scripts and smart directors who have a good sense of casting.

CHAPTER SEVEN

Cutting the Track

Remember *The Blair Witch Project*? I bet while you were watching it you thought, "I can do that!" As far as script and photography go, you probably could. But what you might not realize is that before it was released in theaters, the film's distributor may have spent as much as ten times the entire production budget on a new sound mix. Without excellent sound, no one would have been able to sit through it.

Even if audiences are learning to tolerate lower visual quality (as illustrated by the success of films like *28 Days Later* and *The Blair Witch Project*, with all that miserable hand-held, low-resolution video footage), they show far less tolerance for a poor quality soundtrack. Ultra low budget films like *Blair Witch* or *El Mariachi* invariably have their soundtracks heavily cleaned up and remixed before being shown in theaters.

SOUND MAKES THE SHOW

Sound is the current that propels the show: an unseen force guiding the movement of the visual elements. This is why L and J cuts are so important to smooth editing. Creating a fluid and apparently seamless audio track is critical to keeping an audience immersed in the film.

The problem for most inexperienced editors is that sound is literally invisible, which makes it easy to forget. But underestimating the importance of sound is a mistake.

A successful film depends more on good sound than it does on good visuals. While it's true that our culture is highly focused on visual information, I believe we are more affected by what we hear than by what we see.

Sound has a direct link to our emotions. If seeing is believing, then perhaps hearing is feeling. Think of how powerful music is, how listening to a symphony or even a well-crafted pop song can move you to tears or exhilaration. Images rarely deliver as immediate an emotional impact.

Of course, it's the combination of image and sound that makes film such a powerful medium. This unique joining touches the audience in a complex way by mixing visual information with the emotional power carried by sound. In this way, film can create a more engrossing experience than any other medium.

THE AUDIO WORKFLOW

Traditionally, most audio work is done after picture is *locked*. For example if you need to re-record some dialogue from a noisy scene, you don't want to waste time recording and editing lines that might get cut when you refine the edit. Now, with the added flexibility provided by tools like Final Cut, you can be less strict about this, but it's still a good idea to leave most of your audio *sweetening* until you've finalized all of the timing decisions based on your picture. If you are going to be sending your audio out to ProTools, Logic, or to an audio post production facility, it is imperative that you lock your picture before you export your OMF files. This insures that the audio mix your sound editor generates will accurately sync back up with your final picture. (For more on exporting OMF files, see "Exporting for ProTools" later in this chapter.)

The beautiful thing about audio is that because it is invisible, you can cover up mistakes made during production or fabricate sounds that never existed. You can also enhance sounds for dramatic effect, like adding an impact noise for a punch or crash. It doesn't matter where the sound actually came from—all that matters is that it matches the picture on screen. There are many stories of *Foley* artists creating audio by smashing fruit or squishing mud to make the gory soundtracks for horror films.

Creating the final audio for a film consists of editing the sync sound recorded during production, adding sound effects and music, and then managing the relative levels so that all of the varied elements combine in a clear, intelligible way. This last stage, called the "mix" is usually the final stage a film goes through before it is considered complete.

Capturing Audio

I won't go into detail about how to record audio properly. It's more important for an editor to understand how to capture audio correctly to make the best use of it in Final Cut.

There is no way to adjust the levels when capturing digital audio (from DV, DAT, Digital Betacam, or HD). Whatever was recorded in the field is what goes on your hard disk. This applies only when capturing via a digital connector such as FireWire SPDIF or AES/EBU.

If you are capturing audio from an analog connector (XLR, RCA, Phono, Mini) as you would from an analog tape deck such as VHS or Betacam SP, adjust the audio level by using the Gain control in the Clip Settings tab of the Log and Capture window (**Figure 7.1**).

Figure 7.1 The Gain slider is dimmed if you are capturing from a digital format. Otherwise, use this control to set your input levels.

If you're converting an analog signal (for instance, when capturing from Betacam SP tapes), line up the 0dB output level on the source deck with -12dB on Final Cut Pro's audio meters. This will ensure that your audio doesn't get distorted or *clipped*. To do this, find a section of the tape with a constant output signal of 0dB (the head of the tape should contain a test tone specifically for this purpose) and adjust the Gain slider until the on-screen meters read -12dB.

Audio Shapes

You can capture audio in five different ways, or "shapes" (**Figure 7.2**). In most cases, choosing a shape simply lets the computer know which multi-channel format was used when the information was recorded on the tape in the first place.

Figure 7.2 Audio can be recorded in one of five different shapes based on how it was recorded on the source tape.

How Was Your Audio Recorded?

Most videotapes are designed to record sound on two audio channels. Some formats let you record four different channels, although all four are rarely used. Professional productions nearly always split the two channels. That means if there's just one microphone, it's recorded on one channel. If there are two mics, they are each recorded discretely on the two channels. That way you can control their volumes independently so both can be set at optimal levels.

For example, suppose one channel is dedicated to audio coming from a *shotgun* microphone, and the other channel is recording the output from a *lavalier* microphone. Even if both mics are pointed at the same subject, you will want to keep the signals separate so you can choose one or the other for your sequence—or mix them together in Final Cut to create a more naturalistic sound than the recordist can achieve with a live mix during the shoot.

> ## *Microphone Types*
>
> *Microphones are frequently identified by their pickup pattern*
>
> ***SHOTGUN*** *A shotgun is an extremely directional mic, picking up signals in a very narrow pattern to the front of the mic. Most films use shotgun mics mounted on a boompole to record dialogue. This allows you to place the mic far enough away from the subject to stay out of the camera's view, but still record an adequate signal with very little extraneous noise from the sides or the back of the microphone.*
>
> ***LAVALIER*** *A tiny omnidirectional microphone, typically mounted on the shirt collar or lapel. These mics are designed to compensate for the extra low frequencies they record from being adjacent to the resonating chamber of the subject's chest.*

In other situations, you may have two wireless mics, each pointing at a different subject and each being recorded on a separate audio channel. This is another case where you'd want to keep the channels entirely discrete so you can edit them separately.

One Channel

If your audio is recorded on only one channel, set the audio pop-up to just that channel. Channel 1 is equivalent to left, channel 2 to right. Final Cut Pro will create a clip with one Audio tab, and the audio signal will be *panned* to the center so it comes out of both speakers at equal volume (**Figure 7.3**).

Figure 7.3 If you capture a clip with only one audio channel, you can see the waveform and adjust Level and Pan controls in the corresponding tab in the Viewer.

Two Mono Channels

If your tape was recorded with two audio channels, set the pop-up to Ch 1 + Ch 2. This will bring in the two channels as two distinct tracks, both panned to the center (**Figure 7.4**).

Figure 7.4 If you capture a clip with the pop-up set to Ch 1 + Ch 2 (the default setting), you will get two Audio tabs in the Viewer. Both will be panned to the center.

Stereo Channels

Many consumer-grade camcorders are equipped with a built-in microphone that records sound on the tape in stereo format. Although built-in mics are continually improving in quality, they still can't record a true stereo signal. Proper stereo separation requires placing two mics at least as far apart from each other as they are from the subject (forming an equilateral triangle). If you have one of these stereo tapes, or if your tape has a stereo signal on it for some other reason (perhaps it was recorded directly from a mixing board at a concert), set the pop-up to Stereo. This will create a clip with one Audio tab but two channels; the channels will be panned split, with channel 1 going to the left and channel 2 going to the right (**Figure 7.5**).

After the Fact

If you make a mistake while capturing and later realize you want to treat a stereo clip as two discrete channels, or vice versa, you can change a clip's audio shape after it's captured. However, this change can only be made in the Timeline.

The Timeline identifies stereo clips with a little double arrow icon (**Figure 7.6**). If you select a stereo clip, the Stereo Pair menu item (in the Modify menu) is checked (**Figure 7.7**).

Figure 7.5 A stereo clip displays both tracks in a single tab

Stereo Pair indicator

Figure 7.6 The Stereo Pair indicator appears on stereo clips in the Timeline.

Figure 7.7 A check mark next to the Stereo Pair menu item indicates when a clip is stereo.

By selecting the Stereo Pair menu item to toggle it, you can change the audio shape of a clip. To delete one track entirely, choose that item in the Timeline and delete it.

> **TIP:** *Stereo pairs must begin and end at the same time, and they must have identical level and pan keyframes, so if you select two audio clips with different lengths or different keyframe settings and turn them into a stereo pair, Final Cut will conform the second clip to the first clip's settings.*

Mono Mix

Sometimes you'll encounter a tape on which the sound was recorded on two channels, but you would prefer to treat it as a single track. This might occur if your source tape was recorded in stereo but you want to use it as a single mono track while editing. In cases like these, set the pop-up in the Capture window to Mono Mix. This will mix the two channels into a single track for editing. This does not change the sound quality, but gives you a single volume and pan control for the item.

Working with Dual System Recording

There are many productions that still chose to record sound and picture on two different devices. This is the way all film is shot, since film cameras cannot record audio on the unexposed film. The audio is recorded on a Timecode capable DAT recorder, or occasionally on an old analog Nagra 1/4" reel to reel recorder. Because two different recording devices are used, this is commonly referred to as "Dual System recording." When the audio is recorded directly on the same tape as the picture, it's called "Single System." Sometimes video productions will use dual system recording for a variety of reasons. For example, it may be impractical to run a cable between the mic and the camera when shooting an extreme wide shot (where the camera is far away from the subject), or if the camera is shooting the outside of a car, and the audio is being recorded inside the vehicle. In these cases, dual system provides the needed flexibility.

This means that in post, you'll have to capture the picture and the sound separately and then join them in Final Cut Pro. Once they're joined, you can manipulate the clip just like any other and the picture and sound will stay locked together.

Syncing Clips

In order to accurately synchronize the audio and video, find a point where the picture and the sound can be precisely matched, or "synced." For example, a glass being set down on a table or a hammer hitting a nail. The need to synchronize picture and sound is the reason for the stick, or "clapper," atop the clapboard (sometimes called a slate). At the beginning of each shot, the camera assistant holds the slate in front of the camera and claps the stick, making a short, sharp sound which will be easy to locate on the soundtrack—in the same way that it's relatively simple to find the exact frame of the picture where the stick contacted the top of the slate (**Figure 7.8**). Set a marker in both the video and the audio clips and line them up in the timeline. Once they're lined up, link them using ⌘-Ⓛ or choosing Link from the sequence menu.

Figure 7.8 The slate sound is very apparent when viewing the waveform.

Merging Clips

Merge Clips is a command in Final Cut Pro 4 that allows you to link up as many as 24 audio clips with a single video clip. This creates a new clip in the browser which from that point forward can be manipulated and edited just like any other clip. To merge clips, select the items in the browser and choose Merge Clips from the Modify menu (**Figure 7.9**). The dialog box that appears allows you to sync up the clips based on a variety of options. You can sync the clips based on their in or out point, which you can set manually (visually setting the picture to begin at the slate clap and the audio to start at the sound of the clap), or you can use one of the timecode fields (Primary, Aux 1, or Aux 2). This will line the clips up so that the same timecode numbers occur on the same frames in all the different clips. This may result in the merged clip appearing to have long sections of black or silence in areas where timecode values don't overlap. For example, if your video clip begins at 01:01:05:00 and your audio clip begins at 01:01:10:00, the merged clip will have five seconds of silence before the audio kicks in.

Figure 7.9 Merge Clips allows you to sync up multiple audio clips with a single video clip.

Timecode Slates

Another type of clapboard, called a Timecode Slate or Smart Slate generates timecode numbers and displays them on the face of the board. When working with this sort of slate, the audio recorder (which must be capable of recording timecode on the audio tape) is *slaved* to the slate so the timecode numbers recorded with the audio match the numbers on the slate. This way, instead of syncing up a sound blip to the frame where the clapboard closes, you can use the more precise time-code numbers. Select any frame where the slate is visible and note the timecode number on screen. Then find the timecode embedded in your audio clip (the timecode will have been recorded with your audio when you captured it). This makes it easy to line up video and audio with exact precision. This method is also used to synchronize shots taken from multiple cameras at the same time.

SOUND EDITING

Once you've completed your picture edit and roughed in all of your production audio, you're ready to focus on sound. As you add elements and move others around, it can be easy to make a mess of your sequence, so it's important to establish strict rules of organization. Remember, you may wind up with as many as 99 audio tracks, and sometimes an audio element can be very short in duration. By keeping your composition orderly you avoid the frustration of losing a clip or having it show up at the wrong time. Begin by separating your audio into three categories: Dialogue, Effects, and Music.

Dialogue Tracks

Dialogue or narration is the most information-heavy of your audio elements, and you want it to sound as clear and natural as possible. In fact, it's common practice to *equalize* (adjust the volume of individual frequencies) each voice separately so you can optimize the overall sound quality.

On a traditional mixing board you can assign only one equalization (*EQ*) setting to a given *pot* (input) so each voice is placed on a different one. The equivalent in Final Cut is to put each voice on its own track in the Timeline. Technically, this is not required, since Final Cut Pro allows you to assign different EQ settings to individual clips even if they lie on the same track. However, it's still fairly common for filmmakers to complete their sound mix outside of Final Cut Pro. If that's your plan, you should break out your voice elements on different tracks to prepare for that eventuality (**Figure 7.10**). This can be a large amount of additional work, but external audio mixing systems may require this type of separation.

Good dialogue editing is much more than just ensuring that the lips are synced with the words they're speaking. Remember that you'll commonly be mixing clips recorded at different times and from different positions. Your goal is to make all of these different sounding clips indistinguishable. For example, the mic placement during the close-up may have been much closer to the actor's mouth than it was during the master shot. A good production sound mixer may have been smart enough to adjust the levels so that they are the same volume, but if the mic was farther away, more of the room's *reverberation* will be recorded.

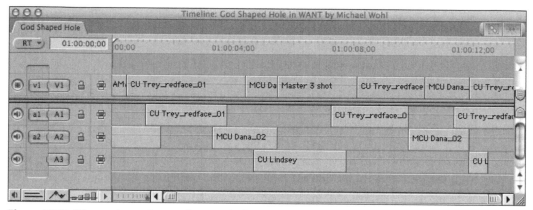

Figure 7.10 It's good practice to place each character's dialogue on its own track in the Timeline.

It's nearly impossible to remove unwanted reverb but if it's not too severe, you might add some to the CU shot so that they match better. (For more on working with audio filters, see "Problem-Solving Filters" later in this chapter.)

One of the first steps in cleaning up your dialogue tracks is to adjust all the levels so that they sound approximately the same. Although the audio meters can be helpful, don't depend on them entirely. Your ear, and a good pair of speakers in a quiet room, is the only reliable judge. Occasionally, barely audible low frequencies can appear to inflate the meter's reading. Similarly, sometimes a high pitched voice can be more penetrating at lower levels than a low pitched voice at higher volumes.

One common situation that can cause sound problems is when two characters are talking to one another in the same room and the CU shots of them—opposing angles—are recorded separately. Perhaps one actor is standing in front of a window and street noise leaks in. When the shots of the two actors are edited together the inconsistency of the background sound will be jarring.

To make the scene sound consistent and natural, you must find ways to smooth out the differences between each shot. This is where EQ comes in. If the street noise produced a low rumble in one shot that doesn't exist in the other, apply a High Pass filter (which cuts out some of the low frequencies). If you're fighting a high pitched sound, apply the Low Pass filter, which has the reverse effect of the High Pass filter. If the offending sound is of the same frequencies as the actor's voice, you may be out of luck. Sometimes a Noise Gate filter can help to cut out sound that occurs in between words or phrases (it works by suppressing any sound below a certain volume), but often there's not much you can do other than re-recording the audio.

Perspective Shifts

Another important trick that makes audio sound more natural is to adjust levels to match cuts or movement within the frame. For example, in a 30 second shot, where two people are walking towards the camera from far away, you wouldn't, in reality, be able to hear them at all until they were within a few yards. For the sake of the story, however, you want to be sure their dialogue is heard throughout the shot. To do this, start the shot with the level audible, but slightly low. As they approach the camera, increase the level. This must be a subtle adjustment, as you don't want the level too low to hear at the beginning or so loud at the end of the shot that it's distracting. The result makes the sound feel much more natural and helps hide the artifice of the medium.

Another example follows cut points. Say you have a scene featuring two girls playing with a music box. The first shot is a WS showing the whole room. The next shot is a MCU of the two girls. Finally, you cut to an insert of the music box. The audio levels need to be adjusted to match the edits. At the first cut point, raise the levels of the dialogue tracks to simulate the effect of moving closer to the actors. In the final shot of the music box, the dialogue levels might not change but you would certainly want to increase the level of the music box sound (**Figure 7.11**).

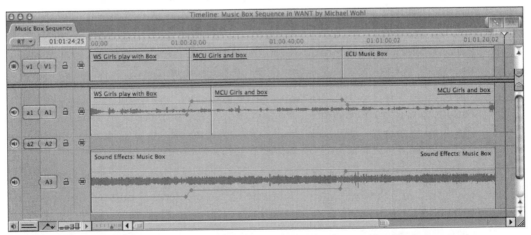

Figure 7.11 Subtle audio level adjustments to go along with changes in visual perspective enhance your overall mix.

These subtle audio adjustments differentiate a professionally mixed film from an amateur production. Some programs, such as corporate communications or soap operas, don't have the time or budget for this level of finesse, and sometimes they don't require it, but if you want that feature film quality audio, you can't skimp on the sound mix.

SOUND EFFECTS TRACKS

After your dialogue edit is complete (or maybe at the same time if you've got several people working together) you begin the most intensive part of sound editing. Fortunately, it can also be the most fun.

Any audio on your soundtrack that's neither dialogue nor music is considered a sound effect. Sound effects can be divided into several categories: Practical sound effects (sounds caused by onscreen objects such as a door closing or a telephone ringing); off-screen sounds (specific noises from the environment that do not occur on screen, such as a dog barking outside a window or distant gunfire); ambient noise (the sound of a particular location, such as a busy restaurant or a boiler room); and non-environmental sounds used to enhance the mood or convey a psychological state, such as a heartbeat or a ticking clock (when no clock is present in the scene).

Designing Sound

When creatively employed, the manipulation of these sounds (along with music) is often referred to as sound design. The idea of "designing" sound to enhance or amplify the tone and themes of a movie is a relatively new one. Most people credit Walter Murch with originating both the term and the idea with his groundbreaking work on films like *The Conversation* and *Apocalypse Now*.

Any sound that occurs onscreen can be recreated and often is. This gives the sound editor far more control. For one thing, the sound can be faded in and out separately from the dialogue track—and creating effects after the fact allows the sound designer to alter the sound for psychological impact.

For example, in the movie *Twister*, about tornado chasers, the sounds of the tornadoes were completely synthetic, fabricated from elements as unlikely as wild animal roars and kitchen appliances such as dishwashers and blenders.

This is the type of work that a sound editor revels in. Building complex combinations of sounds to create a certain effect is the true art of sound design. Some of the elements may come from libraries; some may be recorded specially for the show.

A good sound designer is acutely aware of the frequencies of the sounds being used and how to layer sounds without making mud. For example, if you're creating a sound of a car crash you might begin with a car crash sound effect from a library or perhaps the actual production sound. But don't stop there. To further enhance it, layer in a large caliber gun or bomb blast to fill in the lower frequencies and give the effect more resonance and oomph. Then add some shattering glass to fill in the high frequencies. This fills the spectrum and creates more impact (pardon the pun) on your audience. You might go on to add some "debris" sounds from your library that will linger after the initial crash. These may actually be the sound of plaster falling off a wall or a handful of nails being dropped on a sheet of metal. When your audience hears the combination of all these sounds, once they have been layered and their relative levels adjusted, it doesn't hear the component parts. It hears a convincing, earth shattering car crash.

The Basics

Use the first pass through your film to lay in the obvious sound effects that will be necessary to make the soundtrack feel less naked—practical sound effects and ambiences. You should allocate quite a few tracks in your sequence for these elements. Ambiences will typically run for the duration of each scene and there may be more than one practical sound that needs to occur simultaneously. Final Cut allows you plenty of tracks to work with, so don't be stingy.

Extracting Embedded Sound Effects

Many of these sounds will have been recorded during the production, such as the sound of someone opening a bottle of champagne or closing a door. Because they were recorded along with the dialogue, they will probably be mixed in with your dialogue tracks. It is good practice to extract these segments and put them on their own sound effects tracks (**Figure 7.12**). This allows you to give the sound effects their own EQ settings (that High Pass filter you used on your dialogue really takes the oomph out of a door slam), and it also prepares you for dubbing your film into foreign languages.

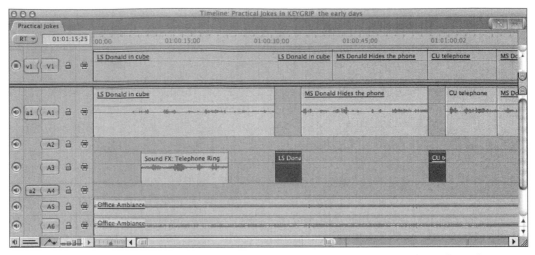

Figure 7.12 Whenever possible, extract sound effects from your dialogue tracks and put them on the designated sound effects tracks

If your film is to be dubbed into another language, all of your dialogue tracks will be turned off, leaving only your sound effects and music elements. If your sound effects (such as that champagne pop) are embedded in your dialogue tracks, the foreign version is going to be missing that sound. If you had extracted it and put it on the sound effects track, all is well. If the champagne pop occurred at the same time that someone was speaking, you may be out of luck. You'll have to leave it alone in the dialogue track. When it comes time for the foreign version, you'll need to go through and re-record all of those embedded sounds.

Adding Additional Sound Effects

There are many practical sound effects that may not have been recorded during production. The director might have simply said "Ring, ring" at the cue when a telephone was supposed to ring. Or a gun may have been left unloaded for safety. Any object in the frame that could make a noise should. Go through and add sounds for that squeaky door, or a passing car, a doorbell, or a computer alert.

Sometimes the microphone may not be properly positioned to hear a cigarette being put out in an ashtray or paper rustling on a desk. If you leave these sounds out, your scene will feel incomplete. In many cases you can rely on sound effects libraries to provide telephone rings or gunshots. More specific sounds, like the cigarette being stubbed out, may need to be recorded specially for the film.

Ambiences

Unless you're floating in outer space, any location has a characteristic sound. If you're reading this in front of your editing station, the hum of your computer is probably one of the loudest sounds you hear, but if you listen carefully you might be able to hear an air conditioner blowing or a clock ticking. Maybe your seat creaks a bit when you shift your weight. If you're really quiet, you may hear your own breathing. Although it takes some concentration to stop and identify all these sounds, if they were absent you would be acutely aware of it.

When a film crew shoots a scene, they make every effort to eliminate all these environmental noises. Streets are closed down, grips drape sound blankets over the windows to dampen extraneous sounds, loud machines and air conditioners are turned off. This enables the recording of the talent with a minimum of ambient noise.

Back in the editing room, however, you have to reconstruct all those elements to create a natural-sounding environment. This is delicate work, but it's one of the most critical components of sound design. You must find just the right mix of background noise to give a realistic ambience. And you can be creative.

For instance, if a scene is set in an outdoor café, and an extra walks by with a dog on a leash, you can add a dog bark even if the real dog never made a sound. Furthermore, you can add it at exactly the right moment, such as in between the actors' lines. This way you get the requisite neighborhood feeling, but the noise won't interfere with the dialogue.

Every scene in your film should have an ambience track (or a combination of several). From the *walla* (human voices) of a restaurant crowd to the machine hum of an office or the revving motor of a sports car; every scene is unique. In an early pass of *Want*, my sound designer found a couple of office ambiences from an old 1970s era library. Since the film is set in the dot-com offices of 1999, the old style telephones and office typewriters stood out so much it was downright funny. Later we found a more appropriate office ambience complete with modern walla including references to email, cell phones, and double lattes.

Room Tone

Even if you eliminate as much background sound as possible during recording, there will still be some white noise in the background. That sound is called room tone, and it's different for every environment. When a crew is finished recording dialogue, they also record some of this unique background noise. Room tone is a critical element for creating realistic environmental ambience.

Room tone is essential for covering up gaps in the dialogue track. For instance, let's say that during a really good shot, one of the crew members had a coughing fit. He managed to do it in between the actors' lines, but you still have to cut out three seconds of the dialogue track so the coughing isn't heard. If you simply drop out the audio, there will be absolute silence for that three-second section—which will sound unnatural. If you lay in room tone, no one will notice the gap, since the background noise *level* will remain constant (**Figure 7.13**).

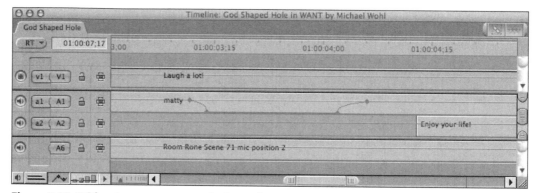

Figure 7.13 Without a room tone track, the audio gap on track A1 would be painfully apparent, since *all* sound would drop out for that section. The room tone provides a constant level of background noise across the whole scene.

Non-Environmental Sounds

Once the "basics" are laid in, your show should feel fully realized and naturalistic. If the dialogue edit is complete, you may be nearly done. However, for some shows, you might want to include sound elements that are not present in the environment. For example, whenever a chart appears in your training film, you might accompany it with a trumpet fanfare.

In *Want,* as the film progressed, we sought to give the audience the impression of delving deeper and deeper into Trey's inner psychological space. One of the main ways we accomplished this was through the sound design: As Trey started to lose his grip on reality, we began incorporating various non-environmental sounds into the mix.

Because one of the factors contributing to Trey's decline was the barrage of marketing messages that saturated his world, we used lots of TV and radio commercials as part of the sound landscape. In the early parts of the film, the sounds of the ads were tied to shots of the TV or radio source. However, later in the film, these ads (with the audio distorted and sometimes layered together) began intruding into Trey's space even when he was nowhere near an actual source.

Using sounds that are not part of the natural environment can break the constructed reality of your film and disrupt the viewer's experience, but artfully employed, this technique can complement the natural elements of the scene, enhance the themes of the piece, and amplify the filmmaker's voice.

Creating Silence from Scratch

What do you do if your sound recordist forgot to capture room tone for "the cough scene"? One option is to steal room tone from another scene, especially if it was shot in the same location or one with similar ambience. But remember that the actors' dialogue tracks from the cough clip are going to include that same ambient noise, so your room tone track must be a good match to blend in perfectly.

*If that doesn't work, scan through the dialogue track of the cough clip to find a section where there's no speech. A fast way to do that is to look at the clip's waveform for silent passages (**Figure 7.14**). Copy that section and edit it into your sequence again and again, dissolving from one piece to the next, until you've stitched together enough room tone for the sequence (**Figure 7.15**).*

Be careful, though: If there's some recognizable sound in the "silence," like a distant car driving by, repeating the clip will sound artificial. In that case, you will need to find multiple sections of silence in the clip and stitch them together.

Figure 7.14 Areas where the clip's waveform is flat, or nearly flat, are good places to use as room tone.

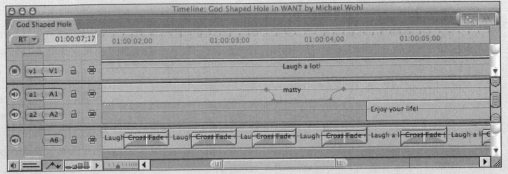

Figure 7.15 By repeatedly copying the silent section into the Timeline, you can create a hand-made room tone track. Dissolving from one piece to the next will prevent audible seams.

MUSIC AND SCORE

There are two types of music that occur in a film. First is practical music; songs that are playing within the environment of the scene on a car radio or a jukebox. Any other music is usually referred to as *score*. Score is the most common type of non-environmental sound. Music can have a huge impact on the emotional tone of a scene, but it requires a careful match to be successful. Using the wrong music can destroy a scene, but finding just the right *cue* can transform that scene into an utterly brilliant sequence.

Don't Use Music to Fix a Bad Edit

Music can make a good scene work better, but it's a bad idea to depend on music to save a poorly edited sequence. Edit a scene until it works on its own before you lay a song on top of it. If the scene doesn't have the right impact, jacking up its emotional level with some piece of music may help a bit, but it runs the risk of alienating your viewers by blatantly manipulating their feelings.

Sophisticated viewers understand that music is often used to tell them what they are supposed to feel, and they tend to resist such attempts at emotional manipulation—especially if the scene doesn't warrant the feelings the music suggests. For example, I got up and walked out of Steven Spielberg's *A.I.* as soon as I heard the third swell of violins.

Temporary Music

It may help your editing if you make a quick guess at some music with the right feeling or rhythm to fit the scene you're working on. Of course, if it turns out to be the wrong kind of music, you may have to scrap the cut you produced under its influence.

I recommend listening to the music *before* you edit the scene, rather than putting it on a scratch track so it will play while you're editing. If a song is floating around in your head, its general feeling and rhythm will influence your editing decisions and help make your pacing and timing more consistent and appropriate. However, unless you're absolutely sure the temp music will make it to your final mix, cutting your picture to the beat or structure of the song can lead to problems. If you do that, when you replace the temp track with the final music, your edits won't match.

Some editors play background music while they work, and this can't hurt, since during the hours you spend roughing each scene together you'll hear a variety of different songs or movements. But that's different from loading a song into your computer and editing your sequence to it.

Don't get too friendly with your temp soundtrack. If you, or your director, fall in love with the song you're using as a temporary placeholder, you may suffer catastrophic disappointment if you fail to acquire the rights to use that song in the final mix. One of the tricks I used to prevent this when cutting *Want* was to lay in the same two temp songs scene after scene. Since I knew I wouldn't want to repeat the music that way in the finished film, it kept me from getting too attached to any one song.

Selecting Pre-Existing Music

Choosing pre-existing music for your movie can be complicated, and finding the right match is often tricky. It's tempting to pick a song that you really like, but resist the impulse. Select music that's right for the scene.

Complement or Contrast?

The first question to ask yourself is: Do you want the music to complement the tone of the scene, augmenting its emotional impact, or do you want it to contrast with the feelings of the scene?

The former strategy comes perilously close to telling the audience what to feel, but of course as an editor you are *always* telling the audience what to feel. The trick is to be subtle about it. Using complementary music can create a clear, consistent message that's easily understood without being patronizing. For example, you might use suspenseful music (a staccato orchestral piece featuring powerful brass and bass lines pouncing on a delicate violin melody) over a scene featuring a character trying to escape his pursuer. In this case, the music would emphasize the feeling of suspense, while a contrasting style of music might dilute the tension of the scene.

Sometimes, however, contrast can be even more provocative. For example, the general feeling of a key scene in *Want,* between Trey and his father, was slow and melancholy. There were long pauses between the lines, and both characters frequently looked at the ground. My first idea was to use music that amplified that wistful sense, so I chose a moody guitar piece with a big synth bed (think Pink Floyd or Radiohead). It worked—sort of: the music made the scene feel even sadder, yet it felt like it was running too long.

I tried to fix it by cutting the scene until I'd chopped out all but the most essential lines of dialogue. It was then quicker, but it had also lost much of what had made it a great scene in the first place. So I went back to an earlier cut and tried different music instead. I found a clarinet solo that meandered between a peaceful melody and occasional bursts of frantic desperation (the way only a screeching clarinet can). I timed the edit so the musical explosions occurred during moments of silence between the two characters. The result was amazing. The music brought out the underlying tension between the characters, and the scene didn't seem too long.

Taking the Music Apart

Music can add a lot to a scene, but the use of some music can be like painting with an overly broad brush. When music is arranged and recorded, it's designed to be complete, including all the elements necessary to give it the musicians' desired impact. Integrating that song into a filmic sequence adds elements to an already finished work that may convolute the character of the music, even kill it. For example, the fast cutting of a chase scene might add an unwanted percussive element to a piece of music based on a syncopated rhythm. While the melody of the piece might suit the scene, the drums and bass compete with it.

One of the best ways to make sure the music in your film is effective is to deconstruct it down to its component tracks and lay in the individual pieces one at a time. That way you are essentially remixing the music so your environmental sounds and images can complete the mix. If the music was composed especially for your film, this may be as simple as experimenting with the tracks, turning the various elements of the song (melodic strings, driving trumpet, percussive rhythm section) on and off. How does the scene play with one or more of these tracks removed? Maybe the visuals of the scene can take the place of the melody, and all you need is the musical foundation. Perhaps the sound effects in your scene conflict with some of the percussive elements, or maybe they could replace them altogether.

An experienced film composer will often experiment this way before presenting you with the final music. As you edit in the music for your scenes, keep in mind that this type of deconstruction is an option you too can employ.

If you're working with pre-recorded music, you might ask a musician friend to re-record the song, one instrument at a time. Maybe she can record just the guitar part or the bass line. It's also easy to throw together a drum track on a sequencer or drum machine; perhaps she'll be able to rebuild pieces of the song one by one. Be aware that manipulating or sampling existing music may infringe on copyrights. Read on to the "No Stealing" section for more information about music copyrights.

Avoid Lyrics

When it comes to score, it's generally a good idea to avoid music with vocals, even if it's going to play over scenes without dialogue. Lyrics tend to be too literal, and their images can compete with the visual elements in your film. They may take center stage and make your images seem to merely support the song—as in a music video. Of course, there are many notable exceptions, including the plaintive lament of the Doors' "The End" playing over the opening sequence of *Apocalypse Now*. Perfectly matched vocal music can complement a film sequence successfully, but this is an advanced exercise. Inexperienced editors should beware of creating a competing focus between the narrative of the song and the narrative of the film.

No Stealing

Using copyrighted material without paying for it is illegal, and the music industry has a legion of disgruntled musicians out to catch every violation of their rights. As well they should. Musicians work hard to create their art. If you are integrating their creative work into your own and benefiting artistically or financially from their labor and popularity, they deserve to be credited and paid appropriately.

Contact the music publisher about using a song. If your show is a documentary or won't be exhibited publicly, you can often negotiate an agreement to use the music for free or for a nominal fee. Many companies have specific "film festival only" rights that enable you to include the song in your film for unpaid screenings. If you later want to acquire broader rights, you will need to renegotiate. If you get caught showing your film at a trade show or film festival using music for which you don't own the rights, you will probably have to pay a stiff fine—not to mention that you will have to go back and create a new sound mix with the offending song removed.

All music has two sets of rights. First there are the rights to the composition, usually referred to as "master" rights. These come from the music publishing company. Almost all songs are registered with either ASCAP or BMI, and one of these two organizations can assist you in acquiring the necessary master rights. Second are the rights to a particular recording of a song. These rights are called "sync" rights. They will come from the individual distributor (look on the CD sleeve for the company name—for example Warner Chappel, EMI, Righteous Babe Records, and so on). If you want to use a song in your film, you need to secure both sets of rights.

Hiring a Composer

If you have the time and money, hire a composer to create music especially for your film (called scoring). It's almost always going to fit better than pre-recorded music. The composer can time elements of the music to sync with key moments (even cut points) in your scene. You also have the luxury of modifying the instrumentation or the tempo to better fit your piece.

You can sometimes get the best of both worlds by using a composer to recreate existing music. This gives you a high degree of control while retaining the power of a familiar song. However, it may be less effective, since the original arrangement and production sound are probably big parts of what attracted you to the song in the first place. In this case, you would still need to secure the master rights, but the sync rights would be free and clear.

Working with Soundtrack

Final Cut Pro 4 comes with Soundtrack, a new tool for building music loops that might just be a way to create much of the music you need for your film. The most amazing thing about Soundtrack is how easily you can build musical loops. And with 4 GB of samples to work from, there's quite a variety of styles and types of music you can create. It's all royalty free so the legal obstacles are gone, and it's designed specifically to work with Final Cut Pro (**Figure 7.16**).

It's easy to use. You simply drag elements from the list on the left into the timeline on the right and stretch the elements to match the duration of your show. By exporting your edited sequence from Final Cut Pro, you can view your movie as you're building your loops, and you can even include special "scoring" markers that Soundtrack can see. This way, if you want a music cue to begin or end at a certain moment, you can see the marker in your Soundtrack timeline (**Figure 7.17**).

When you create a marker in Final Cut Pro, click the Scoring Marker button (**Figure 7.18**) and when you export the movie, specifically choose to include those markers in your output (**Figure 7.19**). I expect other music scoring software will soon be able to see these same markers, so if you chose to work in another tool you'll get the same benefit.

Final Cut Pro 4 also includes a menu item called Export For Soundtrack. This does the same thing as choosing Export QuickTime Movie, but it automatically sets the Markers pop-up to Audio Scoring Markers.

Figure 7.16 Soundtrack is the hot new loop making software bundled with Final Cut Pro 4.

Figure 7.17 Final Cut Pro exports markers that show up inside of Soundtrack.

Figure 7.18 Only markers with the Scoring tag will show up inside Soundtrack.

Figure 7.19 Choose Audio Scoring Markers from the markers menu in the Export QuickTime Movie dialog box.

What's the downside? Well, although there are hundreds of different loop types what's missing are quiet ambient elements to serve as beds or to subtly enhance the mood or feeling of a scene. Most of the included loops will be great for upbeat full volume music cues, but the subtler cues will have to wait. Fortunately, you can import almost any audio type into Soundtrack including loops from the leading loop-making software on Windows, ACID, so go out and buy some ACID loops to enhance your Soundtrack experience and maybe you'll never need to call ASCAP or BMI ever again!

RE-RECORDING AUDIO

Any sound that was not properly recorded during production can be re-recorded during postproduction. Sometimes a location is too noisy or too complicated to record clean voices. Sometimes a technical problem might render the original tracks unusable. Many times the mic was positioned in a way that was unable to capture all of the sounds that occurred at the time, for example, footsteps.

Footsteps?

Yes, one of the most commonly rerecorded sounds is footfalls. On a Foley stage (the place where sound effects are recorded, named after one of the earliest sound designers, Jack Foley) you'll see a half dozen pits in the floor filled with various materials used for recording footsteps: gravel, sand, dirt, pavement, wood, and so on. You may wonder why so much attention is paid to such a seemingly inconsequential type of sound, but there are two things that make footsteps the ideal example of Foley recording. First of all, the production sound mixer is primarily focused on recording dialogue. She will use extremely directional mics so the boom operator can point the mic at the actors' mouths from a safe distance. However this means that most sounds that occur outside of that mic's range will go unrecorded. That includes footsteps. Furthermore, footsteps are a sync sound; they're timed to an actor's individual foot movements. You will almost never find footsteps in a sound effects library since it would be nearly impossible to record all of the variations in speed, shoe type, and ground type. It is far easier to play back the picture, and have a Foley artist walk in place, matching the actor's movements, wearing the appropriate shoes, on the appropriate surface with a microphone conveniently pointed at the ground. In this way you can record any sound effect that needs to be precisely synchronized with an event on screen.

Alternate Dialogue Recording (ADR)

Inevitably, some piece of your production sound will be unusable: A plane or truck will be audible in a scene set in the 17th century, or you'll discover that a wireless mic was overwhelmed by static in the middle of a critical line of narration. Whatever the problem, it's quite common to rerecord some audio to replace objectionable sound. Occasionally a director will use ADR to replace a line reading to get a different emotional effect, even if the quality of the original sound was acceptable.

Professional post-production facilities usually have an ADR stage specifically designed for this process. The scene in question is projected in a loop, over and over, while the original dialogue is played in the actor's headphones. As she speaks along with the line, it is recorded and lined up with the lip movements onscreen. The film continues looping and the process is repeated until the actor gets the line as close as possible to the original. One sound designer I know described ADR as equivalent to sending your film to the best college money can buy. That's because when done properly, ADR results in perfect recording without any of the challenges that occur when recording dialogue in the field; all of the voices are at the same level and are recorded from the same mic placement. Additionally, all extraneous sound effects and environmental sounds can be laid in separately and everything controlled independently. This is all well and good, but poorly recorded ADR can be a disaster. If the performer's lips are not precisely synced to the picture, or if the environment feels artificial or incomplete, it can have the undesired result of disrupting the flow of the film and distracting the audience.

Home-style ADR

If you don't have access to a professional ADR stage, you can do most of this at home. The first thing you need to do is *spot* your scene, identifying the beginning and end of every line that needs to be rerecorded. Presumably you have a *scratch track* (your original, flawed production audio) that you can use as reference. Use Final Cut's duration markers (see Chapter 5) to designate the start and end of each line (**Figure 7.20**). Then set up your station for recording. Ideally you can set up a silenced recording room with a microphone (connected to the computer) and a video monitor (also connected to the computer). You'll also need headphones running from the computer's output so your actor can listen to herself while she records the new version.

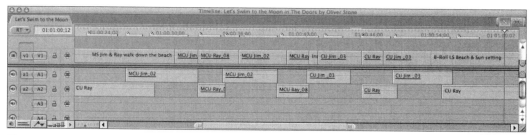

Figure 7.20 A sequence spotted for ADR.

Using the Voice Over Tool

Final Cut features a Voice Over tool that allows you to record audio directly into your sequence while it is playing back (**Figure 7.21**). Set your in and out points around each line (using your markers as guides) and plop your actor down in front of the mic. When you hit the record button in the Voice Over tool, the sequence plays back in the actor's headphones, including an audible countdown to help her know where the line begins. If the first pass doesn't sound right, or doesn't match perfectly with the lip movements on screen, hit record again. Final Cut Pro will automatically add a track to the sequence to make room for the new recording (**Figure 7.22**). This means you don't need to delete the previous version before running it again. Then, when you're finished, sample each of the different versions to find the one that best matches with the picture.

Beware, however, that if you record multiple versions, each previous one will play back in the actor's headphones, which may confuse her. To avoid this, disable each track after it has been recorded. That way the actor will only hear the original scratch audio each time she records a new version.

Figure 7.21
The Voice Over tool.

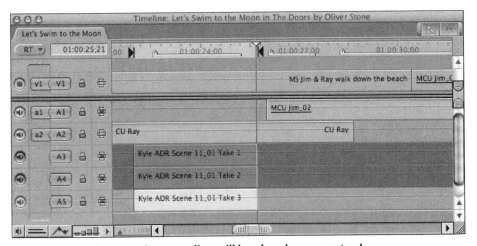

Figure 7.22 Each successive recording will be placed on a new track.

There are limitations to this method of ADR. First of all, traditional ADR systems loop the video playback (hence the nickname "looping"), which allows the actor to anticipate exactly when the line begins and achieve better sync accuracy. With the Voice Over tool method, you have to manually start each new recording, which means an inconsistent time between takes. Second, traditional systems provide a visual cue overlaid onto the picture that indicates exactly when the line will begin. This is another tool that assists the actor in reproducing lines with accuracy and precise timing. Still, despite these limitations, the Voice Over tool is a pretty good quick-and-dirty method of ADR.

TIP: Beware of the sound from the actor's headphones leaking and getting recorded on the new take. Use closed earphones, keep the volume at a minimum, and turn off the beeps that Final Cut Pro plays by default during recording. These beeps are of a high pitch and are often audible over the actor's voice.

An Alternate Method of Looping

If you find the Voice Over tool method unsatisfactory, you can do home-style looping another way, although it takes a few more steps. Rather than recording directly into the timeline, record your new audio on a new tape (DV or DAT, etc.) Turn on the Loop Playback command from the view menu. Set your in and out points around the section to be recorded (you may want to give a little bit of head or tail room for the actor to catch his breath between takes). Begin recording the tape and playback the segment of the timeline using the Play In to Out command (Shift-\\). Let the loop play until the actor nails the line and then stop playback and pause your recording tape. Cue up the next line and repeat the process. The advantage is that the looping rhythm allows the actor to achieve better sync. The disadvantage is that once you're done, you'll need to capture the audio from this new source tape and manually sync up the best new recording with the picture.

TIP: The longer the sections you choose, the more likely your actor is to give an accurate and effective performance. Of course, the longer the sections, the more difficult it will be for him to achieve good lip sync across the whole section. If you record one word at a time, the resulting audio may have perfect lip sync, but the performance will feel stiff or weird. Find the best balance between the two to get a good performance while maintaining accuracy.

Integrating the New Clip

Once you have the new clip recorded, you need to make sure its sound quality matches that of the other clips in the sequence. The more closely you duplicate the original recording situation (mainly by matching the microphone type and placement), the better the sound quality will match. Even so, minor adjustments will help to make the substitution invisible.

Equalizing It

If you're replacing one shot and not an entire sequence, the first thing to do to match the differing tones is to use one of the equalizer filters to modify the sound. Take an acceptable section of the original dialogue and place it in a new sequence immediately ahead of a piece of the rerecorded dialogue. Then experiment with filter settings on the new clip until the two sections of dialogue sound identical (**Figure 7.23**). Once you've settled on the filter settings you want to use, apply them to all the new clips.

Figure 7.23 Place a copy of the new dialog immediately following a piece of the original dialogue and play them back together so you can hear the subtle differences between the clips.

To apply a filter, select the clip and choose the desired filter from the Effects menu. (In this case, we'll use the 3 Band Equalizer.)

To adjust the parameters of a filter that you're applying to a clip, open that instance of the clip in the Viewer. Do this by double-clicking on the clip in the Timeline. To verify that you're editing the instance of a clip used in the sequence, look for the sprocket holes visible in the Scrubber area of the Viewer (**Figure 7.24**).

Figure 7.24 To modify the filter settings for a clip in a sequence, load that instance of the clip into the Viewer. The Scrubber area displays sprocket holes when a clip is currently used in a sequence.

Use the Filters tab to adjust the parameters of the filters applied to your clips (**Figure 7.25**). Final Cut Pro's 3 Band Equalizer is straightforward and similar to equalizers you may have used on your home stereo or other audio devices.

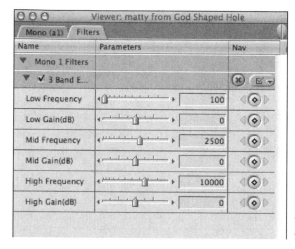

Figure 7.25 Choose the Filters tab to make adjustments to the filters applied to your clips.

For example, if your ADR track has too much bass compared to the original recording, reduce the level of the low frequencies in the clip by pulling down the Low Gain slider (**Figure 7.26**).

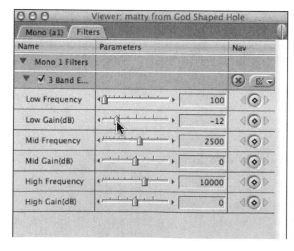

Figure 7.26 By adjusting the Low Gain slider, you can boost or attenuate the level of the low frequencies in your clip.

If the sound you're trying to eliminate is a very low frequency rumble that's too low to be affected by the default setting, lower the value of the Low Frequency slider to include that particular range. To do so, pull the slider down until you hear that the rumble is being affected.

Selecting Specific Frequencies with the Parametric Equalizer

If you prefer, use the Parametric Equalizer filter (**Figure 7.27**). This filter has only one frequency adjustment, plus a Q setting. To filter a specific frequency, start by choosing the precise frequency to be affected. Smaller numbers (starting at 10 Hz) are lower tones; larger numbers (up to 20,000 Hz) are higher tones. Then adjust the Q control to set the "wideness" of the filter (how many frequencies above and below your target frequency will be affected).

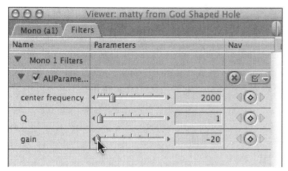

Figure 7.27 The Parametric Equalizer lets you make adjustments to one specific frequency.

For example, let's say you're working with a clip in which some electrical interference produced a high-pitched whistle.

First determine the whistle's frequency. Set your Q setting at 1, which narrows the bandwidth to virtually a single frequency, and adjust your Gain slider to -20dB, which makes your selected frequency inaudible. Now, run through different frequencies until you hear the whistle go away, or at least get a lot quieter. Since it's a high-pitched noise, start at 8,000 Hz to 10,000 Hz and slowly move up, playing back the clip until you hear the whistle being affected.

Once you identify the appropriate frequency, raise the Q level so surrounding frequencies will be affected as well. When the whistle is completely inaudible, you've found the correct Q setting. Now, slowly raise the Gain slider, bringing it as close to zero as possible without hearing the whistle. That way you're reducing the attenuation to the lowest effective level. Over-attenuating even a very narrow frequency range may sound unnatural, since voices comprise so many different harmonic frequencies. Modifying even a narrow band can noticeably change the quality of the voice.

> **TIP:** It's far better to reduce the level of unwanted frequencies than to boost the ones you do want. Equalization is just a way of changing the sound levels of specific frequencies. If you set a level too high, it can become distorted when mixed with other sounds.

Give it Some Space

Once you've matched your new clip as closely as possible to the tone of the original, apply some reverb to match the natural space in which the original sounds were recorded.

Normally, sound waves bounce off the walls of a room and other flat surfaces, creating subtle echoes that interfere with the waves of the original sound. Those reflections are called reverberations. The larger the space, the farther the waves travel before they bounce back, and the more pronounced the echo sounds. That's why a giant church or a huge arena has such a distinct acoustic atmosphere. This echo can be reproduced synthetically using a digital effect.

Final Cut's Reverberation filter is very powerful and can simulate acoustic environments ranging from a small room to a huge cathedral. The trick to getting a natural result is to use small settings to produce a subtle effect. The default settings are a bit too dramatic for most practical purposes. As with the EQ filters, the best way to match clips for reverb is to put a copy of the original clip alongside the new (filtered) clip. Play them back in sequence while you experiment with the reverb settings. When the two clips sound indistinguishable, you've got it right. Now apply that tweaked filter to the other clips you want to affect.

Once you've applied the Reverberation filter by selecting it from the Effects menu, begin by choosing the type of reverb you want to apply (**Figure 7.28**). For realistic effects, I find the Thin Plate settings create excellent natural-sounding effects.

Figure 7.28 Begin by choosing the type of reverb you want from the pop-up menu.

Don't Forget the Room Tone

Once the new clip is thoroughly filtered to match the surrounding clips, mix in the room tone track. Now the sound of the new clip should be indistinguishable from the original. Of course, this scene like every other will require an ambience track that will help mask the difference between the original source and the ADR source.

Check It Out

If it still sounds (or looks) funky, go through the steps again, one by one. First, check that the clip is synced up as accurately as possible. Although the same actor said the same lines while watching her own lips, she may have spoken in a subtly different way that doesn't match the picture. Ultimately, you may not be able to do anything about the discrepancy. This is why medium and wider shots always make for better ADR than close-ups.

Then, recheck the EQ settings, the reverb settings, and the room tone mix—and adjust any of the settings and levels as needed, until the clip sounds as natural as possible. In some cases, you may be better off re-recording an entire scene rather than just one or two problem lines. At least then, all of the dialogue will be identical.

But Wait, There's More!

When you eliminate your original production sound, more than just the dialogue goes away. Scenes in which ADR has been used require a full Foley pass to replace all of the sound effects present in the original recording. After replacing the obvious sound effects (fizzing soda, squeaky chairs, and so on), impact sounds (footsteps, hand claps, objects being lifted or set down, etc.) and adding your ambience tracks, go one step farther.

The Cloth Track

The secret to making scenes with ADR sound natural is to add a *cloth track*. Assuming your actors are clothed, every time they move, jostle, sit, stand, or walk around, that fabric rustles. Of course this sound is subtle, but during production it would be part of the background noise filling out the recording. With ADR, you've eliminated that production track and with it, those subtle fabric sounds.

To record a cloth track, set up just as you would for ADR, but play the whole scene at once. The Foley artist stands near the microphone watching the video play. She holds a sheet or other piece of fabric between her hands and every time someone moves on screen, she makes a small movement with her hands. If someone gets up out of a chair, she makes a longer, more pronounced movement, and if some one is walking she makes a rhythmic hand movement to go along with the movement of the actor's legs. The fanciest productions may record multiple cloth tracks for each character using particular types of fabric, but since the level of this track is so low in the mix, you can probably get away with one pass for everyone in the scene. Typically this is subtle enough that you don't need to worry about absolute precision in terms of sync and it can usually be handled in a single pass.

Once recorded, lower the level of the track until it sounds natural (you don't want the scene to sound like the mic was stuck to the actor's jacket). This may seem excessive, but it's one of the professional techniques that have been used for many years in Hollywood and can help elevate your sound design to a professional level.

How to Record Foley

For synchronized Foley sounds, such as footsteps or impacts, you will probably want to spot your show for these effects, as you did with the dialogue for the ADR scene. Set a marker to indicate the beginning (and if necessary the end) of each needed sound effect. Put your Foley artist in the same room in which you recorded your ADR. Use the Voice Over tool as I previously described and record each sound effect in sync with the show.

> **TIP:** Remember that when preparing a show for foreign distribution, the entire production sound will be turned off, turning every scene into an ADR scene. In this case, every single sound must be recorded. This includes a moment where someone puts her hand down onto a table or scratches her head, an actor writing with a pen or putting a key into a lock, and so on.

AUDIO SWEETENING

Sweetening is a pleasant sounding term for improving the overall sound quality of a show. It might include equalization such as described in the last section, or it may involve cleaning up small problems like pops or hums. Final Cut provides a host of tools for making these types of adjustments to your sound.

Removing Pops

Suppose you have a track that sounds great except for one little pop caused by a faulty audio cable, or a mixing error. The unwanted sound can be easily removed by fading down before the pop and back up after it—so quickly viewers will never notice.

Here's how: As with the slipping control used to micro-sync sound and image, and described in Chapter 6, Final Cut Pro enables audio keyframe adjustments down to 1/100th of a frame. That's not quite down to sample level (there are between 1,600 and 2,000 samples per frame), but it's good enough for most pops.

First, find the pop. Open the offending clip in the Viewer and zoom in until you identify the pop in the waveform (**Figure 7.29**).

Figure 7.29 A pop usually looks like a narrow spike in an audio waveform.

Set level keyframes by Option-clicking on the level envelope (the pink line). Set three keyframes, one directly on the pop and the other two on either side. Then drag the center keyframe down as far as it will go (**Figure 7.30**). The clip will fade out and come back in so quickly that no one will hear the sound of the pop. The closer together you set the surrounding keyframes, the faster that fade-out/fade-in will occur.

Figure 7.30 By setting three keyframes, you can create a very quick fade-out/ fade-in effect to hide the pop.

If the pop lasts longer or there are two pops close together, you may need to set four keyframes and drag the middle two points down so the clip stays silent for a longer period of time (**Figure 7.31**).

Figure 7.31 If you want to silence a longer area of a clip, set four keyframes and drag the two middle ones down. The portion of the clip between the second and third keyframes will be completely silent.

Notice that the fade-outs you just created have a curved line. Final Cut Pro automatically makes all audio level adjustments logarithmically to match the way the human ear hears. A sound at -10dB is twice as loud as a sound at -20dB, not ten times louder. For the most part you don't need to think about this at all, except when you're trying to adjust audio levels numerically.

Just as I recommend making all editing decisions while playing, I also recommend making audio level adjustments based on how the sequence sounds while it's playing.

Problem Solving Filters

Final Cut Pro 4 greatly improves the handling of Audio Filters, enabling real time previewing and adjusting of parameters, introducing support for third parties to make their own plug-ins, and item level rendering— so that in the rare cases when you do have to render an audio filter you can move it around in the timeline without losing that render. Those working in Final Cut Express are limited to non-real time previewing and have fewer filters to choose from, but the overall functionality remains. The filters I describe here are available in both programs.

Reducing Background Noise

There are actually several filters designed specifically to eliminate unwanted background noise. Unfortunately, the nature of audio recording precludes any fail-safe methods of removing one frequency without affecting others. Also, as I mentioned earlier, voices occur over such a wide range of frequencies that if you remove even a narrow band of lows to eliminate a rumble, it's likely to take some of the bass punch out of the voice.

Eliminating Unwanted Frequencies with Pass Filters

When you want to *roll off* (eliminate) frequencies above or below a certain pitch, use the High Pass or Low Pass filters (**Figure 7.32**). The High Pass filter allows all the frequencies above a selected frequency to "pass" into the mix. All frequencies below that are eliminated. Use the High Pass filter to quickly get rid of too much bass or rumble in your track.

Figure 7.32 High and Low Pass filters enable you to define a frequency below which (or above which) sounds will be muted.

The Low Pass filter does exactly the opposite. Use it to eliminate high-frequency noise such as static or the sound of water crashing. (While the narrator might look great in front of that waterfall, don't forget how the location will affect the sound!)

Filtering Out Unwanted Noise

Every audio signal includes a certain amount of noise that's audible in between the parts you want to use (**Figure 7.33**). This is essentially room tone, and in many cases it's desirable, but occasionally you want to eliminate that noise.

For example, let's say you recorded a voice-over narration in a park, and whenever the narrator pauses you can hear traffic noise in the background. You plan to run the narration over a section of the film that occurs indoors. Naturally, you want to remove as much of that traffic noise as possible.

Figure 7.33 The areas where the waveform is small but not flat indicate the environmental noise recorded in between sections of useful information.

This is a job for the Expander/Noise Gate filter (**Figure 7.34**), which is designed to eliminate all signals that fall below a certain volume level.

Figure 7.34 The Expander/Noise Gate filter can be used to cut unwanted segments of room tone from a clip.

Adjust the Threshold slider to the proper value for removing the noise, and use the Attack Time and Release Time settings to determine how quickly the filter takes effect and how long it waits before turning off. (Generally, you don't want to drop out the tiny pauses between words, but you do want to eliminate longer pauses at the ends of phrases and sentences.)

Removing Hum

Use the Hum Remover filter (**Figure 7.35**) to eliminate common hums. This filter works in the same way as the Parametric Equalizer described earlier, but the default settings are designed to remove 60-cycle hum—the most common audio problem. American electricity runs at 60 Hz, and if an electrical signal interferes with your audio (as often happens if a microphone cable runs parallel to an electrical cable on the set), you'll get a 60-cycle hum. (In other parts of the world, electricity runs at different frequencies and produces different hums.)

Figure 7.35 The Hum Remover filter is designed to (surprise!) remove hum. Use the Q slider to control the breadth of the effect.

Since a hum may cause reverberations on additional frequencies (due to the nature of audio harmonics), the Hum Remover has check boxes to apply similar attenuation to harmonic frequencies. If, after setting the main parameters, you still hear remnants of the hum, check the Harmonics check boxes one at a time until the noise goes away.

DePop and DeEss

Recording voices is more of an art than a science. You must choose between many microphones, experiment with mic placements, and overcome a variety of esoteric problems. Voices that are recorded at very close range frequently contain sibilants (hissing S's) and plosives (popping P's, B's, T's, and D's) that can be distracting.

Final Cut Pro provides tools used specifically for solving these problems. Use the Vocal DeEsser filter to remove excessive sibilance. Use the Vocal DePopper filter to remove excessive plosives (**Figure 7.36**).

Figure 7.36 The DeEsser and DePopper are especially designed for cleaning up problems with vocal recordings.

Final Cut Pro and Audio Quality

In the General Settings of Final Cut Pro's User Preferences window there is a setting that controls audio quality (**Figure 7.37**). When this is set to Low, more effects can be played in real time but the overall rendering is done with less precision and can result in slightly reduced quality. This setting is only relevant when you are applying effects to your audio or are converting sample rates within Final Cut Pro (such as using a file from an audio CD in a DV sequence). Ordinary audio clips will not play at reduced quality. Also, whenever you render your audio, all rendering happens at the highest quality. Therefore there is not too much harm in leaving this adjustment at the default "Low" setting for most editing operations.

Figure 7.37 Audio Playback Quality controls how clips are rendered in real time.

When applying filters such as the ones described in this section, switch that setting to High to be sure you are getting precisely the results you expect. In many cases you won't notice any difference, but in some cases, the filter's effect may seem more pronounced with the quality set to High.

THE FINAL MIX

The last stage in sound editing is called the Final Mix. This is when you listen to the entire show and make adjustments to the levels of each individual element to ensure an even and smooth soundtrack. Hopefully you have been paying enough attention throughout the process that there are no surprises at this final stage.

It is essential that you do your final mix in the same type of environment where your likely audience will be hearing the film. For example, if your film is intended for a home TV audience, listen to your final mix playing out of a home stereo or even out of a mono television speaker. If your film is intended to be shown in a theater, do your final mix in a large room with cinema style speakers. If you do your final mix listening to headphones, you're going to be in for a rude awakening when you screen it in a theater and what you remembered as crisp delicate audio suddenly sounds unbearably muddy.

For many independent films, this is one stage that you had better plan to do in a facility. Even if you do all of your filtering and editing at home, before you finalize the show, bring it into a sound studio for the final mix. Most sound studios operate using ProTools software, which is a highly customizable and versatile audio editing environment.

Mixing in Final Cut Pro

You can still do a tremendous amount of your work inside of Final Cut Pro, especially now that the Mixer window is available in Final Cut Pro 4 (**Figure 7.38**). The mixer window doesn't offer much new functionality, but it does provide a new way to monitor and make adjustments to your audio levels.

Figure 7.38 Final Cut Pro 4's long awaited Mixer window accessed from the Tools menu.

Each track in your Final Cut Pro sequence is represented by a slider module in the mixer window. Hide and show sets of tracks using the preset buttons at the top of the window (**Figure 7.39**). Designate one preset to show only dialogue tracks, another for sound effects and another for music. Quickly switch between the sets using the buttons at the top of the window.

Figure 7.39 The presets allow you to hide or show groups of tracks. Each slider represents a timeline track.

Make level and pan adjustments by dragging the level or pan sliders for each track. The real excitement, however, comes from making these changes while the sequence is playing.

Automation

One important new function that arrived with the mixer is the ability to make volume adjustments on the fly. Audio keyframes are added automatically as you adjust the slider for each track. This is commonly referred to as automation.

Using this new function is straightforward. First, be sure to enable the Record Keyframes button in the button bar (**Figure 7.40**). Then, drag any of the sliders up or down to make

Figure 7.40 To record automation in the Audio Mixer, press the Record Audio Keyframes button.

the clip on the corresponding track louder or softer. As you drag, keyframes are added so that the next time you play back that section, the volume changes you've made will be incorporated.

Keyframe Thinning

There is one problem: you may not want every tiny adjustment to generate a new keyframe. This could cause sudden changes in the audio levels, which might sound like mistakes. To alleviate this, Final Cut Pro has a setting in the User Preferences called "Record Audio Keyframes" (**Figure 7.41**). When this is set to Reduced, keyframes will only be placed at the points necessary to make a clean curve (**Figure 7.42**). In general, the reduced setting will be best for most applications. If you're going to be making many subtle adjustments, you may want to switch the setting to All. The Peaks Only setting is useful when trying to create the effect of turning a track on or off when it's dragged up and down.

Figure 7.41 Set your Record Audio Keyframes setting to Reduced to activate Keyframe Thinning.

Figure 7.42 The top example was recorded with All keyframes set. The middle example was recorded with Reduced keyframes. The bottom was set to Peaks Only.

The way this setting is implemented, inside the User Preferences window, makes it difficult to easily switch between settings. I want to be able to change between these different modes on the fly when working in the Mixer window.

As it turns out, there's an elegant way to do just that. Like the other main windows, the Mixer window has a button bar at the top where you can add custom buttons for commonly used commands. If you open the Button List window from the Tools menu, the audio section has a three button set specifically for these controls. Drag any of the three Audio Keyframe Recording buttons and all three buttons are applied (**Figure 7.43**). This allows changes between modes with a quick click. If you prefer to use a keyboard shortcut, use the Keyboard Customization tool to designate the shortcut of your choice.

Figure 7.43 The Keyframe thinning buttons work as a toggle. Only one can be depressed at a time.

Adjusting Level and Pan in Final Cut Express

If you're working in Final Cut Express or an older version of Final Cut Pro, you can still make adjustments to each clip's level and pan settings in one of two ways. All of these methods also work in Final Cut Pro 4.

In the Viewer

One way to adjust an individual clip's level or pan settings is in the Audio tab in the Viewer (**Figure 7.44**). Set either parameter to change over time by using keyframes. Add keyframes by Option-clicking a point on the line, and set the desired value by dragging the point or the line. If you prefer, click the Add Keyframe button and set your desired value with the slider.

Figure 7.44 Adjust audio settings in the Audio tab by clicking and dragging the envelopes drawn over the waveform. Pink is for level, purple is for pan.

In the Timeline

Alternately, you can adjust levels in the Timeline. To do so, first turn on Clip Overlays by clicking the control in the lower left corner of the window (**Figure 7.45**), or by hitting Option-W. When Clip Overlays is turned on, you see the level envelope (or rubber band) drawn over the clips. Set and add keyframes here the same way that you do in the Viewer: Option-click to add a keyframe, and drag the point to the desired level.

Figure 7.45 Levels can also be adjusted in the Timeline.

In Final Cut Pro 4, you have the ability to change the vertical size of each individual track in your timeline. If you like making your audio level adjustments in the timeline, stretch the tracks so you've got plenty of room for making precise adjustments (**Figure 7.46**). To expand a track's height, click and drag on the track header.

Figure 7.46 Customizable track heights can be a boon for adjusting audio levels in the timeline.

From the Menu

You may want to make an adjustment to multiple clips at the same time—perhaps to boost the audio on all the shots containing a particular character's dialogue, or to attenuate background noise in certain shots simultaneously.

To make changes to multiple items, select the clips and choose Levels from the Modify menu. This opens the Gain Adjust dialog box, which lets you set all the selected clips to a new dB level, either by making a relative adjustment (moving all levels up from their current setting by, say, 2dB) or making an absolute adjustment (setting all levels precisely to that value) (**Figure 7.47**).

Figure 7.47 The Gain Adjust dialog box allows you to change the level of multiple clips at once.

Simple level and pan adjustments can be made to clips either in the Timeline or in the Viewer by using the Audio submenu of the Modify menu (**Figure 7.48**). Here you can nudge audio levels up or down by 1 or 3dB and pan clips left, right, or center. The menu lists corresponding keyboard shortcuts.

Figure 7.48 The Audio submenu enables you to make simple adjustments quickly and easily.

EXPORTING FOR PROTOOLS

Final Cut Pro allows you to export the audio tracks from your sequence into an open media format (OMF) file. This file contains the audio information for your sequence, including the actual sound media, as well as the track information. When you import the OMF file into ProTools (or another OMF-savvy application), all the tracks from Final Cut Pro appear in your new document, with all the clips on them—ready to be edited, sweetened, mixed, and output to tape. You can even add handles when you export to allow a little fudge room for editing (**Figure 7.49**).

Figure 7.49 When you export to an OMF file, keep the sample rate the same as the sequence from which you're exporting (usually 48 kHz).

Only one piece of information is lacking in Final Cut Pro's exported OMF data: the levels. That's right, the single most important bit of data is not exported. This means that if you plan to do your final mix in ProTools (or Logic, or another dedicated audio program) you will have to rebuild all of the level settings that you made during your picture edit.

The Advantages of ProTools

Most professional audio mixers and sound designers are trained and proficient on ProTools. It has been the industry standard for many years and although many competitors are beginning to challenge that dominance, there are many qualities that make ProTools a superior audio editing and mixing tool to Final Cut Pro.

There are countless third party plug-ins that can create a wide variety of effects and do clean up in far more robust fashion than the filters currently available for Final Cut Pro. ProTools also boasts extensive hardware support. For example, there are hardware accelerators that can render many of those fancy effects in real time. Also, ProTools can control (and be controlled by) a wide variety of mixing consoles. Traditional sound mixers who, like to adjust rows of physical sliders and dials when they're listening to a sound mix, can use their fancy and elaborate mixing boards, not to mention all of the various hardware effects boxes that have been in use for decades. Another one of the primary advantages that ProTools offers is a basic functionality called *bussing*. This lets you direct multiple tracks into a single bus and apply effects or volume adjustments to that bus. For example, you can direct the dialogue from many individual tracks into a single bus and apply a single EQ or compressor filter to all of them.

You can simulate this ability using Final Cut Pro's nesting capabilities (see "Nest Sequences," Chapter 8), but that feature isn't intended for this use; in practice it proves to be a bit awkward. Lastly, ProTools has full multi-channel output functionality, so you can mix to various types of Surround Sound, such as Dolby Stereo or Dolby Digital (5.1).

Like any technology, the software is not the true advantage; the human operators are the prize. As you can see from all of the details described in this chapter, audio editing and mixing is an art in itself, distinctive from video editing. Finding an expert sound designer is the best thing you can do to improve the quality of your film—and chances are he will prefer to operate on his familiar ProTools rig.

Locked Means Locked

If you are going to work with an outside sound facility or sound designer, it's very important that you don't make changes to your picture after you have exported the OMF. When the sound technicians are finished they'll turn in a single audio file, and you will not be able to make even the smallest timing adjustment. If, in the meantime, you've swapped out a shot or dropped in an unfinished visual effect, be sure that no rippling occurs in your sequence. If you make any editorial changes that affect the timing of edits or the overall duration of your show, you may cause problems that will only be fixable by going back into ProTools and exactly replicating the same edits there. Locked means locked. Besides, you have to stop futzing sometime. Once you send out your audio, you're finished editing. Open a bottle of champagne. Or call that client who's been waiting and start all over again.

INTERVIEW

John Wilson's professional editing career is unique. For ten years he worked exclusively with Peter Greenaway, the highly regarded British artist and filmmaker. Among Wilson's credits are *The Draughtsman's Contract*, *A Zed and Two Noughts*, and the memorable and controversial *The Cook, the Thief, His Wife & Her Lover*. In 2000 he cut the international sensation *Billy Elliot*, directed by Britain's premier theater director, Stephen Daldry. At the time of this interview, he was working with veteran director Lewis Gilbert on a film titled *Before You Go*. Since then, he's been working on *Cheeky* directed by David Thewlis.

MICHAEL WOHL: HOW DOES YOUR EDITING CYCLE WORK?

John Wilson: Good directors will make it quite clear by the way they have shot the material how it should go together. So, for the seven week period of the shoot I'll be putting stuff together as I see fit. Then, when the shoot's finished and the director and I can work together, everything gets particularly interesting. It opens up the possibility of throwing away the script and starting again, if necessary. One has to work with the material rather than following any sort of script; start getting the pace, transitions between scenes, addition of temp music, just to see how it's going to flow and develop. And when we get down to that stage, after maybe four or five weeks of hard editing, we show it to our producers.

HAVE YOU EVER LOOKED AT THE SCENE AND SAID, "I HAVE NO IDEA WHAT TO DO WITH THIS?"

Certainly. There are always scenes that I call my bête noire scenes. Some scenes require a lot more input from an editor than others because of the very nature of the material. Maybe two or three cameras have been run on something, and it's up to the editor to make sense of it. So, yes, there are one or two scenes in every film where you think, "Now that's going to be tricky."

Sometimes you'd like to go off and shoot some more, but often it's very expensive and very difficult: You can't always get your actors back, or the time of year has changed. All these little problems can get in the way. So you have to be creative. There's an early scene in *Billy Elliot* where we see Billy plunking out notes on the family piano, and the father comes in with coal for the fire, and the brother comes in and says he's going to join the picket line for a strike—

we needed to set up an awful lot of things, but that sequence didn't exist in the script. So to construct that scene, we stole bits from other scenes later in the film.

HOW HAS WORKING WITH DIGITAL TECHNOLOGY CHANGED THE WAY YOU WORK?

I'd like to answer that it doesn't change the way I work at all, but of course it has to. It's freed the creativity to a huge degree. On one hand, I just see it as another tool for doing my job. That's certainly true to an extent, but it's such a radical difference. I often say it's rather like giving a caveman an automobile. It's such a huge leap forward in time. People always argue there's not enough thinking time with [digital editing], but I think you've got to make your thinking time, and build it into your schedule. In terms of how one works physically, while you're assembling scenes, you can frequently think, "Well, maybe the director would like it to be this way, I'll put an alternative cut in this little box over here, and dig it out if he says something that's likely to mean that was a good idea." That happened twice today, where I had done that and it was very valuable to do that, and, obviously, that's something we could never do when cutting on film; although we didn't experience it as a frustration at the time because we didn't know anything different. In retrospect, with the benefit of hindsight, the discipline was that you worked on a single cutting copy. You didn't keep umpteen versions of the film dotted around your desktop of your computer, which tends to be what happens now.

HAS DIGITAL TECHNOLOGY CHANGED YOUR AESTHETICS, YOUR STYLE?

It shouldn't. There can be a danger because you're working on machines that so closely represent television. You can get sucked into, perhaps, spending more time on close-ups than you would otherwise have done if, shall we say, one was working on a Steenbeck. Indeed, stylistically, the audience's appetite now is slightly different that what is was maybe 20 years ago. They expect things. Their attention span is very short. They expect cuts to be very quick. I don't hold with that particularly. The whole point of a well-crafted film is that you have staccato moments and you have slow moments, and it's the way those juxtapose with one another that will create the overall feeling of whether the film has got the right pace and structure.

ONCE YOU GET YOUR SCENES WORKING, HOW DO YOU APPROACH THE BIG PICTURE IN TERMS OF THE PACING?

That's a very difficult question to answer. On very obvious things, you cannot really change the pace of a scene from the way it's been shot. And that goes without saying. One is often asked to. It's not a good idea to try that. One thing that [digital editing systems] present you with is an opportunity to have quite a sophisticated soundtrack at your disposal, even though it's temporary. That can actually help a lot of decisions that might otherwise have been left until the sound editors were working, when, theoretically, the picture editor's gone. The use of sound in general [during picture editing] can now be quite sophisticated, whereas it was always restricted previously, to perhaps one strand of sound on your cutting copy. Now you can have three, four, five tracks running. And that can enhance the impression that the over-all film will have further down the line.

In the days when one cut on Steenbecks, you had picture lock and that was absolute—it had to be locked. It very rarely ran over, because the sound editors had a finite amount of time. If he's laying up eight tracks of dialogue, eight tracks of effects, and the editor comes along and says he's taken three frames out of this shot, that involves huge amounts of man hours and labor. Now, of course, it's minutes rather than hours to make those sort of changes.

IS THERE ANY PARTICULAR EDIT OR SCENE THAT YOU'RE PARTICULARLY PROUD OF? SOMETHING THAT YOU DIDN'T EXPECT WAS GOING TO COME OUT THE WAY IT DID?

There are several sequences in *Billy Elliott* I'm particularly proud of. They were pretty heavy editorially. Like the dance he does on the rooftop and then down the street, the dance he does for his dad.

THAT WAS CREATED IN THE EDITING ROOM?

Oh yeah. There was lots of material shot and it was all fairly closely planned. I worked closely with the choreographer, which was an interesting process because that was new. Again, there are moments in all the films I've worked on that I particularly like looking at again. There's a sequence in *The Cook, The Thief, His Wife and Her Lover* when the character played by Helen Mirren, the lover, asks the cook to cook her lover. I admire that sequence not because of its visual content, but because of how we made it work with the material we had. It was a very tricky scene to make work. Going right back to the very first feature film that I edited, *The Draughtsman's Contract*, I'm particularly proud of the sequence where the draughtsman is going through the garden early on and discussing what he's going to be doing with his draw-ings. I think that works very well as an edited sequence. It's very good to revisit films a long time after you've done them and I hope to do it more often than I do.

DO YOU HAVE ANY ADVICE FOR EDITORS GETTING STARTED?

You've got to be very patient. You've got to not mind the fact that you are not known about by the world outside; you live in dark rooms like a mole. Be really determined to do it and you'll do it. I was very fortunate to be very young when I got into the film industry. At the age of about 23 I was an assistant editor, and within 2 years I was an editor. Now some people

I know are still assisting at the age of 40 and beyond. You have to take your breaks when you get them.

HOW DO YOU KNOW WHEN YOU'RE FINISHED WITH A FILM?

No film is ever finished. It can always be improved, but you know you're done when the sound editor is screaming at you for reels to work on and you keep putting him off. Once the executives and the producers have all climbed off, then the film is done. But there are times when you're in the dubbing theater and you think, "If we could only extend that shot there..." You're never really finished, never really satisfied. But that's the organic process of filmmaking, I suppose.

WHAT IS YOUR LEAST FAVORITE PART OF EDITING?

The bits in between when I'm not editing. I love my work, I'm very lucky. I'd like to think I'd be doing this job even if I wasn't getting paid.

CHAPTER EIGHT
Special Effects

OK, you've been working with Final Cut Pro for a couple of months now, and you've edited a few shows. You've been good, too, diligently staying away from all those cryptic menu items—the ones that look intriguing even though you don't know exactly what they're for. Still, there's that longing deep inside. *You've got to know!*

Or maybe it's day three, you've mastered all the editing stuff, and all you want to do is make some cool-looking pictures.

Either way, you're sick of waiting. And you've come to the right place.

One big thing that sets Final Cut apart from all the other nonlinear video editors is its seamless integration of editing and effects. Sure, most other programs have a set of features for doing special effects, too, but the way editing and effects are integrated into Final Cut is both unique and extremely cool: Apply *any* effect to *any* clip at *any* time—and that means seamless workflow.

GETTING STARTED

What is a special effect, anyway?

Any time you alter the video data from the image that was captured in the camera, you have created an *effects shot*. (I'll get to in-camera effects momentarily.) An effects shot can be as simple as applying a noise reduction filter or as complicated as creating a *traveling matte* that composites a video image inside moving words on top of a computer-generated background (**Figure 8.1**).

Figure 8.1 This effect is called a traveling matte. It requires three different layers: the background, the text, and the image inside the text.

Before we get into the nuts and bolts of how, why, and when to create which effects, here are a few general notions to think about first.

Become a Specialist—or Hire One

Just because the software manual says that Final Cut Pro is designed to produce a wide variety of stunning visual effects, many novice editors assume that they can make their cooking video look like *The Matrix*. There's an easy way to disabuse yourself of this notion: The next time you see a major "effects" film, stay in your seat, watch *all* the credits, and try to count how many people were involved in the creation of the special effects. The number can easily run into the hundreds.

You will become very frustrated, very fast, if you buy into the myth that says one person can do everything herself. She can't—and neither can you.

Creating effects is a specialized art, one that's quite different from editing. The two activities require different skill sets and very distinct dispositions. For instance, a word processing program is capable of outputting everything from a love letter to a mystery novel or a technical manual on disarming nuclear submarines—but that doesn't mean the same author is up to all three of those tasks!

Of course, you should experiment with the tools available to you, both to understand what they do and because you *might* have a propensity for effects design in addition to (or instead of) straightforward film editing. But be honest with yourself and with your clients. There are far too many dilettantes dabbling in every area of digital media creation. If you're serious about a career in post-production, you must find a single focus and develop it. Even though Final Cut can do all types of image manipulation, and you'll need one or another of its effects tools from time to time, you don't need to master the whole program.

Employ the Right Tool

If you choose to delve seriously into the realm of special effects, Final Cut Pro may not even be the right tool. You can perform many types of effects much more adroitly with a different application. Some effects, like rotoscoping or 3-D rendering, can't be done in Final Cut Pro at all; others, like organic movements and detailed keyframing, are possible—but are a lot easier to do in a program dedicated to the job.

If you're serious about developing your effects skills, Final Cut Pro is a great place to start. You can experiment with layering, keyframing, alpha channels, and many other elements of *motion graphics,* and the skills you learn will translate easily into the more specialized tools to which you'll graduate.

But it's important to recognize the limitations of Final Cut Pro. Rather than spending hours trying to simulate a randomly generated keyframe pattern by hand, try Adobe After Effects instead and check out The Wiggler. Applications like After Effects, Discreet Combustion, Pinnacle Commotion and the like have specialized features expressly designed for the challenges involved in creating special effects. (See the section called "Getting In and Out of After Effects," at the end of this chapter, for details on the mechanics of moving files between After Effects and Final Cut Pro.)

Don't Do Effects in the Camera

Most modern video cameras are designed with a collection of built-in effects you can apply while shooting. This set of effects generally includes mosaics, posterization, slow-motion capture, and so on. But while they can be fun to fool around with, I strongly recommend against using them on a serious project.

The reason is simple: Once you record the footage, it's all you have. If you record it with some sort of filter applied (such as a pastel effect, which adds a painterly texture to the images), you will never be able to remove that effect.

On the other hand, if you record it clean, you can apply the same effect in Final Cut Pro and exert even finer control over the result, by adjusting the intensity of the filter and customizing various parameters. You can make the effect begin slowly or appear and disappear on a certain cue. If you're applying the filter to an edited sequence, apply it evenly across all the edit points. And if you change your mind about the effect, it can easily be removed—and the original footage will still be perfectly usable.

If you're planning to edit your footage (which is why you bought your G4 and the Final Cut software in the first place), you're far better off doing effects like these in post.

TYPES OF VISUAL EFFECTS

Visual effects can be grouped into four major categories: speed effects, filtering effects, compositing effects, and CG (computer generated) effects. Of course, these are not mutually exclusive. You will frequently combine different categories to create compound effects, such as applying a filter to a title that is composited over a CG background image. You might even filter the background as well, or play it in slow motion, or both.

Organic vs. Inorganic Effects

In another way, any special effect can also be divided into shots that are intended to create realistic images and those designed to alter reality for dramatic or thematic effect. This distinction has ramifications similar to those I described earlier in the book, in which certain editing decisions allow the viewer to lose herself in the narrative, while others interrupt the illusion and draw attention to the filmmaking technique.

Recognizing which is which in terms of special effects is harder than it seems. For example, in real life we *never* experience episodes during which time suddenly slows down to a crawl. Nonetheless, a slow-motion shot is a fairly subtle effect that most viewers will accept without experiencing a disruption of the narrative flow.

On the other hand, compositing two unrelated images into a double exposure would seem to be a jarring, unnatural effect that challenges viewers to make sense of the competing images. It's tempting to classify such a double exposure as a "cinematic" technique with little connection to the real world. But in fact, we see double exposures all the time: When you look out the window of a train, or even out the window of your office, part of the interior is reflected back at you, superimposed over the image of what lies outside.

So, while you can generally drop a slow-motion shot into a narrative sequence with far less disruption than a double exposure, trying to classify effects can get you into deep water. Even though more and more big-budget movies seem to rely on special effects, the current fashion is to create effects that seem entirely real. In most cases, with films like *The Perfect Storm* or *Saving Private Ryan,* the tens of millions of dollars the producers spent on visual effects went to create images that showed no trace of digital manipulation.

Still, part of what makes this medium so powerful is its ability to distort and manipulate images for dramatic impact. Finding a unique balance between real and fake is one important way of defining your own cinematic style. Remember the "bullet time" effect popularized in *The Matrix?* (You know, where they appeared to stop time during the fighting sequences and fly the camera around the actors.) Although that completely disrupted any pretense of realism, the flow of the story was unimpeded.

SPEED EFFECTS

The most familiar types of special effects involve the manipulation of time. A speed effect is any modification to a clip's playing speed: slow motion, fast motion, ramping, and so on. As I mentioned in the previous section, speed changes tend to be one of the least disruptive types of effects.

Change a clip's speed in Final Cut by selecting the clip and choosing Speed from the Modify menu. This opens the Speed dialog box (**Figure 8.2**). Enter a percentage of the clip's normal speed or define a new duration. In either case, only the frames between the In and Out points will be affected. If you want to play a clip backward, enable the Reverse check box. If you want it to play at double speed backward, check the Reverse box and set the speed to 200 percent.

Figure 8.2 The Speed dialog box allows you to set a clip to play at a constant speed, in forward or reverse. Call it up by hitting ⌘-Ⓙ.

Since modifying the speed of a clip also changes its duration, Final Cut has to make adjustments to the surrounding clips in the Timeline. Speed changes cause the sequence to ripple forward or backward to accommodate the change in duration.

For example, if you took a 10 second clip and set the speed to 50 percent, the clip would become 20 seconds long. This would ripple the following clips 10 seconds downstream (**Figure 8.3**). If you're not sure how long you want your clip to be, or if you've got items on adjacent tracks that you don't want rippled, drag your clip onto a new track and lock all the other tracks (**Figure 8.4**). That way any speed changes you make won't affect the surrounding clips until you've decided on the desired speed. At that point unlock the rest of the tracks and integrate the clip back into the sequence.

Figure 8.3 Speed changes ripple the sequence to accommodate the new duration of the affected clip.

Figure 8.4 By dragging the clip to a new track and locking all the other tracks, you can alter the speed without disturbing the surrounding clips. (Option)-clicking the Lock icon for a track "solos" that track, opening it for changes while locking all the others.

Slow Motion

The ubiquitous slo-mo shot is the most common speed effect. Slow-motion shots are used to highlight a dramatic moment (Rocky holding the World Champion belt over his head), enhance the significance of a particular event (the necklace sinking through the depths in *Titanic*), and draw special attention to an event so the details can be understood even though it happens very quickly (the re-enactment of the assassination in *JFK*).

When you slow down a clip, Final Cut Pro has to create new frames to fill in the spaces. Look for a setting in the Speed dialog called Frame Blending (see Figure 8.2). When you enable this check box, Final Cut Pro calculates the new images by mixing together the surrounding frames. If this setting is turned off, Final Cut Pro creates intermediate frames by duplicating the preceding frames, creating a strobe-like effect. The latter technique renders more quickly than Frame Blending but creates a much less natural effect.

How far you can slow down a clip depends on the details of the shot. You can only go so far before smooth movement deteriorates into "steppiness" (even with Frame Blending enabled). And while audiences will tolerate a beautiful slow-motion shot without bouncing out of the story, if the shot begins to step rather than flow, all illusion of continuity is lost.

> **TIP:** In some cases, you can improve the look of a shot slowed to the point of steppiness by applying motion blur from the clip's motion tab.

Fast Motion

It's just as easy to speed up a shot when you want to quicken the pace, increase the excitement, and accelerate how quickly things happen. This is far less common than slowing images down, but it does have its place. While slowing down an event can make it seem overly dramatic, speeding it up tends to reduce its dramatic impact and slide it in the general direction of comedy. Good examples of this are the driving sequences in Steven Soderbergh's *Schizopolis,* or Robert Downey Jr. designing his costume as the title character in Richard Attenborough's *Chaplin.*

Time Lapse

Sometimes you'll want to speed up events so much that what might take hours or days in real time plays out on-screen in only a few seconds. This method is commonly applied to slow-moving natural events such as sunsets or flowers blooming. Traditionally, the effect is performed in the camera using a technique called time-lapse photography. Time-lapse-capable cameras record a single frame at intervals you set: for instance, one every minute, or one every hour.

You can apply time lapse in post, much the same way that you apply other speed effects. You might take an entire one-hour tape and speed it up so it plays in just ten seconds.

Ramping (Variable Speed Effects)

Ramping—changing the speed of a clip while it's playing—is currently enjoying great popularity. You'll see it quite often in TV commercials, music videos, and even feature films. In a ramp effect, the clip may begin playing at regular speed, gradually accelerate until it's playing at 2,000 percent, and then slow back down to a crawl. Director Guy Ritchie featured this effect in the opening sequence of *Snatch,* introducing each character with a ramp shot that slowed to a freeze frame—at which point a title showing the character's name and credit appeared over the frame. Since then that exact effect has appeared in countless commercials, trailers, and title sequences. Now you too can create the same effect on your very own desktop.

Ramping can even be used to go from forward motion to backward motion. Begin a shot by playing forward at half speed, then slow it down to a stop, play it backward, slow to a stop, play it forward again, and so on ad infinitum. Think of this as a visual equivalent of the way a DJ scratches a record. I've seen ramps employed comically in sports coverage, where they show a basketball dunk, then back it up and show it again and again: ball goes in, ball comes back out, ball goes in, ball comes back out. It's a bit nauseating, but it does have a certain charm.

Performing a Ramp Effect

Final Cut Pro 4 added a tool specifically for creating ramp effects called the Time Remap tool (**Figure 8.5**). There are two different ways to use it. Both involve dragging frames around within a clip that's already in a sequence. When you drag a point in a clip you move a new frame to the current time position and cause all of the surrounding frames to speed up or slow down to accommodate the change. This creates a ramp. Alternately, hold down the option key and move the current frame to a new time position.

Figure 8.5 The Time Remap tool can only be used in the timeline.

Let's take an example of a car chase sequence. At the climax of the chase, our hero, out of options, decides he's going to have to drive his car over an open drawbridge. The scene was shot from a profile angle so we can see the car approach the ramp, lift into the air and successfully land on the other side of the bridge. The entire shot lasts ten seconds, and he's in the air for just less than three seconds.

To enhance the drama and sense of peril in the shot, you decide to ramp the shot down to super-slow motion when the car is in the air and then resume ordinary speed when it hits the ground on the other side. You've already got a music track laid in, and you've cued the jump to match up with a single piercing guitar note, but the guitar note lasts for six seconds.

So in this case you want to stretch the middle section of the clip from three to six seconds. To make the effect more natural, you want it to slow down smoothly and then, as soon as the car lands, speed it back up to regular speed. Here's how you do it.

Setting the Markers and Moving a Frame

Begin by identifying the important moments in the clip. You can set markers, but unfortunately the markers don't stick to the frames once you apply the variable speed effect. Still they can prove helpful. In this example, I've set a marker at the frame where the car left the ground and one to identify the beginning and end of the guitar note (**Figure 8.6**).

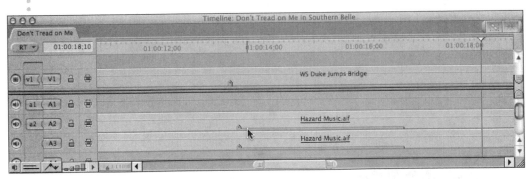

Figure 8.6 Set markers at the moments where you want the speed effect to begin and end.

When you click your mouse with the Time Remap tool, it sets a keyframe at that point in time. As you drag, you move a different frame from the clip to the keyframe position. Because the beginning and end points of the clip don't move, this creates a speed effect. Dragging to the left causes the portion of the clip to the left of your keyframe to slow down and, correspondingly, the portion to the right speeds up. The tooltip that appears as you drag identifies all of this information (**Figure 8.7**). The new video frame that will be moved to your keyframe time is displayed in the canvas as it is during a trim.

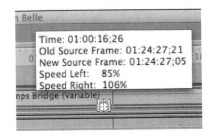

Figure 8.7 The variable speed tooltip identifies the new speed to the left and right of the keyframe, it also displays the timecode number of the old and new frame.)

Adding a Keyframe

Each time you set a keyframe, you establish a new clip speed for a portion of the clip. In our example, we want the car to move at normal speed until it reaches the bridge, so we must set a keyframe at the moment when the car reaches the bridge. By just clicking (with no drag) a keyframe is added that sets the speed to the right and left to 100 percent (**Figure 8.8**).

Figure 8.8 Add one keyframe where the effect is to begin.

Next, find the point in time where you want the effect to end. In this example it's the end of the guitar note (identified by the end of the audio marker). Click to add a new keyframe at that point and drag to the left until the frame where the car completes the jump appears in the canvas (**Figure 8.9**). Now the clip plays at normal speed until the first keyframe, then plays at 50 percent speed from the first keyframe to the second, and plays at 119 percent speed from that point until the end of the clip.

Figure 8.9 Set the second keyframe where the effect will end and drag to stretch the section to the left.

Fixing the Clip Speed

The only remaining problem is that the last section of the clip is now sped up and we want it to play at normal speed. To fix this, click the Time Remap tool on the last frame and drag to the left until the tooltip identifies the left side at 100 percent. Disregard the increasing number to the right since there are no frames that will actually play at that speed (**Figure 8.10**).

> **TIP:** When dragging with the Time Remap tool, holding down Shift constrains the effect to always land on 10 percent increments

Figure 8.10 Modify the final keyframe to reduce the last section to normal speed.

If, after setting your keyframes you want to move them around in time (perhaps you want to stretch it even further than the guitar note), hold down Option and drag with the Time Remap tool. Now, rather than moving a new frame to the current position, the tool moves the existing keyframe to a new position. The tooltip changes to reflect the new behavior (**Figure 8.11**).

> **TIP:** *Variable speed effects do not affect audio clips. Once you apply a ramp effect to a video clip, the audio will no longer sync up with it.*

Figure 8.11 The Option-drag effect of the Time Remap tool allows you to pick a frame in your video and move it to a new location, speeding up or slowing down the surrounding frames.

Visual Feedback

Many people find it is very difficult to comprehend and keep track of this complex speed information without a little help so Final Cut Pro provides several additional tools to help you visualize what is happening.

Speed Indicators

The primary way to keep track of Time Remap settings is with the Speed Indicators (**Figure 8.12**). This control displays tick marks to simulate the playing speed of the clip. When the clip is moving at a linear speed, the ticks are evenly spaced. The faster the clip plays, the closer together they are. When a clip is frozen on a single frame, there are no marks at all. When a clip is set to reverse speed, the marks are in red (**Figure 8.13**).

Normal speed ⏌   Slow motion ⏌   Fast motion ⏌

Figure 8.12 The speed indicators identify a clip's playing speed through the dispersion of tick marks.

Reverse Speed (shows in red) ⏌   ⏌ Freeze Frame (no tick marks)

Figure 8.13

To turn the Speed Indicators on or off, use the Clip Keyframes button in the lower left corner of the Timeline (**Figure 8.14**).

Figure 8.14 The Speed Indicators are controlled by pressing the Clip Keyframes button.

Motion Bar

The Clip Keyframes button also turns on the Motion Bar. This is another tool that can assist in controlling ramp effects (**Figure 8.15**).

Figure 8.15 The Motion Bar can display and allow you to manipulate speed keyframes.

The blue Motion Bar displays the keyframes for any parameters selected in the Motion Bar pop-up menu (**Figure 8.16**). By default, all motion keyframes (Scale, Rotation, Opacity, Drop Shadow, and so on) are visible. If you want to view only speed keyframes, first choose "Hide All" which unchecks all parameters, then select Time Graph from the Time Remap section so the motion bar will display only those keyframes (**Figure 8.17**).

Figure 8.16 Select which keyframes you want displayed in the Motion Bar by control-clicking on the blue bar

Figure 8.17 Set as many different parameters to be displayed as you like.

> **NOTE:** If you enable the Clip Keyframes button and no blue bar appears, don't panic. The Motion Bar will appear only if there are motion settings applied to the clip. Once you add a motion effect such as Scale, Rotation, or Time Remapping, the blue bar will magically materialize.

Each time you click with the Time Remap tool you add a keyframe that is visible on the Motion Bar. Drag these keyframes around on the bar to change their locations in time—just like Option-dragging an existing keyframe with the Time Remap tool.

Keyframe Editor

The Clip Keyframes button also activates one more essential tool, but by default it is not displayed. You must access the Keyframe Editor by Ctrl-clicking on the Clip Keyframes button and selecting it from the shortcut menu that appears. The Keyframe Editor toggles the visibility of a keyframe graph for each timeline track (**Figure 8.18**). However, no graph will automatically appear. You must first select a single parameter from any currently applied filters or motion effects on a given clip (**Figure 8.19**). For control of your variable speed effects, choose Time Graph from the Time Remap section of the shortcut menu.

Figure 8.18 The Keyframe Editor adds a keyframe graph under each track.

Figure 8.19 Use the shortcut menu to select the parameter of your choice to have full keyframe access right in the timeline.

Different speeds are represented in the Keyframe graph by different slopes. When the speed is set to 100 percent, the slope is an even line from the beginning of the clip to the end. When a clip is playing slower than 100 percent, the slope is flatter; when the clip is playing above normal speed the slope is steeper (**Figure 8.20**). When a clip is held in a freeze frame, the line is completely horizontal and when a clip is playing in reverse speed, the slope moves downward (**Figure 8.21**).

Figure 8.20 Slow Motion, Normal Speed, Fast Motion

Figure 8.21 Freeze frame. Reverse speed.

There's no reason to attempt to make keyframe manipulations in a tiny box on your screen. The keyframe editor is resizable by dragging the thin vertical bar at the far right edge of the track header area (**Figure 8.22**). Make the best of your timeline real estate by growing and shrinking the keyframe editor as you need to. If you have specific settings you want to reuse, the height of the graph can be saved in your custom timeline track layouts (see Chapter 4, "Customizing the Timeline").

Figure 8.22 Resize the Keyframe Editor here.

Finalizing Your Ramp Effect

The keyframes you set create a sudden change from one speed to another. In the car jump example, playback went from 100 percent to 50 percent and then back to 100 percent. Most of the time, however, you will want the speed change to be somewhat gradual, so rather than switching from 100 percent to 50 percent all at once, the clip slows down over the course of a few frames.

To accomplish this, change the keyframe from a corner keyframe to a smooth keyframe by Ctrl-clicking on it in the Keyframe Graph (**Figure 8.23**). Bezier handles appear to allow you to adjust the curve manually, but beware; tiny adjustments to the handles can cause unexpected results. The only change I suggest making is to shortening the length of the handles so the change happens more quickly. Be careful to keep the handles completely horizontal to avoid changing the shape of the curve (**Figure 8.24**).

Figure 8.23 Smooth your speed changes using the shortcut menu in the Keyframe Graph.

Figure 8.24 Keep the handles level but drag them towards the point to shorten the speed transition.

Variable Speed Settings in the Motion Tab

The same controls that you use in the timeline to create variable speed effects are also accessible in the Motion tab of the Viewer (**Figure 8.25**). Although you can make modifications here, I recommend against it. The Time Remap tool doesn't work in the motion viewer, so all you can do is move keyframes around to different times and values. I find that decisions are best made in the context of watching your video rather than based on a numerical analysis. The only advantage to working in the Motion viewer is the ability to line up keyframes from other motion parameters and to view values for the acceleration. This is good in case you want to manually paste the same number into several different effects so they all change at the same velocity.

Figure 8.25
You're best off not touching the speed controls in the Motion viewer.

For example if you wanted to zoom in on a clip at the exact moment that the speed effect began, you could align those keyframes in the motion viewer. (See the "Keyframes and Filters" sidebar later in this chapter for more information on how to manipulate the controls in the motion tab.)

Resetting Speed Effects

As you experiment with variable speed, you are likely to get yourself lost and want to eliminate all of the keyframes you have set, returning the clip to its normal unadulterated state. One easy way to do this is to open the Speed dialog box for the clip (⌘-J). Set the pop-up from Variable to Constant and set the speed to 100 percent. This will remove any settings you previously applied (**Figure 8.26**). Alternately, open the clip's motion tab and click the Reset button for the Time Remap section.

Figure 8.26 Reset your clip's speed by choosing Speed from the Modify menu.

What's Wrong with Variable Speed?

Unfortunately, there is a limitation to Final Cut Pro's implementation of variable speed that I find somewhat crippling. If you slow down any portion of a clip, you will not be able to extend the length of the clip in the timeline. Ordinarily, whenever you slow down a clip it gets longer. What happens with variable speed effects is that the clip slows down, but doesn't get longer. That means that the end of the clip is cut off, unless you speed it up super-fast to make up for the amount you slowed it down (**Figure 8.27**). There is a workaround (other than launching Adobe After Effects) but it's a little tricky.

Figure 8.27 Once you slow down a clip, there's no way to get to the added frames at the end of the clip.

Duplicating the Clip

Edit another copy of the clip into the sequence and line up the frames so the speed appears constant across the edit. The best way to do this is to perform a Match Frame to Master Clip on the last frame of the affected clip, clear the clip's In and Out points and set a new In point on the Match Frame. Then edit the clip into the sequence (**Figure 8.28**).

This is acceptable when you simply want to return your clip to regular speed, but if you want to apply more speed changes, it's difficult to create a smooth seam between the same clips.

Figure 8.28 To workaround the duration limitation, Match Frame on the end of the clip and lay in a new copy.

Creating a Ramp Effect in Final Cut Express

Apple may be hoping that features like Time Remapping will encourage you to upgrade from Final Cut Express to Final Cut Pro 4, but if you're not ready to shell out another $500 you can make a pretty close approximation of a ramp effect by using the Razor Blade tool and the constant speed controls.

1. *Drag a clip into a new sequence and chop it in half with the Razor Blade tool.*

2. *Select the first half and set the speed to 150 percent.*

3. *Cut the second half in half.*

4. *Set the first half of that clip to 200 percent.*

5. *Cut the remaining clip in half and set the first half to 300 percent.*

6. *Repeat as needed.*

*The result is that the clip gets faster and faster as it plays. Although this is somewhat clunkier than using the feature in Final Cut Pro 4 (or After Effects), the result is quite similar (**Figure 8.29**).*

Figure 8.29 Create a ramp speed effect by chopping a clip into bits and assigning different speeds to each section.

Freeze Frames

A freeze frame—stopping the action on a single frame—is a common way to end a sequence when you want to leave your viewers in suspense. Or you might use one as a background for a chart or title.

Performing a freeze frame in Final Cut is a snap: Select a clip and choose Freeze Frame from the Modify menu, or press Shift-N. This selects the current frame and opens it up as a still frame in the Viewer. Set In and Out markers to determine how long you want it to run, and drop it into your sequence like any other clip.

In Final Cut Pro 4, you can also create a freeze frame in the middle of a clip and then revert to normal playback. Set two Time Remap keyframes each set to the same frame (**Figure 8.30**). The Keyframe graph displays a flat line and the Speed indicator shows no tick marks for the duration of the freeze.

WS Duke Jumps Bridge (Variable)

**Figure 8.30
A freeze frame in
the middle of a clip**

Fit to Fill

If you need a clip to fill a certain gap in your sequence, but the clip is too short or too long, use the Fit-to-Fill edit style. For instance, suppose you have a 22-second clip in which the narrator describes how to fold a flag. You also have a B-roll shot of a flag being folded, but that shot lasts only 15 seconds. You want the clip to fit the narration exactly, and you don't care if the action is slowed down a little.

Fit to Fill will change the speed of the source clip to make it fit the space you've allotted in the sequence. It's one of the choices on the Edit Overlay, or you can press Shift-F12.

To execute a fit-to-fill edit, you must provide all four points—source In, source Out, record In, and record Out (**Figure 8.31**). If one of these points is missing, you'll get an Invalid Edit error. (Okay, that's not entirely true; if you don't provide a source In or Out, the beginning or end of the media will be used. You'll get the error only if one of the record points is missing.)

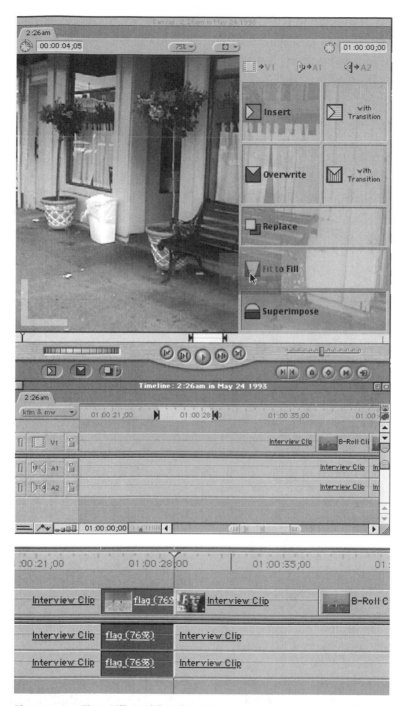

Figure 8.31 Fit to Fill modifies the speed of the source clip, stretching or squeezing it into the space defined in the sequence.

Use Fit to Fill with caution. Many clips can't be slowed down or sped up without the effect being obvious. In general, you can get away with speed changes below 10 percent without anyone noticing, but once you push it much above that, the effect is impossible to hide.

Speed and Audio

Final Cut can apply constant speed effects to an audio clip just as easily as to a video clip. The good news is that audio speed changes don't require rendering (even in Final Cut Express). The bad news is that there's no way to change speed without altering the pitch of the sound. That means if you speed up an audio clip, it will get higher pitched, and if you slow it down, it will get lower. Sometimes this effect is desirable, but if you're trying to make a subtle speed change, this pitch alteration can give you away. It *is* possible to change speed without shifting audio pitch—in Pro Tools.

FILTER EFFECTS

Filter effects are modifications to the pixels within an image. They might include anything from lightening a dark shot to making it look like an oil painting. Final Cut Pro performs these manipulations with the use of filters. More than 80 different filters are built into Final Cut, and each comes with different parameters that can create an amazing variety of effects (**Figure 8.32**). Final Cut will also let you use certain third party filters designed for After Effects. That brings hundreds of additional effects to your fingertips.

Many filters are designed to clean up images or modify them in a naturalistic way, not to create a flashy effect. This includes color correction filters, noise reduction filters, blur or sharpen filters, and certain perspective filters like Rotate or Flop. (Of course, any of these filters can be used to create a dramatic distortion of the original image, if you like.)

Figure 8.32 Filters can be accessed from the Effects menu or from the Effects tab in the Browser.

Applying a filter is as easy as selecting the clip you want to modify and choosing the desired filter from the Effects menu. Or just drag and drop filters onto a clip from the Effects tab in the Browser.

Once you've applied a filter, modify its parameters in the Filters tab for the affected clip (**Figure 8.33**). Remember that each instance of a clip is unique. So if you want to modify the parameters of a filtered clip that's currently in a sequence, you must double-click that clip to open it into the Viewer.

In Final Cut Pro 4, most filter parameters can be keyframed so the effect changes over time. This could be as simple as a clip that gets increasingly blurry—or it could be a complicated effect where many parameters change at different times. Final Cut Express limits your filter usage to constant settings.

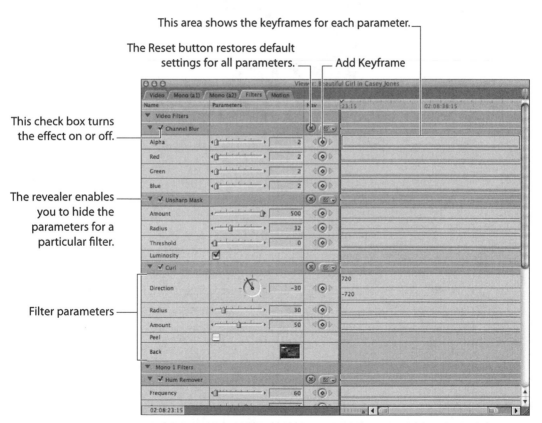

Figure 8.33 Adjust filter parameters by selecting the Filters tab in the Viewer. The order in which the filters appear in the list governs the order in which they will be applied.

When you modify a setting in the Filters tab, the image is processed and the newly generated frame is displayed in the Canvas window. This requires that your playhead in the Canvas be parked on the clip being modified. Alternately, tear the Video tab out of the Viewer, and the changes you make in the Filters tab will be visible there (**Figure 8.34**).

Figure 8.34 By pulling the Video tab out of the Viewer window, you get immediate feedback on your filter manipulations.

Color Correction

When Apple released version 3 of Final Cut Pro in 2001, one of the most hyped new features was its enhanced color correction filters. To a novice this might seem strange: "Are videographers that bad that everyone is depending on software to "correct" their mistakes?" Well, it turns out the answer is no, and yes. Making color adjustments such as lightness, darkness, contrast, saturation, and color balance are a critical part of any production. Typically, this is broken into two categories: color correction and color timing.

Because experienced cinematographers understand the flexibility available to them in post, they will often overlook small errors or inconsistencies between shots. Certain characteristics are not fixable, such as how hard or soft the light source is, or if the contrast is too extreme, but almost everything else about the shot can be modified. Furthermore, because the various scenes in a film are usually shot under different conditions in different environments, most films undergo a pass to unify the "look" across all of the scenes.

Correcting Errors

The term "color correction" implies that something needs correcting. Usually this means you've got a shot (or series of shots) in a sequence that doesn't match its neighbors. Perhaps the shot is a pickup, recorded under different lighting conditions, or the movement of the sun during the course of the day changed the look of the shot. In any case, before you can fix an image you have to know what "correct" looks like.

Comparing Similar Frames

Don't try to match the color for a close-up with a frame from a long shot. Find another close-up so you can compare skin tones apple to apple. Ideally you'll have a shot of the same actor under the proper lighting conditions to use as your reference frame. If not, you may need to find another element in the scene to use as a comparison, such as a red couch or blue sky that appears in both shots.

The Frame Viewer

Final Cut Pro contains a Frame Viewer that enables you to look at two images side by side (**Figure 8.35. See color section following page 460**). Load up any two images in the two sections, including the same clip with and without the filter applied. Choose from the pop-up menus at the bottom of the window (**Figure 8.36. See color section following page 460**). Also, you are not limited to splitting the screen vertically. Drag the blue or green handles to reshape the window however you like (**Figure 8.37. See color section following page 460**).

Using the Color Corrector Filters

Both Final Cut Pro and Final Cut Express include the Color Corrector filter (**Figure 8.38**). This filter is very flexible and easy to use. Final Cut Pro 4 also includes the 3-Way Color Corrector (**Figure 8.39**) that allows you to make different, individual color adjustments to the highs, mids, and lows. It's sort of like a three-band equalizer for audio, but instead of bass and treble, you control the dark and bright elements of the picture.

Figure 8.38 The Color Corrector Filter is your basic tool for manipulating the look of your clip.

Figure 8.39 The 3-Way Color Corrector allows you to manipulate just the Highs (bright parts) and Lows (dark parts) of your image.

Adjusting Contrast

Most clips can benefit from a little contrast correction. This means stretching the luminance, so the brightest pixels are set to pure white and the darkest pixels are set to pure black. Everything in between is stretched accordingly. Setting the contrast this way has the benefit of sharpening edges and clearing a muddy appearance by increasing the range of grays in your shot (**Figure 8.40. See color section following page 460**).

The Color Correction filter has buttons for automatically performing this sort of contrast adjustment (**Figure 8.41**). However, sometimes the automatic settings are not ideal. If your image contains a lot of subtle grays, stretching the luminance this way might wash out or darken your gray areas more than you would like. In this case, individually drag the sliders for the Highs, Mids, and Lows (**Figure 8.42**).

Figure 8.41 The top button sets the white point, the bottom button sets the black point, and the button in the middle sets both at the same time.

Figure 8.42 These sliders control the brightness of your image.

If your image is significantly over or underexposed you may not be able to improve it without adding a significant level of noise or artifacting. Whenever you are manipulating the image you run the risk of adding undesirable noise to the picture. Often you must find the best balance between the darkness of the shot and the tolerable amount of video noise. If you intend to project your final product or blow it up to 35mm film, that noise will be blown up, too, and what looked passable on your editing system may be wholly unacceptable on the big screen. There is not a whole lot you can do in this situation other than request reshoots from your production team.

Broadcast Safe Levels

Another important correction that is applicable to almost every clip is to ensure that your brightness and saturation levels do not exceed broadcast standards. If parts of your show are too bright or too saturated they can cause interference. You may have seen this when watching broadcast TV. Sometimes a commercial will have bright white or bright red text that exceeds the broadcast safe levels. When this happens you can hear a buzz on the soundtrack. If you submit a tape containing these errors, most reputable TV stations will send it back to you. In addition to disrupting the soundtrack, these errors can interfere with neighboring frequencies and the broadcaster can be fined by the FCC.

Final Cut contains a Broadcast Safe filter that automatically clips your video signal to the legal levels (**Figure 8.43**). You may be tempted to nest your finished sequence and apply this filter to your whole show at once. This will bring the entire show into the broadcast legal limits, but it may overcompensate, lowering the whole show when only one or two shots need correcting. For best results apply this filter to each clip individually.

Figure 8.43
Choose the Broadcast Safe filter from the Color Correction submenu to ensure legal video.

Range Check Indicators

Although this solution ensures that your show will be legal for broadcast, it involves applying a filter to your entire show which means excess rendering time, and if you are working in DV it means another lossy compression step that can somewhat degrade your image. Ideally, you only want to apply the filter when it is necessary. Final Cut Pro includes a special indicator to let you know when your luminance or chrominance is exceeding those legal limits (**Figure 8.44. See color section following page 460**).

Using the Scopes

Additionally, Final Cut Pro provides professional style video scopes that allow you to individually analyze the components of the video signal. The Waveform monitor illustrates only the luminance values of a clip (**Figure 8.45. See color section following page 460**). The Vectorscope shows just the color values. A concentration in any one area indicates an abundance of that color in the image (**Figure 8.46. See color section following page 460**). The Histogram may look familiar if you've ever used Photoshop's Levels control. This scope displays the luminance of the clip based on concentration of values. If your clip has a lot of blacks, there will be a large spike near the left side of the graph (**Figure 8.47. See color section following page 460**). The Parade is three mini waveform monitors, showing the luminance values for each of the main colors: red, green, and blue (**Figure 8.48. See color section following page 460**).

Getting familiar with these scopes can greatly improve your ability to perform effective color correction. For example, when trying to match the flesh tones across two clips, other colors in the image may be misleading, but by focusing on the various scopes you can identify exactly what is different about the two shots. Professional colorists can read and compare these different scopes as if they were looking at the actual video.

A Few Words About Hue Match

Final Cut Pro 4 added a new feature to the color corrector filters called Hue Match (**Figure 8.49**). This was intended to assist with one of the most common color correction jobs; matching two shots. Great idea, poor implementation. If you want to play with it, you can learn how by reading the User Guide, as far as I'm concerned, don't waste your time. Hopefully they'll revisit it for the next version and get it right.

Figure 8.49 The Hue Match control is intended to magically match the colors of two clips.

Secondary Color Correction

Sometimes you want to correct a single color in an image without affecting the rest of the image. For example, you could shift the color balance towards yellow to correct for overly red skin tones, but that might make the sky turn unnaturally purple. In this case, you would want to isolate the skin tones and only apply the yellow shift to that. This process is called Secondary Color Correction.

Final Cut Pro 's color correction filters include a handful of additional controls at the bottom of the window to facilitate this (**Figure 8.50**). Use the eyedropper to select the color in the image that you want to affect (**Figure 8.51. See color section following page 460**). Add to the selection by shift-clicking with the eyedropper or by adjusting the sliders in the Limit Effect area. (For more on how to use these controls, see "Keying" later in this chapter.)

Figure 8.50 Twiddle open the revealer to access the Limit Effect controls for Secondary Color Correction.

Multiple color correction filters can be applied to the same clip. They will be applied in the order that they appear in the filter tab of the Viewer. In this way, you could use one filter to correct the skin tones, another to make an adjustment to the sky, and a third to make an overall correction to the whole image.

Color Timing

So far, all of these examples have related to fixing problems in your shots, but you will use the same filters and tools to do another kind of manipulation to your picture. *Color timing* is the process of optimizing the "look" of your video to create a certain emotional tone and flavor. The term "timing" comes from printing color film; in order to expose the film properly, each lights is illuminated for a certain duration to create the right balance of colors. The term has been adopted in video circles to refer to the artistic application of color elements as opposed to "correcting" mistakes.

All theatrical films go through a color timing pass. Usually the audience is completely unaware of this stage of manipulation, but occasionally it plays a significant part in the artistic process. Films such as *Bladerunner* or *Alien* used a cool stark palate to emphasize the human isolation and make the world feel dangerous. The Polish Brothers' *Northfork* used an exquisite drab color scheme to draw out the amazing emptiness of the abandoned town and to enhance the nostalgia of the period, which most of us remember only through black and white or faded photographs. Although the cinematographer must be aware of the intended look of the film to create a unified vision, the colorist is the one who implements that look in the final stage.

Colors Affect Each Other

I'll warn you that in addition to mastering the tools of the art, it takes a certain eye to be a good colorist. Tweaking the various parameters of your picture affect one another. For example, you may determine that a certain shot looks too green and so you shift the balance of the shot towards magenta (the opposite side of the color wheel). That adjustment might result in the image now looking too saturated, as colors on the red side of the wheel tend to stand out more than colors on the blue side. So, next, you reduce the saturation, which brings out the contrast a little too much. To correct for that you reduce the contrast, which brings out more of the green. Can you see where this is going?

A colorist I once worked with proposed a theory that I found useful. He said that green affected contrast, red affected saturation and blue affected lightness. This is not to say that you can adjust the blue values instead of fixing the lightness, but it does illustrate how all the parameters are tied to one another. There are many detailed books on color theory and if you are serious about becoming a good colorist, you should certainly invest in a few.

The most important rule of color manipulation is to make small adjustments. For this reason, dragging the color balance controls in Final Cut is geared-up so that it takes a large mouse movement to make a small change on screen. Override this by holding down ⌘ while you drag, but do so sparingly.

Getting Out of Control

Color timing should be done in short sessions. Your eyes and brain get tired easily when trying to match colors and make subtle adjustments.

Especially when working on a large show, it's very easy to get caught in the trap of endless tweaking. It's very common to find yourself in a loop where you're thinking, "I'll add a little more contrast to this scene... but now that other scene looks too flat.

So let's add more contrast there. But now the first one looks wrong…" It can be like cutting hair, and continually making each side shorter and shorter to match the other. Fortunately, Final Cut Pro's color correction filters all have a reset button (**Figure 8.52**).

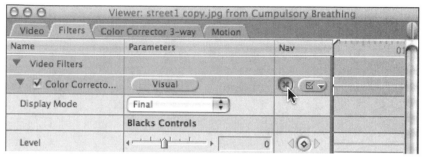

Figure 8.52 Go to the Filters Tab to find the reset button.

Finally, it's very important to make your color timing decisions in a consistent lighting environment. If the room gets darker as the day goes on, you will likely find that the beginning of your show will be darker than the later parts, as the ambient light in the room can't help but influence your perception of the colors on screen. This is another important reason to use the scopes in Final Cut Pro to insure that you use the same settings throughout the day. Of course, you can also restrict your color timing sessions to late nights—just don't get so "creative" that in the morning you wonder what the hell you were thinking.

Do it Last

It's common practice to save your color correction and color timing for the very end of your editing process. Traditionally, this was because these changes weren't made until the film was printed for distribution, but it still makes sense procedurally. You don't want to waste time coloring shots that may be cut from the show, and if you add or replace a shot after this stage, you're going to be stuck trying to match it to the rest of the (already corrected) scene. While your sound designer is building your final mix, you can be working with the colorist to create the look that will give your film its ultimate coherence and consistency.

Do it Uncompressed

If your budget permits, I strongly recommend making your color correction pass at an online editing facility using an uncompressed format like D1. That's right, abandon the nonlinear digital world and make a tape-to-tape transfer, applying color correction shot-by-shot as you go. While this is fairly expensive (these suites cost between $100 and $1,000 per hour), it gives the best results. Not only will you find state-of-the-art color correction tools that far exceed Final Cut Pro's capabilities (million dollar machines with names like Henry, DaVinci, Alex, and Inferno), but they will be operated by specialists who know exactly how to make the most of your images.

Alternately, you can stay in Final Cut Pro, but then you should find a station equipped with a Kona or CineWave PCI card that can input and output uncompressed video and convert your entire movie to that format. Remember that DV is a compressed format and during this stage, you're likely to be making changes to your *entire show*. This means recompressing every frame of your video, which can cause degradation. Also the DV color space is smaller than the uncompressed space so you will have more flexibility and more range if you work with uncompressed video.

Abstract Filters

If you want to create interesting artistic effects, you can also use filters to make a shot look like a moving painting or a ripple spreading across a watery surface. It's rare for an editor to apply these sorts of severe distortions in traditional narrative films, but if your object is to keep the viewer's eyes open during a dull sequence, this sort of eye candy can be just the thing to help the medicine go down.

For example, speaking of medicine, I produced a series of films for a medical equipment firm: educational sales tools designed to explain the details of high-tech medical machinery to doctors and hospital staff. The material was unbearably dry, and even though we used dramatizations to show how the tools were put to work in a hospital, we still needed something to keep the doctors' eyes from closing. So to brighten up the transitions between sections, we used a filter called Find Edges, which identifies areas of contrast in the image and gives them a sort of neon glow (**Figure 8.53**). This abstract visual element helped to offset the methodical details about the medical equipment.

Figure 8.53 The Find Edges filter is just one abstract effect available in Final Cut Pro.

You can find most of the abstract filters listed in the Distort and Stylize categories (**Figure 8.54**), but a few more cool ones are hidden in other places. I recommend playing with the Color Style filter in the QuickTime submenu (**Figure 8.55. See color section following page 460**). And check out the Zoom Blur filter in the Blur section (**Figure 8.56. See color section following page 460**). Don't be afraid to try combining multiple filters: Sometimes just the right combination can create a truly unique eye-pleasing effect.

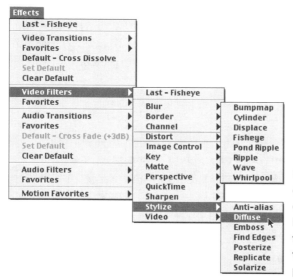

Figure 8.54 The Distort submenu contains filters that apply a physical distortion or texture to your image, like Pond Ripple or Fisheye. The filters listed under Stylize modify the image itself, reinterpreting the pixels in some abstract way.

Figure 8.55 The Color Style filter can create something that looks like an image in a comic book. (This figure also appears in the color section following page 460.)

Figure 8.56 Zoom Blur can simulate the exact effect of a super-fast zoom (called a "smash zoom") with the camera lens, but by experimenting with the parameters, you can create some very interesting variations.

Keyframes and Filters

Final Cut Pro's keyframe architecture is consistent across the program. Once you understand how keyframes work, you can use them for audio levels, filter parameters, motion effects, even titles.

*The basic controls for all keyframes are the Add Keyframe button, the parameter control (usually a slider), the keyframe graph, and the keyframe navigation controls (**Figure 8.57**).*

continues on next page

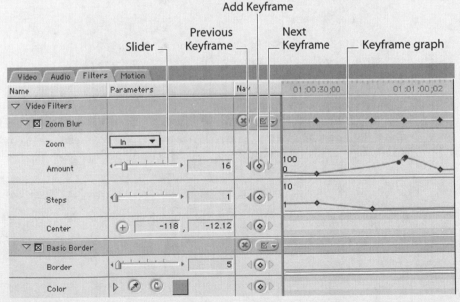

Figure 8.57 The basic keyframing controls are the same in all the windows where they appear.

Keyframes and Filters *continued*

Since keyframes are time-critical, be sure to check your playhead position before creating a new keyframe. Also, once your first keyframe is set, all it takes to set a new keyframe is changing the parameter value at a different point in time.

*For example, if you set the Gaussian Blur filter to a value of 12, it will be 12 across the duration of the clip. If you then tell the filter you want it to be 5 at some other point in the clip, the value will have to change over time to get from 12 to 5. This change will be reflected in the keyframe graph (**Figure 8.58**).*

Figure 8.58 Keyframe graphs are very flexible. You can stretch them by dragging the bottom edge of the graph, and you can zoom in or out on them just as you can in the Timeline. You can also drag the keyframes around in the graph to change their values.

Change a keyframe to a smooth point by Ctrl*-clicking on the keyframe. That will add Bezier handles that allow you to control the curvature of the keyframe envelope (**Figure 8.59**). This has the advantage of smoothing out the time changes of the effect. In the case of the blur, it will go down from 12 to 6 linearly, but it will slow down as it goes from 6 to 5. This creates a more organic-looking effect (see "Easing In and Out," later in this chapter).*

*Once you've set multiple keyframes, Navigate between them using the little Previous Keyframe/Next Keyframe buttons. If there are no more keyframes in one direction, the button will dim (**Figure 8.60**).*

Figure 8.59 Changing a keyframe point to smooth allows you to use Bezier handles to make nifty smooth curves.

Figure 8.60 The keyframe navigation buttons dim if there are no more keyframes in that direction.

COMPOSITING

For many people, this term conjures up images of 3-D football helmets flying across the TV screen, or fancy title sequences for movies like *Seven* or *Fight Club*. But most compositing is far simpler than that. In fact, any time you put two or more images on the screen at once, that's a form of compositing. Every lower third is a composite. So is every split screen or picture-in-picture.

In Final Cut, a composite is represented by two or more clips in the Timeline occupying the same point in time period. Accomplish this easily by placing them on separate tracks.

Superimposing Edit Style

Clips can be dragged to the Timeline and put directly on whatever tracks you want, but sometimes you'll want to line up a clip using traditional In and Out points before you edit it in. The last edit style you'll find on the Edit Overlay is Superimpose; its keyboard shortcut is F12.

A superimpose edit places your clip into the sequence on the track *above* your target track (**Figure 8.61**). One of the most common uses for the superimpose edit is adding a graphic, like a lower third. Set your In and Out points in the sequence and drag the title to the Canvas. If you select Superimpose, Final Cut Pro will automatically drop the clip exactly where you want it.

Once the clip is positioned in time, you must decide where you want to place it in the frame.

Figure 8.61 Superimpose will add a new track, if necessary, in order to put the new clip above the current target.

Motion Effects

Any clip can be moved, rotated, scaled, distorted, and cropped to change its placement in the frame. These are all called motion effects. To perform a motion effect, simply grab the clip in the Canvas and drag (**Figure 8.62**).

Figure 8.62
Modify nearly any aspect of a clip's size and shape by clicking and dragging it in the Canvas window.

If you're going to be moving clips around in the Canvas window, you must set the View pop-up to Image + Wireframe (**Figure 8.63**). Once this setting is enabled, you will see a frame around each clip; when a clip is selected, an "X" will connect the four corners of the clip (**Figure 8.64**).

Figure 8.63 The View pop-up lets you set various display options for the Viewer or Canvas window. When Image+Wireframe, or Wireframe, is set, you can drag items around in the window to reposition them. Toggle between the states by hitting Ⓦ.

Figure 8.64 You can tell if an item is selected by the highlight around the clip and the "X" connecting the corners.

Designing a Picture-in-Picture

Suppose you are doing a picture-in-picture effect and you want to make clip 2 appear in the upper right corner of the frame, superimposed over clip 1 (**Figure 8.65**). Start by putting both clips in the Timeline at the same point in time (**Figure 8.66**). If you remember from Chapter 5 ("Basic Editing"), clips on higher tracks obscure clips below. In this case you will shrink clip 2 so it obscures only part of clip 1.

Figure 8.65 A simple picture-in-picture effect.

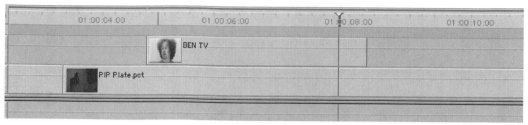

Figure 8.66 Items on higher tracks obscure items on the tracks below them.

Once the clips are properly lined up in the Timeline, you're ready to shrink and position clip 2. Make sure the wireframe is enabled. Then click on one of the corner points to scale the clip. Rotate the clip by dragging the edges, and if you click anywhere within the boundaries of the clip, you will move it (**Figure 8.67**).

Scale   Rotate   Move

Figure 8.67 Depending on where you click, you can modify the clip in different ways.

> **TIP:** Shift constrains or unconstrains clip movement. When you're changing the position of a clip, holding down Shift limits your movement to left-right or up-down. When you're scaling a clip, Shift releases the default aspect-ratio constraint so you can change the horizontal and vertical scale independently (squeezing or stretching the clip). When rotating, Shift constrains movement to 45-degree angles.

Starting and Ending the Effect

You still need to decide *how* clip 2 will appear and disappear. At this point, it's just going to pop on the screen and then pop off, based on the duration of the clip as set in the Timeline. But suppose you want it to fade in, and then, when it's finished, shrink to a point and vanish.

I introduced the Clip Overlays control (**Figure 8.68**) in Chapter 7 ("Cutting the Track"), when I discussed setting audio levels in the Timeline. But that control has an additional function. Not only does it turn on the audio level rubber band, it also turns on the clip *opacity* (transparency) rubber band.

Fgure 8.68 The Clip Overlays control is found in the lower left corner of the Timeline window. Turning it on displays an opacity envelope that lets you fade clips in and out right in the Timeline.

Add keyframes to the rubber band by Option-clicking the line. Then simply drag your new point to the desired setting. See Figure 8.68, which shows our picture-in-picture fading in from completely transparent (invisible) to completely opaque (solid).

Setting Keyframes Near Edges of Clips

One of the trickier aspects of working with keyframes in the Timeline is adjusting them when they're positioned near the edges of the clip.

The problem is, when you try to grab a keyframe that's right next to the clip edge, Final Cut Pro grabs the clip edge instead, assuming you want to trim the clip. This might not seem all that rough, but in real life, almost every time you set a keyframe in the Timeline, you are setting it right at the clip edge. This is how you perform fade-outs and fade-ins. Far too often, you innocently Option-click to set your first keyframe where you want your fade-out to begin. But then, when you try to set the second keyframe at the end of the clip, the program won't let you!

There are two ways to work around this.

*The first is to set the keyframe farther into the clip and then drag it to the edge (**Figure 8.69**). This is the most common solution because it can be done with minimal interruption to your workflow.*

The second option is to switch to the Pen tool by pressing P. Use the Pen tool to set all the keyframes you want, anywhere your heart desires. Then switch back to continue editing.

Figure 8.69 Set your keyframe far away from the edge, and then drag it to the edge to set it.

Using the Motion Tab

To make the picture-in-picture disappear by shrinking into a point, we'll need to fire up the Motion tab.

You can make a clip shrink by dragging its corner point in the Canvas—but it's difficult to get it to a precise setting, especially when you're trying to set the scale to zero! This is why Final Cut also allows you to set the value numerically.

Double-clicking the clip in the Canvas will load it into the Viewer (just like double-clicking a clip in the Timeline). Once in the Viewer, select the Motion tab (**Figure 8.70**). Here you can make numeric changes to every aspect of the clip's size and shape.

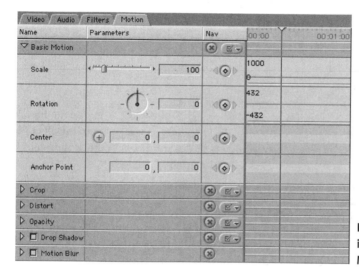

Figure 8.70 Every clip in Final Cut Pro has a Motion tab.

To make the scale change over time (in this case, move from 35 percent to 0 percent), we must set two keyframes. The first keyframe goes one second before the end of the clip, and the second goes on the last frame of the clip (**Figure 8.71**).

Presto! A vanishing clip.

In Final Cut Pro 4 you can set these keyframes in the Motion tab. In Final Cut Express you can do the same thing, but you can only set keyframes in the Canvas window using the Add Keyframe button (**Figure 8.72**).

Figure 8.71 Set keyframes in the Motion tab exactly the same way you would in the Audio tab or the Filters tab: ⌈Option⌉-click to add a keyframe and then drag it to the desired value. Or click the Add Keyframe button and adjust the slider.

Figure 8.72 The Add Keyframe button allows you to keyframe all of the parameters in the Motion tab.

Controlling Clip Motion

Let's say that instead of fading in our picture-in-picture effect, we want it to fly across the screen and land in the designated spot. The trick to position keyframing is to figure out your landing position first. Then go back and set the starting point. This is because in most cases, the ending point of the move is where the item will stay once the move is complete.

First, find the point in time where you want the move to end, and place the clip at its final position. In this example, we want the opening move to be complete exactly one second into the clip, and the resting position to be in the upper right corner of the screen. Once you've set the time and place, add a keyframe in the Canvas by clicking the Add Keyframe button at the bottom of the window (see **Figure 8.72** above). That's to let Final Cut know that this is the ending point of the move.

You may notice that there's no keyframe graph for the Center setting in Final Cut Pro's Motion viewer. That's because the Center parameter determines the clip's position, and those keyframes show up right in the Canvas. When you change the position of a clip over time, a dotted line appears in the Canvas showing the path that the clip will follow (**Figure 8.73**).

Figure 8.73 Motion paths appear in the Canvas and the Viewer to show you how your clip will move over time.

Move the playhead backward until it sits on the first frame of the clip (a perfect time to use ⬆, which moves you back to the previous edit). Drag the clip to your desired starting position in the Canvas. As soon as you drag, a line appears showing the path the clip will follow. Why does the line appear even before you set a new keyframe? Because you've already established that it must be at that ending position at a later time. By dragging it while the playhead is parked at an earlier time, you are automatically setting a new position keyframe (**Figure 8.74**).

Figure 8.74 Drag the element to its starting position.

TIP: *Use the Canvas Zoom pop-up menu to control how much of the viewable area you can see in the current window. If you wish to position a clip offscreen (as we're doing for the starting position in the picture-in-picture example), zoom out so you can see the pasteboard around the viewable area (**Figure 8.75**).*

The Canvas Zoom pop-up allows you to set the current zoom level on the window.

The Fit All setting will display as much extra space as necessary to show every clip currently on the pasteboard.

The Fit to Window setting will force the viewable area of the window to fill the current window size regardless of the zoom level.

Figure 8.75 When the Canvas or Viewer is zoomed out, you can see areas that will never be seen in the finished movie. This allows you to place clips "in the wings" so they can move on- and off screen.

At this point, the picture-in-picture will fly in from offscreen (lower left) and land in the upper right corner. But you're still not satisfied. Now you think it would be much more natural looking if the picture-in-picture followed a curved path. Add keyframes to a motion path by clicking and dragging a point in the path (**Figure 8.76**). That will add a keyframe, and, as you can see in the figure, it will create a curved path by default.

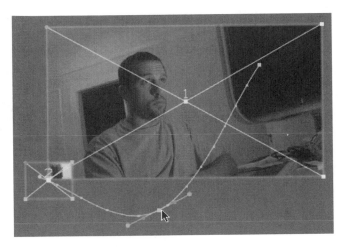

Figure 8.76 Adding points to a motion path is as simple as clicking and dragging. New points appear automatically, set to be smooth points complete with Bezier handles for adjusting the amount and type of curvature.

Easing In and Out

In addition to creating a curved path, you may want to make your picture slow down and stop gradually when it reaches its final destination, rather than slamming to a sudden halt.

This kind of smooth deceleration is called easing in, and the corresponding change at the beginning of a move (slowly accelerating until it reaches full cruising speed) is called easing out. When you're flying clips around on the screen, you should generally use this type of acceleration/deceleration control in order to observe the rules of inertia and simulate the way objects move in real life. Here's how:

Any keyframe can be set to ease in and out via the Shortcut menu that appears when you Ctrl-click the keyframe (**Figure 8.77**).

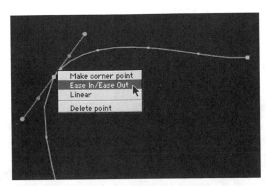

Figure 8.77 Ctrl-clicking a keyframe brings up a Shortcut menu that lets you set the point to Ease In/Out. You can also toggle a point between being a corner point (a hard change in direction) and a linear point (with Bezier handles).

If you're trying to perform precise moves, you will probably want more control over the speed and amount of acceleration and deceleration than the preset Ease In/Out setting provides. Change the acceleration manually by adjusting the tiny subhandles on each keyframe's Bezier handles (**Figure 8.78**). Unfortunately, while this looks kind of cool, I find these controls virtually useless. There is no way to get a precise result, and the range of variation is extremely limited.

Figure 8.78 The Bezier controls contain a second set of handles for controlling acceleration.

To get more precise control I recommend using After Effects. After Effects has wonderfully flexible and accurate control over acceleration settings. And it allows you to control acceleration for every parameter of every clip or filter, so you can control how quickly your blur takes effect, or how slowly a pond ripple slows to a stop.

Previewing Motion Without Rendering

*Depending on the specific effects you use and how powerful your machine is, you may have to render the sequence in order to see your final effect. However, if you want a quick preview of the movement your clips will make, you can do it by setting the Canvas view state to Wireframe (**Figure 8.79**). In this state, all clips turn into simple outlines, but when you play the sequence, the objects perform their movements in accurate real time. This includes all Ease In/Out settings, so you can use this to adjust the timing of your movements. Audio is played as well, so you can time movements to line up to specific audio cues.*

Figure 8.79 Setting the Canvas View menu to Wireframe enables the real-time motion preview. You can toggle between the three view states by hitting W.

Applying Motion Blur

The perfect precision of computer-generated movement can make your motion effects seem phony. One way to counteract this is by applying an effect called Motion Blur. Motion Blur simulates the slight fuzziness that occurs when a camera photographs an object that's moving too fast for the camera's limited shutter speed.

You might expect that viewers would prefer images to be as sharp as possible, but our eyes are so used to seeing this slight blur that when it's absent, moving objects look stiff and unnatural (**Figure 8.80**). This becomes particularly apparent when you combine camera images with movements created synthetically in Final Cut Pro.

Figure 8.80 Motion Blur creates a subtle blurring effect on moving objects.

Turn on Motion Blur in the Motion tab of the Viewer (**Figure 8.81**). There are two parameters you can assign. % Blur controls how dramatic the effect is. You'll need to experiment, since the result can vary depending on how large your object is and on how quickly it's moving. A fast-moving object generates much more blur than a slow-moving object. You can

Figure 8.81 Turn on Motion Blur in the Motion tab.

counteract this by cranking up the blur percentage for slow-moving objects, but that defeats the purpose of the control. Raising the blur amount is similar to lowering the frame rate in the camera, causing more blur in each frame. As an object slows down (as it would during an ease-in), the blur decreases.

The second parameter is Samples. This refers to how many frames are used to create the blur. If this setting is too low, you will see steppy frame edges instead of a smooth blur effect. In general, you should set this value as high as possible to create the smoothest blur, although with slow-moving objects you may not see much benefit from the higher settings. Just remember that the higher you set it, the longer the effect takes to render. Setting it to 8 will take twice as long as setting it to 4, and 16 will take twice as long as 8. Rendering motion blur is pretty slow to begin with, so a high setting like 16 will increase your rendering time dramatically.

Moving Clips in 3-D Space

Another common motion effect involves making the clip or graphic seem as if it's moving forward or backward in three-dimensional space, as though there were physical depth to the screen. You'll see many examples of this effect in show openers, title sequences, and so on, although, like most motion effects, they rarely show up in narrative films.

Flashy motion effects like 3-D can help keep viewers alert, especially when you need to make information on a chart or graphic more interesting. Objects moving in the frame create action, and action creates engagement. So even if your show doesn't include a motorcycle chase, you can add a few 3-D motion effects to spice up that list of safety instructions.

Unfortunately, Final Cut Pro's 3-D options are very limited, so this is another case where you should probably turn to After Effects, Apple's Shake, or Discreet Combustion.

All of these packages offer true 3-D capability, allowing you to move objects along a Z axis as well as the X and Y. You can make one image pass through another on its approach to the front of the screen. Additionally, objects themselves can have depth as they fly around and flip over, so they look like books or boxes rather than flat objects that vanish when seen edge-on. They can also cast shadows.

But if you have no other option, and you want to create 3-D effects within Final Cut Pro, you're not totally out of luck.

Figure 8.35 The Frame Viewer (found in the Tools menu) is an essential asset to successful color correction.

Figure 8.36 Many different things can be loaded into the two sides of the Frame Viewer for comparison.

Figure 8.37 Find the best part of the images to compare and isolate them with the handles for optimum comparison.

Figure 8.40 Auto Contrast improves this image by stretching the luminance of the shot from pure black to pure white.

Figure 8.44 When the Range Check menu options are activated, several indicators appear in your canvas. A Green Checkmark (not shown) means your levels are legal. A Yellow Hazard icon indicates a section that exceeds either luminance or saturation. "Zebra" lines indicate areas in your clip where luminance is within 10 percent of the legal limit (in green) and areas where the luminance or chrominance is above the legal limit (in red).

Figure 8.45 The Waveform Monitor represents the brightness levels in your clip. Levels above 100 percent are not broadcast safe.

Figure 8.46 The Vectorscope displays only the chrominance information from your clip. Points outside the outer circle indicate areas where the color exceeds broadcast levels. The diagonal line in the upper left indicates the range of color typically associated with human flesh tones. In this image you can also see a concentration between red and magenta that represents the flowers.

Figure 8.47 The Histogram maps the clip's grayscale values onto a graph.

Figure 8.48 The Parade Scope discretely displays luminance for each color.

Figure 8.51 The filter is only applied to the colors within the clip that you select.

Figure 8.55 The Color Style filter can create something that looks like an image in a comic book.

Figure 8.97 In the keying process, the key color is removed from the shot, leaving behind a transparent area where the color used to be. Then the image is combined with a new background, creating a composite shot. Adding color correction to both background and foreground can help to enhance the effect.

Figure 8.100 The eyedropper is the easiest way to select the key color.

Figure 8.101 The color that you select turns transparent. Add to the selection until the green is completely gone.

Final Cut's Basic 3-D Filter

The Basic 3-D filter (found in the Perspective submenu of the Effects menu) allows you to make a clip *look* as though it's moving in 3-D space (**Figure 8.82**). This is accomplished by applying graphic distortions to make the 2-D object appear to be tilted or skewed in three dimensions. For a single image the result is nearly indistinguishable from what you get with true 3-D tools, but the Basic 3-D filter lacks a way to define the three spatial coordinates. That means objects can't bump into nor break through objects behind or in front of them.

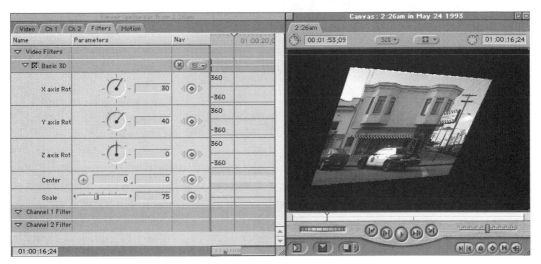

Figure 8.82 The Basic 3-D filter allows you to simulate 3-D movement for a clip.

Using the Secret 3-D Tool

Another cool way to simulate 3-D in Final Cut Pro is to use a fairly esoteric feature of the Distort tool. The Distort tool (**Figure 8.83**) allows you to grab any corner point of a clip and move just that point—which stretches and distorts the clip's shape (**Figure 8.84**).

Figure 8.83 The Distort tool is hidden beneath the Crop tool. Access it from the keyboard by hitting D.

Figure 8.84 You can distort the shape of a clip by pulling on one corner point.

Very few people know that the Distort tool can be transformed into a magic 3-D tool by using the [Shift] modifier. When you view a clip in 3-D space, it's distorted based on the rules of perspective so that the side of the image closer to the front of the screen is larger than the side farther away. When you hold down [Shift] while dragging a point with the Distort tool, it automatically forces the clip to simulate this effect (**Figure 8.85**).

Figure 8.85 The magic 3-D tool is really just the Distort tool with [Shift] held down.

If you combine this special type of distortion with changes to the Scale parameter (which makes the whole clip look closer or farther away), you can create convincing three-dimensional effects without ever needing another program.

Saving a Favorite Motion

Motion settings can be saved and applied to a different clip. Let's say you're doing a training film about environmental responsibility that includes six different episodes providing examples of environmentally responsible behavior. During each section, as soon as the character realizes the right thing to do, you drop in a little animated light bulb from the top of the frame. It swings back and forth a couple of times as text fades in explaining the point you just illustrated.

Once you define the exact motion that the light bulb will follow in section 1, you can save that motion path. Then, in the next section, rather than redesigning that motion, you can simply apply the saved motion path so the second light bulb follows the same exact path of movement as the first.

*Saving a motion path is simple. If you have a clip in the Viewer with the motion applied, or if you have the clip selected in the Timeline, choose Make Favorite Motion from the Modify menu. This will add that motion to the Favorites folder in the Browser (**Figure 8.86**). Once you have it there, rename it and drag it onto another clip. Alternately, apply it just like a filter from the Motion Favorites section of the Effects menu (**Figure 8.87**).*

Figure 8.86 The Favorites folder can hold motion paths as well as other effects.

Figure 8.87 Favorite motions can be applied just like filters via the Motion Favorites section of the Effects menu.

Mixing Layers

Once you've mastered the art of moving clips around, you'll soon find yourself in situations where you've got two overlapping clips on the screen. If you don't want one image to completely obscure the other, you'll need to decide how they should interact visually.

Sometimes you'll want to mix multiple images together to create a background for a title or chart. Other times you may need to create a poetic combination of images. There are no rules, so feel free to make up your own.

Final Cut includes a number of tools to help you resolve situations like these. It's difficult to describe exactly when to fire them up, but if you understand something about what they can do, you'll probably begin developing your own ideas about how and when to put them to use.

Opacity

All clips have an opacity setting, and by default it is set to 100 percent opaque. As you lower opacity, the clip becomes more and more transparent, revealing the clip or the background behind it.

I've already discussed how to adjust a clip's opacity by using Clip Overlays in the Timeline. And you may have noticed that there's an Opacity slider in the Motion tab. These controls are identical: Changing one will change the other. It's exactly like the way the audio level rubber band in the Timeline is identical to the graph in the corresponding Audio tab.

Using Composite Modes

Any time a clip is layered over another clip, you can choose different ways for the images to interact. In Chapter 5, I discussed additive and non-additive dissolves as two variations on how clips could be combined during a cross-dissolve. By setting a clip's composite mode, you gain access to more than ten different ways of combining superimposed clips.

Just as every clip has an opacity level, each one has a composite mode too. By default it's set to Normal. That means that at 100 percent opacity, the clip will be entirely opaque, and as opacity decreases, the clip will fade away in a linear fashion, as in an ordinary cross-dissolve.

However, if you set the clip's composite mode to one of the alternate settings, such as Multiply, Hard Light, or Lighten, you can create wildly different effects (**Figure 8.88**). I can't describe exactly what each setting does, because they are based upon complex mathematics and results vary widely. But I can recommend a few settings. In all these cases, I'm assuming that the bottom clip is set to normal (100 percent) opacity, so the changes I'm describing will be applied only to the top clip.

Lightening and Darkening Effects

Some modes make your image lighter and some darker. This can be tempered somewhat by the effect of the opacity of the clip. Some modes will not change the overall lightness or darkness value of the image at all.

Figure 8.88 You can set Composite Mode for each clip in the Modify menu. (Ignore the Travel Matte choices for now.)

If you're trying to create a background for a logo or title, it may be helpful to create a lighter background (for a dark logo) or vice versa. The composite modes Add, Screen, and Lighten tend to make your image lighter, while Multiply and Darken are likely to make the image darker.

I find the Multiply and Screen modes (which are roughly opposites) to produce some of the most beautiful and useful results. Multiply will combine lighter elements (darkening them) but leave the darker areas alone. Screen will lighten darker elements but leave lighter areas unaffected (**Figure 8.89**).

Figure 8.89 Multiply and Screen are two of the most versatile and attractive settings to use for combining images.

Since Multiply will always remove any areas of absolute white in the combined clips, and Screen will automatically remove any areas of absolute black, you can use them to remove white or black from a clip. For example, if you had an image of a lens flare effect on a black background, compositing that lens flare using Screen would ignore all the black and combine only the flare itself with the bottom image (**Figure 8.90**).

Figure 8.90 Screen will remove the black areas so only the lens flare is combined.

The Overlay setting is unique because it actually combines the effects of Multiply and Screen. Multiply affects only pixels darker than 50 percent gray, and Screen affects only the lighter half. Overlay combines them, creating an entirely new type of effect.

Additional settings include Difference, and Hard and Soft Light. Difference has the effect of inverting the image based on its combined values (**Figure 8.91**). Hard and Soft Light are supposed to give the impression that a harsh spotlight, or a diffuse soft light, is shining on the image. They don't always achieve that result, but they can make for pretty pictures regardless (**Figure 8.92**).

Figure 8.91 The Difference mode creates a type of inverted look.

Figure 8.92 Hard and Soft Light create unique effects that are dependent on the contents of the clips.

Controlling Transparency With Alpha Channels

Frequently, when you're dealing with elements such as logos or other graphics, you will need to control the shape of transparent areas in your frame. For example, if you have a round logo, you wouldn't want to see its square outline when you use it in a sequence. Final Cut Pro (as well as most other programs that deal with computer graphics) controls transparent areas in the frame by using something called an alpha channel. You'll find alpha channels in still images like PICT or TIFF files, you'll find them in 3-D animations, and you'll even find them in some video files (**Figure 8.93**).

Figure 8.93 The alpha channel for an image contains the details of which areas are opaque and which are transparent. Black areas are treated as transparent, and white areas are treated as opaque. Gray areas are semi-transparent.

When you bring a clip with an alpha channel into Final Cut Pro, the alpha channel is automatically recognized and the appropriate areas will be treated as transparent whenever you use that clip in a sequence. Different programs store this information differently, but Final Cut Pro can determine the precise format of the alpha channel and interprets it appropriately.

Occasionally you may import a file whose alpha channel is interpreted incorrectly—or, more commonly, is inverted. (In the latter case, what should be transparent appears opaque, and what should be opaque shows up as transparent.) In these cases, you will need to override the program's assumptions manually.

Reset the alpha channel state for any clip in the Modify menu. Fix an inverted alpha by selecting Reverse Alpha, and fix an incorrect alpha setting (usually identified by a halo or crunchy edge around the transparent object) by selecting a different setting from the Alpha Type submenu (**Figure 8.94**).

Figure 8.94 Clips with an alpha generated against a white background should be set to White. Ditto for Black. Clips with alpha that was generated against no background at all should be set to Straight. Normally this setting is determined automatically when you import a clip. You need to adjust it only if something looks wrong.

Viewing the Alpha Channel

If you have a clip with an alpha channel, and you go into Wireframe mode, Final Cut Pro actually shows you the outline of the alpha channel as a pattern of dots (**Figure 8.95**). This enables you to predict how graphics will show up on the screen. This pattern sticks around even during the real-time preview I described earlier.

Figure 8.95 Graphics with alpha channels are visible when playing a clip in Wireframe mode.

Alternately, choose to view the alpha channel for a clip (or sequence) by choosing Alpha from the Viewer View menu or the Canvas View menu (**Figure 8.96**). If you choose Alpha+RGB, the alpha will be overlaid onto the image as a semi-transparent red layer.

Figure 8.96 Choose Alpha from the View menu to view the alpha channel for the clip you're looking at.

As long as the artist preparing your graphics (in Photoshop or some similar program) understands what she's doing, you can usually forget about alpha channels entirely. Final Cut Pro will see them and take care of them, and the transparent hole for your circular logo will be wonderfully round. But it's important to understand how Final Cut Pro uses alpha channels any time you need part of your image to be transparent.

Which leads us to keying.

Keying

Want to insert a person or object from one shot into a background from a second shot? A *key* is the special effect that lets you accomplish this. First, the subject needs to be shot in front of an evenly lit, solid color field. Then you remove the color digitally, creating a transparent alpha channel where the color used to be. Finally, the subject is composited over an alternate background that shows through the transparent areas (**Figure 8.97. See color section following page 460**). This process is called keying, short for chroma-keying. The color that's removed is called the *key color*. Most often the key color is blue or green. That's because a solid, primary color is easiest for the computer to identify, and human skin tones mostly fall outside of the blue and green range. These backgrounds— and therefore the shots themselves—are called green screens or blue screens.

Constructing a Killer Color Key

Final Cut Pro provides sophisticated tools to help create your matte, but even so, you'll need to invest serious effort in choosing foreground and background elements that match convincingly.

First, make sure that the lighting matches. If the key light in the foreground shot is coming from the left, don't use a *plate* (background shot) where the light source is coming from overhead.

The same goes for lighting style and color: If your goal is to hide the fact that two shots are being combined into one, don't expect a shot filmed in the studio, with diffuse, cool light sources, to match a plate filmed in strong, warm afternoon sun.

Accounting for Camera Position and Movement

If the blue screen shot is low angle, the plate must be as well. If you intend to use camera movement, you must create tracking marks on the set to allow the computer to record the movement. In many cases you will want to use a *motion control* rig. Motion control can recreate the camera moves that were used in the studio so they can be repeated for the plate.

Performing the Key

Final Cut has several filters in the Key subcategory of the effects menu but the only one you need to learn to use is the Chroma Keyer (**Figure 8.98**). This filter can key out a blue or green background, but it can also key out any color at all. You could use this filter to make someone's red shirt transparent, or even to key out a white building so it could be replaced with a computer generated one.

Figure 8.98 The Chroma Keyer is the filter of choice for creating transparency from a green or blue screen shot.

First, you need to arrange the clips in the Timeline. Because the Chroma Keyer filter will make the colored areas transparent, put the plate on the track beneath the key shot. That way when the green area is made transparent, the background will show through.

Apply the Chroma Keyer filter to the top clip, and double-click it to open it into the Viewer. Bring the Chroma Keyer tab to the front (**Figure 8.99**). The controls are exactly the same as the Limit Effect controls in the color correction filters.

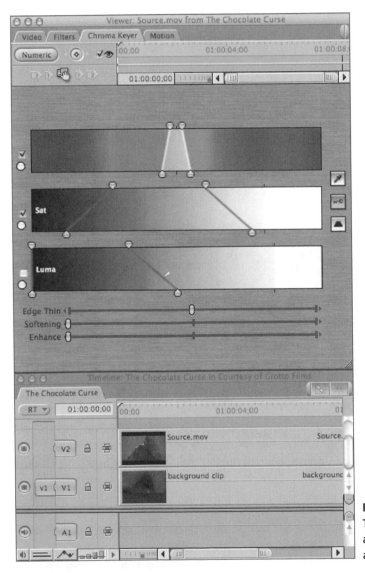

Figure 8.99
The Chroma Keyer allows you to extract a color from a clip.

Identifying the Key Color

Use the eyedropper on the right side to select the color to be keyed from the image in the Canvas (**Figure 8.100. See color section following page 460**). This works similarly to using the magic wand in Photoshop. The area you selected will immediately turn transparent (**Figure 8.101. See color section following page 460**). You can use the eyedropper again and again to make more colors transparent, but you need to hold the Shift key when you click in the canvas. A tiny + symbol will appear next to the eyedropper (**Figure 8.102**).

Figure 8.102 Add to the selection by holding shift when using the eyedropper.

Instead of clicking additional colors, increase the transparent area by manipulating the sliders in the Key filter (**Figure 8.103**). If the area that remains to be removed is a darker green, move the top of the luminance bar to the left. If the area you want to remove is more yellow, broaden the Hue bar.

Figure 8.103 Dragging the top part of the bar broadens the selection, dragging the bottom part of the bar softens the edge of the selection.

Use the eyedropper and sliders until the bulk of your key area has been eliminated. Be careful not to go too far and cause areas of your subject to become transparent. Do not try to clean up the edge of the key using these tools. That's what the sliders below are for.

Examining Your Key

Examine your key using the buttons below the eyedropper. The first button will toggle between the original image, the completed composite, and a matte-only image showing the key in black and white (**Figure 8.104**). The bottom button inverts the key effect.

Figure 8.104 When in Matte mode, opaque areas appear white and transparent areas appear black. Areas that are semi-transparent appear gray.

Finessing the Key Edge

The three sliders at the bottom of the Chroma Keyer tab are all designed to clean up the edge of your key (**Figure 8.105**). Dragging the Edge Thin slider to the right contracts your key edge, eating away at the edge of your key. The Softening slider blurs the edge of the key. Although at first this may seem like a quick and easy way to clean up your edges, if you soften too much it will destroy the realistic effect of the key. I don't recommend ever setting this above 3 or 4. Finally the Enhance slider subtracts your key color from any semi-transparent pixels in your key. If you set this value too high, the opposite color will begin to appear (green becomes magenta and blue becomes orange).

Figure 8.105 These sliders control the edge of your key.

Getting the Spill Out

Often, when you're shooting a green (or blue) screen shot, a bit of the screen color reflects or spills onto the subject, especially if it has any reflective surfaces. That means that your actor might have a slight green hue reflecting off his shiny face. So, even though you may have created a perfectly clean edge between the subject and the background, the foreground shot may still need more work.

Remove this subtle green haze by applying a Spill Suppressor filter to the source clip. This will extract all the green (or blue) from the image. Choose green or blue, and then set the Amount slider to control how much of the color is removed. Slide it down until all the color is gone; then bring it back up very carefully until you start to see the green spill reappear. Bring it back down a hair, and you're there.

Remember that the order in which filters are listed in the Filters tab indicates the order in which they will be applied to the clip. If you apply the Spill Suppressor before you apply the Blue and Green Screen filter, you will extract all the green from the shot, and the key won't work.

Don't Key With DV

Now that you know everything about keying (yeah, right!), let me issue a serious warning: Don't do it with DV footage!

That's right: If you plan to shoot a blue screen shot, don't shoot it with DV. Rent a Betacam, a Digital Betacam (usually referred to as Digibeta), HD, or even a DVC PRO-50 camera and shoot it with that. Why? Remember that DV is highly compressed—and while the compression is extremely intelligent, it is also specifically optimized to fool the human eye. It's not that good at fooling the computer, which stumbles over all the missing data.

The human eye is far more sensitive to changes in light and darkness than to changes in color, so one of the ways DV stays svelte is by throwing away a lot of color data. In fact, it throws away almost three quarters of the color data for each frame! Given that, it's amazing how good it looks. But unfortunately, when it comes time for Final Cut to find the exact pixels where the green screen ends and your actor's curly brown hair begins, the data doesn't exist.

If your final "release print" is going to be a highly compressed Web movie, shooting your blue screens on DV may work just fine—but if you intend to show the finished shot on a movie screen or a high-resolution TV, the key that seemed perfectly acceptable on your computer screen may suddenly look embarrassingly crunchy.

Color Smoothing Filter

Final Cut Pro 4 includes a filter that is designed specifically to improve keying DV footage. The filter is called Color Smoothing 4:1:1 and is found in the Key Filters section of the Effects menu. Apply this filter to your DV footage before applying the Chroma Keyer. There are no parameters to adjust, so there's really nothing to it. This pre-processes the clip and does an intelligent blur that improves keying performance significantly.

Making Mattes

Keying is based on making a matte from the information in a clip, usually a clip that's been shot against a blue or green background specifically for that purpose. But you don't need a colored background; sometimes you can use a separate element to create a matte. Since a matte is just a way of determining what part of the image shows through and what part is hidden, you could use a matte to apply an effect to any part of a picture.

For example, let's say you had a shot that included a window, and the window was overexposed. You want to darken the window without darkening the whole image (**Figure 8.106**). To accomplish this, create a matte using one of the tools described below and isolate the window and then apply a color correction filter to the window to counteract the overexposure.

Figure 8.106 The window is overexposed, but the inside of the room is fine. You can use a matte to apply an effect to the window only.

Cropping

For very simple mattes, Final Cut allows you to crop the visible area of any clip. That means you can hide problems around the edges of your clip such as a light stand peeking into the frame or some video noise introduced during capture. (Some analog capture cards create a few lines of black or colored noise at the bottom or right edge of each clip.)

Figure 8.107 The shortcut key for the Crop tool is Ⓒ.

To crop an image, select the Crop tool (**Figure 8.107**) and drag from one of the edges of your clip to eliminate the objectionable material (**Figure 8.108**). If you drag from a corner point, you crop two sides at once.

Figure 8.108 You can crop an image from any side, or from a corner to crop two sides at once.

Since you're replacing the cropped area with transparency, cropping makes the viewable image smaller. So if the cropped clip is on the bottom track, that area will appear black. If it's on a track with a clip beneath it, that clip will be visible in the cropped areas.

Custom Mattes

Cropping is very limited, since you can create only straight edges and rectangular mattes. When you want to design a matte that's a custom shape (suppose that overexposed window was a porthole in a ship's cabin), the Crop tool's functionality is clearly inadequate.

Here again, I recommend that you cut your losses and launch After Effects. This trusty motion graphics behemoth allows every clip to have custom-shaped mattes controllable via Bezier curves, and what's more, you can have as many of them as you like. So, not only can you quickly isolate that round porthole, you can matte three windows shaped like boat anchors.

Final Cut Pro does include some additional matte tools, and for simple cases they can be useful. Furthermore, they have the advantage of creating the effect right in your editing tool, with no need to pass files back and forth. But they are unquestionably inferior to After Effects' offerings.

Garbage Mattes

Functionally, a garbage matte is no different from any other matte; it gets its name because you use it to get rid of junk you don't want in the frame. It's most frequently combined with tools like the keying filters. For example, if your blue screen shot included a tiny corner of the stage that wasn't painted blue, you could apply a garbage matte to make that corner turn transparent as well.

Final Cut Pro's garbage mattes are an attempt to emulate the functionality that After Effects provides, but they are quite awkward to use. You apply the matte as a filter, which you select from the Matte submenu of the Effects menu (**Figure 8.109**).

Figure 8.109 All of Final Cut Pro's matte tools are applied as filters, accessible through the Matte submenu of the Filters section of the Effects menu.

Rather than dragging the points of the matte where you want them, you must use the Point control in the Filters tab (**Figure 8.110**). You have to click once on the Point control in the Viewer, and then click in the Canvas where you want the point to be.

Figure 8.110 The Four-Point Garbage Matte can create a transparent shape with four points.

Furthermore, forget about true Bezier curve controls. If you want your matte to have a curved edge, you'll have to settle for the Smooth slider. All this does is uniformly round the entire matte (**Figure 8.111**). Create a soft edge to your matte by adjusting the Feather Edges slider (**Figure 8.112**). Don't get me wrong, you can create some cool and useful effects using these tools, but to me it still feels like hammering with a wrench.

Figure 8.111 The Smooth control rounds the edges of your matte.

Figure 8.112 The Feather Edges control softens the edge of your matte.

Mask Shape

The Mask Shape filter can create mattes in simple shapes like diamonds, ovals, and rectangles. (In Final Cut Pro, "mask" and "matte" are synonymous.)

Image Mask

This filter lets you select another clip and use its luminosity as a matte.

Widescreen

Try the Widescreen filter to create a letterbox matte at the top and bottom of your image. This simulates the wide-screen aspect ratio of theatrical film formats. The advantage to using this filter instead of the crop controls is that the Widescreen filter allows you to slide the image up and down underneath the matte. That way, if your subject's head is being cut off by the letterbox, you can lower the image until it fits. Of course, you're just cutting off more of the bottom of the image, but if you want to make a wide-screen image out of a full-frame picture, you have to cut something.

Mask Feather

Apply the Mask Feather filter to soften the edges of any of the mattes you create with these other tools.

Traveling Mattes

The term "traveling matte" refers to any matte that moves. Technically, all of the mattes I've described so far are traveling mattes, since they are all keyframable (in Final Cut Pro)—which means you can change their positions or shapes over time.

What I'm referring to here is a little different: using one clip to act as a mask for another clip, where both can be moving independently of each other. For instance, a good example of a traveling matte would be titles in which images are moving inside the letters while the text is scrolling across the screen. This is one of the most useful mattes in Final Cut Pro.

Travel Matte (abbreviated to save space on the menu) is actually a composite mode. If you set a clip's composite mode to Travel Matte, it will use the clip beneath it as a mask. To use this feature, place the mask clip (for instance, the letters of the text scrolling across the screen) on one track, and place the video you want to show through the mask (for instance, exciting footage of explosions or flames) on the track above it. Set the upper clip's composite mode to Travel Matte–Alpha, and the clip will show through the lower clip's alpha channel (**Figure 8.113**).

Figure 8.113 A classic traveling matte is created by using one clip's alpha channel to act as a mask for a second clip.

If you want to use the luminance of a clip rather than using its alpha channel, set the upper clip's composite mode to Travel Matte–Luma. This is perfect if you've got a simple graphic such as black text on a white background (**Figure 8.114**). If you have white text on a black background and need to invert it, apply the Invert filter (found in the Image Control submenu of the Filters section of the Effects menu) to the mask clip.

If you want to go for broke, put a third clip beneath the traveling matte clips to create a background for your matte (**Figure 8.115**). Be careful to choose something that won't compete for focus with your matte image; otherwise it will just be a big mess.

Figure 8.114 If you're using a clip's luminance for the mask, remember that black is transparent and white is opaque.

Figure 8.115 Most traveling mattes are used with a background element. Pick a muted image that won't make the matte hard to see.

Nest Sequences

Sometimes you may want to apply a single effect to a group of clips. Let's say you've got a two word title with the words in different clips, and you want to fly them on as one entity. Or you might want to apply two effects to the same clip in a carefully controlled order. For situations like these, Final Cut Pro allows you to nest one sequence inside another.

In the simplest case, you may have an interview and a lower third you want to treat as a single item so you can dissolve them together into another clip (**Figure 8.116**). This is a perfect example of how nesting the items can make your task easier.

Whenever you nest items, the sequences become live-linked. If you go back and fix a spelling error on that lower third, the correction will also take effect in the parent sequence.

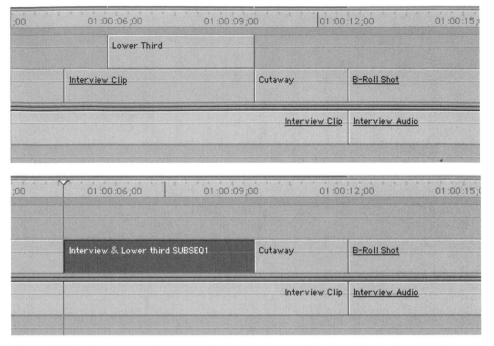

Figure 8.116 We want to dissolve both the interview and the graphic at the same time. By nesting them, we can treat them as a single clip.

There are two ways to create a nested sequence:

Dragging One Sequence Into Another

You can build the two sequences separately and drag one sequence from the Browser right into the second sequence, treating it like a clip. This is fine if you know about it ahead of time. For instance, in the lower third example I just gave, if you knew before you started that you were going to nest the sequences, you could create a new sequence, lay in the interview clip and the lower third, and then drag that whole sequence into your master sequence, where you could dissolve it with the adjacent clip.

Using the Nest Items Command

If you don't think about doing a nest until after you start (which is usually the case), use method number two, the Nest Item(s) command.

Select the items that you want to nest in the Timeline, and choose Nest Item(s) from the Sequence menu—or press Option-C. This will open the Nest Items dialog box (**Figure 8.117**).

Figure 8.117 The Nest Items dialog box allows you to define the new sequence you are about to create.

Don't fail to immediately give the new sequence a good name. Once you begin nesting sequences, you can quickly create a complicated mess. Name the subsequence something that will tell you what's in it, and also that it's used in a parent sequence.

Once you dismiss the dialog box, a new sequence will be created replacing the clips right there within the sequence. The new sequence will be placed on the lowest available track, and from that point on you can treat it as a single clip. The only difference is that if you double-click it, rather than opening into the Viewer, it will open as a new tab in the Timeline, revealing the clips inside the sequence. (If you want to open it into a Viewer—to adjust filter or motion parameters—hit Enter or choose Sequence in New Window from the View menu.)

CG

This last type of effect (the acronym stands for computer graphics, or computer generated) refers to elements created in your computer. These can include titles, background elements such as a solid color field, or 3-D objects (everything from a static logo to an animation of a realistic-looking dinosaur).

In most cases you will import these elements into Final Cut Pro from other applications, but first I want to talk about the ones you can create right inside the program.

Generators

Final Cut Pro includes a group of effects called generators. These are clips that are generated by the program and can be used just like any other clip. They include titles, color mattes, gradients, and noise. Use the motion controls to fly these clips around on the screen, distort or scale them, and add drop shadows. Add filters, use them as part of a complex composite, and customize the titles to suit the aesthetic of your program.

Generators are born in the Viewer window. Select the type of clip you want to create by choosing an option in the Generators menu (**Figure 8.118**).

Figure 8.118 This menu in the lower right corner of the Viewer provides access to all the generators available in Final Cut Pro.

Titles

When you need to create basic titles, try the generators you'll find in the Text category (**Figure 8.119**). When you select an item from the Generators menu, it opens into the Viewer with a new tab called Controls (**Figure 8.120**). All of the generator's parameters can be adjusted there.

Figure 8.119 Final Cut Pro includes several different types of text generators. The simplest one is just called Text.

Figure 8.120 If a generator has any adjustable parameters, they can be accessed in the Controls tab.

The best way to use a text generator is to edit it into your sequence *before* you customize the text and set the various controls. That way you can see the changes you make update live in the Canvas window. Here's how:

1. Select the text generator from the pop-up menu.

2. Set your In and Out points in the Viewer and the Canvas, and perform an edit to get the title into the sequence.

3. Park the Canvas playhead somewhere over the title.

4. Double-click the generator in the Timeline to open that instance in the Viewer. (Be careful! If you skip this step you will modify the wrong instance of the clip.)

5. Open the Controls tab, and change the text and other parameters to create the title you want.

If you follow this procedure, the changes you make in the Controls tab will update live in the Canvas. While the controls are fairly rudimentary, this still allows you to create attractive titles.

> **TIP:** *Final Cut Pro can read only TrueType fonts. If you have a Type 1 font that you absolutely must have for titling, use a shareware utility to convert it to TrueType.*

Using Readable Fonts

You can use only one font for each title. If you want multiple fonts, you must create two generators. Be sure to select a fairly thick typeface. Remember that video is *interlaced* and if you select a font with thin horizontal lines, it will flicker during video playback.

In general, sans serif fonts are best, since they lack the tiny ornaments (serifs) that can get swallowed or distorted because of the interlacing. It's also a good idea to use a large font size. Anything smaller than 30 points will be too small to read comfortably onscreen. In general, I recommend sizing screen fonts between 36 and 96 points.

Final Cut Pro's text generators suffer from overzealous kerning of the space between letters. You'll probably want to adjust the tracking to a setting of 1 or 2. Another problem with text kerning is that the Tracking slider only works if the Auto Kerning check box is enabled. Go figure.

I recommend changing the font color, too. Bright 100 percent white can be harsh when seen on a video screen, and on some TVs it will cause smearing or bleeding. If you want a white title, set the color to 90 percent white. This will still look plenty white but will avoid distortion.

More Text Generators

Final Cut Pro provides an additional handful of other text generators for more specialized purposes. Lower Third is a quick and easy way to whip up title cards for your interview subjects and includes several different styles to choose from. Typewriter creates your indispensable *X Files* type-on effect. (Unfortunately, there's no built-in sound effect.)

Scrolling Your Credits

The Scrolling Text generator is perfect for creating those scrolling credits for the end of your film (**Figure 8.121**). Enter as much text as you want. I recommend typing the list in your word processor and then copying and pasting the text into the generator.

You might want to adjust a couple of special settings for this generator.

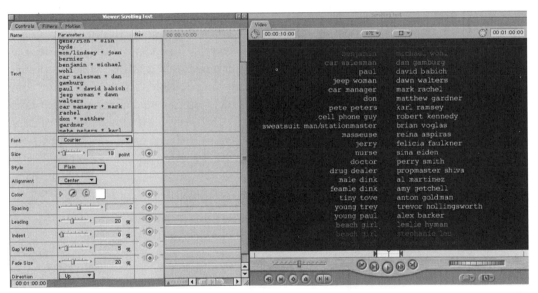

Figure 8.121 The Scrolling Text generator provides that essential for every film: scrolling end credits. The asterisk character is a secret message to Final Cut Pro indicating you want to insert a gap between two columns of text. Only the first * is recognized.

Fade Size

Want to set an area at the top and bottom of the screen where the titles will fade in and fade out? Use the Fade Size slider.

The Secret of Gap Width

This slider has absolutely no effect unless you know the secret way to use it. If you place an asterisk (⁜) in each line of text, Final Cut Pro will read that character as a request to add a tab (or gap) at that point in the line. The Gap Width parameter controls the size of that space. This is especially cool for creating the two columns of information commonly found in credits.

To create your columns, type the text for the first line of the first column, then type an asterisk, then type the text for the first line of the second column. Repeat this for every line of text (see figure 8.121).

LiveType

Final Cut Pro 4 includes an entirely new application for generating titles called LiveType (**Figure 1.22**). While LiveType's interface leaves something to be desired (it's very modal and far too complex for such a simple task), it contains enough canned animations and font styles to keep anyone occupied for days. In that, I find it a wonderful procrastination tool (although not quite as much fun as Soundtrack) and it is ideal for creating wild animated titles. The program is too complicated for me to give full instructions here, but if you get in and start poking around, you can make some pretty fun looking stuff very quickly.

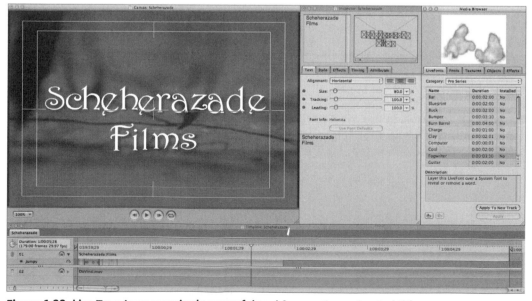

Figure 1.22 Live Type is an amazingly powerful tool for creating animated titles

Integrating your Final Cut Pro sequence into LiveType

Once you've got the hang of it, you will probably want to see how the text will look in your sequence before you finalize it. To do so, export a reference movie from Final Cut Pro. You only need to export the section where the title will be applied. Be sure to include all markers if you want them to appear in LiveType. Alternately you can select Export For LiveType from the Final Cut Pro Export menu, which does the exact same thing.

Once you've saved your reference movie, import it into LiveType. If you select Place Background Movie from the File menu (Shift-⌘-I) The clip will appear in the LiveType timeline beneath any title you may have already created (**Figure 8.123**).

Marker

Figure 8.123 Import your video clip into LiveType to see how your animated titles will look when integrated into your sequence. Final Cut Pro Markers will appear in the LiveType ruler bar.

Outputting Back to Final Cut Pro

When you choose Render Movie in LiveType, you can choose whether or not to include the background clip as part of the output (**Figure 8.124**). By leaving the background out of it, LiveType will save the animated title with an alpha channel so you can import it into Final Cut Pro and do your final compositing there. This is preferable to rendering the background inside of LiveType because it affords you the flexibility of changing the background, or the position and timing of the title, at any time without having to return to LiveType. Once you export your LiveType data, you cannot modify it.

Figure 8.124 Be sure to leave the checkbox for Include Background unchecked so you can do your final compositing in Final Cut Pro

As cool as LiveType is, I confess that most shows call for fairly reserved title treatments, and in those cases, LiveType may be overkill. But keep in mind that LiveType can be used for more than just making titles. The textures and effects are ideal for creating static or moving backgrounds that can be used like any other generator in your Final Cut Pro toolbox.

Creating Color Mattes

Final Cut Pro can generate fields of color. While this capability may seem fairly unimpressive, you'll be surprised how often you need it. First of all, at the end of your movie, when the lead character goes to heaven, you might want to fade the last shot to white instead of black. Or you might want your titles to be black text on an orange background for that big Halloween special.

Also, the Crop and matte tools can turn any clip into a custom shape. That includes generators. Need a small blue diamond to go under your company logo? How about a tiny white oval to fly through a shot of the night sky looking like a UFO?

The most basic generated clip is the simple color matte. By default it is 50 percent gray. The only parameter you can modify in the Controls tab is the color. But remember, as with every parameter, you can change the value over time, so your UFO can cycle through the spectrum as it races across the sky. Also, as with every other clip, you can modify a generator's opacity, add a drop shadow, or apply filters to it to broaden its usefulness.

One great thing to do with a white color matte is mix it with another clip using the composite modes. If you apply a white matte onto an image and experiment with the opacity and the composite mode, it will lighten and soften the image, creating a dreamy, washed out look that might be good for a flashback. Alternatively, to create a nice, light background to use behind a dark title, try the Soft Light, Overlay, or Add settings.

Regeneration

Just as with filters and motion paths, in Final Cut Pro 4 you can save generators in your Favorites folder. I recommend creating a white color matte and adding it to your list. That way you'll always have quick access to it in the Favorites section of the Generators menu (**Figure 8.125**). As you figure out which generators you use most frequently, make them into favorites, too.

To create a favorite generator, open the generator and set the parameters to the way you like them. (In this example, we're setting a basic color matte to White.) Next, select Make Favorite Effect from the Modify menu. If you want to rename it, find it in the Favorites folder in the Effects tab of the Browser window (**Figure 8.126**).

Figure 8.125 If you save a generator as a favorite, it will show up in the sub-menu of the Generators menu.

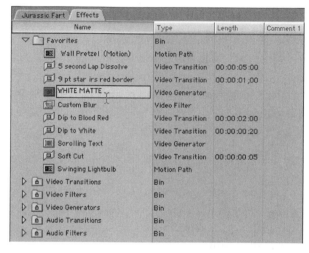

Figure 8.126 The Favorites folder is where the generators you use the most can be edited.

Gradients

A gradient is just a color matte that uses two colors instead of one. Choose the colors in the Controls tab, and then set the gradient's direction and shape. Gradients make nice backgrounds, although they look a bit conservative.

If you need a background for a chart, or even for a narrator who was shot against a blue screen (or some other background you can replace), try this recipe for an elegant moving background:

Set your gradient colors to two shades of a similar hue, such as a medium blue and a dark purple. Next apply a distort filter, such as Wave or Whirlpool. This will create a very slight movement in the background. You don't want something so dramatic that it detracts from the subject in the foreground, just enough movement to make the shot feel dynamic.

A Word About Slug

When you're cutting actual film, it's essential to keep the picture reels and sound-track reels exactly the same length so they stay in sync. If you add a shot you don't have sound for yet, you have to fill in the space on the track reels temporarily with random scraps of film. This filler is called slug. Final Cut Pro borrows this metaphor for the Slug generator.

When you launch Final Cut, the Viewer window is black—but that doesn't mean it's empty. It actually contains slug. That means if you want to throw a placeholder clip into your sequence, you can drag right from the Viewer into the Canvas without ever loading a clip. Slug has both audio and video (the audio is silent and the video is black) so it can be used as placeholder on any track.

Slug is also handy if you need a black matte. Rather than creating a favorite color matte set to black, you can just use slug. For example, there are some third-party After Effects plug-ins that create effects like fire or snow and completely replace the shots you apply them to. If you want to use those filters in Final Cut Pro, you can apply them to a piece of slug.

Importing Files

In most cases, when you use a computer-generated element while editing, it's not created in Final Cut Pro. If it's flat art, it probably comes from an illustration program like Freehand or Illustrator, or an image manipulation program like Photoshop. If it's 3-D art (still or animated), most likely it comes from Maya, Lightwave, or 3-D Studio Max. Final Cut can read a wide variety of file formats, but here are a few tips to make your life easier:

Importing Flat Art

Final Cut can't rasterize vector graphics. That means if you're working for Greenpeace, and someone sends you the logo as an EPS file, Final Cut Pro won't be able to read it. Solution? Open the EPS file in Photoshop and save it in TIFF format. That will convert it from vector art into actual pixels.

Final Cut can read almost any graphics format, including BMP, JPEG, SGI, PNG, PSD, TIFF, PICT, and TGA as well as some Macintosh-specific formats like MacPaint and QuickTime Image. However, not all these file formats can hold alpha channel information. Since PICT, TIFF, and TGA can, any of these formats is ideal for use with Final Cut Pro.

Importing 3-D Animations

If your 3-D program can output its file as a QuickTime movie—and most can—
go ahead and save it that way. You'll be able to import it right into Final Cut Pro.
Just remember to use the Animation codec, with the color depth set to 32 bits.
That way, the alpha channel (the one that separates the dinosaur from the background) will be imported into Final Cut Pro along with the file. The Animation
codec is lossless (when set to highest quality), so you won't be throwing away data
during the transfer process.

Try to avoid outputting your 3-D file in DV, since that will compress it even before
you get it into Final Cut. Nor will it have any alpha channel information. Then,
when you incorporate it into your sequence, you'll have to re-render it (I'm pre-
suming you'll be compositing the 3-D element with some other shot), recompressing it and causing further degradation.

Using a Series of Stills

If you can't export the 3-D animation as a QuickTime movie, your only alternative is to export a series of still images from the 3-D program. The stills can be in
any of the graphics formats I just listed. While Final Cut won't automatically recognize the series of images and turn it into a single clip, you'll achieve the same
result if you follow these instructions.

1. To import the individual frames of your animated sequence, start by changing
    the Still/Freeze Duration setting in User Preferences to one frame (**Figure
    8.127**). This setting defines the duration of every still image you import, as
    well as how long freeze frame clips last.

Figure 8.127 Change the Still/Freeze Duration setting to one frame.

2. Make sure your 3-D program saves all the still images in a single folder, and then import that folder into Final Cut Pro. When you direct Final Cut Pro to import a folder, it creates a bin in the Browser with all of the folder's contents inside (**Figure 8.128**).

Name	Duration	In	Out
▦ Dinosaurs galore	00:00:04;00	01:01:08;26	01:01:12;25
▽ ▢ Tyrannosaurus Rex			
▨ T-Rex_Growl_Final 001.tga	00:00:00:01	00:01:00:00	00:01:00:00
▨ T-Rex_Growl_Final 002.tga	00:00:00:01	00:01:00:00	00:01:00:00
▨ T-Rex_Growl_Final 003.tga	00:00:00:01	00:01:00:00	00:01:00:00
▨ T-Rex_Growl_Final 004.tga	00:00:00:01	00:01:00:00	00:01:00:00
▨ T-Rex_Growl_Final 005.tga	00:00:00:01	00:01:00:00	00:01:00:00
▨ T-Rex_Growl_Final 006.tga	00:00:00:01	00:01:00:00	00:01:00:00
▨ T-Rex_Growl_Final 007.tga	00:00:00:01	00:01:00:00	00:01:00:00
▨ T-Rex_Growl_Final 008.tga	00:00:00:01	00:01:00:00	00:01:00:00
▨ T-Rex_Growl_Final 009.tga	00:00:00:01	00:01:00:00	00:01:00:00
▨ T-Rex_Growl_Final 010.tga	00:00:00:01	00:01:00:00	00:01:00:00
▨ T-Rex_Growl_Final 011.tga	00:00:00:01	00:01:00:00	00:01:00:00
▨ T-Rex_Growl_Final 012.tga	00:00:00:01	00:01:00:00	00:01:00:00
▨ T-Rex_Growl_Final 013.tga	00:00:00:01	00:01:00:00	00:01:00:00
▨ T-Rex_Growl_Final 014.tga	00:00:00:01	00:01:00:00	00:01:00:00
▨ T-Rex_Growl_Final 015.tga	00:00:00:01	00:01:00:00	00:01:00:00

Figure 8.128 The bin contains all the still images for your animation sequence.

3. Drag the folder right onto the Canvas window. Final Cut Pro will edit the images into a sequence one after another, automatically reassembling your animation (**Figure 8.129**).

Figure 8.129 The images are laid into the sequence in order.

That's it! Since the stills are in a different format than your video, this sequence will need to be rendered before you play it back, but at this point you are rendering it as part of your sequence, so it will be rendered only once.

Importing Photoshop Files

When you create a file in Photoshop, you can store different picture elements on different layers. When you import a layered Photoshop file into Final Cut, you get a sequence with each of the layer elements on its own track—allowing you to animate and manipulate each of them independently. This is one of the coolest special effects features in Final Cut Pro (**Figure 8.130**).

Figure 8.130 On the left is the Photoshop Layer palette. On the right is the same file imported as a Final Cut sequence.

You don't need to do anything special to make this work, either. Whenever you import a Photoshop document (PSD), Final Cut will interpret it this way.

Why is this so cool?

Photoshop is the ideal tool for image manipulation and the best place to design all the graphics you want to use in your video. For example, create a chart with each element on a different layer. Once you bring that file into Final Cut Pro, animate the bars independently or fade them in one by one. Or let's say you want to do a title where each of the letters is animated individually. Create each letter on a different layer in Photoshop, and do the animation in Final Cut Pro.

Even existing images can benefit from doctoring in Photoshop before you animate them. I did a job once where the director wanted to animate a series of Marc Chagall paintings. First I imported the images into Photoshop, where it was easy to isolate each element onto its own layer. Then I moved the layered Photoshop file into Final Cut, where I could apply the movement: I made the lamb in *I and the Village* blink, and in *Au-Dessus De La Ville* I made the couple flying over the farmhouse actually fly!

Final Cut Pro imports a lot of vital information from Photoshop, such as each layer's opacity, whether the layers are currently visible or hidden, even composite modes. Each element gets its own track and its own alpha channel in Final Cut Pro and inherits the transparency it had in Photoshop. You cannot import Text layers, Layer Effects, or Shapes. So if you're using any of those features, rasterize those layers before importing the file.

GETTING IN AND OUT OF AFTER EFFECTS

Final Cut Pro is my editor of choice, but it will never replace After Effects as the premier tool for creating motion graphics. So how do you move your files back and forth between them?

After Effects is QuickTime savvy, which means it can open the files you captured in Final Cut Pro right off your disk. So go ahead and open your clips in After Effects, perform amazing feats such as ramping or creating awesome keyframe effects, and export a QuickTime movie you can suck right back into Final Cut Pro.

If the shot you're creating in After Effects doesn't need to be dissolved, supered-over, or combined with any other elements in Final Cut Pro, you can export the After Effects file compressed in the DV codec so it will play immediately in your Final Cut sequence. However, if the After Effects output is going to face potential re-rendering in Final Cut Pro, export it in the Animation codec as I described earlier for 3-D animations. This way you'll avoid unnecessary recompression and retain the highest possible quality.

The only problem with output from After Effects is that it doesn't maintain the timecode track Final Cut Pro creates during batch capture (so you can export EDLs or recapture your footage later). For that reason, you should always keep the original clip in your Final Cut Pro sequence when you drop in the doctored After Effects version (**Figure 8.131**). Put the new clip on a higher track than the original, so you'll see only the doctored version when you play back. EDLs and recapturing will still identify the original clip.

Figure 8.131 Place your After Effects output directly above the original source clip in the Final Cut Pro Timeline.

Automatic Duck

If you begin working on an effect in Final Cut Pro and you realize you would be better off doing it in After Effects, you don't have to start over again from scratch. A third-party plug-in called Automatic Duck will do exactly that. With this plug-in installed you will have a new menu item in your export submenu called Automatic Duck OMF (**Figure 8.132**). A separate plug-in for After Effects (included in the package) adds an item to After Effects' Import submenu (**Figure 8.133**). The result is that your entire Final Cut Sequence is transported into After Effects.

Figure 8.132 With Automatic Duck installed, you can export your whole Final Cut sequence into After Effects.

Figure 8.133 Import your Final Cut Pro sequence into After Effects.

This only works in one direction. Once you move your sequence to After Effects, you cannot bring it back into Final Cut Pro, so you will have to export a QuickTime movie and follow the steps above to integrate it back into your Final Cut Pro project.

INTERVIEW

Paul Hirsch is best known for the Academy Award he won for editing *Star Wars*, but his credits are even more impressive than that, and his career has covered more ground than most editors dream of. He collaborated with Brian DePalma on 11 films, including *Carrie*, *Blow Out*, and *Mission Impossible*, and has cut films as stylistically diverse as *Ferris Bueller's Day Off*, *Steel Magnolias*, *The Empire Strikes Back*, and Joel Schumacher's *Falling Down*. Just before this interview, he completed the Eddie Murphy comedy, *Pluto Nash*. In 2003, he completed *The Fighting Temptations* with Cuba Gooding Jr.

MICHAEL WOHL: DESCRIBE THE PROCESS OF GETTING FROM THE FIRST CUT TO THE FINAL CUT?

Paul Hirsch: Well, it's a bit like doing a mural in mosaics. You have a design that you've been working from, but you've been placing each tile in place from very close up. So, when you step back and look at the whole mural, you say, "Oh God, the eyes are too close together," or "The nose is too big," or "That woman is standing to the left of the tree and she should be to the right of the tree," or whatever. And it's only by looking at the whole that you get a sense of what needs to be corrected. It's a combination of stepping back and looking at the whole, and then going in and focusing on the details.

HOW HAS EDITING CHANGED IN RECENT YEARS? NOT NECESSARILY FROM A TECHNOLOGICAL POINT OF VIEW, BUT IN GENERAL?

When you were working with film, there was an industrial quality to the workplace that kept the executives and the suits out. Editing rooms were always grungy. But as the technology changed, the editing rooms have gotten more inviting and comfortable for executives and producers. At the same time, I mean, all generalizations are false, but many of these people have short attention spans, and very few of them had the patience to sit while you made changes on film. But now electronic editing can happen so quickly that they can see things change in front of their eyes. So the process has begun to be more micro-managed than it used to be.

HOW WAS IT WORKING WITH BRIAN DEPALMA?

I've done 11 pictures with Brian. On some of the earlier pictures he'd often be on location and I wouldn't be with him. A number of years ago I called him and said, "I just looked at dailies, and I'm not really sure what you have in mind. How is this supposed to go together?" He said, "You're the editor, you figure it out." I got off the phone and I was sort of angry. The anger fueled me and I came up with some interesting solutions to whatever the problem was. Brian won't micro-manage unless what you present him is in violation of some sensibility of his, in which case, he'll object. He only gets involved to the extent that he needs to. It is very interesting seeing Brian over 30 years. I've seen him work with different directors of photography, different production designers, editors, writers and, of course, different casts. Yet all his pictures are very distinctive Brian DePalma movies. The people he works with are creative, artistic, talented and they are contributing, yet he has a way of imposing his sensibility at crucial moments, so that the whole thing comes out very much his. I think in his case, in particular, the auteur theory does hold.

ARE THERE DIFFERENT PROBLEMS IN DIFFERENT GENRES, SUCH AS COMEDY, DRAMA, AND ACTION?

The problems are always the same. You have to make a beginning, a middle, and an end. You have to have effective transitions. You want them to be dramatic or comedic in one way or the other. You have problems with pace. You have problems with clarity. You have problems with performance

I really don't approach them any differently. My approach to editing is a very musical one. I come to it from a dancer's perspective. It's more of like an interpretive thing. If a dancer hears music, he'll dance to it a certain way. If the music is slow, he'll dance slowly. If it's fast, he'll dance fast. I take that approach to editing—the material dictates or inspires a certain aesthetic response which is how I approach that particular picture. If it's up-tempo, then that's the way I try to approach it. If it's a slow movement then I play it like a slow movement. I always approach it from a musical sense. I was a percussionist and so to me editing is about time and tempo, pace and rhythm.

DO YOU GIVE PRIORITY TO ONE TYPE OF PROBLEM OVER ANOTHER?

You have to make it all work. You approach the problems one by one and try to make them go away. My wife once asked me, "Can you tell if a picture is well edited?" I said, "Sweetheart, sometimes the biggest contribution I've made on a film is taking a scene out. Take that out and everything flows, it all makes sense. So how can you tell what's been done?" If we do our work really well, the picture should look as if there's nothing to it.

If you've struggled for months trying to make everything clear and all the transitions work and the scenes the right length and the emotions the right pitch, and so forth, and you get to the end and everyone looks at it and says, "Well, of course."

DO YOU HAVE DIFFERENT WAYS OF WORKING WITH DIFFERENT DIRECTORS?

If editing a picture can be compared to driving a Rolls Royce, some directors like to be chauffeured around and some like to take the wheel themselves. I'm happy to do the driving. If some want to take the wheel, that's not quite as much fun for me. I think the best directors that I've worked with encourage editors to contribute their point of view, because directing is sort of lonely and it's always nice to be able have one person that you trust and ask, "Well, what do you think?" Between the two of you, you work out that approach to resolving the aesthetic problems that always come up. The best directors are interested in the picture above all else.

IS THERE A FILM THAT YOU'VE SEEN LATELY THAT YOU THINK IS EXCEPTIONAL FROM AN EDITING PERSPECTIVE?

There are some films now that are doing some very interesting things editorially. They're stretching the ways in which stories are being told. I'm thinking in particular of the two films that Guy Ritchie made—*Lock, Stock and Two Smoking Barrels* and *Snatch*, and also [Christopher's Nolan's] *Memento*, to a degree—where things are not told in a linear fashion. I worked on a picture called *Raising Cain*, which jumped around in time between dreams and reality.

THAT WAS WITH DEPALMA?

Yes. It had a big influence on the way Quentin Tarantino's *Pulp Fiction* was constructed. Going forward and back in time is something that audiences can handle better and better without much explanation, and it lets you do some interesting new things. I also think that Darren Aronofsky's pictures are very interesting from an editorial standpoint.

HAVE ANY OF THOSE FILMS INFLUENCED YOUR WORK?

I'm always influenced by what I see. And if I see something that works in another context...sometimes you're looking for a solution to an aesthetic problem that you're facing and you think, "Maybe I should try this thing that I saw somewhere else." Of course, in a different context it comes out slightly different. You're always looking. It's not that you're searching, but you can't help but be influenced by something you see.

HAVE YOU EVER SAT DOWN IN FRONT OF A SEQUENCE AND SAID, "I HAVE NO IDEA HOW TO MAKE THIS WORK?"

It happens all the time. I shouldn't say that. Sometimes, a script is written really well so that everything falls together and you lock the picture a week after the end of shooting and that's that. That has happened to me.

THAT'S AMAZING.

On *The Empire Strikes Back* we locked three weeks after the end of shooting. Of course, the shooting was extended so we had a lot of time to get it right.

HOW ABOUT A CASE WHERE IT WASN'T SO SMOOTH?

Blowout caused us problems. When we looked at the whole thing, we realized that in the first cut, the John Lithgow character came in much too late. [We said,] "We've got to get this guy in earlier." So we juggled things to get him into the picture earlier, which meant moving scenes that were intended for earlier to later in the movie. We juggled the whole picture trying to solve one problem and then other problems resulted.

DO YOU HAVE ANY ADVICE FOR YOUNG EDITORS?

If you want to be a film editor, it has to be because you love doing it. The financial rewards are good but not great. The extrinsic rewards will frustrate you. The intrinsic rewards of sitting there looking at something that is stymieing you and then suddenly getting an inspiration—a flash comes to you and you know how to solve a problem, that moment is what you do it for. The moment when you think, "Oh boy, this is going to be great." It's that moment when you think, "Oh, I know what to do." That's what you live for. That's what you work for.

CHAPTER NINE

The Digital Future

I don't know about you, but I'm sick of the choices at the local multiplex. As bigger and bigger companies take over the major film studios, we're seeing a striking conservatism limit the kind of material they're willing to produce and distribute. Increasingly, Hollywood is forcing us to choose between:

- TV sitcom-quality comedies that rely primarily on sight-gags and fart jokes.

- Giddy, shallow romantic comedies that reinforce stereotypical gender roles and focus on the helplessness of being in love.

- Action comedies that depend on ever-more-violent images to whip audiences into a heightened state of blood-lust.

Commercial film scripts have often been written by committee (even if the committee is just the director, the producer, and the writer), but lately these committees are getting bigger and dumber—and they are tossing away Joseph Campbell's marvelous rules of storytelling. Instead of turning to myth or character for inspiration, they are poring over the box-office charts, trying to repackage whatever shred of innovation made last year's hits sell.

And so, rather than offering us a variety of fresh voices telling unique stories, mainstream movies have begun to resemble a kind of pornography. Plots are just threadbare fabrics that tie together the moneymaking scenes of violence (for men) or romance (for women). Formulas abound in which hearts are broken or cars get demolished, all glossed over with well-timed, smartaleck punch lines delivered with clever cynicism by this season's bankable actors.

The secret subliminal message? Movies are cotton candy. They vanish in your mouth and still spoil your supper.

If You Don't Like the Movies, Go Out and Make Some of Your Own

Is this it? Is this what cinema, the culmination of over a century of technological and aesthetic innovation, adds up to? Well, it doesn't have to be!

In fact, thousands of independent movies are being made all over the world that do not suffer from the cowardice and failure of imagination that has beset the film studios like a disease of the spirit. If there's one thing I hope you have learned from this book, it's this:

Anyone can make a movie. (Anyone with access to a few relatively inexpensive pieces of equipment, that is.) A DV camera, a computer, and Final Cut are all you need to make films equal to, or better than, the pictures being produced in Hollywood right now for tens or even hundreds of millions of dollars each.

Hope From the Internet

There is a deep irony at work in the film industry right now. While it's getting less and less expensive to make a movie, budgets are growing larger and larger. Stars, sets, and special effects are all costly, of course, but the most outrageous expense is incurred in marketing a film. Since more movies are being released, it costs more to make sure a film rises above the crowd so the public will hear about it.

If your movie costs $40 million dollars to produce and market, you need to sell nearly 5 million tickets (at $8.50 each) to earn a profit. This is exactly why studio execs fall back on lowest common denominators when they plan their next money-making venture. But hope is in sight. The Internet provides a new medium for marketing movies to a more select audience—and maybe even for distributing the movies themselves. If your movie costs only $50 grand, you can earn back your money by selling just 6,000 tickets. The problem of finding 6,000 people and seducing them into seeing your movie is of a completely different level of magnitude than trying to find five million viewers.

MARKETING ON THE WEB

I'm not going to give you a lesson on how to use the Web to market your movie; plenty of other books and Web sites out there are waiting to help you with that. But I *can* tell you that over three years Bare Witness Productions, my improvisational film company, received more than 150,000 hits from 80,000 different visitors to our Web site. And that was entirely through word of mouth; we did absolutely no intentional publicity or marketing, other than submitting our films to festivals.

Doing your own marketing on the Internet is particularly easy if a project is aimed at a clear target audience. For instance, if you're making a film about the human rights abuses of the Indonesian government in East Timor, you can probably find a wide audience quickly by advertising your film on sites devoted to Indonesia, East Timor, or human rights. At the very least, you might be able to get a mailing list from one of the sites' organizers.

If your project is aimed at a more general audience, it may be harder to find such a rich concentration of potential viewers, but you can still post a trailer for the film on general-interest Web sites focused on independent film, such as iFilm, Atom Films, or Eveo. And you'll find dozens of other resources for independent filmmakers online, many focused primarily on marketing and distribution. (See the Appendix for URLs.)

> **TIP:** Don't forget what director Roger Corman said about marketing: Even the most expensive advertising and publicity campaign will fill theater seats only for the first weekend. After that, if people don't tell their friends how great your movie is, you'll die like a dog. In other words, a great movie is the best marketing strategy you can have.

With just a minimal effort like this, you can spread the word about your films to a very wide audience. Combine that with as much traditional marketing (direct mail and ads in magazines and newspapers) as you can afford, and you can probably convince a few thousand people that your film is worth checking out. Then all you need to do is hope they like it. If they do, go ahead and book a *four-wall* tour of a few targeted cities. Who needs a major distributor?

DISTRIBUTING VIA THE INTERNET (WEB CINEMA)

All signs point to the inevitability of Web-based video delivery. Of course, it hasn't happened yet, but the only serious question is how long we have to wait.

I don't want to get *too* starry-eyed about the promise of the Internet, but video delivery over the Web is one of your best avenues for finding enough paying customers to offset your production costs. Let's say only 15,000 of the 6 billion people in the world are interested in ancient Mayan archery; you could conceivably find two-thirds of them on the Internet. If you can also sell them the opportunity to actually *view* your latest production, *Shafts Over Iztacíhuatl,* online, the $25,000 you spent on production would turn out to be a good investment. Filmmaking could actually become a sustainable career without you having to produce ads for tennis shoes or makeup.

Of course, a lot of technological innovation still needs to take place before this dream becomes a reality. For one thing, no one will take Web video seriously until it downloads instantaneously, with image quality equal to or better than television's. For another, that same problem of getting your voice heard above the din exists on the Internet. You will need to develop effective, non-intrusive, personalized marketing to ensure those Mayan archery fanatics find out about your Web site without having to suffer through advertisements for Bullseye brand cologne or plastic replicas of Mayan art. For films aimed at more general audiences, I predict we'll become largely dependent on curators, critics, and popular review sites where the wheat can be separated from the chaff.

Web Video Today

Setting the future aside for the moment, there's nothing preventing you from putting your video content on the Web right now. Your work will be seen, and you will be communicating the information in your movie to the public (albeit a mostly white, urban, and affluent public). At the very least, you'll find out if anyone responds to it.

If you're creating instructive or educational content, it will be added to the wealth of information that already makes the Internet such a powerful and versatile research tool. Essentially, you'll be joining the discussion on your topic of choice and contributing your views to the discourse. And thanks to the compelling nature of film, you'll be presenting those views in the most convincing way possible.

Just don't expect to make any money showing video on the Web. Internet video quality isn't worth charging eight bucks per viewing yet. But a Web presence can help attract the attention of a distributor, who might buy the rights to distribute your film in a more traditional channel.

Outputting Video for the Web

What does it take to put your video on the Web?

Not much! It's incredibly easy to make your show Web-ready. And if you already have a Web site of your own, it's no more difficult to include a video clip on a page than it is to include a static graphic. If you don't have your own site, dozens of sites will eagerly host your video for you.

Uncompressed Standard Def video is approximately 27 MB per second. DV is heavily compressed, reducing the bandwidth to approximately 3.6 MB per second, but that's still far too big for internet playback. In order to stream video across the Web at a reasonable speed, you need to reduce the data rate to between 10 and 50 KB/sec. That's a *lot* more compressed than DV!

Format Wars

How do you select the best format, file size, and type of compression to use for your Web video? There are so many issues to address that I'm going to skip most of them. (A number of other books and Web sites cover nothing *except* those three questions. I've listed a few of my favorites in the Appendix.) However, here are some general guidelines that should be helpful no matter how you approach the problem.

Currently there are three competing formats for compressing video: RealPlayer, Windows Media Format, and QuickTime. In most cases, it doesn't matter which format you choose. All three are capable of relatively high quality, all three are viewable on most computers connected to the Internet, and all three are fairly easy to host. In fact, these days all three are based on the same open-format standard called MPEG 4.

Compressor

Final Cut Pro 4 includes a helper app called Compressor specifically for converting your video into files for Web or DVD playback. Compressor is very easy to use and gives great results and although it is a stand-alone application you can also use it by exporting directly out of Final Cut Pro (**Figure 9.1**).

Compressor is designed not only to make Web movies, but also to make files for DVDs (**Figure 9.2**). When you export your sequence from Final Cut Pro, it is added to the Compressor batch list. Select one or more presets from the pop-up menu (**Figure 9.3**) designate a destination on your disk for the new file and click the Submit button.

Figure 9.1 Export your finished sequences directly to Compressor to prepare them for Web or DVD video.

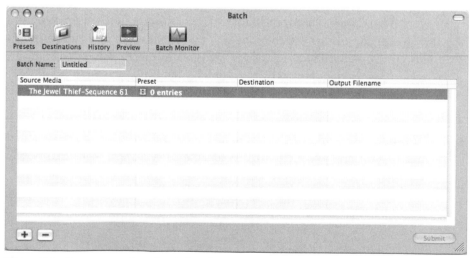

Figure 9.2 Compressor is a simple batch compression tool with very few controls.

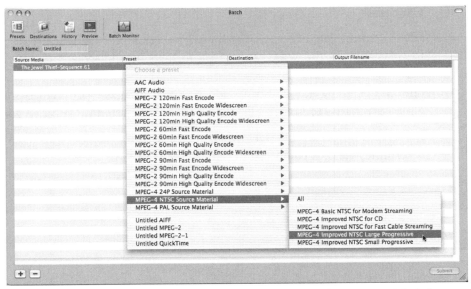

Figure 9.3 Select the preset for your job. MPEG2 settings are for DVDs, MPEG4 is for the Web.

Compressor is built to be a batch processor, so if you have more than one file you want to compress, add it to the Compressor window before you press Submit. Once you submit the batch, Compressor opens the Batch Monitor Window (**Figure 9.4**) where you can monitor your compression jobs just like the OS X Print Center.

Figure 9.4 Start, stop, and rearrange your compression jobs just like files queued to go to your printer.

Cleaner

If you're using Final Cut Express, an older version of Final Cut Pro or you want to create files in the Windows or Real formats, use Discreet's Cleaner (**Figure 9.5**). Cleaner is very similar to Compressor but it offers a slew of additional options including the ability to add hotspots to make your video interactive. Choose from the presets by clicking on the Settings column (**Figure 9.6**).

It also comes with an optional "wizard" that asks you a string of questions and then determines the best compression settings for your video.

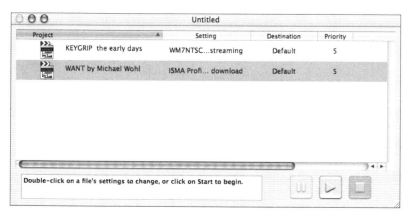

Figure 9.5 Discreet Cleaner is another batch processing tool.

Figure 9.6 Choose from presets for Quicktime, Windows Media, Realplayer, MPEG 2 and more.

Exporting a Reference Movie

To use Cleaner on your finished sequence in Final Cut Pro, you do need to know one special trick. Cleaner works on single clips, and your edited Final Cut Pro sequence is actually hundreds of tiny clips carefully positioned and timed. To turn your sequence into a Web movie, you'll need to export a single file that contains your whole show.

But if you export a new clip with all the data in it, the file will be gigantic. Even if your show is only 15 minutes long, that can still take quite a while to export, and you'll end up with a 3 GB file! To address this, Final Cut Pro allows you to export a *reference movie*. This is a file that contains nothing but pointers to all your original media clips. The file itself is quite small, but it's all that Cleaner needs to turn your show into a Web movie.

Unfortunately, this feature is quite hidden. To export a reference movie, you must select Final Cut Movie from the Export submenu, or in Final Cut Pro choose Export QuickTime Movie (**Figure 9.7**). Then, when the dialog box appears, uncheck the check box called Make Movie Self-Contained (**Figure 9.8**). By unchecking that box, you will be instructing Final Cut to make a reference movie instead of generating a new clip that contains all the video and audio data from the sequence.

Figure 9.7 To make a reference movie, choose Export Final Cut Pro Movie (in Express) or Export QuickTime Movie (in Final Cut Pro 4).

Figure 9.8 Uncheck the Make Movie Self-Contained check box. The movie that is created will require the source clips to which it refers.

A reference movie does not contain any actual video data for the movie; that's what keeps the file size so small. It refers to the video data in your original source clips, though, so be careful not to throw any of those away. If one of those files is missing, the reference movie won't play, and it will be unusable in Cleaner.

Garbage In, Garbage Out

This age-old adage is the first and most important rule of Web compression. The better your video and audio quality is before you compress it, the better it will look and sound after it's compressed. And the smaller the file will be, too.

Unfortunately, even the best Web video is still pretty ugly. The frame is small, the frame rate is reduced to 10 or 15 fps, compression creates distracting artifacts like blockiness or noise patterns, and the audio quality is mediocre. However, if you feed poorly lit, poorly shot, and poorly recorded video and audio into Compressor or Cleaner, not only will the end result be even uglier than necessary, but the compression won't be able to function well, and your resulting file will be significantly larger. That means slower download times for your viewers and more space eaten up on the server's hard disk. The higher the quality of the original, the better a job the compressor can do to preserve that quality and make your file as small as possible.

Preparing for Your Web Audience

If you know you're making a video that will be distributed over the Internet, you should make certain editing decisions differently than you would if you were aiming for television or theatrical distribution.

For example, if the end result is going to be a movie that runs in a postage-stamp screen inside a Web browser, wide shots won't play very well. The details in longer shots will be completely lost on so small a screen. Web video works best with CUs.

Similarly, since the frame rate may be reduced to only 10 or 15 fps, fast cutting might not look right once the video is compressed. To reduce the frame rate, every other frame (or even two out of every three frames) is discarded. If you use edits shorter than one second, the sharpness of the cuts can be completely lost, resulting in a muddy mixed frame. Or sometimes cuts simply won't line up properly with audio cues.

Also, short cross-dissolves look horrible at reduced frame rates. If you have a 5-frame dissolve, and you play that back at 10 frames a second, you'll see only frame 1 and frame 4 of the dissolve. That means you'll get two partially dissolved frames without a smooth transition between them—which will look like a mistake. The same is true for any short-duration transition effect.

Even the production team should think differently if final distribution is slated for the Web. Compression performs poorly with busy backgrounds, so if the camera crew shot an interview in front of waves of grain, or a sparkling lake, or a busy freeway, that background is going to turn into a mushy blob come compression time, or the file will get huge, or both.

Another thing compressors hate is camera movement—especially zooms and hand-held shots. Part of the way compression works is that pixels that remain unchanged from frame to frame can be thrown out; rather than redrawing the pixel, the compressor just says, "Same as last time." But when the camera is moving, every pixel changes in every frame, making your compressed movie bigger. Or, if you insist on a small data rate, it will turn the image to video noise when it can't keep up.

Hosting Your Video

If you are your own Webmaster, you can embed your compressed video clip into your Web page, or create a link so the clip will be played in a special helper application like Windows Media Player. Depending on your HTML authoring program, this is usually no harder than inserting a simple JPEG graphic.

If you don't have your own site, you can send your finished video to one of the popular online movie sites, such as iFilm, which will take care of everything for you. In most cases you can send a DV tape through the mail, and the online site will even do the compression for you. Of course, compression is compression, and the same rules apply.

Also, keep in mind that while your video is extremely precious to you, and you are perfectly willing to stay up all night experimenting with different compression settings to make it look its absolute best, most movie sites compress hundreds of movies every day. Your film will probably get tossed into an automated system that will lack the optimization you could do yourself.

Some sites evaluate your film before they agree to host it and may turn it down if they don't like it or it fails to fit the themes or style of their site. Some sites will host just about anything except outright pornography (and quite a few sites host nothing but). A quick Internet search on "web cinema" or "virtual theaters" will turn up scores of sites that will host your movie, usually free of charge.

For instance, not only will iFilm host your movie, the film will be rated by anyone who visits the site. iFilm claims dozens of success stories in which unknown film-makers posted their work and the films were purchased for distribution in other channels—or the filmmakers sold subsequent screenplays or got jobs in advertising or television. Some have even signed multi-picture movie deals.

What's the Web Good For?

The biggest problem facing the success of Web cinema is bandwidth. If the quality and immediacy of Web video matched that of television, the Internet's unlimited channels and on-demand capabilities might allow it to actually replace the boob tube. But bandwidth isn't the only issue.

While it's not impossible to gather a small crowd around a computer monitor, watching Web video is usually a solo activity. One of the most unique and characteristic elements of movie going is the collective experience of sitting in a theater and sharing your experience with 200 other people. Comedy is always funnier when a crowd is laughing, and even the collective silence created by the tension of a drama or suspense film is palpable. Sitting alone in front of a computer, the "movie theater" experience is impossible.

But it doesn't have to be.

The Web has the potential to support a virtual theater experience where hundreds, thousands, or even millions of other viewers could be present with you when you watch a program online. Although no one has yet to tackle this obstacle, the technology offers the potential to address this issue, creating something combining the best of what television offers with a unique experience based on the community of the World Wide Web.

Already, files can be downloaded from the Internet into existing movie theaters equipped with digital projectors. This allows a true movie theater experience but saves the cost of making and distributing film prints (which can cost tens of thousands of dollars).

Interactive Cinema

And there's something else. One of the most exciting and dramatic possibilities offered by Web video is the ability to create films that incorporate a certain kind of audience involvement never seen or experienced before; a sort of interactive cinema.

Take just one parallel example: When it was first invented, the telephone was considered military equipment. It was highly sophisticated technology for its time, but the only application its inventors could conceive of was to convey brief, urgent messages between high-level officers. The idea of a hot line between Washington and Moscow was inconceivable. So was the concept of ordering a pizza from your car so it arrives at your home just as you do, or trading stocks, or sending faxes, or any of the other things we use the telephone for today—including accessing the

Internet. These commonplace functions were literally unimaginable when the technology was invented.

I believe we are currently in a similar state of ignorance with regard to this emerging technology. Right now, the most intriguing explorations of an interactive interface between the video medium and the computer have been implemented only in games. Many experts feel that interactive video might be more of a sport than an entertainment, and the very nature of interacting is incompatible with the narrative experience.

I don't believe that. I think we can create an entertainment experience that lies halfway between a modern movie and *Star Trek*'s holodeck. If you're unfamiliar with it, the holodeck is fictional technology where the viewer literally steps into a 3-D virtual reality, interacts with narrative elements, and creates an entirely personal experience comparable only to a dream state.

Do What's Never Been Done

Why am I talking about this here? Because I believe it's you, the new generation of video editors, media creators, and filmmakers, who can bring about this reinvention of the medium. I don't think we need machinery as sophisticated as a holodeck to find new ways to use the film medium. The simple technology of making marks on paper was transformed from a primitive accounting machine into an art capable of creating novels that captivate the human imagination. I believe we are on the verge of a similarly significant transformation in film.

Final Cut is just a tool, a way to make the art of film and video editing easier and less expensive. But the intersection of affordable filmmaking tools and the exploding potential of the Web as a distribution medium creates possibilities that exceed the sum of these parts.

I challenge you to see this opportunity with new eyes. Don't simply recreate what's come before. Do what's never been done. A movie streaming to a Web page can have multiple video streams simultaneously. The viewer can click and type and speak to affect which images and sounds he sees and hears. The content of the video image can originate on edited film, or it can be computer-generated material. Live camera feeds can be incorporated on the fly into the video stream. A camera pointing at the viewer, or pointing at a live performance, can be mixed with pre-existing images and sounds in real time. The possibilities are limitless!

I'll give you two examples of how I've tried to explore these concepts in my own work. In Future Cinema, the class I teach at San Francisco State University, we constructed a Web site about commuting and public transportation that incorporated many types of media. We started with four streams of video, all downloading simultaneously to the viewer's computer. Each was a different fictional commute story, edited so they were all exactly the same length. By clicking on different areas of the screen, the viewer could switch focus from one story to the next, controlling which audio stream was heard. Simultaneously, text messages containing traffic statistics scrolled over part of the screen, and a live, interactive map showed the paths of the four different fictional stories. Finally, the site was supported by extensive links to other Web sites about transportation, plus editorial content pertaining to the impact of commuting on the students' lives.

Our goal was to merge the immediacy of the video medium with the entertainment value of four fictional stories to serve as the backbone for a comprehensive multimedia experience about our chosen subject.

Another project I've been developing with my improv company, Bare Witness Productions, is an interactive movie loosely based on Ryunosuke Akutagawa's novella, *Rashomon*. *Rashomon* is a story about a rape and murder, showing how different narrators perceive different versions of "reality." As a written text it was a seminal exploration of subjectivity, comparable to and contemporary with Joyce's *Finnegan's Wake* and Einstein's theory of relativity.

In 1950, when Akira Kurosawa made a film version, it was a masterful artistic statement that reflected (among many other things) the incredible schizophrenia that beset post-war Japan as the USA, its former enemy, spent billions of dollars transforming it into a modern first-world nation.

I plan to bring the same questions of subjectivity and multiple perspectives to bear in order to explore the nature of the interactive cinema experience. How can each viewer create her own narrative experience of an event? And is there one true version, or are all the versions tainted with an inescapable human subjectivity?

We will shoot each event multiple times, from different psychological perspectives, and then present the finished piece as a Web movie in which the viewer can switch between versions, joining any one of the perspectives at any time.

TELL YOUR STORIES

Telling stories is how we make sense of the world and how we bring communities together. Some would argue that it's the single most important cornerstone of civilization. Storytelling is power.

And we all have stories to tell. Nonetheless, over the last few decades the number of voices telling stories has been systematically diminished. Mainstream media has become a bully pulpit on which a tiny minority of storytellers present narratives that are little more than shallow advertisements promoting a culture of consumption and passivity.

Now we have an opportunity to rediscover our true voices.

The tools at your disposal are revolutionary. Take a risk and tell your stories.

The economics of filmmaking have been redefined. Take advantage and tell your stories.

A new medium is being born. You and I are the pioneers who are discovering what is possible. We live at an incredible time in the history of the planet. Get out there and tell your stories.

The world is listening.

INTERVIEW

Walter Murch is one of the most admired and respected editors of our time. His inspiring book, "In the Blink of an Eye," is a definitive theoretical text on editing. More than just a great film editor, he is also one of the most renowned sound mixers in the history of cinema. His editing credits include *The Conversation*, *Julia*, *Apocalypse Now*, *The Unbearable Lightness of Being*, *American Graffiti*, *The Talented Mr. Ripley*, and *The English Patient* (for which he won an unprecedented double Oscar for sound and picture editing). His credits as a writer and director include the dark, moving, and woefully underrated, *Return to Oz*. He took time out from cutting Kathryn Bigelow's *K-19: The Widowmaker* for this interview. Since then he's been working on Anthony Minghella's *Cold Mountain*.

MICHAEL WOHL: WHAT MAKES THE FILM MEDIUM UNIQUE?

Walter Murch: I think every age has a medium that talks to it more eloquently than the others. In the 19th century it was symphonic music and the novel. For various technical and artistic reasons, film became that eloquent medium for the twentieth century. It's partly because cinema synthesizes all of the arts: it's photography, and in a certain sense painting, and it's theater, and it's architecture, music, and the novel—all rolled up into one. And then—at its best—it has become something else which synthesizes and transcends all of its parts.

HOW IS THE LOWER COST OF TECHNOLOGY GOING TO AFFECT THE INDUSTRY?

People become excited about any new technology, particularly when the cost becomes significantly more affordable. A tool like Final Cut Pro, for instance, is at least an order of magnitude less expensive than the Avid. Ultimately, I'm not sure where it will go. Film editing is now something almost everyone can do at a simple level and enjoy it, but to take it to a higher level requires the same dedication and persistence that any art form does. The price of the ticket to get into the park is now much lower than it has been, but the cost of the ride is still ultimately very high in terms of time and dedication. I am excited that there is now the opportunity to give film students copies of uncut dailies from professional films, so that they can practice their craft on top-quality material and then compare their results with the finished film.

WHAT IS THE BIGGEST CHALLENGE FACING INDEPENDENT FILMMAKERS RIGHT NOW

Finding innovative ways to take advantage of the new forms of distribution. By which I mean the Internet—both as a way to publicize the work and a means by which that work can be distributed

Distribution has been the bugaboo of independent films. You can always make a film somehow. You can beg, borrow, steal the equipment, use credit cards, use your friends' goodwill, wheedle your way into this or that situation. The real problem is, how do you get people to see it once it is made?

WHAT DO YOU LIKE MOST ABOUT EDITING AND SOUND DESIGN

At a very early age I fell in love with the tape recorder. What I loved about it (and this is true about film editing now) is that you could instantly capture a fragment of reality, and then you could manipulate that fragment and juxtapose it with other fragments in unpredictable ways. That was intoxicating to me in the early 1950s, and it still is in the early twenty-first century. I also love the collaboration, working with other people, and I'm very interested in emerging technology, how it can be applied, and how parts of the old technology can be maintained and integrated into these new systems.

CAN YOU THINK OF SPECIFIC EXAMPLES OF PROBLEMS YOU FACE IN THE EDITING ROOM?

Well, on a certain level there's always the basic question of "How do you put the shots together?" Like every editor, I have to find ways to choose the right material, and to cut to the right shot at the right time, and be on the right character at the right moment, and make action scenes dynamic and interesting, and come in on schedule, and all that kind of stuff. But those are not primary issues for me any more. I suppose it is a little like learning how to play a musical instrument: Once you get past the issues of fingering and learning how to read a score, you don't think about them so consciously

The things that I do struggle with are the issues of structure, length, and what you might call redundancy. The moving image is inherently redundant: twenty-four times a second it's the same image, but slightly different. That's a metaphor for the whole process, because the art director will read the script and interpret the characters and the situation with set construction. The cinematographer does the same thing with light. The camera operator does the same thing with framing and camera movement. Actors do the same thing with how they act, how they speak the lines. The costumer does the same thing with the costumes.

For instance: Because of something the art director did in scene 3, you may find that the audience already understands something about a certain character. "Oh, if he owns that kind of entertainment center, then I know exactly how much money he makes." So we don't need a later scene about how much money he makes. Nonetheless, that other scene might get shot, and it's only when you see the whole film put together that you realize the extent and nature of all of these kinds of redundancies. Then it becomes a question of what and where to eliminate, at ever more subtle levels

WHEN YOU'RE CUTTING AN INDIVIDUAL SCENE, DOES THAT SAME SORT OF MENTALITY APPLY? ELIMINATING REDUNDANCIES?

Exactly. It's kind of a fractal situation. How long do you hold this shot? Is that look redundant given the fact that the character gave a similar look just before? You don't see all these things immediately. They reveal themselves over time. Looking at a first assembly is kind of like looking at an overgrown garden. You can't just wade in with a weed whacker; you don't yet know where the stems of the flowers are. So you have to gently go through and discover, "OK, that's a weed, that's a weed, there's a flower." Then you start to see the outlines of the garden, and you discover that it might look better if these flowers were over on the left side where they'll get more sun. Then you start transposing, and things start to get interesting

HOW DO YOU GO ABOUT CUTTING A LONG ROUGH CUT DOWN TO FINAL LENGTH?

You need the time to find all of the redundancies. On *The Conversation*, which was the first film that I edited, our rough cut was four and half hours long. And a wonderful one hour, 52 minute film came out of it. But we spent a long time getting it down to that length, and had to jettison many things that seemed at the time to be important parts of the script. So it's not that it cannot be done, but it will take time, and you're putting the patient (the film) at risk. And you're naturally kind of depressed at all of the work that went into the things you are now taking out.

THAT'S WHY ROUGH CUTS ARE THREE HOURS LONG.

Or four and a half. If they were only three hours long I'd be very happy. The last four films I've worked on have had rough cuts that were four to four and a half hours long. My rule of thumb, which seems to hold, is that you can reduce an assembly by 30 percent without affecting it's genetic structure. Or to change the metaphor, you can put that film on a 30 percent diet, but to get below 30 percent you have to do surgery. Meaning you have to remove characters from the film, or situational beats within the script, that seemed to be important when you read the screenplay.

You can reduce that assembly by 30 percent by finding ever more clever redundancies. You begin with the initial redundancies such as, "We don't need him to walk down the hallway, he can just come in the door." Those kind of things get rid of maybe 8 percent. Then, "He doesn't have to say that line, because we already understand what he means." That gets rid of another 8 percent. Then, "We don't really need this scene because we already know that information" gets rid of another 8 percent and then you can micromanage another 6 percent out. But then you're kind of at the limit of that process.

IN LOW BUDGET PRODUCTIONS THE EDITOR IS ASKED TO DO A LOT OF THE VISUAL EFFECTS WORK, BECAUSE THE SYSTEM HE'S USING IS CAPABLE OF IT. I'VE ALWAYS FELT THAT SPECIALIZATION IS GOING TO GIVE YOU A BETTER RESULT, BUT AT THE SAME TIME THERE IS SOMETHING TO BE SAID FOR "A SINGLE VISION."

I'm a hybrid person myself. I am both a film editor and a sound mixer; I do both on the same film. There are certainly advantages to that. I love doing it, but I also like to work and collaborate with people. So I think there is a limit. Let's say you could invent a single box that would shoot the film, edit the film, do all the visual effects, and produce the finished result. It would be viewable on television or in theaters, but one person could do it all. That it would be good on certain projects but on others, I wonder. One of the glories of film is that you have a multi-faceted vision in the end because of the collaboration that goes into it. It's more than just the director's vision. It's the director's vision amplified and scattered and intensified by the fact that the director has to work with other people; sometimes it gets diluted, that's the risk and the down side. But there are also times when the ideas are beyond what the director ever had to begin with. It hits the screen because of this collaboration.

The holy grail down the road is to have the editor working on a machine that is producing the final product—what is coming out of the editing room can be cloned and sent out to theaters. We're not quite there yet, but we can see that time on the horizon.

IF IT'S THE CASE THAT YOU'VE GOT A SYSTEM THAT CAN OUTPUT THE FINISHED PRODUCT, AND IT RIVALS WHAT YOU'RE SEEING NOW IN THEATERS, DOES THAT POSE A THREAT TO THE EMBEDDED INDUSTRY, SINCE MANY MORE PEOPLE WOULD HAVE ACCESS TO THAT SORT OF EQUIPMENT?

No, I think the exact analogy would be with the recording industry. The film industry will change along the same lines as the recording industry has. The difference is, that in the recording industry it is the band creating itself and creating their own work. In film there are some actors who also direct and produce; maybe that will become the norm. On the other hand, film requires more collaboration than the music industry. *The Blair Witch Project* is almost the exact equivalent of a garage band and who knows where the *Blair Witch* filmmakers will go.

This "I now want to see grander and grander visions" tendency, which is part of human nature, requires the mobilization of more and more unexplored territory. The nature of the grand vision is that is explores things that haven't been explored before in a spectacular way, and for the foreseeable future that requires collaboration with other people.

DO YOU HAVE ANY ADVICE FOR YOUNG EDITORS?

When you're starting out in your career, pay close attention to the material you decide to work on. You may not be able to be selective yet, but ultimately don't be afraid to turn things down. There's a common fear that if you turn a certain project down, you'll never work again. But I think what's more to the point is that if you take whatever comes your way without really looking at it, you're potentially chaining yourself to something that doesn't suit you. And therefore you won't be able to do your best work on it, and the result may damage your reputation.

You also have to realize that most of the time you're in the same room with somebody—the director—whose baby this really is. It's not your baby. Well, part of it is, and you have to take responsibility for that part, but there's a certain kind of psychoanalysis that goes on in the editing room, in which you're finding ways to ask the director, "What were you trying to get at here?" And beyond that: "*Why* are you trying to get at that?" You have to develop a feeling for knowing how to ask those questions, because some directors will respond favorably and some might resent it. This applies to many film jobs, not just editing: Half the job is doing the job, and the other half is finding ways to get along with people and tuning yourself in to the delicacy of the situation.

My daughter does make-up for film, and it's absolutely true in her case. Half of the job is getting the make-up right. The other half—she has the actor in the chair sometimes for hours—is making the actor feel comfortable, talking when the actor wants to talk, shutting up when the actor obviously doesn't want to talk, and finding ways to drain off the accumulating poisons of the last twelve hours. She is delivering to the stage an actor who is not only made up properly, but who is prepared to be the character. It doesn't matter how talented she is at make-up if she can't also do that other role, which is just as important.

The same applies to film mixing, camerawork—all of it. Don't bury yourself too obsessively in the technology and the craft of manipulating the material, and blind yourself to this other aspect of it, which is at least half of the job if not more.

Appendix

There's so much to learn about film editing, Final Cut Pro, and the world of digital video that no single book (even mine) could possibly cover it all. So here's a sampling of some of the best places to find more information and continue your education.

Don't forget, though: Reading is good, but cutting is better. Start editing! Nothing can teach you like experience.

BOOKS

In the Blink of an Eye, Walter Murch (Silman-James Press, 2001)

Read this book. It'll change the way you think about editing forever.

First Cut: Conversations With Film Editors, Gabriella Oldham (University of California Press, 1992)

If you like the interviews in *my* book, *First Cut* is a collection of 23 insightful and inspiring discussions with an incredible selection of film editors.

On Film Editing, Edward Dmytryk (Focal Press, 1984)

This simple, elegant look at the aesthetics and technical considerations of film editing is nearly 20 years old, but it's still one of the best books I've read on the topic.

The Hero with a Thousand Faces, Joseph Campbell (Princeton University Press, reprinted 1972)

This book will give you essential information about life in general, but it's especially useful for understanding the underlying structures of stories—something that must become part of every good editor's sensibility.

The Writer's Journey: Mythic Structure for Writers, Christopher Vogler (Michael Wiese Productions, 1998)

Based in large part on the work of Joseph Campbell, this is required reading for screenwriters, and it'll help editors understand the fundamental elements of storytelling.

Nonlinear 4, Michael Rubin (Triad Pub Company, 2000)

You'll find this an indispensable reference on the technology of computer-based editing, especially DV. Also check out the companion Web site: *www.nonlinear4.com.*

Creating Motion Graphics with After Effects (Vols. 1 & 2), Chris and Trish Meyer (CMP Books, 2000, 2003)

From the best teachers on the planet, the definitive guide to my favorite motion graphics program.

Photoshop for Nonlinear Editors (CMP Books, 2003)

An excellent reference for anyone working extensively with Photoshop and FCP. Also useful for folks migrating from the print world to video, translating your familiar terminology into the video space.

Apple Pro Training Series: Advanced Editing and Finishing Techniques in Final Cut Pro 4 (Peachpit Press, 2003)

I wrote about one third of this book of step by step lessons for mastering the advanced features of Final Cut Pro 4. This is required for the Apple Certified Training program.

Final Cut Pro 4 for Macintosh: Visual QuickPro Guide, Lisa Brenneis (Peachpit Press, 2003)

This is the fundamental guide to daily use of Final Cut Pro. 'Nuff said.

The Final Cut Pro 4 User's Manual (Apple Computer, 2003)

This essential reference is not just a detailed description of every bell and whistle in Final Cut Pro, it's full of practical production advice, too.

WEB SITES

2-pop *(www.2-pop.com)*

The 2-pop community of Final Cut Pro editors has been around since Day One. Although this site has changed significantly since its inception, it's still a wonderful resource, and the perfect place to waste hours procrastinating instead of working on your show.

ifilm *(www.ifilm.com)*

This is a very useful site for independent filmmakers—not just because it might host your work, but because it tells you what's going on in the realm of Web video and in the film world at large.

The Internet Movie Database *(www.imdb.com)*

Here's everything you ever wanted to know about the movies, searchable by title, filmmaker names, even plot elements. This is the single most useful film reference work available in print or online. Check out the glossary of movie terms in the "Fun & Games" section.

Adam Wilt's DV Page *(www.adamwilt.com/DV.html)*

Adam is a DV master. His site is a sharp, clearly written source of information about the technology that underlies your editing system. Although it can be a bit technical at times, it's a required bookmark.

DV Creators.net *(www.dvcreators.net)*

This site is host to FCP411, a Final Cut Pro–specific message board, and it provides excellent resources in the way of tech support, tips, and techniques for Final Cut Pro. DV Creators.net also runs the DV Revolution workshops, a three day crash course in digital filmmaking. All in all, it's an informative introduction to every aspect of digital filmmaking, and tons of fun (especially if I'm instructing).

The DV Guys *(www.dvguys.com)*

Another handy source for tips and techniques on Final Cut Pro and digital video in general. The Guys host a weekly Internet radio program, featuring interviews, discussions, reviews, and usually some humor.

IFP *(www.ifp.org)*

The premier national organization for independent filmmakers. With branches in New York, Los Angeles, Chicago, Miami, Seattle, and Minneapolis/St. Paul, IFP provides classes, seminars, screenings, and discounts on filmmaking supplies and services. This Web site is full of great articles and links for independently minded filmmakers.

Filmmaker Magazine *(www.filmmakermagazine.com)*

The official magazine of IFP. Look here for intelligent commentary and news on the world of the independent filmmaker, as well as nuts-and-bolts articles with titles like "12 Tips for Selling Your Film." If you like the site, check out the magazine.

Res *(www.res.com)*

These guys are pioneers in the digital video revolution, as well as the founders of Resfest, the first digital film festival. This site and its corresponding hard-copy magazine are always a great read. Both include lots of useful product and service comparisons. Don't miss Rob Nilsson's monthly commentary. I learn something new with every issue.

DV Magazine *(www.dv.com)*

DV is a solid source of reliable product reviews, how-to articles, and current information on the state of the video art—always well written and intelligent. This site contains much of the magazine's content plus some Web-only features that make it a great bookmark.

Indie Bin *(www.indiebin.com)*

This new site, aimed at the independent film community, is developing a large selection of original content and contains an outstanding set of links to the world of indie film on the Web.

Want, the Movie *(www.wantthemovie.com)*

This is the site for my film *Want*. You've seen so many images from the film in this book, you should pop over, see the trailer, and let me know what you think!

Glossary

ADR Short for "automatic dialogue replacement," also known as looping. This is the process by which actors in a sound studio re-record dialogue while watching playback of a loop of the shot so they can match lip movements on- screen. ADR is frequently used to replace poor production sound or to change the delivery of a line.

ALPHA CHANNEL The part of a graphics file that indicates which areas of the image are opaque and which areas are transparent.

ANSWER PRINT The first print back from the lab with all color timing and dissolve effects included. Once this print is approved, the lab can make multiple release prints, which are sent to theaters for distribution.

ASSEMBLY The first rough cut of a show, which contains all the material in approximately the correct position but not yet cut for style or pacing.

AXIS An imaginary line based on the eyeline of the on-camera subject.

B-ROLL A catchall term used in documentaries to describe all the footage that is neither interview nor narration.

CAMERA ANGLE Refers to camera position: high angle (camera shooting down from above the set), low angle (camera shooting up at the set from the ground), and so on.

CAMERA LOG A detailed journal, made on set during production, recording essential information that will enable the camera crew to re-create the shot if necessary: the camera's f-stop, focal length, position, and so on. It also usually includes information for the editor, such as length of shots, where they are on the film or tape, and comments on their content.

CAPTURE Transferring audio and video from your original videotapes to your computer's hard disk.

CG Short for computer generated, or computer graphic.

CINELOOK Cinelook, Filmlook, and Magic Bullet are all post-production processes that manipulate color balance, frame rate, and aspect ratio to make content shot on video appear as if it were shot on film. Filmlook and Magic Bullet require you to send your video to a facility for processing, but Cinelook is a plug-in that works with Final Cut Pro or Adobe After Effects.

CIRCLE TAKES At the end of the shooting day (or the next morning), the crew usually gathers to watch the dailies. The director will identify the takes she prefers, and an assistant will circle her choices in the camera log. (In the old days, economy dictated that only the circled takes would be printed onto film for editing.)

CLIPPING Audio that's recorded louder than the capability of the recording device will sound distorted. That distortion is called clipping.

CLOSE-UP A shot that usually cuts off mid-neck, showing the face or entire head.

COLOR CORRECTION Part of finishing a show is fine-tuning the color matching for every shot.

COLOR TIMING A film-specific process in which each individual shot in a film is tweaked so it looks its best and matches the others.

COMPOSITE See *compositing*.

COMPOSITING The act of combining two or more images on-screen at the same time. This can be as simple as superimposing a title card on top of an image or as complex as mixing multiple layers with special effects, transparency, and motion. The end result is a composite shot.

COMPS Short for composites, rough versions of completed special effects sequences.

CONTINUITY CUT Any cut that preserves continuity of action, space, time, and screen direction across the edit point.

CONTINUITY In order to make a seamless edit between two shots, it's important that both shots match up in as many ways as possible: props, key lighting, focal length, speed of motion in the frame, screen direction, room tone, and so on. If all the elements match, the shots maintain continuity.

CONTINUITY REPORT Similar to a camera log, this report is made during production and lists every shot and every take in the order in which they appear on the tape. It focuses on continuity elements within the shots: props, costumes, makeup, gestures, and blocking.

COVERAGE The number and variety of shots and angles that were filmed during production in addition to the "master shot." Good coverage means you have lots of editing choices; poor coverage means you have only one or two choices for cutting each scene.

CRANE SHOT A shot in which the camera is mounted on a crane, allowing it to move freely in three-dimensional space.

CROSSCUTTING The process of showing two events that are taking place in two different locations at the same time by alternating shots from each of the events.

CROSS-DISSOLVE See *dissolve*.

CUE A musical element timed to a specific point in a film. It can be as short as a few seconds or as long as a whole song. A cue point is the moment the element syncs in, and a cue sheet is the list of musical events prepared for the sound mix.

CUT A transition between shots in which the second image replaces the first image instantaneously.

CUTAWAY A shot of a neutral element from the location that's *not* part of the current shot but *is* part of the current scene. For a scene that takes place at the beach, a classic cutaway would be a shot of seagulls flying.

CUTTING Another word for film editing. For many years, editing involved physically cutting pieces of film, scraping off some of the emulsion, applying special cement, and reassembling the pieces using a handy gadget called a splicing block. In this book, I used the term generally to refer to any aspect of the editing process.

DAILIES To make sure that the scenes have been photographed successfully, each day's work is reviewed either at the end of a day or the next morning (to allow some sleep after a long or late shooting day or, if you're shooting on film, to give the lab time to print the film). These screenings are called rushes or dailies.

DISSOLVE A transition between shots in which the first shot starts to fade out while the second image is fading in. In the middle of the dissolve, both shots are briefly superimposed.

DOWNSTREAM Events or clips that exist later in the sequence from the point where you're working are described as downstream. Events or clips that exist earlier in the sequence from the point where you're working are upstream.

DP Short for director of photography.

DUTCH ANGLE A shot in which the horizon is tilted.

DV The term "digital video" (in lowercase) refers to any video information that is stored digitally, but the acronym DV (in uppercase) refers to the latest digital technology for recording video images and the specific format it uses. That format may be further specified as MiniDV, DVCAM, or DVCPRO. Some variants include DV50 and DV100.

EDIT POINT The precise moment when one shot ends and the following shot begins.

EDL An edit decision list (EDL) is a text file containing the bare minimum of pertinent information to allow you to re-create your sequence. These files are commonly used to transfer projects from one editing system to another, such as from Avid to Final Cut Pro (or vice versa).

EFFECTS SHOT Any time you alter the video data from the image that was captured in the camera, you have created an effects shot.

EQ See *equalization.*

EQUALIZATION (EQ) Fine-tuning an audio track by boosting or lowering certain frequencies (or bands of frequencies). For instance, you can boost higher frequencies to improve clarity or reduce low-frequency rumble.

ESTABLISHING SHOT A shot (sometimes called a locator shot) that shows the environment in which the events to follow take place. Usually the first shot of a sequence.

EXTREME CLOSE-UP (ECU) A shot in which the subject exceeds the boundaries of the frame.

EXTREME LONG SHOT (ELS) A shot that shows a vast area.

FINE CUT Sometimes called picture lock, this is the final edit of the picture.

FIREWIRE (or IEEE 1394) allows high-speed data transfer over inexpensive cables. FireWire is the technology that connects your DV tape deck to your computer and transmits video, audio, and time-code information all at once, and very quickly. Before FireWire, connecting a deck to a computer meant hooking up as many as six different cables and having a special interface on the computer to plug all those cables into.

FLOP A digital effect where the image is reversed left to right.

FOLEY The art of re-creating incidental sound effects (such as footsteps) in the sound studio, in synchronization with the images on-screen. The term is named after Jack Foley, one of the first sound designers.

FOLLOW SHOT A shot where a dolly is used to move the camera along with a moving subject (for example, a car-to-car shot).

FOOTAGE All the video and audio shot during production.

FOUR-WALL Rather than placing a film with a traditional distributor (a company that will put it in theaters and pay the producer a percentage of the box-office take), independent producers may choose to rent a theater themselves and present their film directly to the public (thereby keeping more of the box-office money). This is called four-walling.

GAP Final Cut Pro–speak for any empty space in a sequence. If you play across areas of gap, you'll either see black video or hear silent audio, depending on which tracks contain the gap.

GRIP The technical crew on a film shoot is usually separated into two categories, based on whether they handle electrical equipment or nonelectrical equipment. A grip handles non-electrical equipment.

HANDLES Extra footage before and after the selected In and Out points. Final Cut Pro can add handles automatically during capture.

HEADS AND TAILS Extra footage at the beginning and end of a shot.

HIGH-ANGLE SHOT A shot filmed with the camera above the subject and looking down.

IN AND OUT POINTS When you're working with a clip, Final Cut Pro allows you to set special markers identifying the frames that begin and end each shot you want to use. These markers are known as In and Out points.

INSERT A close-up of an object or detail within a scene.

INTERLACING Video images consist of hundreds of horizontal lines. Televisions display this information by splitting the image into two fields, with each field containing every other line. The upper field contains lines 1, 3, 5, and so on, while the lower field contains lines 2, 4, 6, and so on. When the TV plays the signal, it paints each field on the screen alternately, creating the illusion of smooth movement. This is called interlacing.

JOGGING A way of moving through a clip frame by frame, using the Jog wheel or S and A to go forward or backward one frame at a time.

JUMP CUT Any cut or transition that breaks the continuity of time, space, or screen direction—deliberately or accidentally—or where the action doesn't match across the edit point.

KEY COLOR See *Keying.*

KEY LIGHT The primary source of light in a scene.

KEYFRAMING Any time you tell Final Cut Pro to make changes (such as fading to black) over time, you must provide different values at different points in time. These markers are called keyframes, and the act of defining them is called keyframing.

KEYING Special effect that allows you to insert a person or object from one shot into a background from a second shot. The subject needs to be shot in front of an evenly lit, solid color field. Then you remove the color digitally, creating a transparent alpha channel where the solid color used to be. Finally, the subject is composited over an alternate background that shows through the transparent areas. The color which is removed is called the key color.

LAP DISSOLVE A cross-dissolve that lasts longer than 2 seconds; in fact, it may last as long as 15 or 30 seconds.

LAVALIER A tiny omnidirectional microphone, typically mounted on the shirt collar or lapel. These mics are designed to compensate for the extra low frequencies they record from being adjacent to the resonating chamber of the subject's chest.

LENS FLARE A spot of haze or discoloration created when a light source shines directly into a camera lens.

LEVEL Refers to audio volume level.

LINKING Final Cut Pro links clips that should remain in sync (such as stereo audio tracks, or clips originating from the same file). If you edit a linked clip, the other clips to which it is linked are affected, too. A Timeline state called linked selection controls whether selecting items in the Timeline observes linking or ignores it. Deactivating linked selection makes it easier for clips to get out of sync but permits finer control of individual elements. Whatever the current state, *s*-L temporarily overrides it.

LOGGING The process of cataloguing your footage and preparing your original source tapes for capture.

LONG SHOT (LS) A shot in which the camera is set back far enough to include the full human figure. While the point of focus is the human being, the environment is clearly visible as well.

LOW-ANGLE SHOT A shot filmed with the camera beneath the subject and looking up.

LOWER THIRD When you superimpose a title or other graphic element over the bottom third of the screen to identify the person speaking in an interview, it's called a lower third.

MARKER A placeholder or bookmark you can use to identify a specific frame (or a range of time) within a clip or sequence.

MASTER CLIP The clip from which a subclip was generated.

MASTER SHOT A shot that is framed to capture all the action in the scene and usually runs from the beginning of the scene to the end.

MATTE More or less synonymous with an alpha channel. When working in film, it refers to a piece of film that blocks out the background in one shot during printing so you can drop in the background from another shot. In the digital realm, it tells programs like Final Cut Pro which areas of the clip are transparent and which are visible. The only difference is that while an alpha channel is embedded in the clip, a matte might be an entirely separate clip.

MEDIUM CLOSE-UP (MCU) Usually a shot that frames the head and upper torso, cutting off midchest.

MEDIUM SHOT (MS) A shot that frames the subject from the waist up.

MONTAGE An extended sequence of short images that are tied together thematically but break the rules of continuity of time and space.

MOTION CONTROL A mechanical, computerized system that records and re-creates camera moves.

MOTION GRAPHICS A subset of special effects focusing on clip motion and layering.

OPACITY The opposite of transparency. The more opaque an object is, the more it obscures objects behind it. The more transparent it is, the more background objects show through.

OVER-THE-SHOULDER (OS) SHOT A shot in which two people are facing one another—one in the foreground with his back to the camera, the other facing the camera.

PAN A shot that turns from side to side. Short for "panoramic."

PAN (AUDIO) An audio track can come out of the left channel, the right channel, both channels at the same time (centered), or anywhere in between. The control that adjusts this is called a Pan control, and the act of moving the audio track from channel to channel is panning.

PICKUPS Additional shots requested by the editor, to be collected after principal photography is complete.

PLATE The background element of a key.

POINT OF VIEW (POV) SHOT A shot that lets us look through a character's eyes and shows us exactly what she's seeing.

POST See *post-production*.

POST-PRODUCTION Everything that happens after the film is shot, including editing, sound design, special effects, and so on. Also known as post.

POT Short for potentiometer. A pot is the control knob (or slider) that adjusts the volume of a particular track or input on a multitrack audio control board. The term can also refer to a single track.

PRACTICAL Any prop or object in a scene that is actually used by the production. For instance, a bedside lamp that is part of the scene lighting is called a practical. Similarly, any device that makes a sound on-screen, such as a car door or water faucet, might be called a practical element.

PRE- AND POST-ROLL In order for Final Cut Pro to capture clips accurately, the deck needs a few seconds before the clip gets up to speed—and a few seconds after the clip ends so Final Cut Pro can close the file properly. Different decks require different amounts of pre- and post-roll; you can set the values in the General Preferences window.

PROCESS SHOT An old-school film term for compositing. On film, if two images are to be optically combined, an additional lab "process" is required.

RACK FOCUS A technique that involves the camera operator shifting (or racking) the focus from one character or object to another within a single shot.

RAMPING Manipulating the playback speed of a clip so that it varies over time. For example, a shot can begin at normal speed, slow down smoothly to a few frames a second, then speed up to a superfast playback rate that's three or four times the normal speed.

REACTION SHOT A shot that reveals how a character reacts to something that just happened.

REFERENCE MOVIE An intermediary file exported by Final Cut Pro and used by Cleaner to turn your show into a Web movie. The reference movie is a relatively small file that contains pointers to all your original media clips.

RENDER When Final Cut Pro can't perform the calculations necessary to play an effect in real time, it needs to stop, process the effect, and write it to a disk file. This process is called rendering. Thereafter, when you hit Play, Final Cut Pro reads the file and plays the effect in real time.

REVERB Echo, usually produced electronically.

REVERSE SHOT Any shot that is taken from the opposite angle of the previous shot. Also known as reverse angle.

RIPPLE EDIT Rippling an edit modifies an edit point by changing the duration of only one of the clips involved. This changes the duration of the entire sequence.

RIPPLE The act of pushing all the items in a sequence forward or backward in time to make room for new material. However long the new material is, that duration ripples through the entire sequence like a wave traveling down a rope.

ROLL EDIT Rolling an edit shortens one clip while lengthening the other—with a single adjustment. It doesn't matter whether it's the outgoing clip getting shorter and the incoming clip getting longer or the other way around; the overall sequence length doesn't change.

ROLL OFF Eliminate unwanted ranges of frequencies.

ROLLING Moving an edit point forward or backward in time by lengthening one clip while shortening another.

ROLLING OUT THE TAPE To make sure they don't run out of tape in the middle of a shot, videographers commonly swap a new tape into the camera two to five minutes before the current tape runs out. However, since editing software like Final Cut Pro requires at least three to five seconds of recorded footage after the last Out point, it's good practice to record a few moments of "junk" after the last shot on the tape so the very last recorded frames aren't ones you intend to use. Filming that junk is called rolling out the tape.

ROOM TONE Unless you're in outer space, the environment around you has a characteristic sound. In a house it might be the soft hum of the refrigerator and the ticking of a clock. In a park it could be wind in the trees and a chattering squirrel. These sounds make up what filmmakers call room tone, an important consideration when recording and editing the soundtrack.

ROTOSCOPING The process of painting digitally on individual frames of the film. It's used primarily for cleaning up mistakes or removing the wires from a model shot.

ROUGH CUT An interim cut of the show, usually containing incomplete sound, placeholders for special effects shots that aren't done yet, and some editing areas that require further work.

RUBBER BAND CONTROL One way to set keyframing. You click and drag a line that represents various values over time—and it stretches like a rubber band.

SCENE CUT A cut that takes the viewer from the end of one scene to the beginning of another.

SCREEN DIRECTION The direction (left or right) that a subject is facing, or moving, in the frame.

SCRUBBER AREA A graphic representation of the length of the clip or sequence. The playhead, In and Out points, and markers are all indicated.

SHOOTING RATIO A comparison of footage shot to finished film.

SHOT Every time the camera frames a different angle or image of the events being filmed, the resulting video or film is a shot. The word also refers to different ways of framing the action, as in "close shot" or "long shot."

SHOT LIST Breakdown of how a scene will be filmed, shot by shot. May be supplemented by a matching series of shot sketches known as a storyboard.

SHOTGUN Microphones are frequently identified by their pickup pattern. A shotgun is an extremely directional mic, picking up signals in a very narrow pattern to the front of the mic. Most films use shotgun mics mounted on a boompole to record dialogue. This allows you to place the mic far enough away from the subject to stay out of the camera's view but still record an adequate signal with very little extraneous noise from the sides or the back of the microphone.

SHUTTLING A way of moving through a clip at variable speed by using the Shuttle control. Hitting the play keys J and L multiple times serves as the keyboard equivalent.

SINGLE Any shot of one person.

SLATE Also known as a clapboard, this tool is primarily used to identify a shot. On productions where the sound and picture are recorded on separate media, clapping the top bar gives a "sync" point that allows the editor to line up the separate recordings in post. The Final Cut Pro icon and box art show a typical slate.

SLIDE EDIT Rather than adjusting the In and Out points of the selected clip, the slide edit changes the In and Out points of the *surrounding* clips, allowing you to slide a clip around within a sequence. Slide will not alter the overall duration of your sequence.

SLIP EDIT This edit changes both the In and Out points of a single clip simultaneously. Essentially, it changes which section of the clip you are using by trimming frames off the front of the clip and adding them to the back—or vice versa. It does not change the duration of the overall sequence, and it has no effect whatsoever on the surrounding clips.

SNAPPING A Timeline state. When snapping is turned on, certain items attract and grab other objects (such as clip edges, edit points, In and Out points, the playhead, keyframes, and markers) that are dragged nearby.

SOFT CUT A very short dissolve that lasts between three and five frames.

SOUND MIX This is the final stage of post-production, after the picture is locked. It involves mixing the sound from many individual tracks into the final, balanced track that will be distributed with the film.

SOURCE/RECORD Traditional videotape-based editing systems comprised two tape decks: one to play back the source tapes, and one to record the master sequence. This model has carried over into the digital realm, even though tape decks are no longer required.

SPLIT EDIT Any edit where audio and video are cut at different points.

STRAIGHT EDIT A cut, as opposed to a dissolve or an L or J edit.

SUPERING Short for "superimposing."

SWEETEN A general term referring to various types of manipulation used to improve the sound quality of an audio element or track. Sweetening might include removing hiss or pops, equalizing a track so it will match a particular environment, and so on.

SYNC SOUND Audio that's synchronized with the image. For instance, the sync sound for a wine-tasting sequence might include the clink of glasses being set on the counter and the tasters' discussion of the grassy overtones of the Sauvignon Blanc.

TAKE A single iteration of a scene or shot, as in take 1, take 2, and so on.

TALENT Film-biz talk for actors.

TELECINE The process of recording film onto video is called Telecine.

THERBLIG Term coined by Frank and Lillian Gilbreth, behavioral scientists whose analysis of human behavior made huge contributions to the technological advances of the 20th century. It refers to the most basic mechanical action a human can make. The Gilbreths came up with 17 or so unique therbligs. Note that "therblig" is Gilbreth spelled backward (almost).

THREE-POINT EDITING Every edit you make has four points: the starting point of the source clip, the ending point of the source clip, the point where it will begin in the sequence, and the point where it will end in the sequence. If you supply three of the four points, Final Cut Pro can figure out the fourth.

TILT A shot in which the camera tilts from down to up—or vice versa.

TRACK Film editors refer to all the sound elements as "the track." It's short for "soundtrack."

TRACKING SHOT A shot that begins in one physical location and moves along the ground to another. Also known as a dolly shot, crab shot, and truck shot.

TWO-SHOT Any shot with two people in it.

UPSTREAM See *Downstream*.

VOICE-OVER An audio-only shot.

WIDE SHOT (WS) A shot in which the camera is far away from the action and captures roughly what might be witnessed with the naked eye.

WINDOW DUB Some video decks can display timecode numbers in a window right on top of the video image, so you can see the exact timecode number for any given frame on the TV monitor. This is known as BITC—short for burned-in timecode, and pronounced "bit-see." A dub made with that window visible is called a window dub. This makes it possible to record timecode values even from a non-professional tape format like VHS.

WIPE A transition between shots in which the second image replaces the first image by taking some recognizable shape such as, for instance, an expanding circle or a moving diagonal line.

ZOOM SHOT A shot that involves changing the focal length of the lens while the shot is rolling to make the subject seem larger or smaller in the frame.

Index